Out Of The Blue Too

More scary and often funny tales from the Royal Air Force
and Friends

Compiled and edited by
Ian Cowie, Dim Jones & Chris Long

Foreword by
Air Marshal Cliff Spink CB CBE FCMI FRAeS RAF Ret'd

HalldaleGroup

Published by Halldale Group on behalf of "The Out of the Blue Foundation"

Halldale Media Ltd
Pembroke House, 8 St. Christopher's Place, Farnborough, Hampshire, GU14 0NH, UK
Halldale Media, Inc.
115 Timberlachen Circle, Ste 2009, Lake Mary, FL32746, USA
www.halldale.com

100% of the profits from the sale of this book will be donated to military charities, with 50% to
the RAF Benevolent Fund and 50% divided equally between the Army Benevolent Fund and the
Royal Navy Royal Marines Charity.

ISBN 978-0-9570928-2-2

Designed by David Malley & Daryl Horwell, Halldale Group

Printed and bound by Clays Ltd, Bungay, Suffolk
www.clays.co.uk

Distribution courtesy of Flostream Ltd,
Slough, Berkshire
www.flostream.co.uk

Featured Aircraft

[1] Auster   [2] Buccaneer   [3] Canberra   [4] Cessna   [5] Chinook   [6] Chipmunk

[7] Commander   [8] Dominie   [9] F-16   [10] Gnat   [11] Harrier   [12] Harvard

[13] Hawk   [14] Hercules   [15] Hunter   [16] Jaguar   [17] Jet Provost

[18] Lightning   [19] Meteor   [20] Nimrod   [21] Phantom   [22] Sea Harrier

[23] Shackleton   [24] Strikemaster   [25] Tornado   [26] Vampire   [27] Victor

[28] Vulcan   [29] Wessex   [30] Whirlwind

Featured Aircraft

[1] Auster   [2] Buccaneer   [3] Canberra   [4] Cessna   [5] Chinook   [6] Chipmunk

[7] Commander   [8] Dominie   [9] F-16   [10] Gnat   [11] Harrier   [12] Harvard

[13] Hawk   [14] Hercules   [15] Hunter   [16] Jaguar   [17] Jet Provost

[18] Lightning   [19] Meteor   [20] Nimrod   [21] Phantom   [22] Sea Harrier

[23] Shackleton   [24] Strikemaster   [25] Tornado   [26] Vampire   [27] Victor

[28] Vulcan   [29] Wessex   [30] Whirlwind

It was a Dark but Beautiful Night

In July 1986, Phantoms and crews of 19 and 92 Squadrons, from RAF Wilden-rath in Germany, were sent on a combined detachment to the United States Air Force Base at Tyndall in Florida, to participate in Exercise Copper Flag. The exercise took place over the Gulf of Mexico, and sorties were flown during the evening and at night. The exercise aim was to defend the USA against attacking aircraft that were using extensive electronic warfare defences. The Phantoms were designated long rectangular areas in the Gulf of Mexico, orientated north and south up to 100 miles off the coast, and attacking aircraft approached from the south.

Midway through the exercise we had the usual late afternoon briefing. The weather was going to be fine, with no moon, but the forecaster did mention (as a joke?) that just off the coast were large shoals of hammerhead sharks and it would not be a good idea to end up in the water. Later that night, we were launched as one of a pair of aircraft to man a Combat Air Patrol (CAP) in our al-located area. The transit outbound was uneventful, and we split into individual aircraft and set up our CAPs, with each aircraft flying a racetrack and taking it in turns to look down the threat direction. Shortly after arriving in our area we felt a thump resonate through the aircraft, and I felt a puff of hot air come through the cockpit ventilation system. Immediately afterwards, the FIRE warning light for one of the engines illuminated. I warned the navigator, saying, "Jimmy, we have a FIRE light on and this is not a practice." As squadron QFI[1], I was so used to giving practice engine fires that I thought I would make it clear that this was the real thing!

Following the normal drill, I throttled back the engine and waited for the FIRE light to go out. It did not, so I turned off the fuel and shut down the engine. However, the light remained on. Now UK Phantom engines (Rolls-Royce Speys) were not equipped with fire extinguishers; so here we were, out over the Bay of Mexico, at night, with what appeared to be a genuine fire, no means of putting it out, and the recurring thought of hammerhead sharks if we had to eject! The other aircraft on CAP quickly joined up in close formation and

[1] QFI - Qualified Flying Instructor

informed us that there were no visual signs of fire. As everything appeared to be under control, apart from a bright red light, we headed for base. The generator of the remaining engine provided electrical power for the aircraft systems and, although we had lost two of our four hydraulic pumps, there was still sufficient hydraulic power to fly the aircraft. At some distance out from home, we aimed to intercept the main runway centreline at five miles, execute a hard left turn and fly a visual straight in approach to land as soon as possible. We declared an in-flight emergency on our operating radio frequency and, as we approached base, we changed to Tyndall Radar Approach Control. At this stage we lost radio contact with the other aircraft but, as he was still in close formation with us, I reasoned that we were obviously not visibly on fire or about to explode! We therefore continued our recovery as expeditiously as possible.

Approaching the chosen five mile point, I throttled back the good engine, commenced the hard left turn to intercept the runway centreline and simultaneously lowered undercarriage and flaps. Life then got even more interesting. What I had not considered was that, with one engine shut down and the other at idle, I was making impossible demands on the aircraft's degraded hydraulic system. With insufficient power to operate the flying controls, at the same time as the other services we commenced a gentle, uncontrolled roll towards inverted flight as the undercarriage and flaps lowered. Immediately applying full power on the good engine restored hydraulic pressure and control of the aircraft, and eventually we ended the correct way up with undercarriage and flaps lowered. At this stage the FIRE warning went out, and we continued the approach for a normal single- engine landing, vacating the aircraft smartly once we were clear of the runway.

Investigation of the engine revealed that the thump we had felt was the engine casing rupturing, thus allowing very hot air into the engine bay. The FIRE light had remained on until final approach when the Auxiliary Air cooling doors, on top of and below the fuselage, opened and ventilated the hot air from the engine bay. Thankfully, the sharks were not offered an extra meal that night!

Knights of the Road

One afternoon in late winter, my driver was taking me back to my headquarters, when we both spotted a BMW convertible firmly lodged in a hedge, down a slope from the edge of the road. The car had clearly rolled but was upright, a front wheel was still spinning, and the headlights were on. Wearing our woolly pullies[1] (mine complete with wings) and our SD hats (mine brass-adorned), Cpl 'Steve' and I leapt from the car, and rushed down to the BMW, where we found a delightful young lady – no, a truly stunningly beautiful young woman - kneeling by the wrecked vehicle.

Pointing with a shaking hand to the top of the hill on the other side of the road, she said "I have just left my sister at her house up there, and I need to call and tell her what has happened. I can't find my phone - could I possibly use yours?" Two mobiles appeared, as if by magic, and she smiled, accepted mine and turned away to make her call. Having contacted her sister, she said she was feeling OK and told us that her sister would be down shortly. She then thanked us profusely for stopping to help and said, "Please drive on, I'm fine really."

As we climbed back up the slope to the road she called after us, "By the way, are you with the AA or the RAC?" I thought my driver was going to have a heart attack, trying to suppress his belly laugh!

---

[1] Woolly Pullies – long sleeved, heavy duty sweaters that formed part of the normal working uniform.

Baptism of Fire: 01 May 1982

Reproduced from his book, Hostile Skies, by kind permission of Orion Books and the author, Lt Cdr David HS Morgan DSC

Grey fingers of dawn tentatively probed the eastern sky as the twelve of us made our way across the gently pitching deck towards the silent bulk of our fully armed Sea Harriers. We moved with the slightly shambling gait associated with the modern fighter pilot. All of us were weighed down with helmet, oxygen mask, anti-G suit, maps, immersion suit and layers of thick-pile clothing, to enable us to survive in the near-freezing water around the Falkland Islands. HMS *Hermes*, the old lady of the Royal Navy, which had sailed millions of miles since her commissioning in 1959 and launched hundreds of thousands of aircraft sorties was, in her twilight years, about to launch her first-ever air strike against the enemy.

In the four weeks that it had taken us to sail the 8,000 miles from Portsmouth, the mood aboard the flagship had changed dramatically. When we first set sail, a large percentage of the ship's company had thought that we were purely the big stick, which would frighten the Argentines into giving up their illegal occupation of those far-flung islands. As we pressed south, however, the mood gradually changed. The Sea Harrier force had always assumed that we would be called upon to show our mettle, an occasion that all fighter pilots anticipate, with a peculiar mixture of eagerness and foreboding, throughout their careers. We had, therefore, set about a daily round of planning and practice that would hone our already considerable skills to a razor's edge before closing the enemy. We practised ship attacks and air combat, dropped an example of every live weapon in the ship's magazines, and planned assiduously for every conceivable contingency.

By the third week in April, when it became obvious that a political solution was impossible, we were confident that we would give a good account of ourselves despite our ten-to-one numerical disadvantage in the air. It was now the first of May 1982; in England, children were celebrating the coming of Spring with traditional dance and jollification. In the South Atlantic, the autumnal storms were gathering, and the Sea Harrier force was preparing for its baptism of fire. The weeks of meticulous planning and practice were now coming to a head. We had completed our final mission briefings, and received our escape and evasion instructions. Each pilot carried a Browning 9-millimeter automatic pistol, together with two loaded magazines, probably more of a psychological prop than for any practical use, even for a passably good shot like myself. After a few half-hearted jokes, we had taken refuge in our private thoughts; some had deposited last letters to wives or girlfriends (or in my case both!) in case they did not return, and most of us were happy to immerse ourselves in the well-practised and comforting routine of preparing to fly.

I mentally ran through my part in the plan as I checked the weapons on my aircraft. It was essential that everyone carried out his individual rôle as perfectly as possible, to preserve the integrity of the attack. I was largely responsible for planning the first assault on Stanley airfield, and was aware that the odds were very much against us all returning safely. I double-checked all the weapons and head-up display aiming data, adding two marks on the sight glass in case I suffered a display failure. These marks both coincided with the weapon aiming point: one seen from my normal sitting position, and a further one seen from a position crouching down behind the gunsight camera, where I suspected I might be during the final stages of the attack!

At 1040GMT (0640 local time) the order came booming over the flight deck broadcast system, 'Stand clear of jet pipes and intakes: start the Sea Harriers'. I held up five fingers to my plane captain, to show that my ejection seat was now live, and he replied with the signal to start as I heard the other eleven Pegasus engines winding up around me. As my engine stabilized at ground idle, I began my post-start checks and, after a few minutes, the flashing anti-collision lights showed that all twelve fighters were ready to go. There was time for a quick glance at the en-route map before *Hermes* turned into the prevailing westerly wind, and the chocks and chain lashings were removed, leaving the aircraft ready for take-off.

As the hands on my watch moved, oh-so-sluggishly, to 1050, I inserted the ship's heading into my inertial navigation kit, re-checked: flaps down, armament master switch live, nozzle stop set at 35 degrees, trim 3 degrees nose-down, and ejection seat live. Exactly on time, the red traffic light below the window of Flying Control turned green, and Tony Hodgson, the Flight Deck Officer dropped his green flag to launch Lt Cdr Andy Auld, ahead of me. My machine was buffeted violently by Andy's jet efflux and, as the grey bulk of his aeroplane threw itself off the end of the ski-jump, I taxied forward to the take-off point. Tony, braced against the jet wash, gave me the green flag and, with a final nod, I slammed the throttle open. Within one second, the power of the engine started to drag the locked wheels across the deck and in two seconds the jet was accelerating at a terrific rate towards the ramp, driven by the ten tons of engine thrust. As the end of the deck disappeared below me, I rotated the nozzles and leapt into the air some seventy knots below conventional stalling speed, accelerating rapidly to forward flight. Within ten seconds of launch, the wheels were up and I was in a tight left hand turn to join up with the leader, as the other aircraft got airborne at five-second intervals behind us.

The initial transit towards the islands went without incident, and we soon settled down into a flexible transit formation, with everyone scouring the rapidly-lightening sky for enemy aircraft. After ten minutes on a westerly heading, we turned south towards our planned landfall at Macbride Head, the most northeasterly point of East Falkland. Almost immediately, I saw a couple of dark shapes, hugging the water and closing rapidly from the east. I shouted 'Break port! Bogies left 10 o'clock low' and, as we all pulled our jets into a screaming left turn, I realised that the sinister shapes were, in fact, our three spare aircraft, now on their way to attack the grass airfield at Goose Green. As Lt "Fred" Frederiksen hopped his formation over ours, we regained our heading and with pulses racing, caught our first sight of the islands.

The coastline crystallised slowly into a dark scar, separating the restless sea from the layers of cloud stacked over the high ground to the south. My first impression was of its similarity to the Scottish coast, which made it quite difficult to believe that we were not on one of our more familiar exercises, rather than bent on an errand of destruction. There was little time to dwell on this, however, as we made our way down the coast towards our initial point near Volunteer Beach. I can remember being struck by the complete absence of trees, the beauty of the white sand beaches, and the sight of a lone cow pausing in mid-chew to watch, with a detached interest, as we swept past on our deadly mission.

By the time we reached Berkeley Sound, with only ninety seconds to run to the airfield, we had split into three sections. Four aircraft were pulling up off

Volunteer Point, to toss 1000-lb bombs onto the anti-aircraft defences, three others were setting themselves up to approach from the northwest, whilst Andy Auld and myself headed for the east side of the pair of 900-foot high mountains to the north of Stanley. I was aware of the increase in tension as I urged my machine as low as I possibly could, towards the craggy outline of Mount Low. I was aware of intense concentration as my eyes flicked between engine instruments, head-up display, and the inhospitable rock-strewn tussock grass that whipped past at over 500 mph, a scant fifty feet below my aircraft.

As I rounded the east face of the mountain, tucked behind and slightly to the left of my leader, the target came into view. At first, I couldn't take in the sight that greeted me in the thin grey dawn light. The airfield and the entire peninsular on which it was built seemed to be alive with explosions. Anti-aircraft shells carpeted the sky over the runway, up to a height of 1000 feet, so thick that it seemed impossible for anything to fly through unscathed. Missiles fired from the airfield and from outside the town, streaked across my path, long wavering white fingers chasing the previous attackers out to the southeast. Tracer fire crisscrossed the sky and, as I watched, a number of guns turned in my direction, sending feelers of scarlet probing towards me. The tracer curved lazily down, rather like a firework display and not initially conveying much feeling of imminent danger. As it got closer, however, it suddenly seemed to accelerate, and began whipping past my ears, bouncing off the grey sea all around me. My brain froze in horror for a fraction of a second, as I realised that this wasn't a game any more and someone was actually trying to kill me! The years of training then took over and, as I took evasive action, I realised that I was automatically flying even lower.

I hauled the aeroplane hard left and then right, to pass between the Tussock Islands and Kelly Rocks, themselves only thirty feet high and pressed on towards the airfield below the level of the sand dunes, accelerating to nearly 600 mph. Inspection of the gunsight film, later in the day, showed that we were flying at a height of between five and fifteen feet as we approached the target! I became aware that a number of Argentine soldiers were firing down at me from the sand dunes on the northern edge of the airfield, their bullets kicking up the water all around me. I dropped the trigger on the front of the stick and squeezed it hard, expecting to hear the roar of the 30-millimetre cannon, and see the eruptions of smoke and flame amongst the enemy on the near horizon. But the guns would not fire. I thought that they must have jammed, but realised later that, in the heat of the moment, I had failed to select the gun master switches on!

As I crossed over the beach, I yanked back on the stick, flattening the defenders on the dunes with my jet wash, and levelled at 150 feet, the minimum height required for my cluster bombs to fuse properly. I instantly took in the damage caused by the rest of the formation; the airport buildings were billowing smoke, and a number of aircraft were lolling at drunken angles, obviously badly damaged. The fuel dump to my right was a storm of orange flame, under a gathering pall of oily black smoke, and huge lumps of debris were still falling from the sky from the explosions of the 1000-lb bombs. One aircraft, which seemed undamaged, was a small civilian Islander transport. I quickly lined up my bombsight raised the safety catch and mashed the release button, despatching my three cluster bombs. The first bomb separated from the wing pylon and after a short safety delay, blew off two sections of skin to expose the 147 bomblets. These were, in turn, ejected to form a cloud of death covering the size of a football pitch. Each bomblet contained a charge, capable of penetrating the armoured hull of a tank and designed so that the case fragmented to provide a vicious anti-personnel weapon. One third of a second after the first weapon dropped, I felt the thump as the second bomb left the centreline pylon, mounted under the fuselage, and fell away towards the target.

Suddenly there was a huge explosion and the aircraft started vibrating like a road drill. It was impossible to read any of the cockpit instruments to check for engine damage, but the aircraft still seemed to be flying so, as soon as the last bomb had cleared the wing pylon, I dived my machine for the smoke beside the control tower. I still have a very clear recollection of passing below the level of the tower windows as I entered the cloud of thick black smoke. When I returned to the airfield after the war was over, I discovered that the tower windows were only about twenty feet above the ground! I waited a short pause inside the smoke, then pulled the aircraft into a hard turn to the east, to clear high ground and run down the beach to safety.

As I punched out of the smoke, my radar-warning receiver emitted a strident, high-pitched warbling note: I had been locked onto by a radar-laid anti-aircraft gun! This was no time for gentle flying; I racked the aircraft into a bone-crushing 6-G break to the left through ninety degrees, to put the radar at right angles to my flight path and flicked out the airbrake to release a bundle of chaff into the airflow. I had thought up the idea of jamming packets of these aluminium covered fibreglass needles underneath the airbrake, and one of the squadron air engineering officers had designed a system of wire and string to effect their release when required. Despite the Heath Robinson design, they did their job; the radar lost its lock and I was able to haul the vibrating aircraft back onto an easterly heading and run out to sea and safety.

As we cleared the target area, we changed radio frequency and checked in. I believed that we would probably lose two or three aircraft on this raid, because of the intensity of the ground defences. There was a huge surge of elation, therefore, when everyone checked in. Once safely clear of land, I slowed down and climbed gently up to 10,000 feet. As I reduced speed, the vibration that had been shaking me so violently, began to reduce to acceptable levels, and I was able to check out the aircraft systems. I was amazed to find that everything appeared to be working correctly except a tiny gauge, which showed the position of the rudder trim. This, in itself was of no consequence to the operation of the aeroplane, but gave me the first indication that damage had been done to the tail of the 'plane.

Once back in the overhead of *Hermes*, I circled at a height of 5,000 feet whilst Flt Lt Ted Ball came up to inspect the damage. After a fruitless inspection of the left side of the aircraft, he swapped over to the right side and after a few seconds said 'Ah yes... you have got a bloody great hole in the tail'. I moved the control surfaces to and fro, and was told that they appeared to be working correctly, but there was a distinct possibility that the reaction controls, critical for vertical landing, might have taken some damage. I therefore let everyone else land before setting myself up to carry out a rolling landing. This entails running the aircraft onto the deck with a certain amount of forward speed and is not an approved manoeuvre as there is a distinct danger of running over the side into the sea. It does, however, reduce the reliance on the reaction controls, and might give me the option to overshoot and try again if the controls jammed.

I selected my undercarriage and flaps to the landing position, tightened my lap straps and set myself up for a straight-in approach to the back end of the ship, from about one mile out. As I got closer, everyone on the flight deck started to creep forwards to get a better view of the impending arrival. This worried me somewhat as, if I had lost control, I might have taken a lot of people with me. I transmitted a short call to that effect to the ship and the flight deck crews soon got the message and headed rapidly for the comparative safety of the catwalks on either deck edge!

I stabilised the speed at 50 knots and adjusted the power and nozzle angle to give me a gentle rate of descent towards the stern of the carrier. Slight adjustments were required to compensate for the rise and fall of the deck, but I managed to achieve a good firm touchdown about fifty feet in and braked cautiously to a halt before following the marshaller's signals to park at the base of the ski-jump. As the chain lashings were attached and I started my shutdown checks, I became aware that I was sweating profusely, despite the biting thirty-knot wind whipping in through the open cockpit canopy. The adrenalin flow also made it difficult to unstrap and undo the various connections to the ejection seat, before standing up to leave the cockpit. Outside, on the windswept and slippery deck, stood a crowd of people staring at my tail. Having given a thumbs-up to Bernard Hesketh, the BBC cameraman, I walked a little unsteadily round the tail of the aircraft to inspect the damage. The hole was about six inches across, and had obviously been caused by a 20-millimetre shell, which had entered the left side of the fin at a grazing angle of about ten degrees and exploded, causing considerable damage to the right hand side of the fin and tailplane. After a little consideration, I realised that the shell had probably passed very close to my head and was actually only one of about forty per second coming from this particular gun.

Thus ended the first sortie. We had flown a total of twelve Sea Harriers against two heavily defended airfields, delivered a total of thirty-six bombs, destroyed a large number of enemy aircraft, set light to a number of fuel storage sites and buildings, and escaped almost unscathed. Euphoria now took over from the concern of the pre-dawn briefing. The first operational sortie, the most important in any pilot's life, was over. The rest would now be easier for everyone.

That evening Brian Hanrahan, the BBC's reporter on the spot, sent his report of the raid with the phrase which became famous: 'I cannot say how many aircraft took part in the raid, but I counted them all out and I counted them all back'.

Post Script

In 2007, I returned to the Islands and was concerned to find a row of high tension cables across the route I had used to escape, in thick smoke, after flying past the control tower in 1982. I was relieved to be informed that they had only been there for a few years but horrified when I received an e-mail after my return to UK from Stanley ATC. They had been visited by some Argentine journalists, who were trying to re-create photos taken in 1982. One of these photos showed an HF aerial array slung between 50 ft poles behind the tower, at exactly the point that I had entered the cloud of smoke. I must have flown beneath them, blissfully unaware of their existence!

Credit: Author

Credit: Martin Cleaver EMPICS

Rotary Tales

My first tale is totally in the 'Duct Tape' category, and occurred when I was on my first squadron, flying the Whirlwind Mk 10 in the Far East. First, a bit of background; unless you flew helicopters in the early days, you would be unlikely to know that the rotor blades were protected by a number of layers of neoprene, for both weather protection and as a 'sacrificial' skin - neoprene being cheaper to replace than the true skin of a blade. The leading edge also had a strip of thick-ish, clear, 'sticky-backed plastic' as extra protection - even cheaper and easier to replace than the neoprene! Sometimes rain or debris would damage or wear away this clear layer, and air could be forced into the gap, causing a bubble. This resulted in a hell of a noise and rotor vibration (whumping) which, after a while, became very irritating.

I was tasked to carry a senior Army officer up-country to visit some of his men on exercise. As luck would have it, the aircraft developed one of these 'whumpers' on the outbound leg and, as I landed, it was obvious that we were going to have to do something about it. It was easy to spot the site of the bubble, so we decided on a common and minor (perfectly legal) repair to the affected blade. Once our passenger was safely on his way, we sought out the Army Signals unit as the most likely source of the necessary repair kit. "Have you got some black bodge-tape? The 2 1/2-inch-wide stuff please, and I need about 4 feet". When asked what I needed it for, I just told them I had a faulty main-blade, and needed to stick it back together before flying home. Of course they didn't believe me but, nevertheless, found some bodge-tape and then followed me back to the aircraft, where they watched me and my crewman climb up on the tail boom to carry out this field repair to the faulty blade. We had no sooner finished than our passenger returned, and so, with salutes all around, we started up and departed. To this day, I am sure that there are three ex-squaddies somewhere who might occasionally recount the tale over a few pints of beer and say:

"...and I'll tell you what. I once saw this RAF Rupert[1] use bodge-tape to stick his helicopter's rotor blade back on. Then he flew off with the Colonel on board." And they'll never believe him!

---

[1] Rupert – One of the more repeatable, junior ranks' slang terms for an officer.

My second tale is also set in Borneo. When engaged in troop rotations (moving a replacement unit to a forward location and recovering the original troops), it was sometimes desirable to operate in pairs. This exercise required a number of return flights but the aircraft would carry sufficient fuel to fly just a single round-trip, so crewmen were located at the pick-up (PUP) and drop-off (DOP) points. The routine then was; a quick suck of fuel, load the fresh troops and their kit at the PUP; fly outbound, land and exchange them for the recovering troops and rubbish at the DOP, then return. The crewman controlled the operation on the ground at each location and, once a pattern was established, with a nice spacing between aircraft, a change-over could be accomplished quite rapidly. Although it was more powerful than the earlier choppers, the Whirlwind was not a massive load carrier. The maximum disposable load was rarely more than 1200lbs and, more usually, it was 1000 lbs - or 4 fully equipped troops. However, in those days, we were allowed to operate without a second pilot, so dropping the crewman off gave you one more man's worth of payload; a 25% increase - whoopee! Sometimes the load was not quite as heavy as expected, so a pilot might even land back on, and get the crewman to load another man or piece of kit. You always wanted to maximize your uplift.

On this particular day, we were well into one of these tasks and had flown about 4 rotations (some 3 hours flying). I had picked up another return load of Gurkhas and rubbish (neither smelling very fresh!), and was settling down to the 20 minute transit across the Borneo jungle. About 5 minutes into the trip, I felt a tap on my foot. I should explain that, in the Whirlwind and Wessex, the pilot sat above those 'down the back,' who could only see the pilot's feet. There was normally no intercom available, other than with the crewman, so tapping was the only way of attracting attention. On looking down between my legs, I saw the smiling face of a Gurkha peering up at me. Having got my attention he then gave me a thumbs up, and proffered a mug of liquid. Nice gesture, I thought, and reached down to take the tin mug. It felt quite warm through my flying gloves and, sure enough, when I put it to my lips I found it to be fairly hot tea (with a touch of rum, if I recall correctly!), so I took a sip and handed it back.

Then it struck me. I was picking up troops who had been deployed for several weeks, and I didn't think they would normally have a thermos-flask; so how come the hot tea? I loosened my harness straps, leaned forward and, by looking down and back (not an easy trick in the old Whirlwind), I could just see some of the troops below me. They appeared to be sitting around a hexamine stove[2], heating their tea. The fuel tanks were immediately below the cabin floor, which was reinforced with a sheet of (usually very oily) plywood, so it was not exactly an ideal surface to have in close proximity to a naked flame. Those familiar with the regulations governing the carriage of Dangerous Air Cargo will have already noticed a number of failings but, in those days, everything was dangerous, so we are only discussing the degree. There was nothing I could do and nowhere to land, other than at the PUP or DOP. The DOP was closer but, if I went back, I would not have the fuel to return home, and no other aircraft could get in to continue the task. So I just re-secured my harness and continued en-route.

Despite my best efforts after landing, we never did apprehend the pyromaniacs. There was no means of communicating with the ground team and, by the time the crewman realised that I needed to talk to him, the smooth off load/on load procedure had left me refuelled and with a new batch of troops. So, with two more 'chalks' to rotate to complete the task, I was up and away and filing another lesson learnt into the memory banks.

When one considers the way we operated back in the 60s, and the general experience level of the young helicopter crews (I was Combat Ready on my first Squadron less than two years after joining the RAF), it is remarkable just how few serious incidents actually occurred. Mind you, it wasn't for lack of trying, as the following incidents demonstrate.

Winching guys out of the jungle with a 60 foot cable, when the trees were up to 100 feet tall - you do the maths!

Having to fly a new blade in to a colleague who was stuck in a clearing (which was only big enough to take a second helicopter after the ground troops had trimmed a bit of undergrowth). Why did he need a new blade? A member of the off-loading team was so pleased to see the delivery of a replacement volleyball net (a favourite pastime, when not on patrol), that he shouted with glee to his friends and tossed the net high in the air - straight into the rotor!

Aircraft returning to base with witness marks on the rotor tips, after slightly misjudging the proximity of a tree or cliff.

---

[2] Hexamine stove – A small, solid fuel, portable stove used by the Services.

Landing as Number 2 of a pair one night, and finding we had flown into the middle of an 'aerial farm', with neither helicopter touching a wire - and we got out again!

A Wessex flying over a vehicle that had evaded a security block, and bringing it to a halt by repeatedly banging the main wheel down on top of the car until the occupants, prudently, decided to stop.

Watching tracer bullets pass below my aircraft when I was flying at about 10 feet above the ground. I later discovered that the 'ungodly' were shooting at me and a fast thinking gunner, in the supporting troops, decided to put down suppressive fire under my aircraft, just as I was about to touch down.

Air-dropping chickens from Beverley aircraft to troops on exercise, when the bottoms of the airdrop baskets broke apart as the parachute opened. Two hundred chickens in semi free-fall is an impressive sight!

Watching a 1000-litre fuel cell, on a 'reefed' chute delivery, break free at 500 feet and plummet to the ground, only to rebound almost to the height of the delivery aircraft - Barnes Wallis came to mind. Then seeing the Beverley having to break hard to starboard to avoid receiving its recently-despatched load back on board!

A Belvedere moving sand and gravel from RAAF Butterworth to the radar site on Batu (the highest hill on Penang Island) by underslung load. Ingenious use of a tarpaulin and cargo net had worked well, until a slinging cable got twisted and dumped the better part of a ton of gravel on the dispatching crew. Fortunately there were no serious consequences for the troops, but a lot of red faces for the movements teams overseeing the operation. The stories (which, thankfully, never made the papers) go on and on.

In conclusion, I recall that, as a (just) 21 year old on one of my first solo tasks as a Combat Ready pilot, my authorizer's out-brief finished with the words, "Right, off you go and we'll see you tomorrow. Have a good time but don't break anything." Well, my Service flying career is now well and truly over and, although I came close a few times, I can safely say that I complied with his brief!

Duck or ~~Grouse~~ Gull

It was on the Navigator Training Unit, an element of 100 Squadron dedicated to preparing students for the Tornado F3 and GR4 OCUs. I was enjoying an idyllic second childhood (some will say only an extension of my first) as a Qualified Pilot Nav Instructor (QPNI) on the Hawk. The sortie was a staff upgrade for a newly-arrived Air Navigation Instructor (ANI), consisting of a pairs' low-level route, including a laydown split attack[1] and a co-ordinated laydown/dive attack, both on off-range targets. We were Number 2, so I looked forward to an enjoyable and stress-free sortie, with the added bonus of no write-up to do at the end.

The ANI's main task was ground instruction, since collocation of student and instructor in the air created a shortage of room for a pilot, there being only the 2 seats in a Hawk. Nevertheless, ANIs had to be able to support student sorties as either lead or Number 2, and demonstrate the correct techniques while doing so. They also had to lead and run 'The Plan', a key part of the process, on which the success or failure of the whole sortie could – and often did – hinge. To assist – or, in my case, complicate – The Plan, we had a computerised, automatic planning system. Although the student navigators might not know everything about procedures and tactics, being 'digital natives' they could play the planning kit like a piano. Most of the instructors, and especially the ANIs could be classed as 'digital immigrants'; I, on the other hand, having cut my ground-attack teeth in planning rooms knee-deep in torn maps, was a digital expat; but, since the star of the sortie had to run The Plan, it fell to someone else to work the computer gizmo – guess who? My ineptitude inevitably led to The Plan being so far behind schedule as we approached briefing time (with a firm Time on Target (TOT) and a planned take-off time to match), that we arrived in the briefing room in a clatter of bits, with the drag curve just about in sight, but not immediately attainable. One of the ways in which we could save a little time – or, at least, avoid losing more – was to opt to wear cold-weather flying kit instead

---

[1] Laydown split attack – Due to the possibility of sustaining damage from the detonation of another aircraft's bombs, there was a minimum time separation over the target, which varied, depending on how much risk of self-damage you were prepared to accept. This interval was achieved by the No.2 taking an extended route to the target, and the subsequent RV achieved by the leader taking a similarly extended egress route.

of climbing into a rubber bag[2] (it was early February). The route for this sortie did not venture over the sea, so this seemed a reasonable course of action – at the time.

The sortie progressed uneventfully until we approached the first off-range target in the Borders. The leader, having been delayed by some nefarious ploy created by his instructor, declared 'Slip 1', which meant that he could not make his TOT, and would delay to his alternative, one minute and 20 seconds later. The SOP[3] was that, provided the call was acknowledged, the Number 2 would carry out his attack as planned, but the pair would then swop egress routes, such that they reached the RV (join-up point) only 50 seconds late, thus making it easier to regain the timeline for the rest of the route. As I headed north from the target, probably concentrating a little too much on the timing indications in the GPS[4], I became aware of a flock of birds dead ahead at fairly close range. I pulled up, anticipating that they would break downwards, as these witless creatures appear programmed to do. This they duly did; however, in any flock there is always one 'billy no-mates', and there he was, on the nose at three foot six, and about to join us in the cockpit - which he proceeded to do by flying through it, instead of waiting for us to open it for him.

Anyone who has had this unpleasant experience will probably tell you that the most immediate sensation is noise. This is accompanied by air-blast - the severity of which is obviously proportional to the airspeed - and maps, and anything else which is detachable, flying around the cockpit. One large and jagged piece of canopy had even managed to fly forward, and I found it in front of the gunsight after landing – I never did quite figure out how it managed that. I was also aware that my helmet visor had shattered, and that there was a length of MDC[5] hanging down in front of my face. The approved solution to this

---

[2] Rubber Bag – In this context, slang for the immersion suit that was worn by aircrew to provide additional protection in the event of having to bale out and ending up in very cold water.
[3] SOP – Standard Operating Procedure.
[4] GPS – Global Positioning System, more commonly known as satellite navigation or Satnav.
[5] MDC – Miniature Detonating Cord. Lengths of explosive which were attached to the inside of the canopy, with the function of fragmenting the canopy on ejection, to allow unhindered passage upwards of the ejection seats. There was an outside chance of it detonating when the canopy was opened or closed, for which reason we kept our visors down and eyes shut, and the ground-crew hid under the fuselage at such times.

dilemma was to leave the throttle where it was (pretty close to the far left corner, as I recall) and get away from the ground which, we were constantly telling our students, had a PK[6] of 1. The latter action would also have the effect of reducing the speed, provided that you could get to a reasonable height without going into cloud, which was probably not a good idea until you were confident that all the instruments were still working.

The next move was to figure out where to take the remains of the aircraft (and the remains of the bird, for that matter). In the brief, as usual, we had discussed diversion airfields around the route, and had nominated Newcastle and Edinburgh for this section. I reckoned that I was about equidistant from the 2 (later scrutiny of the map showed this to be a deal more accurate than some of my other assessments that day); Edinburgh required a 90 turn to the left, but Newcastle a 180 to head south. However, I was now in the cabriolet version of the Hawk, with communications which I had not yet had the chance to check out, and an engine which, although it appeared to be working fine, might well have ingested some perspex from the canopy. The thought of having to explain a forced-landing procedure to a civilian air trafficker, using a dodgy radio, did not fill me with enthusiasm; nor did avoiding civilian traffic and crossing a city with a dicky engine; plus, I was still heading north, so the sensible thing to do seemed to be to head for RAF Leuchars, where the crash crews understood people like me, and were familiar with the hazards of MDC.

And so it was that I found myself (or, more accurately, we found ourselves, although Webby in the back had not, thus far, had a vote) over a very cold sea, in an aeroplane which could not guarantee to keep me out of it, without benefit of immersion suit. It might be all right for the nutters at Blyth on New Year's Day, but it didn't seem like such a good idea to me. The feckless bird, it transpired later, had entered through the right hand part of the main canopy, struck my swede a glancing blow, and continued through the bulkhead and instrument panel to the back cockpit, where it distributed itself evenly in a sort of seagull soup. There was plenty left over, however, to cover the coamings, instrument panels and GPS in the front. Webby's first concern had been whether I was still in control of the aircraft; with my flying, it is sometimes hard to tell. Inter-cockpit

---

[6] PK – Probability of Kill

communication was impossible, and a thumbs-up was not acknowledged due to the Potage du Larus Argentatus covering the blast-shield. However, by briefed movements of the stick, I convinced him that he was not about to clock up his first Captain hours (indeed, his first pilot hours of any description). When we could talk to each other, we discovered that we had both put out a PAN call on Guard[7]; this had been heard by our leader, who joined us on the way to Leuchars, and carried out a visual inspection of our aircraft. He couldn't tell me anything I didn't know already, but he could take a bit of the load off us by talking to Leuchars. The rest of the sortie was relatively uneventful; at some point I had to make the choice between maintaining height and positioning for a precautionary forced-landing pattern, in the knowledge that the act of throttling back to idle might send an erroneous message to the engine that its work for the day was done; or going for a fixed power approach, in which case any subsequent misbehaviour by the motor would result in the swim we had been trying to avoid. I opted for the latter, and was not let down.

There was some aftermath to this. Once we had slowed down on the runway, and the effect of the automatic air-conditioning had reduced, the first thing which struck us both was the smell. I don't know what our erstwhile sparring partner had had for breakfast, but it was pretty evil, and Webby was now covered in it. Subsequent inspection of the engine showed it to have bravely swallowed significant lumps of perspex, but it had gamely kept turning – thanks, Rolls-Royce. It amazes me, looking at a photo of the Hawk and the relative positions of canopy and intakes, how bits from the canopy, when travelling at 400+ knots, can find their way in there, but they do! Once we had repaired to the Med Centre for a check-up, I also discovered that the blood on my face, which I had fondly imagined to belong to the now-deceased, was in fact mine. The Medical Officer congratulated us on our escape, and judged us to be unfit to be ferried back home as passengers in other Squadron aircraft; there then ensued an unseemly wrangle between Leuchars MT and Leeming MT as to who was responsible for transporting us home. After a cunning plan to RV in some motorway service station halfway between the two Stations had been deemed too

---

[7] PAN call on Guard – A radio transmission on an emergency frequency to indicate that a state of urgency exists, although there is no imminent danger to life or the continued viability of the aircraft.

difficult, we found ourselves on the southbound platform at Leuchars Junction, surrendering ourselves to the tender mercies of the rail network – which, it has to be said, were probably distinctly tenderer than those of RAF MT, the more so because, since we were travelling in uniform – of a sort – we were entitled to first-class tickets. Also on the plus side, since our flying kit had all been confiscated for examination (and, hopefully, incineration), the Leuchars Flight Safety Officer had gone on a smash-and-grab raid of Clothing Stores, and we were now decked out in brand new kit, including some items we hadn't even been wearing.

Lessons learned? 1. Work at being a bit sharper on the planning gizmo (I did). 2. Plan the diversions according to where you would actually go in a worst-case scenario, and dress accordingly. 3. Having someone to talk to, who can share the workload and monitor what you're doing, is a wonderful thing.

Mostly, however, every time I went near St Abbs Head after that, I kept a b****y sharp eye out, in case his Mum was looking for me!

Credit: Geoff Lee

June 1953 - The Coronation Flypast

The year 2013 marked the 60th anniversary of Her Majesty's Coronation. At Westminster Abbey, on 2nd June 1953, she had been crowned Queen, and there was a massive military parade in her honour. It comprised huge numbers of servicemen and other citizens from all over the Commonwealth and Empire. At that time there was still a vast British Empire and, together with our allies, we had not long since won World War Two. With that went a great overall loyalty towards the Monarchy and a feeling that, with this new young Queen, we could all go forward together and the future would be ours.

The route that she took in the state coach, from Westminster Abbey to Buckingham Palace, was lined all the way, and the following march-past went on for many hours. The various contingents advanced up The Mall and paid their respects to her, as she stood on the balcony of the Palace returning their salutes with Prince Philip at her side.

Royal Air Force Fighter Command was given the honour of performing a flypast and, in so doing, paying the RAF's airborne respects to the Monarch. This flypast consisted of units from all commands of the RAF, together with others belonging to various Commonwealth air forces, and should not be confused with the one for the Royal Air Force review at Odiham, which comprised many more aircraft and took place later that summer. In the early fifties, the treasury's scrutiny had not yet been brought to bear too heavily on the RAF. Fighter Command was still a large and very potent fighting force, the regular day-fighter contingent of it alone consisting of about twenty fighter squadrons, the strength of each being either sixteen or twenty two aircraft. Such numbers must be regarded with amazement, and probably no little jealousy, by today's members of the Service, which has been so terribly cut down by successive Treasury axes.

Usually either two or three squadrons were joined together on one station to form a wing, sometimes with a night fighter squadron as well. Otherwise, the night fighters were based at their own stations, such as West Malling and Coltishall. There was a string of fighter stations that stretched from Fife in Scotland to Sussex on the Channel Coast, but almost all of them have long since passed out of the world of the RAF; they just remain alive in the memories of an everdwindling, past generation of pilots and ground staff.

The main equipment in 1953 was the Gloster Meteor Mk 8, but this work-horse was coming to the end of its operational days, and was generally regarded as being inferior to the swept wing fighters, which had entered service with the USAF and the Soviet Air Force. However, those of us fighter pilots who flew the 'Meatbox' every day, and had done so for some years, knew that we could still give a very good account of ourselves if it ever came to war with Russia, and we were faced with the real thing. We often mixed it with the F86 Sabres from the American squadrons, based in East Anglia, and knew all the tricks there were about taking on swept wing fighters. The Meteor might have been outdated, but it was a great aircraft and we were at one with it. Our morale was very high, just as it should be with fighter pilots.

Six Meteor wings were picked to make up the formation that would fly over Buckingham Palace, and provide our contribution to the parade. These were based at Duxford, Waterbeach, Wattisham, Horsham St Faith, Odiham and Biggin Hill. The honour of forming this flypast fell mainly on 11 Group squadrons, as it would take place in their area, but they were joined for the occasion by one from 12 Group, the Horsham wing, whose base was near Norwich. The Royal Canadian Air Force wing, which was equipped with Sabres and under the control of Fighter Command, was based at North Luffenham, in Rutland, and would make the number of wings taking part up to seven. Each wing would consist of two squadrons, each made up of twelve aircraft flying in three flights of four. That added up to 144 Meteors and 24 Sabres, a total of 168 fighters all together - a huge number to form just a single, close formation.

The four aircraft of each flight would fly in box formation. These boxes would form an arrow head, with one flight on either side of, and slightly stepped back from, the leader. Thus, each squadron's three flights would form what was known as a 'Vic'. The second squadron in each wing would position directly behind the one in the lead, so making the wing into a solid block of twenty four aircraft. The first three wings would form up, again one on either side of the leader and slightly stepped back from him, so making one large vic. Behind the three leading wings, in line astern to them, would come the RCAF Sabre wing, whilst the three remaining Meteor wings were to form up as another block behind the Canadians. This was really a vast conglomeration of fighters, all in close formation, in the same patch of sky, at the same time, and, on paper, the whole thing might have seemed to be a bit of a muddle. Well, in the air it had the possibility of being more than a muddle; it could have the makings of a most horrendous pile up, but none of us thought like that in those days.

The Duxford wing had the honour of leading the whole formation, though, of course, we felt that honour should have been ours. Their leader was Wing Commander Jimmy Wallace, the OC Flying on that station. Only three years before, he had been our CO on 41 Squadron, so we felt slightly mollified. We flew slightly stepped back on his right, whilst the Odiham wing, led by Wing Commander Denis Crowley-Milling, formed up on his left. Then, in line astern behind the 24 RCAF Sabres of their 401 Squadron, came the Meteors of the Wattisham wing with the Horsham St Faith wing, led by Wing Commander 'Billy' Drake, stepped back on their right, and the Waterbeach wing, led by Wing Commander 'Paddy' Barthrop, on their left.

We were to fly at two hundred and fifty knots, which was the normal cruising speed for Meteors at low level, if you were not in any hurry. At that speed, the controls were positive and gave a good response to your inputs. Also, the early jet engines, such as the Rolls-Royce Derwent which powered our aircraft, were very thirsty at that height, so revs needed to be kept down to a practical minimum. The whole thing would be organised and controlled by No11 Group, of which we were a part and in whose sector we would be flying. The commander of the operation would be the Air Officer Commanding 11 Group, Air Vice- Marshal the Earl of Bandon. Throughout the whole Royal Air Force, he was much respected and known as the 'Abandoned Earl', or 'Paddy' Bandon. The command post for the operation was to be situated on the roof of the RAF Club, near Hyde Park Corner in Piccadilly.

Because we were the only regular squadron in the Biggin Hill wing, just for this operation No1 Squadron, whose base was Tangmere on the Sussex Coast, were joined up with us. They had been at Tangmere since pre-war days, and that station was always thought of as their home. Now they flew in to work with us for the practices, and then again for the actual show itself; so together, for the flypast, we formed the Biggin Hill Wing. No1 were another superb fighter squadron, and the two of us were used to working together. The only other squadron at Tangmere was a night fighter unit, so we were fairly often required to make up a day fighter wing on exercises, flying from either of our two stations.

Any pilots who served on No1 might disagree about it, but as a member of 41, I can vouch for it that 41 was, by perhaps only just a narrow margin, certainly the best of the two - but both were outstanding. Each month, the two of us were at the top of the published lists of such things as Command gunnery scores and flying hours. Consequently, there was a very healthy rivalry between the two squadrons. In March 1953, we received the official word that we were to take part in the planned Coronation Day flypast and practice flights would start in April. We were officially told what our position would be in the formation and that, with No1 Squadron, we would be described as the Biggin Hill wing.

For some reason, possibly because of the Auxiliaries who were based there, Biggin Hill was different in a number of ways from normal RAF stations, one being that our station commander was a wing commander, Wing Commander 'Splinters' Smallwood, not a group captain, as was the usual thing. Also, the OC flying was only a squadron leader, not a wing commander. In this case, the wing would not be led by our OC flying, but by our station commander. We would be the lead squadron of the two, with No1 behind us; naturally, we had no doubt that this was the correct way of going about things - we had the place that we duly deserved. Our CO, Squadron Leader 'Dusty' Miller, would fly as Splinters' No3, and be the deputy leader. Well, if he could not be the out and out leader, then naturally he should be the deputy, though he would rather have been leading his own squadron.

The first important thing was that the wing leaders had to perfect their joining up technique. This would be one of the great difficulties, and their navigation and timing needed to be absolutely accurate, literally down to a split second over check points. All turns would have to be made very gently, and no last moment steep banks to get into the correct position could possibly be acceptable. The leaders of wings on either side of the one at the front had to be equal distances apart, and not too close. There were a lot of fighters to fit into the patch of sky between each of those leaders, and being too close to one another could cause horrendous pileups between the wings. The first practices were for the leaders alone, although, on some, their deputies flew with them as a pair. I had no idea then just what the real difficulties were, and I remember being rather surprised one afternoon when, after they had landed, I saw Splinters and Dusty talking together with very serious expressions on both their faces. They shook their heads and I heard one say, 'Well, that's something that really must be sorted out'. We were just anxious to get going, and had what could only be termed as a sublime faith in the people who would lead us. They led us on day-to-day exercises, during our ordinary training, and we never doubted them. Only a few years before, most of them had led fighter squadrons in combat.

Each wing would form up quickly into its own two squadron formation pattern during the turn, immediately after take-off from their base. This was not difficult, and was something that we always had to do as part of our everyday flying, though it was usually forming into battle formation, not accurate close formation as this would be. As the formation proceeded along its route, the various wings joined up with one another. The leading Duxford wing came past Southend in Essex, and then headed in a straight line towards the South Coast, across the Thames Estuary and over the Isle of Sheppey. Having flown directly from Biggin, we slid in on their right and took up our position in the formation as they crossed Sheppey. Then, on reaching the Channel coast, we all turned right and followed it along in a westerly direction. We turned again and headed inland, at a point which led us in a straight line directly over Biggin Hill, so passing at right angles across the Mall, just in front of the Palace. The Odiham wing, which was the last to join, slipped in on the left of the leaders as we crossed the coast. We would be approaching from Her Majesty's right, instead of coming directly up the Mall, as flypasts have done ever since. In the event of bad weather, we were told that we would fly with all seven wings in line astern to one another. The difficulty with such a formation, though, would be the possibility of a whiplash effect, which could be very dangerous and uncomfortable at the rear. Also, in order to avoid slipstream, each wing would be stepped down from the one ahead of it, and so the aircraft at the rear would be dodging the trees and chimney pots - rather nasty for everyone concerned.

Our first practice was on April 7th, and we had eleven more altogether, before Coronation Day itself. There were no hitches to the programme, or 'dicey dos' during the flights. Anyway, from where I was, I would not have seen anything go wrong, unless it happened in my immediate vicinity. All I ever saw was the wing tip of the aircraft that I held formation on. That's all you do see when you are flying in close echelon formation, wing tips in line, and head just about opposite the roundel on the other aircraft's fuselage. The weather for that first practice was fine, just as it was for all the rest of the practices. If the weather was ever unsuitable, the practice was cancelled, so there were no problems on that score. In fact, the whole thing became more or less routine, which is just the way such an operation should be. Also, it made an interesting change to our normal day to day work of practice quarter attacks, battle formation drills and interceptions.

Of course the weather was just waiting to turn itself on for Coronation Day, and anybody who remembers 2nd June 1953 will know that it poured incessantly with rain. All those taking part in the parade, and lining the streets, were soaked through, just as were the spectators. Clouds were low and ragged, dragged by a strong, gusty, southwest wind, and some would say that it was typical English weather for June. It was exactly what all the Commonwealth forces, who had travelled from the ends of the earth in order to take part, had always been led to believe about Britain - that the weather there was always just terrible.

We went to met briefing as usual in the morning, and left there not expecting to do any flying that day, certainly not a large formation flight such as had been planned. The met man had told us that the foul weather would last all day, and that it was likely to go on raining without any respite. As usual, we went back to our crewroom afterwards, and started the dreary business of just hanging around. We confidently expected to be stood down, and that, after all the rehearsals, the show would not go as planned. Sadly, the RAF, in the form of Fighter Command, would not be paying its respects to the Sovereign on her Coronation Day. This was all rather depressing, but the planned flying in such conditions was just not on. Word came through from Group that no decision would be made until the absolute last minute. So it became a day of waiting and wondering, and putting our heads out of the door to look at the weather, every so often. We always hated waiting, our instinct was inevitably to get up and get on with it, but wait we had to.

The weather did not appear to let up in any way; for once the met man had been right. The cloud base looked as if it was at about one thousand feet, but it was ragged and wind-torn, with scattered, broken bits below. We also knew that the gusty wind would make formation flying very difficult, and not in the least comfortable. It would have to improve a great deal for the Air Officer Commanding (AOC) to feel that he could risk a large fighter force in such conditions.

In any case, it was certainly not the kind of weather in which any of us might want to go flying, unless it was simply a case of climbing straight up through the muck, and coming out in the fine clear air above it all at about thirty thousand feet. The flypast was programmed to be the last item of the parade, and we were not scheduled to pass over the Palace until about six o'clock that evening. So we had plenty of time to watch all that wild weather and wonder what the decision was going to be, but we couldn't believe that we would actually fly.

We were quite wrong! Any Royal Air Force Air Vice-Marshal, such as our AOC was, could not possibly consider doing something which might harm the reputation of the Service in any way. To make it appear that RAF pilots could not cope with weather like this was just unthinkable; of course they would be able to put on a good show. At the last moment, just as planned, the word came through from Group: it was 'On', and we were to fly the standard formation that we had practised, not the bad weather alternative.

At the appointed time, on six RAF stations in the Southeast of England and one RCAF station in the Midlands, 168 fighter pilots climbed into their cockpits and started their engines. Just as was our normal every day procedure, we took off in pairs with a ten second interval between each. To avoid slipstream as much as possible, the first pair would remain low directly after becoming unstuck then, in order to get above the jet blast from the aircraft ahead of them, the second pair had to pull up steeply as soon as they were off the deck. For all those following, the drill of low high, low high in turn would continue. With this system, 24 aircraft would take just two minutes to get airborne. As soon as he was safely clear of the ground, the leader would start a turn and, in this case, with the number of aircraft that there were behind him, it would have to be just a gentle one. Each pair's leader would then turn inside the aircraft ahead of him, as soon as he safely could and so close into his position. Thus the join up was never difficult, and just normal routine to us.

This time it was a bit different. There was no slipstream problem, as the howling crosswind blew all the jet blast well clear, away to the side of the line of flight along the runway, but the turbulence hit us as soon as our wheels were off the deck. It was incredible, and lasted throughout the whole flight, making formation keeping really hard work. There was no smooth, gentle movement of controls; it was just a case of fighting things all the way and forcing your aircraft into the position you needed it to be, in relation to one that you were formating on. I am unable to relate anything much in the way of details about the flight, except that it was all pretty hairy. I was able to think of only one thing all the way really, and that was just working as hard as I could in order to hold tight to my position in the formation. Where we might actually be at any one time, I could never say. There was no looking over the side and relaxing my concentration on what had to be done, for even a moment. It did not really matter to know where we were anyway, except that, at the appropriate moment, we needed to know that we were approaching the run-in to the Palace. At that point, we would have to make an extra effort to fly in exactly the correct position, and as smoothly and steadily as possible.

Two marvellous radio calls during the flight have remained firmly in my mind, and I laugh whenever I think of them. In fact, the first could have been far from a laughing matter, but somehow, perhaps just by luck, there was no trouble. As we were heading towards the Isle of Sheppey to start our join up, one of the other wing leaders needed to know just where the Waterbeach wing was in relation to him at that particular moment. He called, "Paddy, Paddy, where are you now?" Back came the answer from Wing Commander Barthrop, "Over Southend at one thousand feet in cloud." "Oh my God", came the answer from the first wing leader, "So am I!" They found one another safely and that all worked out with nothing more than a frightening moment or two. Our leaders were brilliant and, thanks to them, everything went off as planned without some ghastly accident.

Then, after passing over the Palace, as we continued on to the north, the AOC came on the radio: "Well done chaps. We've been standing out here on the roof all afternoon getting soaked on the outside, now we can go indoors and get soaked on the inside." As soon as we landed, we all headed straight for the bar in the Mess, and also got soaked on the inside. Our route had taken us directly over Biggin Hill on the run up to London. The people on the ground there told us that they rushed out to watch us pass over, and then rushed back inside to watch us on the television, coming over the Palace.

In 2004, the BBC made a short film about Coronation Day, including the parade and the flypast. Together with Roy Tappenden, another pilot from the squadron who had flown that day, fifty years before, I was asked to take part. We met in the RAF Museum at Hendon, where each of us in turn sat in the cockpit of a Meteor 8, whilst we answered some questions. Amongst other things, both of us were asked what the crowds of people and the marchers looked like from the air as we flew over. The interviewer seemed surprised when we both said the same thing, "Heavens, that's the last place that we would ever look when flying in formation in such conditions. I never saw a thing except my leader's wingtip!" Using old takes from the day, the film showed just how wet it was and how soaked everyone had become. The Coronation medal might have come out with the rations, but I know that we all earned ours that day, just as did all the service personnel who marched or lined the route in the pouring rain. But at least we stayed dry in our cockpits!

Credit: RAF/Crown Copyright

Dangerous Domestos

It was the summer of 1975, the Air Officer Commanding's annual visit to RAF Luqa, Malta, was imminent, and each crew on No 203 Squadron was allocated one of our Nimrod MR1 aircraft to clean internally, the groundcrew being responsible for the external appearance.

As the captain of Crew 2, it was up to me to decide how to allocate the various tasks for the areas to be cleaned in XV241. I thought that, if I detailed one of the NCOs to clean the toilet, he would feel that 'yet again' the NCOs were being stigmatised; but, if I asked one of the officers to carry out the task, he would feel that it really wasn't the sort of thing that an officer should be asked to do. So I decided to set a democratic example by cleaning the wash basin and Elsan myself.

On the day that XV241 was available for cleaning, I arrived at work armed with cleaning clothes, Domestos, Jif and the like, and duly embarked upon my self-imposed task. By lunchtime, when we had finished cleaning the aircraft, it was 'as good as new', with nowhere more gleaming than the toilet. However, what I hadn't even considered was the chemical reaction between the Elsan fluid and the cleaning materials that I had used!

On getting home to my hiring near St Paul's Bay, my wife greeted me with a gasp and our two young sons didn't recognise me – my face was so swollen up that my hat perched on my head like the proverbial pimple on a pie crust. I never associated this with my toilet cleaning activities so, next morning, I was at the front of the queue at the Medical Centre, seeking an explanation and treatment for my condition – which the Doc quickly diagnosed, not as some terrible tropical disease but as the result of the fumes coming off the Elsan, caused by a reaction between the Domestos bleach and the Elsan oil. Outcome: grounded for one week and lesson learnt!

The final sting in the tail was that, after leaving the Doc's consulting room, I passed my flight engineer in the corridor. He walked right past without even recognising me.

Toilet Notice

In an attempt to make the toilet in the Nimrod easier to clean after flight, and to try to reduce blockages, copies of this notice were attached to the wall adjacent to the Elsan:

> **Before You Sit Upon This Crapper,**
> **Put Some Paper On The Flapper.**
> **Then The Seat, When It's Replaced,**
> **Will Dispose Of All Your Waste.**
> **Please Don't Use Your Private Tissue,**
> **Use The Paper That We Issue.**

Pretty much to the point!

Credit: Geoff Lee

Blackpool Illuminations

I had just arrived at my squadron, after the Central Flying School course, as a newly-fledged Qualified Flying Instructor on the Jet Provost 5A. My squadron checkout at night was carried out by a charismatic ex-Lightning pilot – a really great guy. Not wise to the ways of such folk, I looked forward to seeing how things were done with fighter flair. The normal procedure of launching all the first wave of some 6 aircraft at the same time was in operation. Things got off to a brisk start; having got airborne we left the circuit, said goodbye to RAF Leeming, a base on the east side of the Pennines, and set off to the West. A few minutes into the flight, my mate turned off everything – navigation lights, transponder and also stopped talking to Air Traffic Control. This was something new, so I asked what we were up to. "Off to see the Blackpool illuminations!" came the answer.

Staying above safety altitude, which meant that we would not bounce off the Pennines on the way over, we arrived to see the colourful display of lights clearly on a pitch-black night and, with Blackpool tower in sight and well below the airways, we let down off the coast. We then had a great time – rushing up and down the beach, below the level of the searchlight on the tower, as it scanned the skies desperately (and unsuccessfully) trying to find us. Safely over the sea, we weren't in the least bit worried.

Eventually it was time for the fun to stop, so we climbed back above safety altitude, and sauntered back towards base. In due course all the electrics were turned back on, we chatted to Leeming again, and did several "touch and goes" to get the correct number of night landings out of the way, thus completing my night currency.

Feeling pretty smug, in that the night check had been completed satisfactorily, we signed the aircraft in, and went to the crew-room for the inevitable coffee before the next flight. The other crews joined us, and very casually we commented on what a smooth night it was, if a bit dark in the absence of moon/ starlight. Very gently someone steered the conversation onto what sort of flying might be suitable for such a night. To my mounting horror, the first crew boasted of having wandered over to see the Blackpool illuminations, they were then joined by others who also started to look just slightly ashen-faced. We each realised that what had stirred up the searchlight on Blackpool tower was not just the noise of a single aircraft, but the awareness that, just perhaps, there was more than one of them out there in the dark.

Sometimes you get lucky!

Credit: Arpingstone/Wikipedia

You Will Go To War

'Gentlemen, you will go to war in this theatre!' After 10 or so hours flight by Hercules, via RAF Akrotiri in Cyprus, these were the first words spoken to us on our arrival at the Tornado Detachment in Muharraq, Bahrain; it was October 1990 and Operation Desert Shield - the international coalition operation to halt Saddam Hussein from expanding his conquests in the Middle East - was well under way. The person who spoke these words was the Air Commander, Operation Granby, the code name for RAF ops in support of Desert Shield. There we were, 8 of us standing there in the planning room, four 31 Squadron crews. A picture of Baldrick from Blackadder Goes Forth adorned the door, announcing he had 'a cunning plan' – right there, at that moment, we certainly hoped someone did. We had been deployed to augment 14 Squadron, who had been in theatre from the initial deployment in August. Having had one week's notice, here we were in a potential war zone, the first time for all of us! Quite a sobering thought. We rightly anticipated that this was going to be the most 'interesting' deployment any of us had ever taken part in. It was becoming clear that the international war of words was little more than 'mouth-music' and that, as things stood, we would indeed go to war in this theatre.

I had been posted to 31 Squadron almost exactly a year before, a re-tread from 7 years on Buccaneers. I had enjoyed the mighty banana jet, but felt that it was time for new pastures, a new challenge and a chance to see a bit more of the world. My front-line flying career started on the Operational Conversion Unit at RAF Honington. Stepping onto the wing of my first ever Buccaneer for my familiarisation flight, I was a little perturbed to see two gaping holes in the wings. It appeared that the ginger-beers[1] had omitted to refit a couple of not insignificant panels in the middle of the wing after the last service. I was gently informed that the panels would normally cover the wing fold joint, but more often than not, they buckled and, for that reason, they were never fitted. Mmmmm, didn't recall that little snippet from ground school! Hey ho, off into the wide blue yonder, thundering skyward (compared to a Jet Provost 5A, or even a Hawk, this was quite something). We completed a high- level transit to

---

[1] Ginger Beers – Engineers.

the Northumberland coast. During planning, I had been a little perturbed that, despite checking and re-checking the coordinates, the plotted turning point always turned out to be just off the coast - odd. However, the reason became clear when I asked my pilot instructor to turn right and begin the descent to low level over the sea. There was Holy Island, right under our wing. Putting two and two together for once, I informed 'Wings' that the turning point was directly beneath us. We found a few ships on the radar and did a bit of 'homing in' on them. 'Wings' then proceeded to show me some of the Buccaneer's finer handling points. As we sank lower, and lower, and lower, the sea became a blur; we were hurtling along at nought foot six and 580 knots. It was at this point that 'Wings' held both hands above his head, to demonstrate the inherent stability of the old beast. Well what can you say 30 feet above the sea, close to 600 knots, and nobody holding the controls – incredible. A quick blast through Wainfleet range, a couple of Medium Toss DHs[2] (yeah, right), and back to Honington for tea and medals.

I was the first of my course to fly, and so the other navs were naturally curious to hear how it had all gone. I enthused about the wave-height, high speed dash with some relish. It was a little later in the day that 'Wings' invited me into a quiet corner of the hangar, to explain about flight authorisation, minimum separation distances, discipline at all times but, more importantly, the art of knowing when to keep 'schtum'. However, it was also satisfying to hear him discreetly asking one of the instructor navs if the high level turn point of FAM1 was an island off the coast, and even more amusing to hear his 'oppo' say he hadn't a clue! Honours even!

And so to 12 Sqn and RAF Lossiemouth. There were no Married Quarters available for a recently- married Flying Officer, with no kids and not even enough points to warrant a hiring. With no home to go to, the only course of action was to get our first mortgage and a beautiful cottage, just a mile or so away from the airfield - best move we ever made! But back to the Bucc. My time on the force followed the usual progression of 2, 4, and 6-ship lead, QWI[3] course et al. We were principally a maritime attack wing, utilising TV and AR

---

[2] DH - Direct Hit.
[3] QWI - Qualified Weapons Instructor.

Martel[4] and conventional 1000lb retarded and freefall bombs; later weaponry included Paveway laser-guided 1000lb bombs and Pavespike laser designation. I often wondered how we would fare against a Kirov[5] battlegroup, firing only 4 TV and 4 AR missiles per attack from 10 miles out. What a blessing it was that Maritime HQ's strategy was to task us against relatively unarmed oilers on the way to refuel their fleet!

Whilst the Germany-based 'overland gang' were a little disparaging of us maritime types, there was a great sense of satisfaction to be had when, after a bit of air-to-air refuelling and a 2 hour transit, the ship of your choice turned up under your TV Martel crosshairs. Just prior to my departure from Lossie, the force was reequipped with Sea Eagle, which significantly changed the odds. Now 24 sea-skimming missiles could be launched per 6-ship from over the horizon, with a correspondingly higher chance of collecting the aforementioned tea and medals! We had also, by this time, been equipped with an inertial navigation platform which was pretty accurate. However, its principal reason for being there was to provide the Sea Eagle with precise launch parameters. Whilst it would have significantly improved our bombing accuracy as well, that upgrade was never funded. We were still very much in the map and stopwatch mode of navigation for overland and sea as, on occasion, a slight overheat in the avionics bay could see indicated speeds in excess of 1000 knots on the inertial nav display – even in the circuit!

Fighter affiliation was always interesting. Whilst the Bucc was outstanding at running low and fast in straight lines for a very long time, 'mixing it' with any credible modern air defender was just not on. I do remember vividly on one maritime exercise being overtaken by a flight of Tornado F3s as if we were standing still, despite the ASI showing 580 knots; oh for a bit of reheat (oh, and a tanker near at hand!).

The buddy-buddy tactical tanker role of the Buccaneer was of course legendary for the lower, longer, further profile often sung about in Happy Hour.

---

[4] Martel - An Anglo-French anti-shipping missile, the product of a collaboration between Hawker Siddeley and Matra, with 2 variants, TV-guided and Anti-Radiation. The name is derived from Missile, Anti-Radiation, Television.
[5] Kirov - The first of a class of 4 battle-cruisers, built for the Soviet Navy in the Cold War, and the heaviest and most powerful non-carrier surface ships in the fleet.

This capability was trialled to extend the range of a Tornado (also often sung about at Happy Hour, but not in such adoring terms!). However, it required one Tornado, one Buccaneer and a fleet of VC10s, similar in concept to the Black Buck raids during the Falklands. The two fast-jets were topped up from VC10s, as close to bad-lands as was prudent. We then accompanied the Tornado to low level, topping him up as far down track as we could. We returned to the tanker for a further plug, descended to low level again, met the Tornado at a predetermined point (us using DR[6] essentially), topping him up on our way back to our chaperones for the return journey. Quite what we thought the opposition would be doing whilst we conducted these intricate manoeuvres, I'm not sure.

I don't consider myself a superstitious type and, in my 7 years on the Bucc, I only occasionally found myself reaching for the wooden handle on the canopy winding mechanism for 'good luck', or so I thought; one of the Navy's finer ideas. But time for a change, and so there I was, 1989, 1500 hours of good flying behind me, and off to the swing wing Jaguar... sorry Tornado; the joys of Cottesmore, and the Tornado Tri-National Training Establishment (TTTE).

Groundschool left my head feeling that it had been placed in a microwave; I was disbelieving at the number of buttons required to get any simple task done, and astonished at all of this crew cooperation talk - wasn't that what two-seat aircraft crews did? And the amount of time spent looking in! Not that I was much of a whizz at spotting the bounce, more a need to keep the world in view to reduce my predilection for chucking up! When, in one lecture, we were informed that the TFR[7] would 'alarm off' if more than 60° of bank was detected, I asked the Italian instructor how, then, one coped with the clangers going off, if one ridge-rolled[8] with the TRF up and running. 'Reeedge rolling ? What is this reeedge rooollling?' Not a sign of things to come I hoped!

It took quite a time for me to get it into my head that an attack run started 10 or more miles from the IP[9] rather than, as on the Bucc, when you eyeballed the IP and declared 'over to you, Wings'. Weapon package, fix/attack/ stab and

---

[6] DR – Dead Reckoning navigation.
[7] TFR – Terrain-Following Radar.
[8] Ridge-rolling – The technique of rolling the aircraft on its back and pulling down when crossing a ridge, in order to minimise the 'ballooning' effect over the ridge crest.
[9] IP – Initial Point.

the radar centred on your IP or chosen update point. A green haze shimmered in front of you, a bit of tilt and a bit of gain and maybe, just maybe, a picture resembling what you had highlighted on your 50-thou ordnance survey map would appear. If you hadn't updated your height channel by overflying some conveniently flat piece of ground, then what looked like a good mark to you might appear to the pilot as suspended in mid-air or buried under the nose! And still, with all this technology, we were planning on overflying our heavily-defended target to drop something that was designed in 1944! And we won't even go into the efficacy of the enforced tactical rigidity of night TFR!!! Still, it was quite remarkable what could be done with a 128K computer - yes 128K, not even 1Meg never mind 5 Gigabytes!

I had been a little over a year in Germany when Saddam ordered the invasion of Kuwait. Lots of speculation on the who/what/when abounded before, in August, 14 Squadron was tasked to deploy from our base to Bahrain, as the RAF attack contribution to Desert Storm[10]. I kept assuring my wife that there were plenty more experienced chaps on the squadron and that, if 31 were called upon, I was unlikely to be selected etc, etc, etc! Fortunately I'm not a betting man. At the end of September, 31 were tasked to supply a 4-ship to augment the Bahrain detachment. I was planning to tell my wife after we had been to a party that weekend. But, as we left the bash, my wife with car keys in hand, one of the chaps asked her what she thought about me being selected to go off to war (thanks mate!). So I took the car keys from my now somewhat stunned wife and (not thinking) drove back onto the base. I will always be grateful to the Corporal on gate duty that night. He asked me if I had been drinking; after a pause, I said that I had just had the one before leaving a party. He looked me straight in the eye, paused, and then waved me through. Mitigating circumstances or not, it was a close shave.

My intended pilot for the deployment had just been posted onto the squadron that week, from a sister Bruggen squadron, and we hadn't met. So, arriving for the briefing, and noting a new face, I walked over to him and said, "You must be Mike, how do you fancy going off to war?" As it transpired, we didn't

---

[10] Desert Storm - A war waged by coalition forces from 34 nations in response to Iraq's invasion and annexation of Kuwait.

fly together, but what a way to meet a new squadron mate!

And so there we were. Facing this Air Commodore, telling us we would go to war in this theatre. We soon fell into a routine; high level transit to Oman, with air-to-air refuelling; fighter affiliation, either against the Jaguar detachment from Thumrait, or one of our own; occasional weaponry on Misierra or Fahad ranges; lots of night flying, lots of TFR. There was always something alluring about desert flying - or, maybe it was just the complete absence of bird sanctuaries/old folks' homes/ industrial avoidance sites/towns etc, etc, etc. The RAF operated a 3-month rotation and so, in late November, 14 Squadron handed over the detachment to 15 Squadron, and we remained as augmentees. We were cleared to fly at 50 feet, (just like my first day on the Bucc OCU!). There were some amazing incidents; on one occasion, we were pulling round a turn, when I looked over my shoulder to see what must have been the wingtip vortex carving a groove in the sand! Oh, for a bit of wood in the cockpit! We pulled up a wee bit after that. One wag at Shareholders[11] suggested that we should exceed an operating limit each day and report back, so that we could expand the flight envelope prior to the big push! After a pregnant and incredulous pause, the Boss thanked the contributor for his suggestion, but reinforced that the normal operating and never-exceed limits were there for a good reason, and were quite adequate for the job.

There was a feeling that the invasion of Kuwait and Iraq might kick off in November, but that came and went. The Jaguar detachment redeployed from Thumrait to Bahrain, much to their disappointment. At about this time, two crews from each Tornado 4-ship were on rotation as QRA[12], should Saddam strike first. When on duty, we were equipped with bleepers. It did not matter what time the bleeper went off/where you were/what you were doing; your task was to get to the base, get kitted-up and be airborne ASAP, to conduct a retaliatory strike from medium-level, delivering our aforementioned 1944 arsenal. Well, one night, in the very wee small hours, our bleeper went off...my trusty front-seater didn't stir! For some reason, I thought I would give the number

---

[11] Shareholders - Periodic squadron aircrew meeting.
[12] QRA – Quick Reaction Alert.

from the pager a ring. Not quite the SOP[13], but - it turned out that the Jaguar night duty aircrew bloke, being a bit bored, decided to ring all the pagers on the callout list he had, to see who was on the other end! I politely informed him of the purpose of the pager he had just rung, thanked him for his interest and suggested he went off and found something else to do! Not a little relieved, I rolled over and went back to sleep.

Apart from the JP233 'runway buster', our inability to hit targets with precision was a concern. One evening, in the bar (a significant advantage of Bahrain, as compared with either of the other two bases), I suggested that the Buccaneer Wing should be deployed with their Pavespike kit, to act as designators for Tornado carrying Paveway bombs. In fact, I suggested, why didn't we leave the Buccaneers to do the precision bombing whilst the Tornado fleet continued to do area bombing. I found myself pinned, none too gently, against the bar wall by some rather irate through-and-through Tornado type. Only a joke mate! (well, sort of). It was about this time that I sent what must be the only operational deployment postcard in military history. The card showed the 5 Star Diplomat Hotel in Manama city, with a short note suggesting that, if they were going to go to war, this was the place for them - quite prophetic, as it turned out.

It eventually became clear that Operation Desert Storm, as the liberation of Kuwait was to be called, was going to kick off in mid-January. Our 3 months were up and, despite now being some of the more experienced crews in theatre, we were promptly shipped home, to be replaced by crews from RAF Laarbruch who had yet to set foot in the desert. So, after 3 months of training 'to go to war in this theatre', we departed, with the prospect of watching the whole thing on television and leaving the fighting to someone else! However, no-one anticipated the early loss rate of aircraft. So, almost immediately after hostilities began, we started to find ourselves, in the wee small hours, bidding our families farewell and reporting to the squadron, packed and ready to trail our jets to whichever of the 3 Tornado bases needed us; the deal being that we would definitely be deployed to one of the detachments within 7 days. Turning up on the last of these days, and expecting to go, we were, yet again, put on hold. It had, after all, been

---

[13] SOP – Standard Operating Procedure.

decided to deploy the Buccs with their Pavespike laser designation capability; it would appear that my postcard to the squadron had finally made it up the decision chain to Strike Command! The Bucc/Tornado combination was a great success. The Thermal Imaging And Laser Designation (TIALD) pod for Tornado was also rushed into service, and performed very well. Sitting at home, for the duration, I certainly got more 'tea' than you could shake a stick at and, thanks to our Boss, a medal as well. As a footnote, it was to be a full decade later before I was to earn my wings in combat, over Belgrade at 2 o'clock in the morning. But that, as they say, is another story.

So, 2500 flying hours later, what of the mighty Buccaneer and the Tornado? Quite different roles and equipment and capabilities, but equally enjoyable to operate. There is no doubt that the Tornado has matured into a very capable weapons platform, but one will always wonder what a Mk3 Buccaneer could have achieved!

Credit: Geoff Lee

Baby Valetta

When I took over as Commanding Officer of an overseas RAF station, many years ago, one of the surprising things I was told by my predecessor was that I was a godfather. What's more, I had to visit my goddaughter as soon as possible. It was 1966, on the East Malaysian island of Labuan, off the coast of Borneo. RAF Labuan had become a key operational base during the period of confrontation between Indonesia and Malaysia, and the whole place was full of aeroplanes – fixed-wing and rotary – from all three Services. The Royal Navy had four helicopters, the Army several Scouts and Beavers, and the Royal Air Force presence there comprised Hunters, Canberras, both Single and Twin-Pioneers, Argosies, Beverleys, Whirlwind helicopters and Valettas. Most of the time, some of each type were based there on permanent detachment from Singapore, while others flew in as operationally required. For a simple fighter pilot like me, this was a new and exciting world. But this story centres on just one of these types – the Valetta.

Before I arrived at Labuan there had been a 'hearts and minds' mission to take a young Malaysian lady from her jungle village to hospital, because she was having trouble with her pregnancy. She was airlifted from the kampong (settlement) by Whirlwind, and transferred to a Valetta for a flight to Jesselton (now Kota Kinabalu), the Sabah provincial capital, where there was a good hospital. The Valetta took off from Labuan with a crew of three, plus a doctor and nurse with the patient. But by the time the aircraft reached Jesselton the POB[1] had risen from six to seven. You've guessed it of course; there had been an airborne birth in the Valetta.

Members of the RAF have always been charity-minded, and never more so than when, in 1966, news of the airborne baby reached Labuan. A fund was immediately set up to provide for the child; she was named Baby Valetta, and the CO of the day was to be her godfather. So, having taken over as CO, I set up an early visit to my goddaughter and her family in the jungle. The British press had somehow got hold of the news and came along too. Having landed, by Whirlwind, in the jungle clearing, we were treated to a memorable day of

---

[1] POB - Person(s) On Board.

generous hospitality in the kampong longhouse. Local thoughts may have been on what was by now a substantial trust fund, but the Valetta medevac mission had genuinely captured hearts and minds.

The press wanted lots of photographs, and a special one with me holding the baby, "like a proud godfather" they said. Encouraged by the villagers, I had no choice but to oblige. Sure enough, this shot featured prominently in the wide coverage of the story which subsequently appeared in the UK press. It prompted many enquiries from anxious family and friends at home, wondering why I had gone native so quickly!

Baby Valetta was a happy story, from a Cold War military support episode now long forgotten - but the story doesn't end in 1966. About a quarter of a century later, in the RAF News, I spotted an announcement from a lady whose father had been flying a Valetta from Labuan to Jesselton, when a baby was born on board. Did anyone know about such an event? I made contact and passed on the whole of my side of the story, discovering that this lady planned to visit Malaysia on holiday, and would dearly like to track down Baby Valetta. On arrival, she went to Sabah and Labuan, diligently exploring a line of contacts, including the bank where the trust fund had been lodged when RAF Labuan closed down. She eventually found the girl, who was by now a proud mother herself, living in the kampong which I had flown into all those years ago. The family wasn't rich, but the trust fund had enabled Valetta, her husband and her children to live happily ever after!

But what of all those other aircraft at Labuan? To the simple fighter pilot, who thought he knew all about flying, their operations were an eye-opener. The challenging jungle setting required flying skill and professionalism of a special order. For a start, navigation aids were rudimentary; no GPS[2], just stopwatch and accurate flying, from which to build up some sort of a picture of the area. Two types and roles impressed me in particular. Firstly, the Beverleys that were used for supply drops to British and Malaysian forces in the interior. I flew on the flight deck on several missions, witnessing the flying skill which, after a shallow dive and wings-level pull-up, placed the aircraft in an ideal position for the drop into a small clearing. Most people would agree the Beverley was a big and

---

[2] GPS – Global Positioning System, more commonly known as satellite navigation or Satnav.

ungainly aircraft, but seeing it hauled around the sky like a fighter was revealing! Then there were the resident Whirlwind RAF helicopter units, 230 Squadron permanently based at Labuan and at full strength, together with a sizeable detachment of 110 Squadron aircraft from Singapore. The units were led by young COs and flight commanders, with several first-tourists[3] among the remaining pilots. Until then, the helicopter force had seemed (unfairly) to some to be non-mainstream, with their work, perhaps, lacking some of the glamour which other operators liked to confer upon themselves! But here, during 'confrontation', the helicopter force was at the forefront of operations. Apart from his flying skills, a young pilot, not all that long out of training and working in the interior, could find himself exercising or sharing leadership and decision-making with all sorts of military and local people – maybe the head of a village, a troop of the SAS, or a flown-in diplomat. I have always thought that the outstanding reputation of the rotary-wing element of today's Royal Air Force has many of its roots in the way helicopter operations came to the fore in the Borneo jungle during the 1960s.

However, coming back down to earth, much as I had seen and learned a great deal from active operational involvement with the wider Royal Air Force, I had lost none of the enthusiasm for my original trade. Some time later, I was therefore delighted to return to the world of fighters – in this case, back to the Lightning.

---

[3] First-tourist – Someone on their first operational posting after completing flying training.

A Cock and Ball Story

The Red Arrows shunned night flying but, in order to comply with some Air Staff Instruction or other, and to cater for a possible night transit (perish the thought), they had to keep current. So it was that, one spring evening, the 'Reds' took to the gloaming – individually – from RAF Kemble in Gloucestershire, to get their mandatory hour of 'almost' flying in the dark. As they strolled back into the crew-room after landing, a very sheepish Red 9 sidled up to the Boss.

"Boss, I think I need to tell you something. I used the smoke to draw a 'design' in the sky at 30,000 feet, but I forgot what the met man had said about the upper winds being east to west. So I think my artwork has probably just arrived over Cheltenham and Gloucester!"

"So, what's the problem?" asked the Boss.

"Well," said the pilot, "It was the outline of a cock and balls."

There was nothing much more to be said, really.

Credit: Ronnie Macdonald/Wikipedia

Flying With Roly Beamont

In late-1976/early-1977 the RAF Germany Air Defence Wing, 19(F) and 92(F) Squadrons, exchanged their Lightning F2A aircraft for Phantom FGR2s. As part of the stand-down celebrations of 19(F) Lightning Squadron, at the end of November 1976, the Boss, Bob Barcilon, invited Roly Beamont, the original Lightning aircraft Test Pilot, and his wife Patricia, to visit the Squadron at RAF Gütersloh. The itinerary for Friday 26 November was a morning flight in the Squadron's T4 two-seater (XM 991) followed by an afternoon sight-seeing tour in the local area and a formal Ladies Dining-In Night in the Officers' Mess.

As the Squadron QFI (Qualified Flying Instructor) I was selected to fly with Roly and, under the direction of the Boss, I planned a mixed-profile sortie containing: some low flying in the area south of Gutersloh; a climb to height for two 1v1 medium-level PIs (Practice Interceptions); some general handling; and a visual recovery to base for some circuits and a final landing. Having retired from formal test flying some years previously, although still working at Warton, Roly was concerned, prior to the sortie, that it was some time since he had handled a Lightning. However, there was little evidence of rustiness as we took off and transited south at low level in what I can only describe as challenging conditions, even for the North German Plain. His low level handling was spirited and precise and he coped well with the target run down the Möhne Dam, although we were a little higher than the Dambusters had flown the profile! The low-level element complete, we climbed to height and undertook the two PIs, with John Spoor as our target; here some rustiness did show through but, with a little prompting, we managed to end up in the right place and achieve a 'kill'. Then, after about 5 minutes of adventurous general handling, most of it on the edge of the flight envelope, we commenced our recovery to Gütersloh for a few circuits and the full-stop landing.

Before I recount the next phase of the sortie, a few words on the landing technique that RAF Lightning pilots were taught at the Operational Conversion Unit might be apposite. The aim was to make a calculated threshold speed, around 155 knots, at the appropriate point and a few feet above the runway, and then to enter a slight flare[1] with power on and reducing speed. After touchdown,

---

[1] flare – in this context it means to move the control column rearwards, thus causing the nose to rise and rate of descent to reduce.

the nose-wheel was immediately lowered and the throttles retarded to an Idle/ Fast Idle position, the latter allowing the AC electrics to remain on-line and for a fast engine acceleration in the event of a go-around, should the brake parachute fail to deploy. Once the chute was deployed, both throttles were set to idle and the brakes applied as required. The main pitfall in the whole procedure was the risk that either too slow a threshold speed or an over-rotation of the aircraft in the flare could result in the tail-bumper striking the runway, with the consequent severing of the chute attachment lines which ran around the perimeters of the two jet-pipes. I should also observe that, at 7,400 feet, the Gütersloh runway was considered short for Lightning operations.

With this in mind, I was slightly concerned on our first 2 approaches for low-overshoots, when Roly flew speeds around 10 knots slower than those advocated, and the same applied on our approach to land. My concern increased further when, having crossed the threshold at around 145 knots, he started to gently flare the aircraft and to allow it to float, airborne, down the first 1000 feet of runway, with a high nose-attitude and reducing airspeed. I resisted the temptation to take control as the aircraft was being handled in such a smooth and controlled manner. Having touched down, Roly proceeded to raise the nose even further to aero-dynamic brake; he eventually lowered the nose and streamed the chute at 90 knots. Little wheel-braking was then required, and we cleared the runway at about the 4,000 foot point – a landing roll only two-thirds of the norm!!

All-in-all, I had been fortunate enough to experience a master-class in the finer points of handling the Lightning, conducted by none other than the Master himself; an experience that I will never forget. Needless to say, we all enjoyed the Ladies' Dining-In Night that followed.

A Break in Denmark

I remember it as being my first, proper sortie in the left-hand seat. I had recently completed the conversion course, and was looking forward to some "operational" flying in the Victor SR2. 543 Squadron's most pressing task, at that time, was a survey of Denmark, on behalf of the Danish government. Photographic Reconnaissance (PR) was one of our specialist roles and, with the weather set fair, a sortie a day was being despatched across the North Sea. A few days later, it was our turn, and I remember being both excited and slightly nervous as I strapped into the aircraft. I was still flying with the people I usually flew with. The five of us, two pilots, two navigators and an air electronics officer (AEO), were a 'constituted crew', and fully trained in the various, disparate roles that the Squadron undertook; all that was different was that John and I had swopped seats at the front end. Ultimately, of course, he still retained responsibility for the safety of the aircraft and crew, but he had made it clear that he expected me to shape up, and had no intention of taking over unless it was absolutely necessary. In one sense I felt it was good to have the back-stop if things went pear-shaped but, in another, it added even more pressure. Nobody would want to hand over control - apart from anything else, the rear crew would never have let me live it down!

We ascended into a virtually cloudless sky, set course for foreign parts, and were soon under Danish control and in the descent to begin our PR runs. Once at operating height, the Nav Plotter made his way down to the nose where he would spend the next few hours. This required us, at the front, to raise the large, hinged, fuel control panel until Terry had squeezed his not- inconsiderable frame through the gap. We then dropped the tray again so that he was, effectively, trapped in the nose. However, this was the only way to ensure the level of navigational accuracy required. Terry would visually map-read us along the photo runs with Paddy, the Nav Radar, providing support and additional information from the back. The camera crate, in the Victor's bomb bay, contained some high quality optical equipment but, in order to get the best results, we had to fly within very fine limits. Heading adjustments on a photo run could only be made between camera exposures, which were every few seconds, and were normally a matter of one degree or less. The latter was commonly referred to as a 'gnat's c**k', that being the smallest measurement in common aircrew use.

There was a bit of turbulence from isolated cumulus clouds, so I used a mixture of auto-pilot and manual flying, but the runs went like clockwork and it was soon time to go home. I was manually flying the aircraft when we finished and called for climb power without delay. We were not flush for fuel, so I wanted to get us up to cruise altitude as soon as possible, where our mpg would be much better. I had advised Terry of my intentions before we started the last run, and he was quite happy to remain at the front, sorting out his maps, until we were established in the climb, when we would let him return to his seat in the back.

A couple of seconds after the increase in power, there was a muffled bang and the aircraft shook violently. John immediately checked the engine gauges, and reported that the JPT[1] on Number 3 engine was climbing above limits, and the engine RPM was decreasing slowly. I had just asked him to reduce Number 3 RPM to flight idle when the fire warning light for that engine illuminated. However, it then extinguished, and the JPT dropped as the RPM decreased. We completed an engine shutdown on Number 3 and, without prompting, Paddy gave us a heading and distance to the nearest available airfield. Air Traffic Control then piped up and asked us to confirm that we were squawking Emergency[2]. Tony, our AEO, had also been quick off the mark in letting the world know that we had a problem. After a brief discussion we declared a PAN[3] and requested a diversion to Karup, a nearby Danish Air Force Base.

The vibrations had stopped when we shut down Number 3, and Number 4, the engine next door, appeared to be fine, so we all breathed a little easier, and settled down into the descent, on heading for Karup. John asked me what my intentions were, and I replied that we would carry out a low-speed handling check with the undercarriage and flaps down, and then do a straight-in, 3-engine landing. At around this time it all went silent in the cabin, at which point a little voice piped up, "Can I come out please?" In the heat of the moment I/we had completely forgotten about Terry who, to his credit, had kept quiet and let us get on with sorting out the problem. John raised the fuel tray, and Terry

---

[1] JPT – Jet Pipe Temperature.
[2] Squawking Emergency – Using an on-board electronic transponder system to indicate (squawk) to a radar station that we had a problem.
[3] PAN - A state of urgency exists although there is no imminent danger to life or the continued viability of the aircraft.

scorched past us and was back in his seat, strapped in and with his parachute on, in Olympic time. This lightened the atmosphere considerably and, after some exchanges of dark aircrew humour (which I will not repeat), we carried out our emergency checks and landed at Karup without further incident.

After landing we were directed to a spare parking bay where we shut down the aircraft. A Danish military pilot was waiting to greet us as we climbed down the steps, and, in impeccable English, he said, "Double engine failure, eh guys?" DOUBLE engine failure?! John and I walked around the nose and looked back at the engine intakes on the starboard wing. He was right! Both engines had bent and broken compressor blades[4], although Number 3 undoubtedly looked the worse of the two. However, Number 4 engine had behaved impeccably while we were airborne, and had given us no reason to suspect that it was anything other than 100% operational.

We spent a pleasant few days in Karup, enjoying the Royal Danish Air Force's hospitality, and assisting the ground crew with a double engine change. A quick air test did not reveal any problems, so we hot-footed it back across the North Sea with our precious cargo of film, and all was, once again, well with the world. It transpired that a compressor blade at the front of Number 3 engine had failed and then wrought havoc with the internals, causing the engine to surge violently, which was the bang we had heard. This spat broken bits of blade out of the front of the engine, which had immediately been sucked into the neighbouring intake of Number 4. The Rolls-Royce Conway engines fitted to the Victor were a double-skin bypass design, and this ensured that nothing had come out of the side through the engine casing, which could have had serious repercussions. However, their inherent sturdiness also masked the damage that had clearly occurred to Number 4 engine. We probably got off lightly that day, but it was certainly a baptism of fire for me in the left hand seat, made so much easier by the professionalism of the other members of the crew. And, Terry, I'm sorry – we hadn't really forgotten about you.

---

[4] Compressor blades – The front section of a jet engine consists of a series of linked fans that compress the air.

Ditties From The Desert

For as long as British industry and Her Majesty's Government have been supplying friendly nations with aircraft, British servicemen and ex-servicemen have been sent on loan service to help introduce them into service, instruct, operate and maintain them. Performing these functions in an alien environment and culture can generate some unusual situations...

Me in the front seat, turning finals to land. Man in the back seat mumbling something or other.

"Are you asking me to recheck 3-greens[1] Abdullah?"

" No, I am praying to my God for a safe landing!"

At which point, I raise both my hands in the air, and say, "He has control!" The response is immediate. "No, no Mr Mick – you fly the jet!!"

For weeks, I had tried to get the young students to understand Electronic Warfare and the role of the BOZ and Sky Shadow countermeasure pods on the Tornado. Each morning at met brief I would ask questions, such as, "How many flares are there in the BOZ Pod?" The students would respond with random numbers such as 30, 50 or 70. "No", I would answer, "There are 32." Finally, one day, one of the brighter students responded '32', at which point they all seemed to get it! The next day I asked: "How many flares does the Tornado carry?" "32", they chorused. "No", I said, "The answer is 33 – 32 in the BOZ pod plus the WSO[2]. If you eject him, the flare from his seat will be number 33!" Cue much laughter from the pilots.

A couple of weeks later I was in the back seat, with a young student pilot in the front; we had been tasked to drop a Phase 1 bomb on a FRA (First Run Attack – 200 feet agl[3], 500 knots) and then deploy 3 flares. As we approached the range, I selected the BOZ live, but realised we only had one flare loaded.

"B****r – we'll be in trouble with the Boss, because we only have one flare", I informed my young pilot.

---

[1] 3-greens – Cockpit lights indicating that the undercarriage is locked down.
[2] WSO – Weapons Systems Officer.
[3] agl – above ground level.

"No Mr Mick", he responded, "We have two."

"How can you know that?" I replied, "Only I can see the BOZ controller, and it confirms we have just one flare'.

"No Mr Mick, we have two, one in the BOZ pod...and you!"

Credit: Geoff Lee

What If?

From the distance of forty years, I often look back fondly on my short RAF flying career, even happily remembering dodgy moments, such as my Canberra having an engine failure after take-off, or bouncing around inside a big cumulo-nimbus cloud on a night climb out from RAF Leuchars, with thunder and lightning, the full son-et-lumière effects in surround sound, and a touch of icing just to spice things up a bit. But there is one short scene that keeps replaying in my mind, which still sends a chill down my spine, and has me asking, "What if?"

In this scene, still vivid, a fully loaded Victor tanker is struggling into the sky, about 20 feet above the 'numbers' at the end of a runway. And there, in the pre-dawn gloom, an enormous parachute is billowing and flopping about on the runway right underneath the Victor...and the 'what if' pictures keep popping up. What if – a gust lifted the parachute a few feet, or maybe the Victor was a few feet lower? What if - it got sucked into the air intakes, or covered the front of the aircraft, or wrapped around a wing? What if the scene turned into a howling screeching ball of flame, with yet another V-bomber crew inside? And where would that leave me? Because I had just put that parachute there!

It was another of those V-force dispersal exercises, where we put up with the sense of unreality of preparing to nuke Russia with our obsolescent Vulcans, in exchange for the fun of flying them. That night, the honour of being number one in a four-ship scramble fell to our crew, and I loved being in four-ship scrambles. As the co-pilot, part of my job was working out the load, weight and balance, and take-off distance. It always seemed to be around 3,500 to 4,000 feet, but this time it was shorter because we were carrying a light fuel load. On the next desk was a co-pilot from one of the two Victor tankers, which would be scrambled after us, so I compared notes. With about half the engine power of a Vulcan and a full load of fuel, I was a bit surprised (Duh!) to see he was going to need some 8,000 feet of the 9,000 foot runway. "So what happens if you get an engine failure?" "We go off the end of the runway!" (Stupid!)

At some moment in the early hours, the tannoy wakes us. "This Is The

Bomber Controller: This Is The Bomber Controller: for Bomb Lists Echo, Golf, Kilo (etc. etc) Five Minutes Readiness: Five Minutes Readiness" *(Yes, they really did manage to speak with capital letters at the front of every word)*. We grab our bags and stumble out to our crew coach. Careering round the perimeter track, our AEO (Air Electronics Officer) looks up at the rest of us; "I think the Orange General just threw a six" he says, before reverting to his semi-comatose state. So we clamber into the cockpit, strap in, and then – hurry up and wait. The real surprise of the night is that next, we get the order to "Scramble", from cold, instead of the more leisurely increase to two minutes readiness, when we would have had the engines running. So, as the first two engines fire up, my captain lets the brakes off and we start rolling. Accelerating through 100 knots, he announces that we've only got three engines running. A moment later, he declares an abort. I see that we are 15 knots above the speed where we are required to deploy the tail-mounted brake parachute. This is to avoid burning the brakes out in an emergency situation, but I ask, "What about the three behind us, and the Victors?" (there was a third, SR Victor[1] behind the two tankers). We are only the first of seven V-bombers, launching down that runway at 15 to 30-second intervals in the dark.

He says we'll hold to one side of the runway, and orders; "Stream the chute!" I'm now in a dilemma: if I carry out the order, I know that the next thing will be the decision to drop the brake chute on the runway, right in front of the Victors, at about the 8,500 foot point. This is to avoid damaging the parachute shackles, which can happen in gusty conditions if the Vulcan turns off the runway with the chute still attached. I ask, "Are You Sure? We still have 6,000 feet of runway left." Which is to say, if we just close the throttles and don't bother with any brakes, we will be at a standstill with the best part of a mile of runway in front of us. We're going to have to keep power on just to get to the end! And I'm thinking, what happens to me if I disobey a direct order? But we could easily cause a crash here. And, just as he starts raising his hand towards the switch, where my hand is

---

[1] SR Victor – Strategic reconnaissance version of the Victor (Mk2) with much better performance than the Vulcan.

already, I chicken out, and stream the chute. We're now about 5-10 knots above the required chute streaming speed.

By the time we get to the end of the runway, a minute later, I feel resigned. We've heard the other three Vulcans roar above our heads, and when the order to drop the chute comes I give it only the lamest query of "are you sure...?" before I hit the switch. And, as it is a right turn off the runway, I see what nobody else in our aircraft can – the Victor clawing its way into the sky just above all that parachute. And I ask myself "what if – I had summoned the courage to obey common sense, and disobey an order", "what if – the Victor hadn't made it". But there was no crash, no fireball, nobody got hurt, we all got on with our lives. And yet, forty years later, I still ask myself "What if?"

Credit: Sgt. David S. Nolan, US Air Force/Wikipedia

Weight Watchers, Mugabe and Moi

When Ian Smith made his Unilateral Declaration of Independence (UDI) in 1966, Harold Wilson's government persuaded the UN to impose sanctions against Rhodesia, now Zimbabwe. The nearest sea port to which Rhodesia had access for imports, particularly oil products, was Lourenço Marques (now Maputo) in Mozambique. Madagascar accepted that surveillance patrols of the Beira Straits, between Madagascar and Mozambique, could be mounted from the town of Majunga (now Mahajanga) in North-West Madagascar. This was achieved by positioning a couple of Shackleton Maritime Reconnaissance aircraft at the local airport. They carried out patrols every other day, reporting vessels suspected of running the blockade to Royal Naval ships for investigation. Most RN vessels had to linger in the area for a month, when sailing to or from the Far East.

Royal Air Force Detachment Majunga existed from 1966 until 1972. Aircraft were provided initially from squadrons based in the Far East or the Middle East, more latterly from UK. Capital Aircrew and ground crew did 2-month stints, whilst a small number of officers did 6-month detachments, and the Wing Commander CO did 12 months.

As a young Flying Officer, not two years out of Cranwell, I took over the grandly-named appointment of Officer Commanding Supply and Movements Flight in Majunga in January 1971, the latest in a succession of chaps who had served their 6-month stay in that beautiful country. The flight consisted of a Corporal, a Senior Aircraftsman (SAC) and moi (this was a French-speaking job in the former French colony) – which was fine for the Supply bit of the job. To cope with unloading and loading the fortnightly re-supply aircraft, the Movements Team had to be augmented by whichever SNCOs[1] and airmen could be persuaded to get involved in what was invariably heavy, hot and sweaty work. They were MT mechanics, administrators, cooks, and anyone who did not move fast enough when my persuasive Corporal was looking for reinforcements. We had neither forklift truck nor much in the way of handling

---

[1] SNCO – Senior Non-Commissioned Officer.

aids, with the exception of an apparatus known as a Britannia Freight Lift Platform, specifically designed for lifting loads up to the height of the freight access door in a Britannia. Britannias were programmed for a leisurely 24-hour turn-round, and the Air Load-Master generally stayed with the Movements Team to help, whilst the rest of the crew went into town for a cultural visit (of which more later).

Early in my stay, it was decided to use C-130 Hercules instead of Brits on what were called tactical turn-rounds, of 15 hours only, with aircraft arriving mid-afternoon and leaving at about 0600 the next day. This departure time was important, as the first leg back to the UK, from Majunga to Muharraq, was about 14 hours flying and near the limit of the Herc. To get off the shortish run-way at Majunga, with maximum fuel on board, required a take-off in the cool temperature of the early morning; but this small civilian airport, on which we were squatting, only operated from 0800 to dusk. Airport Air Traffic, Meteorology and Fire crews were manned to allow take-off at 0600, but the Fuel Supplier was not. That meant refuelling the Herc the day before, sometimes before we had off-loaded all of the incoming freight, and certainly before we had loaded the outgoing freight – most of which comprised aircraft and vehicle spare parts and tools. Unlike with Brits, we were not aided by the Loadmaster, as Herc crews abandoned their aircraft to our tender mercies, and went off to town for a "tactical" rest, with an admonition to make bloody sure she was ready for the 0600 take-off.

A C-130 with maximum fuel is inherently tail-heavy – and from this basic fact developed a sphincter-tightening episode. Now, listen carefully – there'll be a test at the end. This particular afternoon, we had to empty the aircraft and re-fuel it before re-loading it. The on-board winch was unserviceable, so everything had to be man-handled aboard, either carrying it, or pushing and pulling it up the tail ramp if it was too heavy to carry. All was going well, until I was told that there was a last-minute item which simply had to return to UK for overhaul – a Shackleton engine, known as a Griffon power-plant. These weighed, from memory, about 4500 lbs, and were normally mounted on an air-transportable stand, which was lightweight and had a horizontal bar set high enough to allow the stand to be pulled by the winch up the Hercules ramp, and over the hump where the ramp met the aircraft freight deck. A quick re-calculation of the aircraft trim sheet showed that the aircraft, even with all that fuel and this extra weight at the rear, would still be just within permissible limits.

However, as Rabbie Burns had it – the best-laid plans an' a' that. Observant readers will recall that the aircraft winch was unserviceable. Initiative was quickly unleashed, and we decided to run a chain from the engine stand into the aircraft, through a lashing fitment, and back out to the airport fire engine, a machine of 1940s vintage. Driving the fire engine away from the aircraft, enveloped in thick clouds of fumes from the exhaust and the burning clutch, had the effect of pulling the stand up the ramp and into the aircraft. Decidedly dodgy stuff, and written nowhere in any guide for loading aircraft. But I was not Cranwell–indoctrinated in getting the job done for nothing.

Re-enter Rabbie Burns – the best-laid plans etc. This last-minute, unplanned engine for repatriation was not mounted on an air-transportable stand, but on a normal stand for use in workshops. The horizontal bar at the bottom of this stand was right at the bottom, unlike that on its air-transportable brother. This meant that it could not breast the hump at the top of the ramp to enter the aircraft, without grounding and sticking. Forcing it with our fire-engine-and-chain lash-up would damage the aircraft ramp, and potentially render the aircraft unserviceable. The only apparent option was to decline to return the engine – which would be highly unpopular, as they were always in short supply, and could ultimately have an impact on Shackleton availability to meet the Beira Patrol task. Then that accursed initiative reared its ugly head again. If we got the engine onto the ramp and then raised the aircraft ramp, the angle to be breasted at the top would decrease to the point where the stand could cross over without scraping. So... the fire engine moves away from the aircraft, and the engine on its stand crawls up the ramp. So far so good! The corporal activates the ramp control, and the ramp begins to rise. Great - but hang on! As the ramp rises, the rear end of our tail-heavy Herc starts to go down towards the ground. If that continues unchecked we'll damage the underside of the aircraft, and it won't be able to leave as scheduled. End of promising young officer's career.

Help was at hand from an unlikely source. A Shackleton had landed a few minutes earlier, after a 12 hour sortie, and was being worked on by a post-flight team led by a Chief Technician who was, shall we say, struggling to maintain the lithe profile of his youth. Here were 20+ stone on the hoof, with another half-a-dozen chaps who would weigh in at about 12-14 stone each – getting on for 1500 lbs of fully-mobile, ballast weight. Said team was easily persuaded to climb into the Hercules cockpit, thereby counter-balancing the weight of the engine stand by just enough to stop the Hercules sitting on its a**e, as we lifted the ramp and eased the engine into the freight compartment.

In the slang of the day, we hacked it. The Hercules load was completed, and the trim sheet was closed off. Very early next morning, the crew returned from their evening's entertainment in Madame Chabaud's "leisure complex", over which it is best, dear reader, to draw a veil. Passengers were loaded, aircraft and trim were accepted by the crew, tyres were kicked, and off they soared to Muharraq.

Fortunately for this young officer, in the early 1970s much less attention was devoted to ensuring personnel were fit and kept their weight under control. Had Weight-Watchers and the like held sway as they now do, that Chief Technician would not have come to my notice, and I would not have thought of using him and his team as "make-weights". That Hercules would have been damaged or that Shackleton engine would not have left – and then who knows? The inability of the Shackletons to fly their patrols might have left Ian Smith's regime in place, and Robert Mugabe might be coming up to a well-deserved retirement as a lecturer in Economics at the LSE.

Mugabe and I both owe our careers to an overweight Chief Technician.

Credit: RAF/Crown Copyright

Fox 2 – Splash One Jaguar

Jaguar GR1 14 Sqn XX963 versus Phantom FGR2 92 Sqn XV422.
Ejected 1247 Zulu, 25 May 1982.

I was StanEval Weapons at RAF Bruggen, responsible for the standardisation of weaponeering between the four squadrons on the base. As such, I flew with all of the squadrons, not only to assess standards but also to maintain my own general proficiency in the various roles of the Jaguar.

Thus, on 25th May 1982, I was operating with 14 Squadron, as wingman to Flt Lt Paddy Mullen, on a forward air controller training sortie on the North German Plain. We had completed a most enjoyable sortie, and were recovering to RAF Bruggen in loose fighting wing formation, when there was a violent bang, the aircraft started yawing violently to the right and did not respond to the controls. I think that the canopy shattered and it became very noisy; however, I could hear Paddy's voice from the other aircraft yelling, "Eject! Eject!" My rather confused thought processes were - he must know what is going on because I certainly don't! Result – I followed his wise advice and ejected.

There was a violent explosion and my head was driven down to the breast plate of my lifejacket. I had a vision of the floor of the cockpit dropping away, felt the snatch of the parachute opening and a wrenching pain in my right hand (fool, let go of the seat handle!), and experienced a moment of blissful quiet before I landed, completely out of control, in a field - and it hurt! Herr Gerd Molleken (the farmer whose field I had landed in) and his daughter appeared and helped me to my feet. While gathering my parachute and various bits together, a lone Phantom (F4) flew overhead very low down. I asked the farmer if he had seen what had happened but he had not. I had no idea myself, except that I thought that it was odd for the F4 to be alone – they normally flew as pairs. Could I have had a mid-air with his mate? Questions for later, since a bottle of brandy had now been produced and hospitality offered. Pausing only to make a quick phone call to Bruggen to relay the news (apparently disturbing the Station Commander during the Annual Formal Inspection lunch) we attacked the bottle. Remember, this was in the years before compulsory 'medicals' following accidents; today, I would certainly have compromised the blood test.

Still, morale, welfare and not offending the farmer were much higher priorities in my mind at the time.

The sound of a chopper was soon heard, and a lift back to Bruggen given, courtesy of the German Air Force. I was rushed to the medical centre for a quick check-up, to be met by Paddy, and other members of 14 Squadron, with bottles of beer stuffed in their pockets. I was then waved off for a rather wobbly ride to Wegberg hospital, for x-rays etc, with still no idea of what had happened. Even Paddy was in the dark. He had just happened to look back at me in time to see the aircraft explode, and had the presence of mind to immediately call for me to eject.

What had happened? There I was, minding my own business at 1350 feet, returning to Bruggen with Paddy, when the radar unit we were using warned us of conflicting traffic ahead. The radar warning receiver lit up, which was not an unusual event in the "corridor" routing aircraft to and from Bruggen and Wildenrath. Aircraft went out at 750 feet and back at 1350 feet for deconfliction. The F4s from RAF Wildenrath often "painted" aircraft on their airborne radar, to ensure safe separation. What was unusual was that the CWI band vector[1] moved from front to rear; 'Still', I thought, 'I could be picking up the Hawk surface-to-air missile site to the north, although that would be a fair distance away'.

Hours before this, the alert hooter had sounded at RAF Wildenrath (the Phantom FRG2 base) in the early hours of the morning, announcing the start of a station exercise. In accordance with normal policy for exercising quick reaction forces in NATO, aircraft and crews were generated and the aircraft loaded with live weapons. Once the required number of live-armed aircraft had been achieved, the aircraft would be de-armed and prepared for training sorties, loaded with acquisition rounds (inert missiles, but with real heat-seeking heads). The crews would then stand by to fly training missions, as directed by the Sector Operations Centre (SOC). For the purpose of such exercises, other RAF Germany aircraft were regarded as hostile targets, and fighter controllers scrambled the F4s to intercept them.

One crew, who shall remain nameless, were scrambled for such a mission

---

[1] CWI band vector - An indication on the Radar Warning Receiver that the aircraft was being illuminated by a continuous-wave radar in the I frequency band.

in Phantom FGR2 XV422. They took off from RAF Wildenrath to mount a combat air patrol under the control of the SOC. At approximately 1247 hrs they were vectored onto a pair of Jaguars, and told to engage the "hostile" aircraft. Following standard procedures for a simulated attack, the Phantom closed on the Jaguars and, when in an ideal position to complete what, until that moment, had been a typically routine engagement, the pilot pulled the missile release trigger. This should have produced only a witness mark on the radar film to record the intercept. Instead, as the pilot said later, the 'growl' from the missile seeker transferred to the other ear (the missile on the other wing) and the missile which had acquired then launched! Dumbfounded, he watched, powerless to influence the outcome, as the missile exhaust trail headed off towards the target - my Jaguar. The AIM9G Sidewinder hit my aircraft, and the warhead detonated. The complete tail section behind the wing broke away, and the front part of the aircraft (with me still inside at that stage) entered a flat spin.

Obviously the accident was the result of a monumental cock-up. Unsurprisingly, the Board of Inquiry found the crew of the Phantom to be negligent, but they were, it subsequently transpired, not solely to blame, and were simply the last link in a classic accident chain. They had been called out late, had missed the start of the exercise, were briefed hurriedly, and were the last to be allocated an aircraft, which was live-armed[2]. A simulated bomb incident then forced them to evacuate the aircraft shelter, and they were allocated another aircraft, which was also still armed with live weapons. The navigator noted that this aircraft had no red tape over the master armament switch (which would have denoted that the aircraft was live-armed). Halfway through a pee-break (flying- and NBC[3]-kit

---

[2] live-armed - This was unusual, but not unheard-of. In a previous Tactical Evaluation (Taceval), the inspecting team had doubted the Station's ability to launch a high proportion of fully armed aircraft within the required time scale, and also the validity of generating aircraft without bringing them to a fully armed state. The Station also believed that future Tacevals might not be in two parts ie: generate live armed then fly disarmed. Up to the time of the accident, it was unusual for Phantoms to be flown armed with live missiles other than when scrambled from Battle Flight (Quick Reaction Alert) or at Missile Practice Camp. However, the Station confirmed with Command HQ that it could fly armed aircraft in accordance with the relevant Air Staff Instruction, which it did for some of the sorties in this exercise. Thus the crew obviously saw nothing untoward in accepting an armed aircraft, although it was not the norm.

[3] NBC - Nuclear, Biological and Chemical protection equipment

hindering a speedy execution of this manoeuvre), they were scrambled by the SOC, which was also on exercise. The accident train was under way!

The report of the Board of Inquiry revealed that all the safeguards relating to the carriage of live missiles, provided for in the Command and Station Operating and Engineering Air Staff Orders, were either ineffective or had not been complied with. The circuit breaker for the firing circuit was found not to be an effective safety device, even though it had been pulled to render the system inactive. The SOC fighter controller had not made a "Check Switches Safe" call because he had not been informed that the aircraft was carrying live weapons. Indeed, the Operations Officer at RAF Wildenrath had not passed the information to the SOC because he was not aware of it himself.

Despite these factors, and the absence of the vital tape on the master arm switch, the crew were deemed, by the Board of Inquiry, to be negligent and (eventually) faced a Court Martial which resulted in them being found guilty of negligence. The Severe Reprimand awarded by the Court, which was the lightest punishment available, indicated that the crew was not solely to blame. The organisation behind them was also seen to be at fault and, following a comprehensive review, numerous changes were made to procedures.

The ejection turned out to be good practice for my next 'adventure' some 4 months later, when I left the burning wreckage of Jaguar XX760 (another 14 Squadron 'loan' aircraft) in a peat bog in Scotland. By incredible coincidence, Flt Lt Paddy Mullen was also in that formation, which I was leading, and both parachutes had been packed by the same person, Senior Aircraftsman Cusak!

Both images: Geoff Lee

Not Again!

The date was 13th October 1978. I was a junior, first-tourist pilot on No 31 Squadron, a strike/attack squadron based at RAF Bruggen in Germany. The squadron was on detachment to the Italian Air Force base at Decimomannu, in Sardinia, for the annual Armament Practice Camp. This was an intensive few weeks, spent practising all of the various weapons delivery profiles our roles required, utilising Capo Frasca range which was close to Decimomannu, and taking advantage of the better weather than in Germany. The local beaches and associated 'activities' were also an attraction!

I was detailed to lead a 4-ship (which included the Boss) for an FRA (First Run Attack) toss-bomb profile, followed by more toss bombing, retard bombing and strafe (guns) attacks. Having split the formation into trail for the individual attacks, we ran in at 200 feet and 480 knots. As I approached the IP (Initial Point), there was a bang and the No 1 (left-hand) engine fire warning light came on. I aborted the attack and carried out the fire drill. The light went out, and a visual inspection by the Boss confirmed that the fire had gone out, but that there was a hole in the engine door. Turning towards Decimomannu, I left the Boss to tell air traffic (excitable Italians) what was going on and dumped fuel to reduce landing weight. After flying a visual approach I made an uneventful single engine landing.

The cause of the fire was established as a fracture of the No 1 engine Combustion Chamber Outer Casing, where the P3 air offtake boss was welded[1]. This allowed burning fuel/air mixture to leak into the bypass duct, at a flame temperature of 1600 degrees centigrade, which quickly burned through the bypass duct and into the engine bay, triggering the fire warning, and also burning through the engine bay door. The P3 boss was in the 10 o'clock position on the engine (when viewed from behind) and, being the No 1 (left hand) engine, this meant that the 'explosion' went outboard – this is relevant later on! Fortunately

---

[1] In bypass jet engines, some of the air from the compressor at the front is routed directly to the turbine at the rear, 'by-passing' the combustion chambers. This means that it is designed with two skins, one within the other, with an air gap (duct) between. Inside the engine, air at various temperatures and pressures is tapped off to power or feed other systems. The P3 offtake is one of them.

the fire drill extinguished the inferno on this occasion.

Fast forward 4 years to 1982, and I was back at Bruggen, this time as Staneval Weapons - an Operations Wing post responsible for standardisation and weaponeering standards on the Station. I had been tasked to organise and run a trial to work up tactics and profiles for Jaguar aircraft to drop laser guided bombs (LGBs), with Buccaneer aircraft designating the targets with their Pave -Spike laser target pods. The procedures were worked out in Germany and dummy profiles were flown there, after which a detachment was organised to RAF Lossiemouth, in the north of Scotland, from where we could test the procedures on Garvie weapons range, using live 1000lb LGBs.

On the morning of 13th September (the 13th again!) I took off from RAF Lossiemouth, as the lead aircraft of a mixed formation of 4 Jaguars and 2 Buccaneers. I was once again flying a No 14 Squadron aircraft (see 'Fox 2 – Splash One Jaguar'), this time XX760 (AA), OC 14 Squadron's named aircraft. Flt Lt Paddy Mullen (see 'Fox 2 – Splash One Jaguar'again) was also in the formation. This was the first sortie of the detachment and was to include dry runs through Tain and Garvie ranges, prior to flying with live weapons. Having completed a dry attack on Tain range, we were transiting at low level (250 feet) towards Garvie range when there was a bang, and the No 2 (right-hand) engine fire warning light came on. I carried out the fire drill and started a gentle climb, telling the formation that I had a fire. This was confirmed by my wingman who said, "There's a bloody great flame at the back!" Meanwhile, the No 2 engine fire warning light had gone out, to be replaced by both reheat[2] fire warning lights, the No 1 engine fire warning light and the Fire Detection Integrity light. All rather confusing, but a glance in my rear view mirrors cleared my mind, since I could see the flames engulfing the spine and tail of the aircraft! I told the formation that I was going to eject, thinking "not again" (this was only some four months since I had been shot down). The ejection sequence again worked as advertised (SAC Cusak had once again packed the chute – grateful thanks and beers owed to him for the second time), although the parachute-landing roll was less than perfect, since I landed thigh deep in a peat bog. The aircraft apparently

---

[2] reheat - AKA afterburner, produces considerable, additional thrust by injecting fuel near the rear of the engine.

hit the peat and disappeared completely, starting a peat fire.

I was picked up pretty sharply by the search-and-rescue Sea King helicopter from RAF Lossiemouth, and was soon debriefing the 'wheels' on what had occurred. After a quick check-up at the local hospital, it was back to the Mess and a beer or two. OC 14 Squadron was quite good about me having 'lost' two of his aircraft in the short space of four months, especially since this one had his name on it! Although I had no injuries from either ejection (indeed I had played golf the day after being shot down), that was the end of my participation in the trial, and I returned to Bruggen, not being allowed to fly for a few days just to make sure I had no back problems. However, not all the Squadron Commanders at Bruggen were as relaxed as OC 14 Squadron. OC 20 Squadron issued a local flying order stating that 'Staneval Weapons is not permitted to taxy any 20 Squadron aircraft until further notice!'

There was quite a long delay in the investigation of the accident, since the aircraft had buried itself deep in the peat bog. It was finally dug out, and examination of the No 2 (right hand) engine showed (surprise, surprise) that the P3 offtake weld on the Combustion Chamber Outer Casing had fractured, exactly as that on the No 1 engine had at Decimomannu some four years before. This time, though, the blast and 1600-degree-centigrade jet of flame from the 10 o'clock position on the engine was directed straight into the F4 fuel tank, which was positioned above both engines. The result was the "bloody great flame at the back", as the fuel in the F4 tank cascaded into both engines and caught fire. Needless to say, the P3 welds on all Jaguar and Hawk (same engine but without reheat) engines were inspected after every flight until modified.

As a postscript, Flt Lt Norman Browne, the navigator in the lead Buccaneer, was sharp enough to use the television camera in his targeting pod to film the whole event - which is quite a memento!

Making A Show of Yourself
(and the value of advice from senior officers)

Decades ago, I spent 4 years displaying the Harrier GR3, in an era when such flying was just an additional duty, to be fitted in alongside the normal work of a squadron pilot. I can now look back on that period and see that I was fortunate to gain lots of experience and learn many lessons, all without serious personal mishap.

The display work-up syllabus for the first season included a check ride with the squadron commander. We did a few minutes of something resembling a Harrier display in a T4, before the Boss declared it far too risky, and I should carry on in the single-seater (a few years later, another new display pilot tried harder in the T-bird 2 seat version, leading to a modified front end after contact with the runway at the same airfield). Anyway, I produced a nice safe routine to demonstrate to the Senior Air Staff Officer, a venerable Harrier pilot of old, for public display approval. He duly cleared me, but suggested that the first deceleration to the hover would look much more punchy if done towards the crowd line, rather than parallel to it. That idea lasted until the first hot weather (= reduced performance) display, when I saw the crowd in rather more detail than I would have wished.

At my very first display, in Denmark, I learned another weather lesson without even getting airborne. There were two complete display programmes during the day. In the morning, I saw the American F15 roar off down the runway, pull into the vertical, and disappear into the 1000 foot overcast, returning 10 minutes later to land. In the afternoon, I was in my cockpit, listening to the radio, with the weather looking unchanged, when off went the F15 again. Lots of noise was followed by a 90° pitch up, then a radio call of, "Aw, shit. I done it again. Gimme a steer, will ya?"

Halfway through the season, with the normal run of Tacevals[1], Minivals[2] and detachments still ongoing, I was the duty authoriser on the desk, midweek

---

[1] Tacevals – Tactical evaluations of NATO declared units by NATO staff.
[2] Minivals – Local exercises to prepare for a tactical evaluation by NATO staff.

after a couple of display weekends. The squadron's affiliated doctor popped in to the Ops Room in the PBF[3], and we passed the time of day before he went on his way. The next visitor to the Ops Desk was the Boss, who sent me home for a couple of days. It was not apparent to me, but the Doc had spotted the effects of my working continuously for so many days.

Because it was an interesting venue, with two days of displays, two of us, from different squadrons, went as display pilots to Bex in Switzerland. Arriving on the Friday, at a grass airfield in the bottom of a scenic valley, we were greeted by the bad news that there was no hotel accommodation for us. The good news was that we would stay at a girls' finishing school instead. Looking at the single road along the valley, we realised that driving from the school to the airfield on show days might be difficult. But we had an RAF Wessex (helicopter) there too, and there was a big clear area next to the school's swimming pool where we could park it - so we had a plan. Unfortunately, because of two accidents at the previous Bex display (one involving an RAF Spitfire), the whole weekend was being closely supervised by the Swiss civil aviation authority. So, as some display practice went on, our Wessex pilot engaged the supervisor in conversation regarding the advisability of using the helicopter as a taxi. At this point, another visiting Brit, from Booker[4], drew my attention to an aircraft about to take-off, telling me it was a rare Morane 230, another example of which was being restored by his company. We watched as it lifted off at low speed, stalled one wing, yawed so that this picked up but then stalled the other, and drifted over what would be the public enclosure the next day. At this point, the wingtip hit the ground, causing the aircraft to cartwheel. As the propeller broke, the big radial engine revved up and went bang, then the aircraft came to rest upside down with the two, open cockpits pointing down and the inverted fuel tank now the highest component. To our amazement, two figures rapidly emerged and ran away. It turned out that one was a reporter being carried as a passenger; for some reason, media presence seemed to be a factor in quite a few accidents around that time.

So, having driven to and from our accommodation, my colleague flew the

---

[3] PBF - Pilot Briefing Facility, the hardened operations bunker.
[4] Booker - A small civilian airfield near High Wycombe.

Saturday display. With all the aircraft parking alongside the short grass strip, the airfield owners had invested in a U-shaped piece of tarmac to minimise wear as aircraft turned onto the most-used runway. It was neatly painted, with piano keys and runway number, but ended just beyond those. Our man lined up his jet on the pristine surface, completed the usual Harrier checks of engine acceleration, nozzle operation and pressure to reaction controls, and roared off into his display. What he didn't see was that, as he rolled off the tarmac, the Pegasus blast lifted the whole U-shape, bodily flipping it over to land in 1000 pieces. Fortunately, no-one was hurt, and the organisers swept up all the bits to sell to the crowd as souvenirs!

Later, back in the UK, we hosted a visit to RAF Wittering by the Army Staff College. I was to fly a display for them, and my Station Commander was keen to emphasise that the RAF could always be relied upon to do the job in hand. However, the dense fog was a bit of a problem; so, forgetting my earlier lesson about persuasion by senior officers, I agreed to do what I could, even if that was just a little hovering. At the advertised time, I taxied out along the southern parallel taxiway, to go between the runway and the control tower, aiming to use the stretch of runway in front of the tower, where the visitors awaited. When the controller called that he could see my aircraft lights before I was able to see the tower, I decided to go no further. I performed a rolling vertical take-off from the taxiway (to avoid damaging the surface) and transitioned into a lowish hover. Turning to face the tower, I thought that was probably about all I could manage. But as I sat there, in the hover, a sort of FIDO[5] effect caused a big bubble of clearer air to form around me. I then decided that I could do a bit of sideways transition. That was a very bad idea, as tilting the direction of my engine's thrust blew my clear bubble away down the taxiway. I stopped, recovered my composure, turned to point back down the taxiway, and completed a rolling, vertical landing. Now I was safe and could relax. Or at least, I did until I realised that I was taxying downhill. That meant that I had gone past the turn-off for my squadron, and was entering the 1 (F) Squadron area. This necessitated a quick

---

[5] FIDO – Fog Investigation and Dispersal Operation. A WW2 method of dispersing airfield fog, by burning fuel in rows along either side of the runway.

U-turn, hopefully unseen, and a slower taxy back home.

Around that time, I received another piece of senior officer advice. My Air Officer Commanding (AOC) was hosting a visit by the commander of the French tactical air force. The plan was that he would accompany the visitor to see the Tornado at RAF Honington, then I would take the General as a passenger on a tactical low level demonstration of the Harrier, landing at RAF Boscombe Down, where the AOC would be waiting, having re-positioned by HS125 (executive jet). Yet again, the weather was rubbish and unfit for any low level in the UK. So I asked the AOC if it would be a problem if I arrived before him at Boscombe. He replied to the effect that such an outcome would be "severely career limiting for you, flight lieutenant." A lengthy IFR[6] transit followed. However, I did survive another AOC clash at a 1(F) Squadron anniversary celebration, for which I flew a display. Because of the proximity of the A1 main road, and wishing to avoid distracting drivers, I changed the axis of the display to fly parallel to the road, rather than across it and along the runway centreline. At normal display height, this necessitated flying at high speed on a line that seemed to spectators, through some strange optical illusion, to be between the lighting stanchions. It was later reported to me that an apparently unimpressed AOC immediately asked for the pilot's name. Fortunately, alongside him was the senior guest, MRAF[7] Sir Dermot Boyle, who joined in with, "Yes, I'd like to know too, and shake him by the hand for that excellent display."

It's outside the display arena as such, but the story of the accompanying head-on shot of a Harrier GR3 bears telling. I was on a ground tour at RAF Gütersloh and keen to get any available flying, while the Operations Wing Adjutant was an ex-ground photographer, who wanted any interesting pictures. I was also the chairman of the Gliding Club, one member of which was the German civilian in charge of PSA (Property Services Agency), where their own cherry-picker[8] had been replaced by a bigger one while the original was being repaired. The final part of the jigsaw was that a IV(AC) Squadron jet needed a test flight that included a functional check of the undercarriage. Not many

---

[6] IFR – Instrument Flight Rules
[7] MRAF – Marshal of the Royal Air Force
[8] Cherry-picker – an elevated work platform

people witnessed the event and, once the pictures became public, many doubted their authenticity. When the Station Commander heard the story, his words to me were, "That was a good idea, Bob. You won't be having any more good ideas, will you?"

Well, I did have one or two, but they are, perhaps, a little too recent to be shared just yet.

Credit: Wayne Palmer

A Fishy Tail

Flying that "Queen of the Skies" – otherwise known as the Hunter – in the Far East, circa 1965, was a dream come true for a naïve, innocent, New Zealand schoolboy, who happened to find himself on 20 Squadron at the height of the "Confrontation" campaign against Sukarno's Indonesia.

As a bachelor, I was happy to do more than my fair share of the regular detachments to either Kuching or Labuan in Borneo, from where we used to fly regular border patrols. I never ceased to enjoy the thrill of getting airborne in the Hunter FGA9 and flying, at low level and 420 knots, over the magnificent land and seascapes of this beautiful, tropical country, with its myriad fascinating features. It was like a David Attenborough kaleidoscope.

On this particular occasion, I was No 2 of a pair doing the early-morning patrol, which started at Tg Datuk, on the northwest tip of Sarawak. From Kuching, we coasted out and soon settled into our regular battle formation over the sea, at our normal operating height of two foot six. The downwash from the Hunter, at this height, made an interesting pattern on the calm sea surface! It was a glorious day and the scene was spectacular as we creamed across the South China Sea, with the mountains of Sarawak in the purple distance, and the starting point for our patrol still several minutes ahead.

Picture the scene then, as suddenly – left - 11 o'clock – level - range 10 yards, a huge manta ray reared up out of the water! Suffice to say that the odour in my cockpit changed dramatically, and I've often wondered since what Spry[1] would have said about a "fish strike" in Air Clues. Would I have been unique?

Credit: Bartosz Cieślakk/Wikipedia

---

[1] Spry – Wing Commander Spry was a mythical character, who commented on aviation matters in the RAF's flight safety magazine, Air Clues.

Action at Mirbat

By 1972, the war in Oman had been ongoing for nine years. As a result of the various measures undertaken by the Omani government, groups of SAS-trained surrendered enemy personnel and regular Sultan's Armed Forces, the rebels (known as the *Adoo*) were being deprived both of local support and supplies from the Peoples Democratic Republic of Yemen (PDRY), across the border from Oman. In order to retrieve the situation, the *Adoo* mounted a major attack on the coastal town of Mirbat during the monsoon season (*Khareef*) of 1972. On 19th July 1972, approximately 250 *Adoo* attacked the small town, which was defended by a motley crew of assorted local guards, paramilitary askars (armed police) and a small detachment of nine Special Air Service personnel, known at that time as the British Army Training Team (BATT), who were due to return home the following day.

I was one of a pair of Strikemaster pilots on alert on the morning of 19th July, at our base at RAF Salalah. Sean Creek was to lead the pair, and we were in our rooms at just before 6 am when we were called by the squadron ops officer. This was very unusual at that time of the morning, and particularly during the *Khareef*, when low cloud was a daily impediment to aviation. The south-east monsoon usually lasted from June to September, and had a significant impact upon flying operations - so much so that many Strikemaster pilots were away on R&R up at Muscat, or flying Beaver aircraft on hearts-and-minds support missions elsewhere in the country. It was usually a quiet time on the fighting calendar.

We jumped into our Mini-Moke scramble vehicle and set off for the squadron, where we arrived at about the same time as the strike squadron commander, Bill Stoker. The cloud was almost on the deck and, with only a basic instrument suite in the Strikemaster, and no precision radar at RAF Salalah, we had to wait for at least a 200 foot cloud base – and even that was strictly speaking illegal! Over the next hour it became clear that the town of Mirbat had been under attack since before first light from a large enemy force, something that had never happened before. The guerrilla tactics employed by the *Adoo* were to attack in small groups and break contact when it was prudent to do so, as large scale attacks were too difficult for them to co-ordinate. Information was beginning to filter through to ops, from the Army HQ at Um al Gwarif, that the situation at Mirbat was becoming desperate. The met forecast for the morning was not good, but we still had a discussion about what we might do, if we were ever able to get airborne. Mirbat was a coastal town, at the same sea level elevation as Salalah, so we needed sufficient cloud base to be able to launch, and were prepared to divert to Midway (now Thumrait) if required. We also discussed weapons options, and quickly dismissed the use of 540 lb bombs, as we were never going to be able to get enough dive angle for safe release. We had no retard tails or delay fuses for those bombs, and quickly dismissed the silly idea of tossing them. We narrowed our discussion to the use of 80mm Hispano SURA rockets and the two 7.62 machine guns which we always carried; however, with a very basic, fixed sight, and never having released rockets from Strikemasters at anything less than about 20° dive angle, what were we going to use for a sight depression? I had some experience of firing 3-inch 'Drains' from shallow dive angles, from Hunter aircraft on a range near Sharjah, and knew that we would have to increase the depression, but from that moment it had to be TLAR[1]! The aircraft were prepared with 32 SURA rockets, and both 7.62 machine gun magazines were full. Suffice to say that we came up with a vague plan but, as the situation on the ground at Mirbat deteriorated by the minute, and with the first BATT casualties requiring a CASEVAC recovery, the pressure really was on to get the Strikemasters into the fray. There was also more than a little concern about enemy small arms fire, particularly from the recently acquired 12.7 mm Shpagin heavy machine guns used by the *Adoo*; the Strikemaster was no A-10[2], lacking any form of armour.

As soon as the cloud base reached 200 feet, we decided to give it a go, so serious was the situation now at Mirbat, with more BATT casualties being reported. The first trick after take-off was to stay below the cloud base at all times, as we transited east along the shore line with hearts racing. The visibility was poor, with no horizon, and it was hard enough keeping each other in sight, let alone finding the headland adjacent to Mirbat. There then followed a radio 'faff',

---

[1] TLAR - That Looks About Right.
[2] A-10 – An American aircraft specifically designed to provide close air support to ground forces, with a fuselage incorporating over 500 kgs of armour plating.

as Sean Creak tried to call the BATT on a UHF SARBE[3] frequency. The lack of response suggested to me that we were trying the wrong frequency, so I called us across to the VHF frequency often used by the BATT, something Sean had forgotten. We quickly established 2-way communications, and were informed that the enemy were on the town's perimeter wire in great numbers. We were asked to attack anything forward of the fort – no time for proper forward air control! Sean and I had a plan to fly a racetrack in trail; each attack run would be followed by a leg out to sea. Sean pushed up to above 350 knots, strafing and launching a salvo of 8 SURA rockets, but he was hit on his first pass. With the caution panel illuminated, and with the risk of fire consequent on having lost his hydraulics, he pulled up into cloud and headed for Salalah, urging me to continue with the mission – not that it took much persuasion! We kept in touch, to ensure that no further help was required from me.

Another three passes and I was out of bullets and rockets – time to return for a re-arm back at Salalah, only some 30 miles away. I had rarely actually ever looked into the eyes of the enemy we were attacking before, since we normally flew above 5000 feet to avoid ground fire, diving steeply to attack. But, on that day, there were hundreds of them out there, plain to see. As I left the target area for home, the BATT controller informed me that we had made a huge difference to the situation on the ground, and would have to send another pair ASAP, a message that had already reached squadron ops at Salalah.

After I landed, Bill Stoker approached my aircraft and informed me that he was coming as my No 2 for the next wave. I remember him being very keen to get in on the action from first light. We had a quick wing-top briefing as my aircraft was rearmed, and we were soon underway. By now the visibility had improved a little, and the cloud base was close to 400 feet, making pairs attack in trail a whole lot safer. We each made one attack run and, when Bill Stoker came in for his second pass, aiming to take out the *Adoo*'s Shpagin on the Jebel overlooking the town, he was hit by a 12.7 mm round. This punched a gaping hole in his port wing, causing a serious fuel leak, and, from his radio call, he was clearly in a bit of a state. I told him to climb into the cloud, head west for Salalah, and I would join him on top after one more attack. I duly released the

---

[3] SARBE – Search And Rescue Beacon Equipment.

remainder of my ordnance in one pass, and climbed to join up with Bill Stoker, above the cloud layer at around 3500 feet. Once in formation with him, I was able to carry out a visual inspection of his aircraft and help out with radio calls to assist with homing into the overhead of Salalah. The aim was to get Bill to climb as high as possible, to increase the chances of gliding to base as his fuel state was now becoming critical. When on the Salalah frequency, I pushed out a MAYDAY call and flew formation on Bill. Once overhead, Bill selected idle power and commenced a controlled spiral downwards, with him concentrating on flying while I made the radio calls. We emerged from a 400 foot cloudbase, fast, but with the airfield in sight, and Bill began to position for a forced landing at Salalah. We did not practice forced landings often, and Bill came over the threshold hot and high, but eventually managed to get his aircraft down on the runway. As he trundled off the end into the scrub, I positioned for a low level circuit to land behind him.

Soon thereafter, the BATT and Omani dead and wounded were extracted, along with the *Adoo* dead - later to be dumped from a Bedford truck in Salalah's main square as a warning to the populus at large. They usually took their dead with them, but numbers were too great on this occasion. It only became clear later in the day that this had been the biggest attack ever launched by the *Adoo*. A small detachment of only 9 BATT, supported by a few Omanis, had faced a massive, coordinated *Adoo* attack, in the greatest action in which the SAS has ever been involved; many have compared it to the famous battle at Rorke's Drift. Since they were in Oman covertly, and never as SAS, little was reported concerning the action in which they fought and some died. However it was, for me, a privilege to be part of that day in July 1972.

Credit: Geoff Lee

Midnight Cowboy

In my logbook is an entry for 23rd June 1977. All it says is Gnat T1 XM 705, Self, Solo, Weather Check, 2.00 hrs Night.

It was a beautiful, warm, humid, summer night. Whenever night flying took place at RAF Valley, and solo students were flying, we were required to have an instructor airborne, keeping an eye on the weather. On this particular night, I was chosen for the role and duly got airborne. I climbed up to about 30,000 feet, selected a low power setting and prepared to fly for endurance. As I flew a racetrack pattern, north and south over Wales, I was completely relaxed, listening to the radio and monitoring the night's flying activity. After an hour, I expected to be relieved and to land back at Valley. However, my relief went un-serviceable and I was asked to stay airborne until another aircraft was produced.

Now the Gnat was not renowned for carrying a lot of fuel, so, to eke it out to the last minute, I needed a cunning plan. I decided that, if I stayed at height until the last minute and then did a maximum rate descent to a visual run-and-break into the circuit, I would be on the ground, having used practically no fuel for the recovery. My relief got airborne, just in time, as I was positioning myself over the airfield at 30,000 feet, with absolutely minimum fuel remaining. With a sigh of relief, I dived down to initials as fast as I could with the throttle at idle, and broke into the circuit - at which stage things started to go wrong. What I had not taken into account was that the aircraft canopy had been soaking in very cold air, at 30,000 feet, for some time. At the low power setting I had been using at high level, there had been insufficient warm air circulating in the cockpit, so, as I rolled out downwind in the circuit, the whole of the aircraft canopy became opaque with ice and mist.

In order to clear the canopy, so that I could see out to land, I needed lots of hot air through the aircraft demist system. This required a high engine power setting which, in turn, required lots of fuel. As I was now short - very short - of the latter, the pressure was on. In my mind, it became a balancing act between running out of fuel and being able to see to land. I cleared the circuit at low level out to sea, opened the throttle, set the canopy demist to hot, and flew around at low level and high speed. When I could just see out of the front of the aircraft I requested a base leg join and, with minimum power settings, landed as soon as possible from a steep, high speed, final approach. I taxied back in to dispersal with the fuel low level light shining brightly.

Afterwards, thinking about the events of that night, I realised that I had put myself in a ridiculous position for no good reason. In reality, would it have really mattered if there had been a gap in time between airborne duty instructors? Was the weather really suddenly going to deteriorate? I think not. In addition, as an afterthought, even when you think you have everything covered, always assume that there is a GOTCHA out there waiting to get you!

Credit: Arpingstone/Wikipedia

Support Helicopters are Different

In what would be considered the dim, distant past to most still serving, but what seems to be only a few years ago to me, I joined a rather large and exciting Royal Air Force with a dream of flying helicopters. I had just enough native 'nous' to realise that, at the Biggin Hill aptitude testing and interviewing, I needed to spout the party line 'I want to be an officer first, and a pilot second' and 'fast-jets are my aspiration' etc, thinking that, if lucky enough to clear this hurdle, I would be home and dry! The dream was maintained throughout my time on the University Air Squadron, the staff seeming to believe that I would soon grow out of this naive perversion. I even managed to keep the dream alive during a somewhat patchy time at RAF College Cranwell, while learning how to keep my mouth shut (never did master that) and 'do it the RAF way'. However, within seconds of turning up at the Flying Training School to fly the mighty Jet Provost, (at the wonderful, but now again defunct, RAF Church Fenton) I was disabused of this notion. We were 'Fast Jet or bust,' the RAF needed pilots for the then MRCA[1], and best we got used to it. The 'chop' rate was 50%, the alternatives Valley or the airlines, and the MRCA, soon to become the Tornado, was the future. I was firmly advised (in an un-PC way) that helicopters were rather like fat girls and mopeds, great fun, but not something one should admit one had a penchant for!

After another somewhat patchy period, this time at Basic Flying Training, I ended up as one of the many training risks who were – quite rightly, given my ability to get lost at low-level in a microsecond - suddenly 'chopped'. Given the choice of nothing or a rare, Multi-Engine (ME) slot, I took a few milliseconds to consider my somewhat mediocre career so far and opted for the ME slot! Thereafter I found myself at RAF Finningley, learning to fly the not-so-mighty Jetstream, hence onwards and upwards to the ME front line. After a slightly less mediocre spell on an ME type long gone from the modern inventory (exact details omitted, as I'm still alive and those of us who started as 'plank-wing'

---

[1] MRCA – Multi Role Combat Aircraft; the pre-production name for the Tornado that was developed so slowly many thought MRCA really stood for Must Refurbish the Canberra Again.

drivers are few enough to be traced), I ended up a happily married, experienced chap on a happy squadron with a chance of a career. However, the Rotary Itch (not the 28 Squadron Hong Kong version!) wouldn't stop until I'd scratched it. Nascent career jettisoned, advice from old and bold, execs and Boss all ignored, and despairing wife in tow, I found myself at Shawbury. Despite an inability to hover for at least the first half of the course (a failing that many a crewman would rudely aver I never lost), I finished up in Northern Ireland on the Wessex, an aircraft that was possibly the most anachronistic old p**** of s*** I'd ever seen. It was an aircraft that I had hated whilst learning to fly it, yet one that I would grow to love for her strength, reliability, tail-wheel and gentle manners - especially when you 'porked' another approach into a dark, wet field at maximum weight.

To be honest, I thought that I had nothing to learn, but I was very wrong. After my cushy, spoilt, ordered and regulated life as an ME chap, I simply didn't get it at first. What a learning curve! It started one day when the aircraft's rudimentary stabilisation-system (the ASE to the cognoscenti) failed whilst on task. Having treated such a failure as a major event at Shawbury, I phoned the Duty Authoriser to be told, "Man up, wet-pants. Turn the stick trim off and, by the end of the day, you'll be fine." Somewhat surprised, I discovered that indeed, by the end of the day, I was fine. In fact, I was better, my hover had improved (not difficult) and I had developed some (small amount of) finesse. The learning experience continued, including the value of a bucket of water down the exhaust to wash the fuel out after a failed start (Westland had mounted the engine upside down, because they could!) and how to change igniter plugs and thump relays. I also learned how to get wet when it rained, somehow get wet even when it didn't rain, how to put out the fire when the wiper motors decided to pack in, the fact that the absolute limit for nose up was 57° before a tail rotor strike, that the landing gear was indeed made of girders (who needed an undercarriage that went up and down if you were going to keep forgetting it), and how to develop a life-long hatred of the designer who decreed that the Wessex didn't need the manual computer control ability fitted to the identical engine in the Sea King. That last one will never leave me, but the inevitable limping around with a computer frozen/run down/up did develop my Rotor RPM control and limited power skills to actually somewhat above the mediocre. I'd arrived; I was an SH

(Support Helicopters) 'Shag' (and not in the Jaguar sense either). I'd learnt that you couldn't carry 'fuel for Mum' unless you were a Chinook driver (which was apparently a bad thing, but nowhere near as embarrassing as being a Puma Mate), and 55lbs fuel a side into Bessbrook was 10lbs too much gas, and you'd undoubtedly come home from tasking a tad too early. In fact, if you didn't flame out in the flare to the fuel point (translates to - run out of fuel just as you were landing to re-fuel: Ed), you'd been a wimp. I could even sing all of the verses of the Rotary Song, at night, in the rain on Night Vision Goggles and limited power, and do so whilst navigating on a wet, chinagraph-smeared OS map!

Northern Ireland was an 'interesting' tour and much of what happened is well recorded; mostly sad, wasteful and not something I would wish to document, even if I could. But sometimes we had moments of pure comedy gold, and the Royal Ulster Constabulary supplied one of them during a relatively simple but enjoyable exercise - Vehicle Check Points or VCPs. Dependent on the situation, one or more Wessex would sidle around an area, dropping off troops to stop cars for a 'check'. Others would fly top cover, stop vehicles behind, look for 'Leakers', 'Runners' and other 'Players'. This was often done under the control of the one RUC person on board, who would tell the crew what to stop, where to go etc. One day, I think the only sunny day in 5 years or so, but my memory isn't what it was, we had a pair of Wessae, 2 'sticks' of troops, and a pair of RUC chaps, to carry out VCPs in the middle of nowhere. Off we trundled, limping airborne in the inevitable 'cushion creep' wobble of a fully loaded Wessex at a 'crewman's 13,600lbs and 3.2 torque' (max weight and max torque for the mighty beast; some crewmen were better at maths than others, and some were a tad optimistic about weights but it all added to the fun!). Here I must thank Westland again, for fitting a coupling gearbox that couldn't take all the power of the 2 engines. The positive effect was that the Wessex was a fantastic single-engine performer. The negative was that she was a terrible 2-engine performer when loaded, and you soon learned how to squeeze the last lb of torque from her. If you really want to know more about in ground effect, cushion creep, limited power, translational lift and other such rotary 'stuff', either find an old QHI[2] or, more interestingly, try reading Chickenhawk by Bob Mason.

---

[2] QHI – Qualified Helicopter Instructor.

Anyway, back to a pair of Wessae, off into the wild blue yonder to do VCPs. We soon got into a rhythm and it rapidly became apparent that we were doing random VCPs, where the RUC guys used their well-developed noses to spot something suspicious. I expect that those sharper than me would soon have worked this out, but I was relaxed, naive, enjoying myself and had not a care in the world. Even Walter Wessex was playing fair, not a hint of trouble, it wasn't raining and I had fuel available just five minutes up the road, which always made a Wessex driver happy. We waited a while before commencing, as per the RUC's wishes that day, then we stopped a pretty red sports car. Nothing found, then another trawl before stopping a black cab, before another red saloon was sighted and stopped. This sequence was repeated: we would find a red, then dive glee-fully onto a coloured car, before trawling the back roads for anything suspicious. Suddenly, the eagle-eyed crewman, who was in on the game, spotted a pink car. Off we went in hot pursuit, which could take a while into wind in the Wessex, and stopped it. Then I was told that the last car we searched for had to be a black. Then it dawned on me – The 2 RUC were competing in a game of VCP snooker. They might have denied it later, and I will never be able to prove that it wasn't random chance, but I remain convinced!

Another interesting 'learning experience' occurred during a routine Search And Rescue (SAR) training sortie. The Wessex in NI had a standby SAR role, and was surprisingly capable, given its age. When compared to the Sea King flown by the real 'SAR- Buoys', it lacked a certain amount of range, payload and endurance. However, if your survivors had the decency to ditch/fall/crash/sink within your range, and to do so in small numbers and in daylight, it was an easy and pleasant hover platform, with good visibility from the cockpit and cabin door and a reasonable winch and cabin for the crewman/winchOp[3]. Therefore, before a planned SAR training sortie, my brave and trusty crewman, who was to be the winchman on the day, arranged an RV[4] with one of the new-fangled SeaCat fast ferries from Belfast to the mainland. Since we had a genuine need

---

[3] WinchOp - The Winch Operator remains in the aircraft cabin, gives hover instructions to the pilot and controls the winch in response to signals from the Winchman, who is on the end of the cable.
[4] RV – Rendezvous.

to train with the various ferries and coastguard vessels, in case we had to winch someone from their decks and we as individuals had not previously winched onto such a high speed platform, this seemed like a capital idea and, after a quick check, we worked out that we should be able to do this within the winching speed limits. Off we lumbered, and soon saw the Sea Cat easing out of harbour. The skipper was very cooperative; he was soon on a stable heading and speed, and we were cleared to winch. Putting the winchman onto the deck was a piece of cake. The SeaCat proved to be a very stable platform, we had enough references for pilot and winchOp to see what was going on, and we were nicely in translational lift, thus making us safe in the hover if we lost an engine (again, ask a QHI or read Chickenhawk). We peeled off slightly to stay adjacent to the SeaCat, and the winchman popped into its wheelhouse, had a cup of coffee and chatted with the skipper. All so far so good! Before long, the winchman was back out on the deck, we were cleared in and started to winch out.

Then the problems started! The winchOp was an old hand, and had already weighted the empty cable as, without the extra weight of the brave winchman, it would tend to stream behind the 'cab'; a Navy term, and SH-speak for helicopter, very important to use it, as it winds up the fast jet and Truckie mates. Well, despite the extra weight, we were now towing a trailing aerial, not a winch cable. The next few attempts were abject failures so we peeled off and, probably for the first time that day, had a proper think. The SeaCat, meanwhile, continued walloping along towards the mainland, further away from my fuel and further towards the point of no return when I would abandon my winchman, suffer intense and well-deserved embarrassment, and undoubtedly purchase vast quantity of beer for most of the Squadron. This was because, given the aforementioned limitations of the Wessex as an SAR cab, we were running out of gas somewhat faster than I had anticipated. The simple option of the winchman jumping from the deck into the sea, and being recovered therefrom - very effective if a boat sports tricky masts and cables that endanger winching - was not so much use when the deck in question was higher than the average house, and doing 45 knots! The winchman was remarkably relaxed during our quick conflab with the skipper on Marine FM, maybe already imagining a return trip as part of the SeaCat crew, the free meal he might be able to blag from the boat, and the beer I would have to buy him. This confirmed my view that all winchmen are brave, resourceful, not easily ruffled, and somewhat mad, but soon we had hatched a plan. The skipper would be able, at some cost to him, to trim a few knots without coming 'off the step' and suddenly decelerating, costing him significant time and fuel. We would attach everything we had in the cab to weight the winch, including my navigation bag, and we would attempt to start at the front of the SeaCat, and gently move backwards in relation to the boat, thus slightly reducing our airspeed and its effect on the empty cable. It was not a recovery that the full-time SAR-Buoys would have found pretty, but it worked. As we moved aft, along the length of the SeaCat, the trusty and brave winchman quickly attached himself 'en passant', and was immediately and unceremoniously snatched from the deck, backwards and away, with a lovely swing and spin on the wire, to give the many interested passengers something to talk about. Thankfully, in those days, no one had a mobile phone with a handy little camera attached!

There are other fond memories which I'll never forget, such as the day a radio operator ran for the entrance door with his 20 foot 'Mr Whippy' aerial extended. I forget the exact height of the rotor disc of the Wessex, but this one was going to be close. Then, as if by magic, his upper body suddenly stopped while his legs continued to run; he'd been grabbed by the beefy Staff Sergeant behind him. Good job thought I, as I watched the Staff Sergeant then detach said aerial and wallop the poor RadOp on the backside with it – lesson learnt I guess! I remember the day someone found a bright yellow speed camera in the wilds of Scotland, en route to some mainland 'training'. We took great delight in practising quick-stops and low (but obviously not below our authorised minimum, we were high-spirited, not hooligans) passes over this thing, until we reckoned it had flashed so much it couldn't have any film left in it. After hearing that some Chinook mate had tried to beat the TT lap record with the crewman sitting on his motorbike (which just happened to be strapped to the rear ramp at the time), we immediately tried to beat the NW 200 lap record. Sadly we failed, proving how slow the Wessex was and how bl**dy fast the riders were! We even invested in stocking and high heels, so that when the Royal Marines were in Province they could look up at the 2 pairs of heels/hairy legs above them in the cabin and enjoy the joke. (Note: At this point, the editorial team would like to point out that none of them flew helicopters)

Eventually I had to leave the joys of 72 Squadron and the Wessex. Shame of shames, I became a Chinook Mate. I suppose it could have been worse, and I could have gone to Pumas. I will never forget the Mighty Wessex and 72 Squadron, the crews and engineers who kept that wonderful old bird going, the way she forgave me my cack-handed mistakes, the way she taught me to fly, and the way you could plant her into a boggy field, nose up, out of power and ideas and come to no harm, day after day, night after night. One day I might write something about the Chinook, but I imagine my stories would pale in comparison to anything written about the bravery of all of the SH fleet post 2001, so maybe someone 'new' should write that one!

Credit: Army/Crown Copyright

Operation Attune

The log-book entry reads:
Date: 7th June 1971
Sortie Number: Katina Two
Aircraft: Victor B2 (SR) XL161
Crew:
Captain: Flight Lieutenant Tom Barnard
Copilot: Flying Officer Julian Collis
Navigator Plotter: Flight Lieutenant Roger Willson
Navigator Radar: Flight Lieutenant Pete Gallagher
AEO: Flight Lieutenant Mike Beer

Take Off: 0300Landed: 0910
Flight time: 6 hours 10 mins(4.00 hours night 2 hours 10 mins day)

From 1966 to 1974, the French government conducted 41 atmospheric nuclear tests on the atolls of Fangataufa and Mururoa in French Polynesia, in the South Pacific. The test weapons were detonated on barges, suspended from helium balloons or dropped from aircraft. Each series contained up to eight tests of triggers and warhead devices, and the detonations produced clouds of atmospheric radioactive dust that were blown, by the prevailing winds, towards the coast of South America.

Victor SR2 aircraft of No 543 Squadron were modified to collect the radioactive dust via filter baskets, fitted behind extension cones at the front of the underwing fuel tanks. These were electrically controlled (open and close) from switches on the Air Electronic Officer's (AEO) panel, in the rear cabin. The presence of radiation was detected by sensors that were fitted to the airframe, and connected to meters on the AEO's desk. They measured radioactive intensity and also provided coarse azimuth and elevation information, to assist with sample location. Crew safety measures included a selectable vacuum pump that was fitted to the cabin conditioning system. It provided additional filtering of air used for cabin conditioning and pressurisation, once the cloud had been detected, and crews were also issued with individual dosimeters and photo-sensitive badges.

Before flight, the AEO was given a table of radioactive measurement figures for the sortie. These included the level at which to open the baskets to start collection, the maximum level to reach before closing the baskets and an aircraft background figure. The aircraft were continually measured for exposure to radioactivity during the detachment, to establish their background reading. This affected the calculations of how much to collect and when to break off contact. It was important that sufficient samples were collected to meet the investigative requirement without over-contaminating the aircraft, which would have rendered it unsafe to fly for long periods.

There were several deployments over the years. 'Operation Alchemist' and 'Operation Aroma' prior to 1971 and, in 1971, the operation was codenamed 'Operation Attune.' On each occasion, a detachment of three aircraft, with support crew and specialists, operated out of Jorge Chavez International Airport at Lima, Peru. Each detachment lasted for five months, with personnel rotated at the halfway point. The French test site was Mururoa Atoll, some 3600 miles from Peru, and the detachment came to readiness when the French government issued an international safety notice to mariners for the area. The detachment had its own Meteorological Officer, who interpreted the weather data to forecast when and where the safest portion of the radioactive cloud would come within range. Initial attempts at collection were made at high level (above 50,000 feet), which was the portion of the cloud that would come into range first, due to the stronger winds at altitude. If this was unsuccessful, subsequent sorties would step down in height.

On 7th June 1971, our crew was tasked as the second sortie covering a French test, the first sortie having been unsuccessful in locating the radioactive cloud. We had been on standby for some time, and were fully rested when the bus collected us from our hotel, in the middle of Lima, for the short drive to the airport just outside the city. The pre-flight briefing took place in an upstairs store room, and was led by the Squadron Commander, Wing Commander Gordon Harper. His briefing team was formed from squadron aircrew (doubling as reserves in case of crew sickness), the Met man and a 2-man team from Aldermaston, one a medical health specialist and the other an equipment engineer (I had been a briefing team member and spare AEO for the previous year's deployment, Operation Alchemist). The Met man and the Ops Team navigator had planned the route, and briefed us on the search profile, which was a "W" shape. The initial leg aimed to pass through the predicted trailing edge of the radioactive cloud, and subsequent legs moved eastwards to try and make contact. The aircraft would continue to fly the "W", until achieving a successful collection or reaching minimum fuel to return to Lima. Diversion airfields were Santiago in Chile and Pisco in Peru, and our search altitude was to be as high as possible, up to 55,000 feet.

We crewed out to the small complex beside the aircraft, where we changed into flying clothing in a blow up 'igloo', which housed our support personnel and mobile communications team. As it was to be a high altitude sortie, we dressed in G-suit leggings under, and a pressure-jerkin over, our flying overalls. These safety items would inflate if the cabin lost pressurisation at high altitude, ensuring that we remained conscious and able to enter an emergency descent, while being force-fed with oxygen at high pressure. Finally, we waddled out to the Victor.

We were the only aircraft movement when we got airborne at 0300, so Air Traffic allowed us to turn directly towards the on-task area. Despite being at maximum weight, the Victor climbed easily to 45,000 feet after take-off, and then commenced the longer cruise-climb, to edge up higher as the fuel burned down. The task area was 3 hours away, which allowed us plenty of time to get to 55,000 feet. Just before reaching the start point, we switched on the air conditioning vacuum pump, finished consuming our rations and stowed them in thick, polythene bags. No more food or drink! Next, each of us went through our safety drills; gloves on, cuffs over the top, neck covered, oxygen masks on with safety pressure[1] selected. Then we started the search. For the first three legs, the meters registered only the aircraft's background count but, as we reached the end of that leg, the elevation indicator flicked. I passed the information to Tom, who headed the aircraft towards my bearing indication. The azimuth seemed OK, which was fortunate, as the aircraft was turning sluggishly between 55,000 and 56,000 feet and would probably not climb higher. The intensity meter then

---

[1] Safety pressure – In common with most military aircraft, the oxygen system had a number of modes of operation. Safety pressure delivered 100% oxygen to the crewman's mask, at a slight over-pressure. This ensured that any leaks would be outwards and, therefore, no contamination could enter the wearer's breathing system.

started to increase, indicating the presence of radioactivity in our vicinity, and it soon reached the briefed figure for opening the collection baskets.

As we rolled out of the turn, I opened the baskets. It was just starting to get light and Tom reported that he could see a yellowish cloud in the atmosphere around us. I then continued to give directions, Tom used his eyeballs and, between the two of us, we chased the cloud. After about 30 minutes of collection, the reading reached the 'come-home' figure, so I closed the baskets and we descended (rapidly) out of the contaminated air. Job done, I passed the successful code-word back to Lima on the HF radio (spooky - an action I was to repeat on Operation Black Buck 1, some 10 years later!).

There was not much to do on the three hour transit back to Lima. We couldn't eat or drink anything, with our oxygen masks still clamped tightly to our faces, and I remember trying not to think of running water. I contacted Air Traffic when we were finally in range, and Tom's approach and landing were uneventful. After landing, we were marshalled into an area set aside for successful collection sorties. Only the Aircraft Servicing Chief was allowed to approach the aircraft, in order to swab the external intercom socket, ground power connection and door handle. Before climbing down the ladder to exit the aircraft, we had to seal our crew equipment and waste in polythene bags and hand them to the Crew Chief. We then waddled back to the quarantine area where we undressed, took a shower, were checked for residual contamination (if necessary, took a second shower!), and put on spare flying overalls. In the meantime, the Aldermaston specialists were removing the filter baskets from the aircraft, and preparing them for safe transportation to the UK. The safety team were also busy, bagging up all our flying kit, which would then be taken away to be measured and monitored, and subsequently returned for further use or destroyed. Finally, the word came through that a sufficient sample had been collected and the detachment stood down.

That night we did the rounds of our normal watering holes. I looked at myself and the rest of the crew to make sure that we were not providing the proprietors with free lighting and heating, but no one was glowing - until the sixth Pisco Sour[2].

---

[2] Pisco Sour – A much favoured, South American cocktail.

Editorial Post Script
In the vastness of the Pacific Ocean there was never any guarantee of a successful contact with the cloud. So one of the boffins would routinely take a casual
stroll along the section of the flight-line reserved for international flights, with
a small(ish) Geiger counter concealed about his person. On one occasion he
came rushing back to the Ops Room, and excitedly announced that there was
no need to fly any more sorties chasing the latest cloud, which was proving to be
particularly elusive. A recently arrived Braniff International flight could provide
us with a perfectly usable sample!

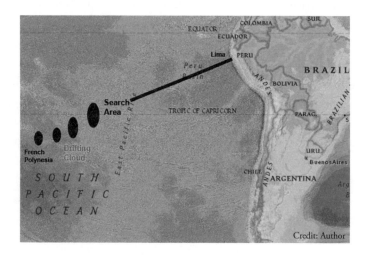

Credit: Author

Bog Roll Bombing

Back in the mid-1980s, there were two fast-jet Operational Conversion Units based at a northern Scottish airfield and, despite the inevitable rivalry, relations between the aircrews of these units were generally pretty good. However, in the run-up to Christmas one year, one OCU decided to have a big lunchtime hangar party, but for some reason decided not to invite anyone from their neighbouring OCU. Needless to say, we were pretty put out by this.

In the event, it was a typical balmy day in NE Scotland, and we noticed that their hangar had its doors open at each end. I also noticed that the hangar's orientation was pretty much in line with the main runway, and an idea sprang to mind. I asked for a Buccaneer to be made ready for a test flight to determine whether the landing gear was retracting properly but, at the same time, asking the ground crew to load the inside of the large airbrake with a selection of bog rolls; some cut in half, others complete, but all held in place by bodge-tape. A hasty perusal of the weapons manual gave no assistance or advice on appropriate sight settings for this ordnance load, so it would be reversion to 'seaman's eye' technique, regularly used by Buccaneer aircrew. Meanwhile, the party on the other side of the airfield was gathering momentum.

I got airborne, immediately reported that I had '3 reds'[1] on selecting the landing gear up, and requested a low, slow fly past the Air Traffic Control tower for a visual inspection. This was the usual routine in this event and the innocents in the Tower granted my request without hesitation. I lined up with the invitingly open hangar, flying quite slowly at 180 knots and about 100 feet. As the hangar disappeared under the nose I opened the airbrake fully. The Tower reported that I appeared to be clean[2], but that something might have fallen from the aircraft as I passed them. I decided to land to see what had happened.

As I taxied into our dispersal, I noticed the Station Commander's car waiting by our line hut, so I had a pretty good idea that this was not a courtesy call he was making. After a short, one-way discussion with him, well out of the earshot of others, he relented and recognized that it was all done in good fun;

---

[1] '3 reds'- A cockpit indication that the undercarriage was not locked either up or down.
[2] clean – In this context it meant that the undercarriage appeared to have retracted fully.

no one had suffered much from bog rolls cascading through the hangar at 180 knots and that, provided we cleared up the mess, we could all go to the party. Those were the days when you could get away with such antics! The Buccaneer had proved to be an ideal bog-roll bomber and harmonious relations were duly restored between the two OCUs.

Credit: U.S. DoD/Wikipedia

A Bit of a Flap

I was in my office, in Engineering Operations, at the RAF Germany Harrier Base at RAF Wildenrath, late one winter afternoon in the mid-seventies, when a message came through that a Harrier had crashed in Holland, and that the pilot had ejected but had not survived. Shortly thereafter came the glad tidings that I was to be the Engineer Member of the Board of Inquiry.

The aircraft had crashed not far from the RNethAF base at Twenthe, just across the border. By the time we arrived in the area, it was too dark to think of visiting the scene of the crash, already being guarded by personnel from 431 MU (Maintenance Unit).

Arriving at the crash site, early next morning, the magnitude of the task facing the Board, and particularly facing me, dawned on us. At that time the Common Market, as it was then, was paying a premium for pigs through its agricultural policy so that, in Holland, there was a "pig mountain" - rather like a butter mountain, but smellier. A rather unappealing side effect was that the pig farmers found it very difficult to dispose of the resulting effluent; the solution was to spread it, about 3 inches deep, over their fields, as had the farmer of the field chosen by our Harrier. Not only that, the aircraft had come down inverted at an angle of about 30 degrees and at a high rate of knots, and had exploded on impact, scattering debris over a large area. It had missed the farmhouse by about 75 yards, and the effect of the impact can be judged from the fact that the two Aden guns from the belly of the aircraft had travelled over the house and were found about 75 yards beyond. Fortunately all the pigs escaped injury; they were billeted on the ground floor of the farmhouse whilst the family lived above, at that time a not unknown way to implement central heating!

When I got home after the first day at the crash site, my wife refused to allow me inside until I had taken off my boots, combat jacket and trousers, which were then hung outside to air, ready for the morrow. As one can imagine, with no washing facilities at the crash site, eating one's lunchtime sandwiches lost a lot of its enjoyment! With bits of aeroplane scattered far and wide, producing the crash map took three days and, even then, there were a lot of pieces of aircraft buried that were not found until later, and in all probability some are still there. The debris was recovered by 431MU, who had to use an excavator to recover the core of the engine, which had buried itself about 15 feet deep. Everything recovered was taken to the 431MU base at RAF Bruggen, hosed down and placed in a Dutch Barn, with just wire netting for sides. In all, we estimated that we had over 2000 individual pieces of debris, the largest being a pair of flaps[1]. No one had witnessed the crash or the events leading up to it, as the pilot was Number Two in a tailchase at the time, so we had no clues as to what might be the cause, not even a radio message. Fortunately, HQ RAF Germany had appreciated the problems we would face in analysing the debris, and had arranged support from the Air Accident Investigation Branch (AAIB) and Hawker Siddeley Aviation (HSA). This very sensible move was to have repercussions later in the investigation.

Readers will be able to imagine the magnitude of the task that faced us, exposed as we were to the elements in a German winter, whilst we sorted through the massive pile of rather smelly bits and pieces that surrounded us. From the excavated debris, it was clear that the engine had still been under power at impact and had not suffered catastrophic failure, so we could discount that. Amongst the larger pieces of debris, the flaps were virtually intact, except that the starboard one had a large hole in it, which neatly fitted the tail cone of one of the underwing fuel tanks that the aircraft had carried. This had us scratching our heads, as to why one flap should be so affected and not the other. All became a little clearer a few days later, when we found the titanium flap operating crank in two pieces. However, it was not immediately obvious whether the fracture was pre or post crash, as there was no visual sign of the striations normally associated with a fatigue fracture, but then neither was there any sign of impact damage; and, although both flaps were essentially intact, the aircraft had impacted at a dive angle of about 30 degrees, and inverted, so perhaps this was to be expected. On the other hand, what had caused it to impact inverted, or was this just coincidence?

At this point, I should perhaps explain how the atypical flap mechanism on the Harrier worked. The two flaps were connected by short torque tubes to a single crank, driven by a hydraulic ram. The hydraulics had been designed

---

[1] Flaps -Devices used to improve the lift characteristics of a wing. They are normally mounted on the trailing (rear) edges of the wings.

so that the flaps, when selected, could blow back towards the stowed position, commensurate with airspeed. One less thing, then, for the pilot to worry about! However, one was not supposed to deploy the flaps above, I seem to recall, 200 knots, to avoid overstressing them. Not surprisingly, as we subsequently learned, there was a tendency amongst the pilots not to worry if flap was selected a little above this speed, as they would blow back and so not be overstressed, wouldn't they? And, no doubt, they helped to manoeuvre the aircraft in, say, a simulated dogfight. However, as they blew in and out and were buffeted by the airflow, the mechanical loads on the drive would vary and often reverse.

Discussing the implications of our findings, the AAIB man and I thought we had identified the cause of the crash. The sequence of events, we postulated, was that the pilot had selected flap and, shortly afterwards, the crank had failed. This had allowed the starboard flap to float freely, and be driven to the up position by the airflow, whilst the hydraulic ram, suddenly offloaded by the disconnection of one flap, drove the port flap to fully down, putting the aircraft into a very rapid, uncontrollable roll. On subsequent impact, there was nothing to stop the freely floating flap from swinging forward and impaling itself on the pointed rear end of the starboard underwing tank. It seemed to us all very logical since, with the aircraft inverted on impact, it was likely that the disconnected flap would have been swung forwards, impaling itself on the end of the fuel tank, rather than the tank having been driven rearwards into the flap. Whilst I and the AAIB man were convinced we had deduced the cause of the crash, the HSA man was adamant that it would be possible to hold the aircraft against the ensuing roll using full aileron. I and the AAIB man were unconvinced, I had faint memories of an Elizabethan (civilian aircraft) crash caused by asymmetric flap some years before, but the HSA man was adamant, so the search for clues continued as we combed through the mountain of debris, with what seemed like permanently frozen fingers.

After about another three weeks of ploughing through the debris, examining smaller and smaller pieces of Harrier, and having found nothing else that could have possibly caused what we had assumed to be a sudden and catastrophic loss of control, the mystery was solved for us. A Harrier from RAF Wittering was the lead in a tailchase, when suddenly the following pilot saw one flap come fully down and the aircraft immediately go into a vicious roll. He called the lead aircraft, telling him to retract flap, and the aircraft was recovered to base. Subsequent investigation showed that the flap drive crank had failed in the same way as had the one we had found. And the reason for the failure? Poor machining had left tool marks on the crank, which had acted as a stress-raiser, promoting eventual fatigue failure.

To say the least, this second event was more than a little embarrassing! So, we had come up with the correct diagnosis after all. However, in mitigation of our failure to pursue this, both the man from the AAIB and the engineer from HSA were relatively inexperienced in accident investigation, as indeed was I. It turned out that the latter, who was a structural engineer not an aerodynamicist, had not, as we had thought at the time, referred our argument back to Kingston. But then, neither had the AAIB man asked the question of his colleagues at Farnborough! I have never been at all happy with my part in the outcome of this enquiry, not least because it could so easily have cost another fighter pilot his life, simply because these basic confirmatory checks were not made.

Why didn't we recognise that our flap drive failure was due to fatigue, and must have occurred in flight? Until then, neither I, nor my co-investigators, had ever seen a fatigue failure in titanium, which does not show the same clearly defined striations found with steel. And the moral I drew from this brief story? Have the courage of your convictions, and make sure that they are explicitly verified one way or the other.

Postscript

No doubt, some are wondering what caused the demise of our pilot. It was a million-to-one chance. Deduced from an actual demonstration, it was concluded that the pilot's build, combined with the violent manoeuvring of the aircraft during the ejection, had allowed a harness shoulder strap to come free, thereby interfering with proper deployment of the parachute.

Bardufoss By Bike

As part of its operational commitment to SACLANT[1], a tour on 12 Squadron offered the opportunity to explore the north-eastern corners of the NATO region, as well as the sunnier climes of the Mediterranean. On my 4-year tour on 12, I was fortunate to visit almost every airbase in Norway and Denmark, sometimes just for a weekend on an overseas Ranger flight, or on exercise for up to 2 weeks at a time.

My first trip to Norway was to Bardufoss Airbase, which sits some 69 degrees north of the equator and, thus, some 180 nautical miles inside the Arctic Circle. It was November 1974, and the squadron had been there on exercise for about a week, operating in the twilight hours of the Arctic winter off an icepack runway. It was an exercise in extreme flying and I, and my novice USAF[2] Exchange pilot, had been deemed too inexperienced to participate fully. However, our reward for our forbearance was that we were to fly to Bardufoss, on the last Friday of the detachment, to join the team for the final party and a weekend in north Norway. We departed RAF Honington on a cold November the 8th and, having climbed to cruising altitude, crossed the North Sea towards Stavanger and picked up the airway that paralleled the coast of Norway. The sky was beautifully clear as we flew on a north easterly heading, tracking the coastline visually past Trondheim and Bodo, before reaching the 'top of drop' for our descent into Bardufoss. The planned flight time from Honington to Bardufoss was 3 hours and, with the sun well established over the southern hemisphere in November, there were only 90 minutes of useable daylight at Bardufoss. Arrival timing at our destination was thus critical, to ensure a daylight landing. We touched down, after 3 hours and 5 minutes, on a hard-pack, snow-covered runway and slid gracefully to a halt as the sun finally dipped below the horizon for another 22 hours. Within 30 minutes of landing, it was pitch dark and, with nothing else to do, we dumped our bags in our on-base rooms and joined the rest of the 12 Squadron team at Happy Hour; it was about 1430! After some 4 hours of drinking, 10 Kroner were extracted from my hand and I, and a large handful of

---

[1] SACLANT – Supreme Allied Commander Atlantic.
[2] USAF – United States Air Force.

the 12 Squadron throng, armed with cans of beer, were encouraged away from the bar to a laundry room in the bowels of the Officers' Mess. There, a RNoAF conscript was running a movie show that, as far as I could make out from my lofty perch on an airing rack, involved pigs, donkeys and naked women doing unspeakable things to each other. At a very early age, I discovered what it was that kept Norwegians occupied during the long dark nights of the Arctic winter.

The following morning started at about 1130 hours, when the sun eventually appeared above the horizon. I joined a motley crew which had assembled, in full 'Nanook of the North' kit, to brave an expedition to a local beauty spot, where we could walk on (frozen) water and admire the beauty of the frozen north. As a youthful 25-year old, I was not normally entranced by nature's wonders, but I have to say that the scenery was outstanding, and the sight of the 2-inch long, ice-formed fern leaf patterns took my breath away – as did the bloody temperature! With the sun in decline at 1330 hrs, we headed back to the Officers' Mess for a cold but inviting beer, stopping on the way to purchase a full reindeer skin to adorn my room in the Mess at Honington. Back at Bardufoss, a party was already in full swing and it didn't take us, who had braved the cold, long to get into the rhythm of it.

By about 2000 hours on that Saturday night at Bardufoss, two of my usual partners in crime decided that it would be a bloody good idea to go into the local town, Andselv, and scout out the night club there. Drawn into their plan, I pointed out a number of facts that they had clearly overlooked in their attempt to locate an alternative hostelry to continue the night's revelry. First and foremost, it was pitch dark outside and about Minus 20°C. Moreover, whilst it was a crystal clear night, and I was qualified in astronavigation, I was not keen to put it into practice whilst shivering from both the cold and an overindulgence of alcohol. Critically, Andselv is about 4 km from the main gate at Bardufoss, along a narrow road that skirts a forest and, in the prevailing weather conditions and without a vehicle, it was likely that we would freeze to death before we arrived at our planned destination.

"Aha!" said Wings. "But we have a vehicle!"

"Yeth!" slurred Art, "we've got bikes!"

"Bikes!" I echoed, "We'll freeze even quicker on bikes or die under the wheels of a car, as we skate across the icy road out of control! Anyway, you may have bikes but I don't!"

"Yeth you do" from Art, "we've done a recce, and the command spare is leaning against the Mess wall, go and get it".

So I did, more out of curiosity as to how the evening might develop than for the devilment of the events unfolding before me. Soon I was joined by Wings and Art on their 'acquired' transport, and the unlawful 3-ship departed the main gate of Bardufoss heading out for the delights of Ands Inn! It was, frankly, a ludicrous adventure. It was almost impossible to stay upright on 2 wheels on the icy road surface and with that much alcohol inside you. Three drunken RAF officers in a foreign land, on stolen bikes, in a frozen waste, under a starlit sky and convinced that their crime would go undetected! I guess I must have been the least drunk, as I soon found myself some 300 yards ahead of the other two, who were constantly giggling and falling off with much clatter. Then tragedy struck, an almighty crash followed by a hollow moan that pierced the night air!

"Dave! Dave! Get back here quick!"

"What's happened?" I called out to Wings.

"Get back here quick, it's Uncle Arthur, he's broken his leg!"

I turned my bike around and pedalled back along the road as quickly as I could on the ice. When I got back to the point on the road from which the voices had come, there was nobody there, only pitch blackness and the still night air.

"Dave, for God's sake! We need help, Uncle Arthur's fallen off his bike in a ditch and he's broken his leg!"

I searched around in the gloom for Wings and Art and, by following Art's quiet moans, I located them both with the bikes on top of them in a ditch on the edge of the forest. As I approached, they started to giggle and it was then that I noticed the open bottle of Teacher's whisky and the top, brimming with the amber liquid, being supped by the pair of them.

"Shit, Dave, it's f*****g cold" said Art, "do you want a wee nip to keep you warm?"

As we sat in the freezing ditch, drinking the whisky and laughing about our adventure, we saw headlights approaching from the direction of Bardufoss.

"Get down" said Wings, "it might be the cops".

As we peered out of our hideaway, we saw the distinctive markings of a military police jeep, travelling northwards to Andselv! It's at this point, as I relate this story some 40 years on, that I ponder on why we didn't turn south, sneak back onto base and return the bikes whence they came. But we didn't. We climbed back onto the bikes, and followed the disappearing lights of the police waggon towards Andselv, where we hid the bikes behind a bus shelter before entering Ands Inn. It wasn't long before the police arrived in the club, and it wasn't much longer before we realised that the individual with them was the owner of the bike that I had been riding. I owned up immediately, and offered my abject apologies to the young Norwegian officer, who had just popped out to the Officers' Mess to get some beer, only to discover that some drunk had pinched his bike whilst he was doing so. As is the way with military personnel, and the camaraderie that they share, he fully accepted my apology and the beers that we bought him in Ands Inn that night. The police were content that it was but a merry jape and departed, taking the three bikes with them back to camp and leaving the four of us to enjoy the rest of the evening together. We shared a taxi back to Bardufoss at the end of the night and no word was ever spoken of the event – until now!

Credit: Geoff Lee

Scramble, Scramble, Scramble!

Under normal, day-to-day operations, it took about an hour to check everything and get a Vulcan airborne, an interval that was hardly compatible with the four-minute warning, which was the worst-case Cold War scenario. True, it was assumed that there would be a period of increasing political tension before anything drastic was likely to happen, and the Cuban Missile Crisis was a prime example of this extended warning, which allowed the V-Force to disperse all over the country.

All the major UK military airfields, together with some civilian ones, were provided with Operational Readiness Platforms (ORPs), which allowed four V-aircraft to be placed at readiness, and able to get airborne with the minimum of delay from every dispersal airfield. These ORPs were ideally located at the edge of the main instrument runway, at the touch-down end. However, with this minimal taxiing requirement, it still took some time for a Vulcan to get airborne, even if the cockpit switches and aircraft systems had been set for a quick getaway. Each of the Vulcan's engines had to be started individually, the elevon powered flying controls had to be started one by one and, while the two pilots were busy getting things going in the front cockpit, the rear crew had to bring all their equipment on-line, piece by piece. So it took a minute or two before the aircraft was able to move forward off the ORP and onto the runway. Then, in May 1963, along came SIMSTART.

This was a wonderful piece of kit that revolutionised scrambles, and No 83 Squadron at RAF Scampton was the first to be so equipped. Instead of starting all the aircraft bits and pieces one by one, the captain merely had to push a single button and everything started at once. All four engines, all the powered flying controls, all the electrics and all the essential equipment; it all came on line and was operational in seconds. As we were the first squadron to have SIMSTART and, as Bomber Command was obviously very proud of this new capability, No 83 Squadron was tasked with forming a scramble demonstration team, to show off how SIMSTART would enhance our ability to get airborne.

I was No 4 in our scramble team; John Sewell was the lead aircraft and I seem to remember that John Nowell and possibly Colin Adams, were the middle two. We had several trial scrambles at Scampton and eventually established some

Standard Operating Procedures of our own, to allow our scramble team to provide a quite spectacular demonstration. All our aircraft would be on the ORP at
the end of the runway, and the only things running were the external Houchin
generators, which were plugged into each aircraft. We also had telebrief plugged
in, which linked us all to the Bomber Controller at High Wycombe. These
plugged-in attachments were designed to automatically disconnect as the aircraft moved forward. The technique we followed was to set the throttles slightly
open and sit on the ORP with the brakes off. When the Bomber Controller
came through with his 'Scramble, Scramble, Scramble', all four SIMSTART
buttons would be pressed and all four aircraft would move forward at the same
time onto the runway, adopting right, left, right, left alignments relative to the
centre line. The lead aircraft would apply full power, just before he was straight,
and would be on his way. Almost simultaneously, the other three aircraft would
follow, belting down the runway, virtually blind in the black smoke from the
aircraft in front. At rotation[1], successive aircraft would pull high, stay low, pull
high and stay low, and angle off just a fraction, to get out of the smoke of the
man in front. We had really got this down to a fine art, and I became quite
skilled at keeping straight on the runway by looking out sideways at the runway
edge, the only useful reference point I could see!

The first official demonstration scramble we did was for HM The Queen,
when she came to Scampton to present a Squadron Standard to No 83. Once
the Royal party was in the viewing stand, the order came through from the
Bomber Controller – 'Scramble, Scramble, Scramble.' We pushed the SIM-
START buttons and off we went - noise, smoke and trusting to luck that the
man in front didn't abort his take-off. My Navigator Radar timed us and, from
the first 'Scramble' call with nothing running, to the moment our wheels left the
runway, as the last in the stream, took just one minute and nine seconds.

---

[1] Rotation – Rearward pressure on the control column that lifted the nosewheel off the runway to initiate the take-off.

First Mission

Waiting... and Thinking

Sitting in my Tornado, all systems up and running, but still 40 minutes before we taxied out, I had time to reflect. This was not welcome. Time for some mental rehearsal for the mission ahead was fine; but, insistently, my mind kept coming back to the possibility that I just might not see again the things I could see around me at that precise moment. After all, the war was only a week old and we'd already lost 5 Tornados in action. I reflected on the chain of events which had brought me to this place, on this night, about to fly my first war mission. There just seemed to be such an inevitability about it all. From my father's example in the RAF during the Second World War, to my early and enduring fascination with aircraft and warfare, to the career I'd chosen and the progression that I'd made. Somehow, it seemed that this night was just always going to happen.

That didn't mean I was looking forward to what lay ahead; far from it. I would have been perfectly happy if we'd had a radio call to say that the Iraqis had pulled out of Kuwait, the war was over and our mission was cancelled. But I knew that wasn't going to happen and I knew that, by now, I didn't really want tonight's mission to be cancelled. I just needed to get on and get this done. Was I scared? Of course I was, although I'm sure I wouldn't have admitted to it at the time. Fear was a perfectly natural and rational reaction to the danger I was about to face. Without some sense of fear, you don't really appreciate risks and the potential consequences, and you become a danger to yourself and others. How much danger I was about to face was an unknown, and the anticipation of the unknown is always a fearful thing in itself. All I needed to do was make sure that fear was not the dominant emotion. Fortunately, a couple of other things were more important. One was the demands and general busy-ness of the task in hand. The other was the 'don't screw-up factor' – the fear of professional failure, especially in the eyes of one's colleagues. It was the case, for me at least, that the prospect of not succeeding on this mission was worse than putting myself in harm's way.

Twenty minutes to check-in. The second engine was started and the sights, sounds and smells of a desert airbase were shut out as the canopy came down; to be replaced by the steady hum of the cockpit, the dim glow of the cockpit lighting, and the radios as our only contact with the outside world. It was time to see what the next 5 hours would bring.

Airborne

It was impossible not to be impressed by the sheer number of aircraft in the night sky. South of the border, running into other aircraft was perhaps the biggest risk, so everyone kept on as many aircraft lights as possible. Once we'd found our tanker – one amongst an enormous number – it was anti-collision strobe lights off, slide in behind and beneath the starboard refuelling hose, give thanks for the absence of significant turbulence, stabilise behind the drogue (dimly outlined by luminous bulbs and the red light from my aircraft refuelling probe) check for amber lights in the tanker refuelling pod to indicate clearance for contact, slide gradually forward, a final small correction up and right as the probe approached the basket, and into contact. Keep the power on, push the basket forward another 20 feet, green lights come on, fuel flows, settle into the 'in contact' position for the next 10 minutes or so. I had a temporary feeling of relief that this part of the sortie was fine, before the inevitable moment of recollection that this was really just the easy bit.

We stayed with the tanker to a point half way along the Saudi/Iraqi border, until everyone had refuelled and it was time to make our 'push' time across the border, a hundred miles or so to the north. In the cockpit, we ran through our 'fence' checks – checking our counter-measures, checking IFF[1] settings, weapons switches, switching off unnecessary kit which might emit and betray our position, giving each other a verbal reminder of the combat rescue details for that day. As each aircraft got to the appropriate point in the checks, the aircraft external lights around us went out, and what had looked like a busy sky turned into an apparently empty one – for all that I could see outside the cockpit, we might now be the only aircraft heading into Iraq. The radio told a different story; one box was on our internal formation frequency, the other on an anti-jam net, and it provided our link to the world; situational awareness and threat information from the E-3[2] and communication with the rest of our package of

---

[1] IFF –An electronic means of identifying aircraft (Identification Friend or Foe).
[2] E-3 – Airborne Early Warning and Control Aircraft.

aircraft. Frequent 'picture clear' radio calls reassured us that someone friendly was looking out for us. Soon enough, the moving map display showed the approaching border. I looked at the time on the clock on the right side of the cockpit coaming, then down at my kneepad; about an hour still to go to the target from here, followed by a little under an hour back to the border, so in only 2 hours I would be back here and through it all - hopefully. There was nothing to mark the transit across the border. The desert below was equally dark and apparently as empty on one side as on the other, but I had one of those momentary tightening knots in the stomach as I realised that I was now in 'enemy territory.'

North of the Border
Continuing north in the darkness, there was nothing visible outside to suggest that we were not by ourselves. Sticking rigidly to our assigned height, to minimise the risk of mid-air collision, I started a gentle weave either side of track. The aim was to see into the large area of the ground which would otherwise be obscured by the nose of the aircraft from our height; we might then have a better chance of spotting unguided missile launches or AAA[3] coming up at us. Manoeuvre also made us just that little bit less predictable and therefore less vulnerable, besides which it just wouldn't have felt right to be flying straight and level, like we were on a high-level transit in Europe. This was war after all! As I reversed one of the gentle weaves to the left into a turn to the right, sudden flashes appeared out in the one o'clock position. Instantly I thought 'threat', but it was quickly apparent that they were some way off and, as the initial brightness settled into a duller glow on the ground, I realised that I was looking at another strike 'going down'. Gradually more pockets of brightness came into sight – strikes going down and clusters of AAA fire around targets. Iraq as a whole was in complete darkness – strikes on power infrastructure on the first night's raids had seen to that – but we were steadily leaving behind the virtually empty desert, which had stretched north for perhaps a hundred miles from the border, and approaching the more populated and militarised areas along the line of the Euphrates River. There was no obvious threat to us at this point, and we had planned our route to stay clear of towns and known defended areas until we had

---

[3] AAA – Anti Aircraft Artillery.

no other option but to head into the badlands if we wanted to get to our target. The minutes ticked by, and I could start to see distant dull traces of light out to the right, two o'clock position, in the area of our target. There were no indications on our RHWR (Radar Homing and Warning Receiver) of hostile SAM[4] systems looking at us, just a reassuring number of 'F's from the 'Friendly' fighter aircraft around us. As we gradually edged our way around the final turns onto the attack heading, dull areas of light started to resolve into individual streams of tracer bullets. Several thoughts ran through my mind: this was random, un-aimed, low-calibre gunfire, so we weren't specifically being targeted and we felt fairly immune at this height. The colours were vivid against the otherwise complete darkness, with an especially arresting green-coloured tracer coming from one point; only one round in seven was tracer, it was said, so there was an awful lot more metal in the sky than it appeared! Those who had described the pattern made by the tracer in the sky as like a flailing hosepipe had it about right; none of the 'big stuff' – heavy calibre AAA which could reach our height and beyond – was visible, but who knew what else might be out there and around us.

Target
None of this was at the front of my mind though; more important was getting the job done properly and not screwing up. Making sure we were in the right place, at the right time, at the right height; getting the pre-attack checks done and then going through them again, just to make sure; making the switches 'live' and, for me, mentally reminding myself, again and again, to keep my finger on the 'commit' button on the control column until all the weapons had released. We were so used in training to just dropping one weapon at a time, that it would be easy to take your thumb off the button after the 'thump' of the first release, at which point the release sequence would stop and you would either have to re-attack or take the rest of the weapons back home, which would be embarrass-ing. The Time To Go (to weapon release) circle in the HUD[5] started to wind down from one minute – it seemed like a very long minute - the AAA of the

---

[4] SAM – Surface to Air Missile.
[5] HUD - A transparent, electronically generated Head Up Display that projects data directly ahead of the pilot, thus reducing the need to look inside the cockpit (head down) at instru-mentation.

target started to disappear under the nose of the aircraft and I felt increasingly vulnerable, unsighted and non-manoeuvring, at what was the riskiest point of the mission. Just before our weapon release, I was aware of bright flashes underneath at the target – our leader's bombs detonating, good we were in the right place – and then, with my right thumb jammed on the commit button, a rapid series of 5 thumps as our stick of bombs released. It seemed like a long time, and with my heightened awareness I felt that I could sense each individual thump, even though they were only a fifth of a second apart. Immediately, it was into a sharp turn off the target by about 90 degrees, to make our flight path unpredictable again, and to ensure we didn't fly directly over the target. The other good reason for turning off the target quickly was that we wanted to get ourselves into a position from which we could see the detonation of our weapons. However, there was no military value in this as they were unguided weapons, so nothing we did could now alter where they were going to hit. I'd never seen one of our bombs detonate at night before, so I hadn't realised that they would explode with such an intense, electric blue flash; followed almost instantaneously by a blue circular shock wave spreading out over hundreds of metres in a fraction of a second. There were 5 rapid fire pulses of this light as I looked down and slightly behind. Regardless of the effect of these weapons, I felt that I'd delivered some impressive military force. There was no AAA visible in the area of the target now; instead, there were the beginnings of some orange fireballs, so obviously at least some of the weapons were hitting the right sorts of oil storage and production things. Someone said 'it's a burner' over the radio – a phrase which seemed to capture the right sort of feeling. But then it was quickly back to wings level and time to run for home as quickly as possible.

Recovery

It was impossible not to start relaxing as we flew back into the complete darkness of the southern Iraqi desert, heading to the west of south to make sure we stayed well away from Kuwait. Dangerous to a degree because we were still in hostile airspace, but experience already showed that the danger lay around the targets, and that, barring the risks of aircraft mechanical problems and mid-air collision, we should be fine out here. Back in Saudi airspace I was just keen to get back on the ground as soon as possible. What were my feelings? I thought nothing about the target from the viewpoint of its significance to the campaign, or of the consequences for anyone on the ground in the target area; all I had was the personal and professional interest in whether we'd succeeded in doing our job. I was satisfied that we had. It was not precision bombing, but it was still good enough to cause a sizeable amount of damage to a target the size of an oil refinery. I felt relief that I'd got through this first mission intact and without error, and that I'd undoubtedly had an easier first mission than many of my colleagues a week or so previously. I was also starting to feel very tired as the tension and adrenalin started to subside, to be replaced with the realisation that it was about 4 in the morning and that I'd been awake for some 20 hours. And creeping insistently into the back of my mind was the realisation that relief was purely temporary, because I was going to have to do all this again in short order. I would be flying again the next night – which, in reality, meant later today – in fact, I would be back over Iraq in less than 18 hours' time. That was a thought for later though, one to worry about soon enough, but for now we continued heading into the lightening sky in the east. The sunrise looked beautiful.

Credit: Geoff Lee

Just How Low Can You Get?

There I was.........enjoying my tea and toast in the Officers' Mess at RAF Little Rissington, on a winter's afternoon, early in 1967, during my Central Flying School course. I picked up the latest edition of *Flight International* magazine, turned to Roger Bacon's *Straight and Level* page, and could not believe my eyes - there was a picture of me in my Hunter FGA 9!

I had left 20 Squadron the previous autumn, and had swopped the sweat of Singapore for the chill of "Hell on the Hill", but the memory of that flight in Borneo quickly warmed my spirit. I was the pilot authorized to do some Forward Air Controller training for a group of Australian army officers, while John Lumsden, another of the Squadron's pilots, escorted them and supervised them from the top of a hill in the middle of the jungle. At the end of their training, I was asked to give them a fly-past. As they were on top of a conical hill, it was easy to fly past the assembled officers, close to them and at the same height. I had climbed away to return to Kuching, when John radioed to ask me if I would do another one but, this time, fly over them from an approach up the hill. I had no idea how I was going to do this but, keeping them in sight, I did a wide circuit and positioned myself for a descent that would take me to the bottom of the hill. That bit went well, but now, picture the scene; I was at the bottom of a hill, at very low level, doing 420 knots, and I had no idea where the summit was – let alone the gathered throng of critical army officers! Image my consternation, but I was committed - so I kept calm and blundered on. As I bunted[1] over the top of the hill, a blur of khaki uniforms flashed beneath the aircraft. I thought no more about it.........until many months later when the photograph flew out of the page in the 'Just How Low Can You Get?' series as I sat in the Mess at Little Rissy.

I eventually got the explanation from John. He had shown the photograph to the Boss (Max Bacon) who had asked for a copy, sent it to Roger Bacon, at *Flight International* and got paid £15 for his trouble. I'm still owed my share!

---

[1] Bunted – Pushed forward on the control column to fly an arc which, in this case, was meant to follow the outline of the hill.

Pianos, Arrests and the RCMP

As a young officer, I noted that there always seemed to be a piano around in an Officers' Mess. The piano is a wonderful instrument of entertainment, in one form or another. I should explain further.

I was privileged to Command a Tornado Strike/Attack squadron in Germany in the mid-1980s, in the good (or was it the bad?) old days of the Cold War. I had served in the role and theatre before, in Phantom and Jaguar aircraft. This was to be a very busy and challenging tour; the Jaguar units at the air base were to be reformed as Tornado squadrons on a four-month rolling programme. In the beginning, I arrived in theatre as the squadron commander, with one other junior officer. No aircraft, no aircrew, no groundcrew and a building site under construction was the starting point. The brand new jets were delivered on time, straight from the manufacturer's production line. An experienced cadre of flight commanders soon arrived; but, thereafter, while I had hoped for men to form the unit, the posting people seemed to send us only boys, mainly first tourists[1]. The groundcrew followed, again with a small cadre of Tornado aircraft engineers, but, in the main, the troops came from other roles. Spares were a bit short initially, but we had 3 months to get up to full strength. A steep learning curve for all was required.

The initial task was to achieve combat-ready[2] status in the strike role, and to qualify in all the essential procedures and tests associated with special weapons control and safety. Drill and ceremonial also had its place, and we managed to get the disparate team of aircrew and groundcrew together, to march around the hangar looking like guardsmen (well nearly) for the formal formation ceremony attended by the top brass. Being a new unit with a new aircraft, particularly in a new role for Tornado, we hosted a plethora of visits from politicians, VIPs and senior military folk. No sooner had we qualified in the strike role, than the work up began to gain combat-ready status in the attack role. The alert hooter, signalling yet another base exercise, seemed to blow on a regular basis, as each

---

[1] First-tourist – Someone on their first operational posting after completing flying training.
[2] Combat Ready – Sufficiently equipped and trained to effectively discharge the squadron's operational role.

squadron on the wing gained combat-ready status and was tested by NATO's Tactical Evaluation Team. Overall, the conversion of the wing from Jaguar to Tornado was a great success, and the programme ran to schedule.

Once we were up and running as a unit, a series of deployments followed to North America, where we developed tactics for day and night all-weather, terrain-following operations. Operational Low Flying, down to 100 feet, and live weapons training were completed, culminating in the Red Flag[3] series of exercises in the Nevada desert. This location was also rather too close to the distractions of the city of Las Vegas. Without doubt, to get the squadron to this level of training some stick-and-carrot encouragement was required from the boss and flight commanders, to keep the troops motivated and focused on the demanding flying and engineering tasks. The commitment and determination of aircrew and groundcrew to get the job done was inspiring, but the days were often long and very busy, with frequent, lengthy deployments and separation from families back home. While on deployment, the aircrew did get high-spirited and 'beer calls' became very lively at the end of the duty week. The conflict between maintaining esprit de corps and controlling the high spirits was often a difficult path to tread, without ruffling the feathers of our hard-working team. It was not surprising therefore, that on one dark winter's evening under a full moon, on a remote airbase in Labrador, Canada, a fiery glow became evident in the snow outside my quarters. Soon, klaxons wailed and the base fire crews arrived, followed by the military police detachment and the local constabulary in the form of a member of the Royal Canadian Mounted Police - although on this occasion he had no horse! The glow came from a blazing, occasionally exploding piano, loaded with jet fuel, firecrackers and other incendiaries; which our talented squadron pianist was not playing at the time.

As the senior officer present, I was summoned to a military police interview and was questioned on the meaning of it all. Without knowledge of this mysterious incident, and without an adequate explanation, I was arrested and

---

[3] Red Flag - An advanced aerial combat training exercise, hosted at Nellis Air Force Base, Nevada and Eielson Air Force Base Alaska. Its purpose is to train aircrew from the United States and other NATO countries. In a typical Red Flag exercise, Blue Forces (friendly) engage Red Forces (hostile) in realistic combat situations.

conveyed to a place of incarceration, whilst fire suppressant foam was sprayed on the blazing musical instrument (and me). I did note that my Canadian Air Force interrogators were somewhat gleeful, having recently adjourned from Happy Hour. Consequently, their interrogation technique was quite unconvincing and somewhat incoherent. I suspected a stitch-up. Handcuffed, I was eventually returned to the Canadian Officers' Mess in a dishevelled state. For those who have encountered Canadian Air Force officers of the fighter squadron variety, you will know that Friday night in a Canadian Officers' Mess is a particularly lively place to be. Once inside, I was greeted by the Canadian base commander (clearly involved in my arrest and incarceration) and reunited with my squadron aircrew, by now in a particularly raucous condition and forging diplomatic relations with their Canadian counterparts. The assembled throng were being entertained by our talented pilot pianist, playing on the only remaining serviceable piano in Labrador. A rousing rendition of the squadron anthem was quickly followed by a melodious, musical tribute to Canadian lumberjacks. At some stage, I recall the Canadian base commander making it very clear that the piano currently being played was not to be interfered with - by any British officer, under any circumstances. Our most junior officer was thus appointed piano protector and when we redeployed back to home base, a few days later, we thankfully left behind an almost pristine piano.

On reflection, I suppose that, as the boss behind the stick-and-carrot regime to keep the boys motivated, I deserved to be stitched up and locked away on a Friday night. The most enjoyable tour of my life, as a squadron commander, was all-too-soon completed. I still like pianos, cannot play them, but, when I see one, I do think a lot about those grand companions I served with on a fighter squadron. They were the boys! I never did find out who owned the piano that we blew up, and sadly rendered well beyond repair.

The Cornfield Club

When accidents are analysed, most show that, somewhere along the line, somebody, usually the pilot, rushed it all, didn't think things out, and started a train of events that led (inevitably) to a prang.

After a lifetime of flying, I am often asked if I've ever had a crash. The question is usually asked in jest, but I get the feeling that the person asking it wants a thrill. Well yes, I've had more than one and this is the story of the most spectacular. I hope people enjoy reading it, but the real reason I have written it is to illustrate how I failed to think ahead, work things out carefully and act as I should have done. Though this happened well over fifty years ago, and the type of aircraft involved has long since vanished from the skies, the lesson has not altered and, if what I've said causes just one pilot who reads it to slow down, think something out and avoid an accident, then my writing about it has been well worthwhile.

Almost every day, during the early 1950s, you could read in the papers about a crash involving a Meteor or a Vampire, the two standard RAF jet fighters at that time and, apart from the loss of the aircraft, the pilot was usually killed. It was a waste of life and years of expensive training, which were far more important than the fighter. The attrition rate was horrendous, and said by some to be higher than might be expected from enemy action in wartime. Many of these accidents were officially categorised as 'unavoidable', as this one was, but I was lucky and got away with it, not being blamed in any way. Looking back now, though, I know that the verdict was wrong; so let's see what we can learn when we go over it all.

A fighter squadron in those days was made up of a bunch of highly-charged young men, living non-stop at the peak of their ability, absolutely sure that they were the tops and that their squadron was the best. Morale was generally sky high and, to prove that they were the best, pilots put everything they had into giving the highest performance of which they were capable - I hope fighter squadrons and fighter pilots are still like that. At the time, I was based at RAF Biggin Hill in Kent, just to the south of London. It is now well known as a large centre for general aviation but, in the 1950s, it was a front line fighter station with three squadrons based there, one regular (ours) and two auxiliary, known as 'weekend warriors'. We flew Meteor 8s, and our job was the defence of the Capital. Of course we knew that, whatever anyone else might have said, we were far and away the best of all the squadrons in Fighter Command. Since those days, I have spoken to some people and read magazine articles which often implied that the Meteor was a dangerous aircraft to fly, with many bad traits. That's rubbish; it was superb, though a pilot needed to respect and understand some things about it which could bite him if he was not careful. That, anyway, is exactly the case with almost every aircraft that I've flown. The Meteor's only real fault was that it did not quite have the performance to match the Russian Mig 15, which we expected to have to fight.

One of the routine exercises that we practised was air-to-air gunnery. We fired at a target which was towed on a long line behind one of our normal squadron Meteors, and was attached to it by a hook fixed onto the rear of the belly tank. The target was a large flag, about thirty feet long and six feet wide, with a thick metal bar at the front which had a large lead weight on one end, to hold it up vertically in the slipstream. Painted in the middle of the flag was a black circle, about a foot in diameter, which was the aiming point. The bullets had paint splashed all over their noses, with a different colour used for each aircraft that fired on a particular flag. In that way, each attacking pilot's hits could be identified.

At the beginning of WW2, the RAF's pilots had to relearn all the lessons that had been so painfully drummed into the previous generation during WW1. As part of our training, we were shown gunsight film from the early period of the Battle of Britain. You could clearly see how fighters were opening fire from a long way off and, therefore, out of range. The only way to achieve hits was to get in as close as possible, preferably line astern of the target, where there was a minimum of angle-off, and then only fire short bursts when the gun sight was actually on the target. The angle-off is the angle between the line of flight of the bullets and that of the target. It would be near zero when the fighter was astern but, in that position, the attacker was also a target for a bomber's defensive armament. Obviously, we could not shoot at our towed targets from line astern, because of the risk of hitting the tug, so the strict rule was that you must never shoot at an angle-off of less than 15°. This was something that you had to judge and learn from experience. We carried gun cameras, which filmed the target when we fired, and this was later assessed so we could see just how good our shooting was – or wasn't. We could also get an accurate idea of the angle-off; less than 15° and you were in trouble! Anyway, the tug pilot was one of us, a squadron pal, who we certainly did not want to shoot down.

We attacked by flying a curve of pursuit, which meant closing in with a continuous turn from the beam position, where we started the manoeuvre. As we closed, so the angle-off decreased as did the range. The tighter the turn, the closer you could get before you had to break off at what you judged was the fifteen degree point, by pulling up hard over the banner. This exercise was carried out in designated areas out to sea, always firing away from the land whilst the tug pilot kept a careful lookout for shipping. One fine day, during the summer of 1952, we were out to sea off Littlehampton, and I felt quite sure that I was doing well. I was getting in very close each time, really clobbering the flag, but confident that I had not allowed the angle-off to get less than the critical 15°. At this point, it is worth mentioning that it was not unusual to put a 20mm cannon shell through the tow rope, sending the banner into the sea. Unsurprisingly, this was not popular with pilots who had already fired on it, because they would never know their scores. Anyway, the crunch came for me when, having used up about half my ammunition for the exercise, I was curving in tightly on another firing run...and got too close. I also shot the banner off and, as it momentarily hung there in front of me, I had insufficient space to pull up in the normal way and break over the top of it.

Had I not shot the banner off there would have been no difficulty but, in this case, I broke new ground by flying into it. Nobody had ever done that before; they had shot it off or flown into it, but not both at the same time. I was confident that the angle-off had never got less than 15°, but could not be sure until my gunnery film had been assessed. At that moment, however, I had other things to think about! There was a tremendous crash as I collided with the metal bar, and its lead weight hit the leading edge of the starboard wing, between the engine and the fuselage. The aircraft yawed hard to the right (normally the first symptom of a sudden starboard engine failure), so I straightened up with full opposite rudder, settled everything down, then got rid of the asymmetric load with left rudder trim - no problem there. I checked the instruments, turned for home and went through the standard engine failure drills. All indications were that the engine had failed, which was something that had happened to me more than once. On each previous occasion, I had come home and landed on the one remaining engine with no particular difficulty. Therefore, my first thought was that this is what I would do, and I didn't think much more about it.

The inboard leading edge of the starboard wing was a horrible sight. The weight had struck at just about the mid-point between the engine and the fuselage, and was lodged there amongst a mass of mangled metal. All around it, the slipstream was pulling the broken skin away and making it peel back across the upper surface, which caused a lot of extra drag. All the controls and instrument connections to the starboard engine were routed inside the leading edge of the wing, so they were now jammed or broken, with the electric cables severed. On the instrument panel, the RPM[1] and JPT[2] gauges for the starboard engine read zero, while the throttle was loose, and could be slid backwards and forwards without any restriction to its movement. This was just as might be expected under the circumstances, so I was fat, dumb and happy about it; well, not happy, but I thought that I knew exactly what was wrong. The drag from the damaged wing continued to cause the aircraft to try and yaw hard to the right. That, together with the zero reading on the instruments, was all I needed to make me believe I had a straightforward starboard engine failure. In hindsight, it's now obvious to me that I should have looked (and thought) further.

Part of the engine failure drill was to turn off both high- and low-pressure fuel cocks. The high-pressure cock itself was situated as an engine accessory, and controlled the fuel flow to the injectors; the connecting rod to it ran along inside the leading edge of the wing. The low-pressure cock simply opened and closed the pipe from the main fuel tank, which was situated in the fuselage, not far behind the cockpit. In the Meteor, the high-pressure cocks, one for each engine, were large levers situated beside one another on the cockpit floor, either side of the ejector seat. They were reached by the pilot, who had only to lower his hand straight down in order to operate them; raising them mechanically switched off the fuel. In fact, we never normally moved the low-pressure lever, which was awkwardly placed and therefore left on all the time. In this case, I could not

---

[1] RPM – Revolutions Per Minute.
[2] JPT – Jet Pipe Temperature.

move the high-pressure cock; it was solidly jammed fully down. The connecting rod to the low-pressure cock could not have been affected in any way as it just led back through the fuselage, but I could not get to it easily and, as a matter of course, just left it in the 'On' position. Without further thought, I made up my mind that the starboard engine had ceased operation, and that was all there was to it. I never considered doing a very positive low-speed check to note if all the extra drag had affected either the stalling speed, or the single-engine critical speed[3]. I completely glossed over all the indications, without thinking what the problem might really be.

All the time, my squadron pal, who had been flying the tug aircraft, remained alongside me in case anything further went wrong. It didn't; I came into the circuit at Biggin Hill and prepared for what I expected to be a normal single-engined landing on runway 04. Everything seemed to go well with the approach until I rounded out and throttled back the port engine in the normal way, prior to touch down. The aircraft did not touch down! Totally unexpectedly, it just swung hard to the left, away from the side where all the trouble was, and kept staggering through the air, low over the ground and not slowing down at all.

It came to me suddenly, in a great flash of enlightenment, that the starboard engine was still running and producing power, but just how much power I had no idea. I reasoned that it must be about what I had selected when I hit the flag, but I could not remember just what that might be. Possibly I had started to throttle back for the break-away, possibly it was still what I had on when I started the actual attack on the target. Whatever it was, I just did not know, and had no means of finding out at that moment. When flying a fighter, you operate the throttles instinctively, not moving them gently to a carefully considered boost or RPM setting, as you do in an airliner.

Now I was in difficulty and thinking very quickly, probably for the first time since the collision. If I tried to climb away, with the intention of learning more about the problem when I had reached a safe height, I would need to apply full power on my port engine. That could be very dangerous, because I was now some way below single-engine critical speed and, if the starboard engine was

---

[3] Single-engine critical speed – The speed below which, in the event of an engine failure, insufficient rudder authority is available to maintain directional control, while using the full power of the remaining engine.

only producing a small amount of power, the Meteor would roll to starboard, possibly right onto its back, before I could stop it. At my current height, it could only mean a horrible mess, with me underneath it all. I voted against that straight away, and decided that my only chance was to spike the aircraft down onto the runway, and do my best to slow down.

The wheel brakes on a Meteor were not very brilliant; they were pneumatically operated, and the system was prone to leaks. If operated in little more than short jabs, they could easily overheat and fail. On the squadron, we had what we called the Cornfield Club. Its members consisted of those pilots who had gone off the end of Runway 04, crossed the wide grass area between it and the boundary, through the hedge, past the haystacks and into the field beyond. Whatever the crop growing there might have been, it was always known as The Cornfield. I easily beat that, and joined the Cornfield Club in quite the most rapid fashion that anyone had managed up to that time. As I went through the hedge, seemingly having slowed down hardly at all, it also became evident that the starboard engine was still producing a great deal of power, which had been masked by all the damage to the wing.

On the fast-approaching far side of the field, there was a narrow belt of woodland, what country people call a shore. I went straight into it, and my first thought was that it was rather a noisy business. When I had got my 'A' Licence at White Waltham before joining the RAF, the instructors were all ex-wartime ATA pilots, who had a fund of stories about their experiences. One, which always brought guffaws when told in the bar, concerned 'Old So and So', who had, for some reason, landed a Hudson in a wood. He had slipped neatly between the trees, which sliced off both his wings, but left the fuselage undamaged and him unhurt. I did exactly that, and remembered the tale as it happened to me, thinking that I must go back to White Waltham and tell them all about it. In fact, I never did so.

Unfortunately, there was a catch to this shore; on the far side of it was a steep drop of about ten feet. I did not measure it exactly at the time, and have not gone back since to check. Anyway, it was what finally stopped my headlong rush. The undercarriage was wiped off, and we slithered gently along and came to a halt in the stubble. I knew that I had to get out, and do so very quickly. Smoke was coming up into the cockpit and, naturally, I was rather dazed. I expected the whole thing to blow up at any second and that the ejector seat might easily do its thing; which would be curtains for me. I undid all my straps and the oxygen connection, and desperately tried to open the hood. It was jammed shut, and I could not move it or jettison it in any way. That is where my memory ends, and I have no idea how I got out of the aircraft. For about 55 years since, my mind has been a complete blank, but I obviously got out - somehow. The next thing I remember is sitting in the stubble about a hundred yards away, watching everything that was going on. The aircraft continued to smoke but never caught fire, and I expected the cannon to start firing off the remaining ammunition, but that did not happen either.

I became aware that the fire engine and its crew were stuck on the far side of the shore, and could not find a way through and down the bank. Then, suddenly, I noticed Sergeant Gowath, our orderly room sergeant, running as fast as he could towards the aircraft. He was someone whom we always looked upon as a friend and, when no senior officers were around, he called us junior pilots by our first names, and we called him Sergeant Garbage. Now he was running towards an aeroplane that was about to blow up, shouting, "Mike, Mike, are you in there. Get out, get out". That was what brought me round. I tried to shout and wave at him, but that ghastly starboard engine kept persistently running and easily drowned out my shouts. Luckily he saw me, came over and helped me up and away to the ambulance.

Next day, the Station doctor sent me and my sore back to the RAF hospital at Halton. The friendly Group Captain orthopaedic doctor who examined me there told me, "Well, lad, your back has been damaged a little, so you now have a choice. You can either be strapped to a wooden board for six months, which will put it right, or you can go straight back to your squadron and fly, letting it right itself in its own time". The answer was obvious as far as I was concerned, so he just added, "Good luck and don't play any more rugby for a year".

As soon as I got back, the questions started. My gunnery film had survived the crash, been developed and carefully assessed. It showed that I had got so close to the flag that it was impossible for me to have avoided it after I had shot it away; more importantly though, it showed that I had not fired below the vital $15°$ angle-off. Until that was said officially, the tug pilot, who is still a friend I'm happy to say, had naturally been looking at me rather sideways. As is usually the way in such cases, all the evidence, plus my statement, was sent up to 11 Group Headquarters, and I had to wait for a few weeks whilst the 'Powers' there deliberated. During that period, I remained on flying duties, was kept as busy as usual, and remember not being at all worried about the potential outcome.

In the event, I was officially told by the Station Commander, Wing Commander Smallwood, that it had been designated an 'Unavoidable Accident'. He subsequently congratulated me on surviving in one piece, and I began to realise that I had had a very close shave. Also it would have been a black mark against the squadron.

Over the ensuing years I have thought a great deal about what happened and, after a lifetime of professional flying, remain convinced that the verdict was wrong. It was, however, entirely consistent with the prevailing culture of the first-generation jets era. Basically, it all boiled down to not carefully evaluating the whole thing right at the start, and going through the emergency drill correctly. I had plenty of time to do so, all the time that it took to get back from the range to Biggin Hill; but I rushed everything and did not work it out properly. If I had been more determined, got my fingers properly round the low pressure cock and pulled it up as I should have, it would have shut down the damaged starboard engine. I also should have carried out a low speed handling check, at a sensible height, to assess the modified flight characteristics near to the stall, and the new single-engine critical speed. In any case, a low speed check on its own would have instantly alerted me to the residual power of the starboard engine when I closed the port throttle. The aircraft would probably have flicked over onto its back, but I could easily have recovered from that and, knowing the new stalling speed and critical speed, I could have flown the approach accordingly. It would certainly have been rather faster than normal, and I would probably have rolled off the end of the runway, but not as far as The Cornfield.

Editorial Note

Further stories of target flying include the Canberra pilot, who was towing a banner off the south coast for the benefit of naval anti-aircraft gunners. After one pass, and somewhat perturbed by the Navy's erratic fire, he calmly transmitted, "Please be aware that I am pulling the b***** target, not pushing it".

On another occasion, a certain fighter squadron was detached to Malta for the purpose of conducting air-to-air gunnery, on their annual Armament Practice Camp. As the days passed, it became evident that they were not having much success. Banner after banner came back with nary a bullet hole between them, and there were many furrowed brows, earnest discussions and long briefings. I was one of the tug pilots and duly got airborne one morning during week two, towed my banner out over the Med. and awaited the first fighter. It turned out to be the squadron boss, who was clearly in a foul mood, and advised me that he would be speaking to my detachment commander after landing. The three crews that followed were also uncharacteristically terse, but it wasn't until I got back on the ground (with the banner still intact) that I realised why. Earlier that morning, our ever-resourceful ground crew had acquired a pot of black paint and a brush. In large letters they had then written BARN DOOR on my banner.

Credit: RuthAS

Revenge is Sweet

I have always liked good hi-fi with its excellent frequency response and handling of deep bass notes. As a bachelor, having some decent kit to play my vinyls on, as it was then, was quite important to me, and so I had some big American Bose speakers and a matching industry Bose amplifier. They not only produced a great sound but also a very powerful sound at 600 watts RMS per channel, for the more technical amongst us. The mess electrical system took a hammering though, because the lights used to dim when I switched it on, so I was convinced that the National Grid dipped a volt or two as well. It also provided some welcome heating in the room during the colder evenings. Such was the power of this kit, I was only able to turn up the volume fully once when I temporarily had it in a hangar following a charity event.

I was approached one day by a fellow bachelor, let's call him Pete, who complained to me about the noise a couple frequently made in the room above him. The Officers' Mess at Northolt is a lovely old Fighter Command building, but had been constructed with relatively thin walls in the original section and, when the lady above had her boyfriend stay over, little was left to the imagination and the noise was quite intrusive, if not impressive. Pete wanted to return this lack of consideration in kind and wondered if I had something in my record collection that might dampen their ardour. I told him that I had something in mind and that he was welcome to use my hi-fi but that I would need help moving it as the power amp alone weighed some 50Kg.

It is worth mentioning that the lady in question had a propensity to exaggerate and too often try and impress others with privileged information to help improve her social standing. Clearly, this didn't go down too well with many and so Pete had further motivation for some retaliatory action.

A short time later Pete told me that he'd heard she was expecting company that night, and I told him that I had selected a good track from my collection of BBC sound effects records. Of the 13 albums in the set, I had chosen the Military Aircraft record and on that, there was a 10 second clip of a formation of Lightnings doing a low pass at full power. Pete became very enthusiastic at the prospect, so we moved my hi-fi to his room, drank coffee and sipped malt whisky until just after midnight, when the 'performance' began above. He hadn't exaggerated about the noise by the way. It was now just a case of gently lowering the arm onto the selected track, turning up the volume, putting our fingers in our ears and waiting for the approaching flight of Lightnings. One could not only hear the roar of the engines but could actually feel it. The whole room shook and I could have sworn that my chest was caving in. Just after the Lightnings had disappeared over Ruislip Lido, we could hear the sound of someone running heavily across the floor above, some hushed conversation and then, magically, peace and quiet. Mission accomplished, we rolled on the floor in hysterics like kids, with tears streaming down our faces, hardly containing our laughter and trying to imagine the scene above.

However, as it turned out, that wasn't the end of it. At lunchtime the following day, I met the certain lady (let's call her Jo), who asked me if I'd heard the noise in the night. I said I had and that I'd wondered what it was. She confidently told me that an aircraft had gone over very low but by the time she had run to the window, she hadn't been able to see anything. I then realised that the prank had much more mileage left in it and that we could capitalise on this.

Some of you will know that Northolt is situated some five miles to the North of Heathrow, a fact, regrettably, even better known to those pilots who have mistaken it for Heathrow. The gas tower on finals was even painted with 'NO' to indicate that it was Northolt ahead and not Heathrow. Jo worked in the air traffic tower at Northolt and I happened to know that the SATCO[1] was on leave. It was Friday when I called the tower and, putting on a refined London accent, I asked to speak to the SATCO to give credence to my call. I was told by the duty sergeant that the SATCO was on leave but that he could pass me to the local controller which was Jo, who then took my call. I said that I was from the Air Accident Investigation Branch at London Heathrow, and that I was investigating an incident that had taken place a couple of nights ago, and would she be kind enough to check their log for that night to see if any entry had been made at about 0020 hours. She said that Northolt would have been closed at that time but asked what it was all about. I said that the incident was under investigation and that I would be unable to divulge anything. She was clearly disappointed but then I said that, although this was very hush-hush, if she promised not to

---

[1] SATCO – Senior Air Traffic Control Officer

tell anyone else I could pass on what we knew, but that it hadn't come from me. She perked up and readily agreed, so I said that a Boeing 747 had been lining up for an approach to Heathrow but missed the turn-in point for the ILS[2] to the runway. This took it over Harrow on the Hill, where it clipped some TV aerials and some fencing that was later found on the undercarriage after it eventually landed. I stressed how secret this information was and she had to promise to keep it to herself.

We knew that Jo would be at Happy Hour later that day, so Pete and I briefed those present before she walked in and quietly found someone she felt she could trust, who happened to be drinking a pint at the bar. I could see from the body language that she was just busting to tell him her news and, in hushed tones, she duly related the events. The more animated she became telling her story, the quieter the bar became, until she eventually stopped, looked round, saw everyone smiling and realised that she'd been set up. Sad to relate though - in spite of our success the noise continued unabated, and Pete was eventually forced to admit defeat and move rooms.

Credit: Makaristos/Wikipedia

---

[2] ILS – Instrument Landing System

Alarums and Excursions

The Shackleton Mk 1 was designed in the late 40s and came into service in 1952. It was followed about 5 years later by the Mk 2 and, in 1955, by the Mk 3. The Mk1 had its radar in a radome under the 'chin', and had a tail wheel. The interior was matt black and lacked soundproofing. In the Mk 2, the radar was fitted in a retractable radome, and the aircraft was fitted with twin 20mm Hispano guns, but still had the tail wheel and an unchanged interior. The Mk3, however, had a tricycle undercarriage and a new electronics fit, and the interior had been fitted with some soundproofing between the skin and the coffee and cream panelling. It also had tip tanks, each of 256-gallon capacity, giving it a maximum fuel load of 4208 gallons. There was a valve in the bottom of each tip tank, which allowed the fuel in it to be jettisoned in an emergency.

Some of the Mk1s were converted to T4s, and used to train new crew members. They flew well into the 1960s, and the Mk2 continued as an Airborne Early Warning variant into the 90s. Not so the Mk3s. They were modified three times, each mod adding to the weight. In the last version, the Mk3 Phase 3, the increase in weight created by the upgraded equipment fit proved too much for the engines to cope with at take-off; so, two Rolls-Royce Viper turbojet engines were added, one behind each of the outboard engines, making the Mk3/3 the only six-engined, eight-propellered aircraft in the world.

I was young, and therefore immortal, and thought little of risk to life; but when I thumbed through my log book in later years, and noted the number of RTB (returned to base due to a major fault) entries, I realised that the Mk3 Phase 3 was downright unsafe. Then there were the losses: on my own squadron of six aircraft, we lost two. One had an engine failure just after take-off; a piston broke up, and the connecting rod came through the crankcase, severing the fuel lines on that side of the engine and also the engine feathering control. Petrol from the severed fuel lines caught light, the engine was still getting fuel from the other side and so it over sped, tore itself out of the aircraft and fell into the Beauly Firth; the pilots managed to crash-land the aircraft at Culloden, with no major casualties (indeed, the ambulances etc arrived to find the crew enjoying the hospitality at the local dance).[1]

---

[1] See Out of the Blue, Volume 1 – 'MAKING YOUR MARK'.

The second crashed into the Moray Firth, with the loss of all aboard. Losses on other squadrons included one into the sea off the Cornish coast (two survivors), and one lost in transit to Ballykelly (believed to have iced up). There was never a suggestion that the aircraft should be grounded, but there was obvious concern about the power-to-weight ratio, and the effect of shifting the Centre of Gravity while in flight. As a weight-saving measure, even the soundproofing (fibreglass matting) was removed, and, if the aircraft was heavy and one of the pilots wanted to visit the (chemical) toilet at the rear of the aircraft, another crew member had to take his place at the front to maintain the C of G. The only Mk2 that I remember crashing, ditched into the Indian Ocean – another engine fire. Some of the most exciting moments in a Shackleton rear-crew-member's life, however, had to do with catering.

We had been in Sharjah for three months, during which time I had shared a room with our engineer. It was our last night there; tomorrow we flew home, taking some of the ground crew as passengers. Our first stop was to be for fuel at Luxor (Egypt), then on to Malta for the night. Neither of us slept well, and we agreed that, once out of Luxor and established in transit, I would take over the engineer's panel, while he got his head down on one of the bunks.

Morning came, I had a shower, felt refreshed and we all trooped aboard. I got out the food for breakfast and put a tin of mushrooms in the oven, before moving to the radar position prior to the start [engine] checks. With half an ear, I listened to the usual litany:

'Start 3'…'Switches 3 '…'Contact 3'…'Turning 3'…and No 3 engine had just spluttered into life when I heard a voice call, "FIRE!"

I learned then how quickly one thinks. My thought process ran: 'That's interesting. If a fire is detected before engine start, you attack it from outside with a fire extinguisher. If after engine start, you wind up the engine and hope to blow the fire out. As the engine hasn't quite started, I wonder what they will do.'…then the voice continued – "IN THE GALLEY".

I shot out of my seat and back to the galley, where I found the oven door swinging on its hinges, the air full of water vapour and the contents of a tin of mushrooms fairly evenly distributed around the area. Muggins had forgotten to pierce the tin, and it had exploded. I made my apologies to all and sundry, and crept back to the anonymity of the radar tent. The ground crew kept the split tin and, once back at Kinloss, had it mounted on a home-made plinth bearing the inscription 'From the Groundcrew to the Aircrew, for the most exciting in-flight meal' - but back to the Gulf.

We landed at Luxor and refuelled without incident - apart from my asking a local for a drink in the middle of Ramadan - and took off for the leg to Malta. As agreed, I sat at the engineer's panel and looked at all the pretty dials. At the end of the hour, I did the fuel calculations, then came up on intercom saying, "Captain, Eng. Your all-up weight is xx,xxx pounds," and thinking what an easy job an engineer had. Sometime after that, the co-pilot asked, "What's the T's and P's [temperatures and pressures] like, Eng?" Frankly, I hadn't a clue, but as the sets of gauges for all four engines showed identical readings, they were all either all right or all wrong. The former seemed more likely so, with confidence, I replied that T's and P's were normal and within limits; then, as I watched, the oil pressure on No 3 engine fell gently from 52psi to 48psi, and just as gently returned.

"We've just had a 4psi fluctuation on No 3" I said.

"Roger" he said, then "We're losing it!"

"Roger" said I, "You feather it (shut it down) and I'll start the Vipers"

The standard drill was to start the Viper on the same side as the failed engine first, then the other, and entailed making various switch changes before holding the START switch on a panel, under a lid on the engineer's desk. Being left-handed, I found myself holding down the starboard (right) START switch with my left hand, while making switch changes on the left of the panel with my right hand. Just then, the (real) engineer arrived, and took over. My recollection is that he threw me out of the seat.

With both Vipers running, we were still not out of the woods. They were intended for use on take-off only, and would run out of lubricating oil if left on too long. We had taken off with a full fuel load but, with one engine failed, we needed the Vipers to maintain height until we had burned off enough fuel (lost weight) to enable us to fly safely on three engines. Off intercom (we didn't want to alarm the ground crew), we set about identifying what items could be thrown out of the door, and securing those we couldn't. It was a close-run thing, but we made it safely to Malta, where we remained until a new engine was flown out - not a happy experience for men who were expecting to be reunited with their families after three month's separation. Having blown up the galley and been involved in an engine failure, I was now seen as something of a jinx. Someone suggested locking me in the nose on the last leg home – a rather cruel suggestion in mind of my other Shackleton incident, which I shall entitle 'Crack(ed) Head'.

The Shackleton had the facility for mounting twin machine guns (20mm Hispanos as I recall) in the nose position. They were elevated, depressed and swivelled by a hydraulic motor controlled by the gunner. We used them perhaps once a quarter, dropping a smoke marker in the water and using it as a target. The guns were highly unreliable; you pressed the firing button and a couple of rounds were despatched, then the gun sight fell off and one gun would jam, followed a couple of rounds later by the other. Consequently, every crew had someone who was qualified to clear stoppages and our crew had two, one of whom was me.

On the occasion in question, I was the gunner and all went as usual – two rounds, gunsight on the floor, two more and the port gun stopped, followed by the starboard gun. I put the Fire/Safe switch to Safe, got out of my seat, and began to clear the port stoppage, following the procedure from my checklist lying on the seat, and wearing gloves and bone dome as required. I couldn't reach under the magazine without depressing the guns and so, raising the magazine, I reached up and pushed the control stick down. On reflection, this was not a wise move, as the response from the hydraulic motor was less than precise. In this instance, instead of moving vertically, the gun tracked down and to starboard, and the magazine end tracked up and to port, trapping my head between it and the port bulkhead.

So there I was, feeling just as a walnut must at Christmas, with my head jammed between the bulkhead and the magazine, and with only a wayward 1800psi hydraulic pump between me and release – or something quite different. I had visions of being stuck there until we had landed, when the hydraulic pump could be stopped and I would be manually released. I came up on intercom and reported that I was trapped: the other stoppage-qualified crew member came up behind me, reached over for the control stick and moved it to bring the gun away from my head. It almost worked but, instead of tracking to the right, the magazine crabbed up and left, and I heard a nasty splintering sound before losing consciousness.

I came to fairly quickly and was helped back to the galley area, where I lay on the top bunk until we landed some hours later. I was not in any pain, nor was there much blood – less than from a cut finger. The only real evidence of damage was that the right side of my face was much flatter than the left: the magazine had caught me on the high point of my cheekbone, and fractured it in three places, driving it inwards and – fortunately – crushing the zygomatic nerve in the process. The aircraft was met by an ambulance, I was taken off to Raigmore Hospital in Inverness and operated on the following day. I say 'operated on', but in fact there was no cutting involved, the surgeon used the surgical equivalent of a tyre lever and pushed the cheekbone back into place – but I had half of my head shaved just in case real surgery was needed.

In true service fashion, a Board of Inquiry was convened to establish the circumstances of the accident, and to determine where the responsibility lay. The Board must have been convened with some speed, because they took my evidence from my hospital bed, at a time when I knew how close I had come to death and was grateful just to be alive. Frankly, I didn't care what conclusion they came to. However, as I had been wearing bone dome and gloves, and had been reading from a checklist at the time, it was determined that I had acted with 'excusable negligence'. I was medically grounded for 3 months, but it took at least a year for feeling to return to the right side of my face. It was a very strange experience; I could feel the left side of my face but not the right, with the border running down the centre of my nose.

Finally, I sent my only distress message in the early hours of a February morning in 1982. We were on Search & Rescue (SAR) standby, and had all gone to bed, to be wakened around 0200 by the SAR klaxon sounding and the tannoy message, "DINGHY, DINGHY, DINGHY. SEARCH AND RESCUE SCRAMBLE. I SAY AGAIN DINGHY DINGHY, DINGHY. SEARCH AND RESCUE SCRAMBLE."

SAR callouts have three levels of priority – 'Advanced', 'Immediate' and 'Scramble'. 'Scramble' means 'Get airborne as soon as you can. You will be briefed once airborne'. Nobody hangs around. I got out of bed, climbed into my flying suit and boots, grabbed the 'Secrets' bag from the locker, opened the window and climbed out. We got into our van, abandoned it at the aircraft and got our backsides off the ground.

The Greek tanker Victory was in a storm, about 350 miles west of the

Azores, when she broke in two. The front section, from the bows to just forward of the wheelhouse, sank immediately. A lifeboat, with 13 crew aboard, was lowered, but broke up on contact with the water. The remainder of the crew were gathered on the bridge. It was still dark when we arrived. I spoke to the ship's captain who told me what had happened. I asked him how much longer he thought his ship would float. "Two hours" was the reply. There was nothing we could do until dawn but, as soon as light permitted, we made two passes across the boat, each time dropping two multi-seat dinghies, each joined by about 50m of buoyant rope. Both drops were successful, so the crew now had two dinghies on each side of the ship, and connected to it by rope. There was nothing else we could do directly, but we stayed to provide moral support, and to send updates back to the Rescue Coordination Centre.

We were making a pass along the side of the ship, when there was a loud BANG from the navigational equipment bay. All the nav kit and screens went blank, and a cloud of black smoke came billowing out of the crate; we had a fire in the air. We climbed away, fought the fire, and I put out my first and only MAYDAY. By the time it was answered (by a yachtsman!), the fire was under control, but we had lost the use of all our navigational kit. We downgraded our MAYDAY to a PAN[2] and, using the sun as a guide, set off roughly easterly for the Azores. When we were about 100 miles out, we were met by an American P3/Orion and shepherded into the USAF base at Lajes.

It wasn't until we were safely in our rooms that the next problem showed itself: when the klaxon had sounded, we were out of bed and into flying suits; now it was out of flying suits to reveal – pyjamas! We were stranded with nothing but the clothes we stood up in. Fortunately, the Captain managed to borrow money from Base Accounts, on the understanding that the MOD would repay. With my portion I bought a shirt and a pair of jeans, and a nightly wash of shirt, socks & underwear enabled me to survive for the five days it took for spares to arrive.

However, the story had a happy ending for all concerned. The Victory remained afloat for a further 24 hours and the crew members were safely lifted off by a helicopter from a Dutch frigate.

---

[2] PAN - A state of urgency exists, although there is no imminent danger to life or the continued viability of the aircraft.

Herc Detachment - Cameroons

Back in 1988, I was the captain of a Hercules from RAF Lyneham, support-ing British troops on an exercise in the Cameroons. The detachment, lasting over three weeks, gave the troops the opportunity to practise their long range navigation techniques over unfamiliar terrain, jungle training, air re-supplies, parachuting, strip procedures and also assisting the local forces. There are sev-eral stories from this detachment, but the final exercise was probably the most memorable for the Hercules crew.

An exercise was planned with the Cameroon forces who were to defend a mili-tary airfield where they were holding hostages. The airfield, although disused, still had a serviceable runway for our use. Our troops were tasked to recover the hostages and, if possible, carry out destruction of the vital locations on the field. This would take place over a period of a week, with the opposing forces not knowing what might happen and when. A plan was formulated, and it was decided that we would drop an advance party of troops into the local area, using a High Altitude Low Opening (HALO) parachute drop. The group would then carry out reconnaissance missions, some days prior to the main assault and re-covery phase, and mark out the runway for our landing. The main assault would commence with a tactical landing on the runway, at night, to unload two Land Rovers and troops, who would then link up with the ground party and carry out the hostage rescue. The landing strip would be marked by troops using infra-red devices, either chemical lights or modified torches. Infra-red devices cannot be seen by the naked eye, but are visible to Night Vision Goggles (NVG) up to 5 miles away in good conditions. The phase was planned to coincide with a visible moon, which would greatly enhance the use of our NVG.

The tactical strip would be laid near to the end of the runway, using a system called a 'box and 2'. The start of the strip would be marked by 2 troops standing 60 feet apart then, 1000 feet further on, another two troops would mark the end of the box, again 60 feet apart. A final two troops would then mark the end of the strip, another 1500 feet further on, making a total strip length of 2500 feet. As captain of the Hercules, all I had to do was to land the aircraft within the 'box' and, by using maximum braking and reverse thrust, the aircraft would, in theory, stop before the end of the strip. The Hercules is a remarkable aircraft and, despite its large size, can stop almost on a sixpence. The tactical approach speeds are not far above the stall speed, and around 25 knots lower than for normal operations. Of course there are lots of performance characteristics such as weight of aircraft, wind, temperature, altitude etc that would affect the over-all performance, and these would be considered in the planning stage. On the night, all I had to do was to land within the 'box' - simple!

Prior to landing, and in order to achieve a rapid unload, troops take positions in their vehicles and all restraints, with the exception of a final restraint, are removed. The rear door of the Hercules is partially opened, and then the engines of the vehicles are started. On landing, the rear door is opened further, so that it is almost touching the ground (ready for the aircraft to stop) and the vehicle final restraints are removed. As the aircraft stops, the door is fully lowered, as are the tactical ramps, and the vehicles rush out of the aircraft to their tasks. The ramps are then folded, the door closing commenced and, as soon as the door is clear of the ground, the aircraft starts its tactical take-off run. In all, this whole procedure only takes a few seconds to carry out and is most impressive to watch.

Landing on a long strip or runway means that the aircraft does not need to make a 180 degree turn before taking off, saving lots of precious time. As we were landing on a runway, that was our plan on this occasion. We would immediately take to the air, and then await the call to return and make a tactical recovery of the troops and vehicles, assuming that their mission had been successful. On our final departure, small charges that had been laid on the edge of the runway would be remotely exploded, simulating runway destruction charges.

A rehearsal of the airfield assault was scheduled using another similar airfield, one that we had used during the day and were familiar with. For the rehearsal, I positioned a crewmember on the ground with a radio, to act as a safety officer. The rehearsal went completely according to plan, apart from one slight problem. On the final departure, the small charges were remotely detonated but, very shortly thereafter, the frantic voice of our safety officer came over the radio, "The airfield is on fire, the airfield is on fire". I made a turn back to the field and, sure enough, we could see fires burning brightly. No-one had thought that the small charges would do any harm, but the dry grass on the edge of the runway had ignited. Fortunately, this airfield was close to a couple of villages, and their occupants, who had been watching the evening's show with interest, helped in putting out the bonfires.

The following evening, we were given the green light to proceed with the assault and, having loaded the vehicles and troops, we departed for our target. Nearing our destination, we made contact with the advance party, who informed us they were having problems getting to the runway, due to the local troops and the terrain. The assault was therefore delayed. We then had to position ourselves far enough away from the airfield, so that the noise of our engines was not heard on the ground, but close enough that we still had contact with the ground party. A suitable downwind holding point was quickly established. We all know that time can almost stand still when you are waiting for something to occur, and this is what happened to us that night. One hour passed, and we still had no clearance. Another 30 minutes ticked by, and the moon slipped away, leaving a very dark picture. Our NVGs suddenly did not work so well, leaving the co-pilot and me a little uncomfortable. With good moon conditions, wires on electrical pylons and animals in the fields can be seen; however, in zero moon conditions, and especially when cloudy, it is not easy to even see such major items as roads, houses, and bridges. Sometimes cultural lighting can help the situation but, in this event, there was none at all.

Finally, clearance was given and we set off to make our approach. Normally the co-pilot would map-read to the target but, on this occasion, all we had were 1:500,000 maps, several years old, and a few photographs. This was also the era before the Hercules was fitted with GPS navigation equipment, but the navigator did have an inertial setup and, thanks to him, we hit the run-in track, and spotted 4 of the infra-red lights. Both the co-pilot and I were searching hard for the 2 far lights knowing that they would appear when suddenly I saw a blur close beneath the aircraft exactly as the co-pilot screamed "Pull Up, Pull Up". Needless to say, the aircraft was already making its move, following my rapid control inputs. "Was that trees?" I asked, and the co- pilot confirmed that it was. There was no way we were going to be able to make a suitable approach to the runway with those trees on the extended centreline. Of course the trees did not appear on the charts, as they were so old and not detailed enough. The decision to abort the assault was quite an easy one to make, so we departed back to our mounting base, all ready and willing to have a beer and discuss the evening's events.

However, this wasn't the end of the tale, as the following day we were informed that the advanced party had subsequently found out that the local troops had placed some large boulders on the runway, a little beyond the end strip markers. Had we managed to land and unload the vehicles, we would have run into these obstructions on the take-off roll, making rather a mess of one of Her Majesty's aircraft and, more importantly, our crew!

Credit: RAF/Crown Copyright

My Second Parachute Jump

I joined the RAF in 1968, not as a pilot but as a Physical Education Officer (PEdO). In those days, the PEd Branch consisted of an elite cadre of Parachute Jumping Instructors (PJIs) and 'others'. Consequently, an essential initiation rite to the branch for a newly-commissioned PEdO was a 4-jump parachute 'taster' course. My course was duly programmed, in the winter of 1968/69, at the then Parachute Training School at RAF Abingdon.

On arrival, my 'newby' PEdO colleagues and myself joined up with a Parachute Regiment intake for the first 4 jumps of their 'wings' course. All the jumps were to be static-line jumps, where the main parachute is opened automatically on exit. The first two jumps would be from a basket, under a balloon tethered at 800 feet, and the final two jumps from an aircraft.

The course commenced with four days of intensive training, simulating an exit from a balloon or aircraft and the subsequent flight and landing. The command 'Red on, green on, go' is repeated at you so many times during those four days, that you wake up in the night shouting it to yourself. However, the training was huge fun. Most of the equipment used was the sort of stuff that people pay to enjoy, nowadays, in any self-respecting adventure park. There was the 'fan jump' from the rafters of an aircraft hangar, designed to float you to the ground at parachute descent speed. Then there was the zip wire; specially designed so that even vertically-challenged people couldn't avoid colliding with the ground at high speed, and in a posture that guaranteed severe pain. And finally, the 90 foot hydraulic vertical drop, to simulate exit from a basket underneath a balloon. Because it was midwinter, the oil in this last contraption remained thick and viscous, resulting in a distinctly false impression of what would actually happen on jump day. Indeed, since I was still slim and sylph-like in those days, I had trouble making it down to the ground at all, floating like a butterfly in the Oxfordshire breeze.

All too soon it was Friday, jump day, and we were packed into coaches for the short ride from Abingdon to RAF Weston-on-the-Green, the school's local Landing Zone (LZ). The atmosphere was a mixture of nervous trepidation, overlaid with the bravado of youth. On arrival, we were divided into groups of three, consisting of a PEdO and 2 Paras, and each group was then allocated a

Sgt PJI, who duly marched us off to one of the balloons tethered around the LZ. Main chutes, reserve chutes and helmets were strapped on for the big event, and then the PJI barked, "The officer will now enter the basket and stand opposite the door." In turn, the two Paras entered the basket ,were positioned either side of the door and, finally, the PJI entered and took his position by the door, before sliding the metal 'safety bar' through the retaining eyelets on either side of the door. Clearly, this lash-up 'safety bar' was well in advance of Health and Safety taking over the world! "Raise the balloon to 800ft," boomed out the PJI, and up we floated. Past two hundred feet and then four hundred, when it starts to become very quiet as sounds from the ground begin to fade, and nobody feels like talking. At six hundred feet Oxfordshire looks magnificent spread out below, then the balloon is at eight hundred and it's time for business.

The PJI says to the Paras, "The officer will now show you Paras how it's done", turns his attention to me and commands. "The officer will now step forward to the door." As I move forward, the balance of the basket suddenly changes with a lurch and, with every subsequent step, the door descends further and further below me, until I seem to be looking vertically down at the LZ below. This wasn't mentioned in the bloody brief, and that platform on the hydraulic drop trainer didn't move an inch. The PJI encourages me to move forward from the position that my brain had told me to stop at 'until you can feel the safety bar against your thighs sir.' I shuffle forward, connect with the safety bar, and then experience the extremely disturbing sensation of it sliding across my thighs, as it is withdrawn with agonising slowness. I steel myself not to panic; I'm an officer, and I've got to set an example. I await the jump commands, transfixed by my view of the LZ below, but nothing happens. I risk a sideways glance towards the PJI for some help, and I am struck by the wicked grin on his face as he softly says, "In your own time, sir". I have no real recollection of what seems like the next five minutes except that I am falling - just like in those awful dreams, when the overwhelming urge is to wake up - and I am woken by a sudden jolt as my main chute opens. Training kicks in: check canopy; check bodily functions normal; check for drift, and use the lift lines to position for landing. Remember that you don't want a backwards landing; the saying for one of those is 'Heels, head, arse, and hospital.' I'm suddenly aware of the ground rushing up to meet me, and the megaphone-loud voice of the LZ PJI cutting through my brain fog, commanding, "Assume the position, sir". I don't have time to appreciate the humour in his remark, before the ground and I embrace at a velocity far in excess of any previous training landing, and I hold onto the earth's embrace as I realise that I'm OK. I slowly become aware of the LZ PJI standing over me bellowing, "You're a bloody disgrace, sir. You dribbled over the edge of that basket and curled up in a ball for the landing like a bloody hibernating hedgehog". That may be so, but the sound of an ambulance speeding across the LZ tells me that I've fared better than some other poor sod!

And so to the subject of this story; my second jump. Twenty minutes later I'm back at eight hundred feet, prepared for any PJI-inspired initiation ceremony at the basket door to welcome me to the Branch, and I'm determined not to 'dribble.' In the event, as I shuffled across the basket, my subconscious took over and reminded me that it knew what was about to happen, and didn't like it one little bit. Personal pride and the overwhelming need for 'the Officer' to set an example were the only things that were going to get me through this. I have no clear recollection of what the PJI said or did at the door, but my debrief confirmed that I had performed a magnificent mega-dribble. Apparently it was a bit like one of those cartoon characters trying to claw its way back onto the top of a crumbling cliff, when the outcome has already been determined. I do, however, recall my longest ever orgasm until my chute opened, followed by me assuming my already proven hedgehog position for the landing.

The subsequent two aircraft jumps, one from an Argosy (for those of you with long memories), and the final jump from a Hercules, proved positively enjoyable. However, I remained unconvinced that life as a PJI was for me. Shortly afterwards I applied for, and was granted, a transfer to pilot training. I subsequently spent the next 39 years sitting on an ejection seat, flying military fast-jets and, fortuitously, I was never called upon to prove the validity of my parachuting techniques ever again. Oh, and I am thinking about a freefall jump to celebrate my 70th birthday!

The Gutersloh Runway Saga of 1970

In 1970, the main runway at RAF Gutersloh was resurfaced, and the resident squadrons had to 'bolthole' to other airfields. I was on No 92 Squadron at the time, flying the Lightning F2a, a very fine aircraft. After 3 or 4 happy months at RAF Bruggen, the time came to recover the aircraft back to Gutersloh, as the resurfaced runway had been declared fully operational. In traditional 92 style, the Boss, Ron Stuart-Paul, a first-class squadron commander, decided that the main body of the squadron would return as a 9-aircraft formation, and announce our arrival with a very noisy and spirited, shall we just say 'co-ordinated piece of flying'. The sortie was carefully briefed and the Boss concluded by saying to his team that 'no-one flies lower than me, understood?'; we did!

We departed Bruggen, with a little bit of farewell razzamatazz, and flew to Gutersloh where, after our 'arrival', there followed what we hoped would be an uneventful landing on the new runway surface. It was really nice to be back at Gutersloh, but the final landing proved to be not quite as uneventful as expected. I was No 8 in the nine-aircraft formation, and I remember that the approach was quite normal, but that, on the landing roll itself, it felt like I was landing on sandpaper. I burst a tyre and blocked the runway. The aircraft behind me, which included aircraft not in our formation, were diverted to the German Air Force F104 Starfighter base at Hopsten, about 30 nautical miles away and the usual crash diversion for Gutersloh. All this, of course, caused a massive disruption to the welcoming party at Gutersloh. I remained in my aircraft on the runway whilst the tyre was changed, and I was then unceremoniously towed back to the squadron line where the Boss was waiting! He was just starting to give me a bollocking for bursting a tyre, when the squadron Senior Engineering Officer (SEngO) approached him and said, "Sir, you need to know that every single tyre on every aircraft that has just landed is shredded and needs to be changed!" Welcome words that saved me from further wrath. Suffice to say, it transpired that the coefficient of friction of the runway surface was all wrong and further work was required. Until that time I had never realised the importance of the texture of a runway's surface and the phrase 'coefficient of friction' was not even in my dictionary!!

Back at Gutersloh, we were, of course, unable to fly while the remedial work was carried out. Ground training absorbed some of our spare time but so did the infamous 92 partying instinct, both on and off base, and team spirit remained high. I won't go into the full detail, but it reminded me of another time at Gutersloh when, at the end of a good party, I ended up in station sick quarters. I had eaten the raw egg, I had eaten the wine glass and, for the first time, I was persuaded to have a go at a bit of flame-throwing. Well, I failed spectacularly; I hadn't taken into account 'blow back', and burnt my throat, luckily not too severely. However, it still cost me three days in sick quarters, during which time my brother pilots kept me discreetly supplied with beer to lubricate the throat. When I was finally released, the Boss summoned me and said, in his strong Scots accent, "Everyone does something bloody stupid on their first tour, Rick, and you have just done yours." He then awarded me three extra stints on Battle Flight[1] – which suited me fine and kept me out of further trouble!

But I digress! After a week back at Gutersloh, and with the runway supposedly fixed, we were tasked to test the surface. We again flew a 9-aircraft formation, and this time we planned to get airborne, fly to Hopsten and Hannover for formation flyovers to 'show the flag,' and return to Gutersloh. We got airborne without apparent incident, although the weather, as I recall, was not great, and set off in formation for Hannover. We were in and out of wisps of cloud (or probably rather more cloud than that), when air traffic called the formation to say that someone had burst a tyre on take-off as they had found shredded tyre strips on the runway. There then followed an airborne inspection within the formation and, sure enough, we quickly located the source of the problem. This time it was the turn of that great Lightning pilot, John Spencer, to be in the spotlight. We all returned to Gutersloh and, fortunately, landed without further incident. John was the final one in, but I can't recall whether or not he took the arrestor wire[2]. That afternoon it was deemed OK for us to depart from Gutersloh by air for another month on detachment/bolthole at RAF Wildenrath, whilst further runway repairs were carried out. The experiences of that week will remain with me forever, in particular, the 'esprit de corps' of a great squadron.

---

[1] Battle Flight – Also known as QRA (Quick Reaction Alert) and refers to aircraft and crews that are held at a high state of preparedness.
[2] Arrestor wire - A system installed at the end of the runway to stop an aircraft (suitably equipped with a hook to grab the wire) from overshooting the runway.

Hats Off!

In days of yore, officers had to wear hats, both on and off duty. Even in the late 60s this was an anachronism, but in the Cold War 'Standards Had To Be Maintained'.

The scene was West Berlin in 1969. I was attached to a celebrated Scottish Infantry Battalion, and A Company had been sent to Berlin, so that the resident British battalion could get out for their annual holiday to charge around on exercise in northern Germany. Our duties were to defend West Berlin from any Soviet incursion and, amongst the treats in store, I was to take my turn as "Alert Platoon Commander" British Forces Berlin – the definition of which seemed to be that, for 24 hours at a time, I was not allowed to take my boots off so that I, and the rest of my platoon, could rush out to our defensive positions at 2 minutes' notice. Fine, we could manage that, but a wrinkle was that I had to be briefed and inspect the various sensitive positions around the British Sector. With ponderous military logic, it was decided that, to carry out the reconnaissance of those bridges/electricity sub-stations etc, we officers had to see them at first hand. Alongside that, there was the imperative that the bad guys should not know where these key locations were, or realise that we had an interest in protecting them. So we - this group of half a dozen officers in civvies - were solemnly led in procession around said sensitive areas. Perhaps we could have got away with it, but, frankly, I suspect that any observers, watching a group of short-haired, smart and, above all, be-hatted young men, may just have smelt a rat.

I had, by this stage of my Army secondment, adopted what I deemed to be a suitable uniform. On arrival with the Scottish Infantry, I had been issued with a Tam O'Shanter, complete with a square of regimental tartan. Delighted by this, but realising that I was not really entitled to the regimental cap badge, I affixed to the plaid the Crown from a Royal Air Force officers SD hat. That worked well and, given the absence of any field kit from the RAF, I equipped myself with some combat trousers scrounged from the Army stores which, with the flying boots and flying jacket I had from my standard aircrew issue, pretty much set me up with what I needed on a day-to-day basis. A few weeks after I joined them I must unknowingly have passed some strange test set by my platoon of Jocks (as they referred to themselves) and, during a fairly intense social evening with them in the Company bar (most details of which remain a little hazy), I became at some point the very proud owner of a Glengarry – presented to me by the platoon. This red and black chequered fore-and-aft cap, resplendent with tails at the back, also had a patch of the regimental tartan on it – to which I attached another RAF badge. If you are still with me – I then had a rather fetching but definitely non-standard uniform.

Back to Berlin. When not on the Alert Platoon, one of the duties which we had to carry out was a patrol of the wire between West Berlin and East Germany. Although the Berlin Wall got a lot of publicity, dividing as it did the middle of the city, it was less well-known that the city as a whole was separated from the rest of East Germany by a much longer-standing series of huge barbed wire fences, minefields, attack dogs and watchtowers. It was our duty to patrol our side of the British Sector, which I did at dawn three times while we were there. Just a note here: on every occasion, there was both single-shot and automatic fire on the other side of the wire, but whatever was happening was out of our sight in the trees. Might have been rabbits hitting the trip wire – or not.

Anyway, there was a series of Goon Towers on the other side, whence the opposing team watched us as we charged up and down in our Ferret armoured vehicles and Landrovers. We, of course, did not have goon towers, but we did have stilted observation posts. At the appointed position, I climbed up to take my turn at looking across the void. I had forgotten that I was not dressed the same as my companions, so was initially puzzled when the opposition appeared to be taking rather more of an interest than usual. The thinks bubble over the guy with the binoculars was almost visible. He then pulled out from his desk what I can only assume was the East German Big Boys' Book of British Uniforms. He studied this strange figure on the British side, flicked at length through this tome, and then got onto the telephone in his tower. Short pause. Eventually, an East German jeep came hurtling along the access road, and a mate leapt out of the jeep with what appeared to be the EGBBBoBUs Volume Two. He rushed up the tower with it, and the pantomime started again. In fact nothing visible to us happened after that, but I would love to have seen the intelligence signals fluttering back to the Soviet HQ about the presence of a hitherto unknown special Scottish military unit with a new cap badge!

Note

I was used to my own uniform when I was with the Army but, as my parent unit was notionally RAF Gutersloh, I had to pitch up there from time to time. As a lowly Pilot Officer, I entered in my Scottish splendour with some trepidation – to be greeted by the Flight Lieutenant in charge of our motley crew of FACs. On seeing me in the doorway he stormed towards me and bellowed that from now on...every time I turned up at the Officers' Mess dressed like that he... - I waited for the axe to fall – ...would buy me a beer! Job done!

Credit: Author

Life With The Kipper Fleet

In 1964, I was fortunate enough to be posted to Gibraltar, as Squadron Engineer on 224 Squadron, the resident Squadron equipped with Shackleton MR2 aircraft. I travelled out accompanied by my wife and 6 year old daughter. Contrary to what we had been led to believe, no married accommodation was available and we were put into a hotel. Indeed, apart from houses for the CO, OC Eng, OC Admin and the Squadron CO, there were just 12 flats on the base, all full of other ranks; the rest of the officers had to find accommodation in the town.

Communication between the ground crew, on the ground floor of the Squadron building, and the aircrew, on the floor above, was not one of the Squadron's strong points, and my predecessor had left the next morning, on the aircraft in which I had arrived. So it was with some surprise that one morning, after a less than week in post, I was asked by the B Flight Commander where I had put my kit. The Squadron was going on detachment for a month, with four aircraft, and no one had warned me! I had to rush back to the hotel, pack my bag and return to the Squadron, telling a very apprehensive wife and small child they were on their own for a month! Fortunately, the Families Officer swung into action, and soon found temporary accommodation with a local family, where I joined them on my return. It was another month before we got a flat of our own, in the centre of the town.

That detachment threw me in at the deep end, but ensured that I got to know my men and the aircrew far more quickly than usual. We went first to RAF Ballykelly, in Northern Ireland, where it is said that if you can't see the mountains it is raining, and if you can, it will be soon. It was during these two weeks that I learned why the grass in Ireland is so green. Running off the runway would result in the aircraft being bogged down up to the axles of those giant main-wheels, as one of our pilots had demonstrated sometime earlier! One night, at about 10pm, I was called to one of the dispersal pans, to an aircraft which had just landed, trailing an errant sonobuoy[1] under the rear

---

[1] Sonobuoy - A small sonar system that is dropped from an aircraft conducting anti-submarine warfare.

fuselage. After inspecting the damage, which was largely superficial, I was feeling distinctly glum as I trudged back, heading for the lights of the crew hut in
the distance. In the dark, I stepped off the pan and promptly sank up to my
shins in mud. This did little to improve my mood, and I was very circumspect
where I put my feet after that!

Weekend relaxation was a trip into Londonderry on a Saturday night,
culminating in a visit to the local dance hall. Here a game called Shirt was
played. In those days, and perhaps even now, Derry was the home of Van Heu-
sen shirts, and the girls from the shirt factory were regulars at the dance hall.
While dancing with them, you would ask if they worked at the shirt factory
and, if so, which piece of the shirt they made. The winner was the first one to
assemble a complete shirt, and was supposed to shout "Shirt" as he collected
the last piece. Rather fortunately, perhaps, I never heard of anyone managing
to put together a complete shirt.

One of the pleasures of being on a Shackleton squadron was the opportunity to get some time in the air, and to go on land-aways and detachments. For
us, these included occasional two-day stops at the USAF Base at Lajes Field
in the Azores. One of these outings culminated in a weekend in Casablanca,
as a consequence of a Grade 1 emergency diversion during our flight back to
Gibraltar. Unfortunately we were without any money, as the Imprest (fund)
Holder had, somewhat unwisely, allowed a crew member to squander what
remained on a camera, before we left Lajes. After landing, our financial situation deteriorated even further, when the duty Attaché announced that he did
not have access to Consulate funds at weekends. He did, however, condescend
to pay our hotel bill. All these detachments were great fun, but one major
disadvantage of flying was contracting 'Shackleton Ear', a well-known prelude
to complete deafness. On the plus side, I have many wonderful memories, including, on one occasion, looking up at the side of RMS Queen Mary during
a rather exhilarating flypast.

Apart from the UK and Norway, the two principal detachments whilst
I was there were to Aden, during the time of the troubles, in support of the
resident Shackleton Squadron (No 37). The flights there and back were conducted at relatively low level, which made for some wonderful sightseeing
opportunities, including a marvellous view of the Nile and the pyramids as

we overflew Egypt. Night stops were either in Cyprus or El Adem where, on one occasion, we had to land during a sandstorm. In Aden, we were billeted about two miles from the base, in transit accommodation known as the Red Sea Hotel, a large building with some unique features. To the rear of our dormitory-type room was a shoat market, which did not encourage languishing in bed. For those who are not familiar with this unusual animal, a shoat is the sterile result of crossing a sheep with a goat. The advantage of the pairing is that they produce both milk and wool; the disadvantage is that they display the noisy and smelly attributes of both parents. At the front of the hotel was a disused filling station, which could have been mistaken for a scrap yard. It had become a place where itinerant locals would lay out the beds that they carried with them, seemingly everywhere, on their backs. One inventive pair had a stripped out an American car body (minus wheels, doors and just about everything else) which they would tip over during the day, from one side to upright to the other side, to shield them from the sun; while another resident pair used a Rolls-Royce Griffon aero engine packing crate as a home. The hotel never had a particularly welcoming vibe, which was confirmed when, on the day we left at the end of our second detachment, a terrorist bazooka shell hit one of the rooms we had been using!

In general, the Shackletons remained remarkably serviceable, but we did have one or two unusual incidents. A sparrow-sized bird managed to fly through the propeller blades without being diced, and made a neat round hole in the mesh covering the air intake. But perhaps the most unusual defect was when water-methanol (used for boost at high power outputs), on the No 2 engine of one aircraft, came on, without being selected, every time the forward camera cupola was lowered. The engine fitters were highly suspicious that someone was having them on. But no, on a ground run, sure enough, the No 2 water-meth came on when the forward cupola was lowered. You didn't need to be a genius to deduce that we had an electrical problem. The difficulty was determining why and how. After some time spent poring over circuit diagrams, and playing with AVOs (a meter for measuring amps, volts or ohms), the mystery was eventually solved by physically following the cables. It was discovered that the cables for the water-meth and the cupola were in the same loom, and that this ran around the edge of the bomb-bay rear bulkhead, inside the rear fuselage. It transpired that, a week earlier, the rear bomb bay seal, which was retained with blind rivets, had been replaced, and the trades-man concerned had inadvertently drilled into the loom and caused the short circuit.

The social life in Gibraltar was as good as it usually is overseas. Time off was spent either on the Mess beach or across the border in Spain. However, following the election of the Wilson Government in the autumn of 1964, we found ourselves very much confined to the Rock. Every autumn there had been a maritime exercise with the Spanish, but Wilson cancelled UK partici-pation. In retaliation, the Spanish closed the border with Gibraltar to vehicu-lar traffic. Having not been long in post, we weren't accustomed to nipping across the border at every opportunity, but others found the new restriction very difficult to live with. We were quite content to explore the Rock in some detail, and it was still possible to walk across the border; so the ladies con-tinued to use the hairdressers in La Linea, and the menfolk the bars. As time went by, the Spanish relented to a degree and allowed one car through every half-hour, so visits to Spain became restricted to holidays. However, even then, there was the risk of being delayed four or more hours, and of having your camera confiscated by Spanish Customs, to be retrieved on your return. We could still go to Morocco on the daily ferry, but, whilst fine for a quick visit, it was a risky place to take a holiday. One colleague, who tried camping with his family, woke up on the second night looking at the stars. The tent and all their belongings had acquired a new owner!

There was an alternative way of crossing the Mediterranean. Gib Air, a subsidiary of BEA, used an old Douglas DC3 for a daily service between Gi-braltar and Morocco. The aircraft was not hangared and, when not in use, would sit on the tarmac in front of the terminal building. One evening, after the staff of the terminal had left, an enterprising Cpl from the Fire Section took a pot of red paint and a brush, and added YO before the airline name on each side of the fuselage. Thereafter, the DC3 was known affectionately as Yogi Bair to all on the Rock, much to the chagrin of the local BEA manager.

After two very enjoyable years I was short-toured and posted to RAF Cranwell to attend the Advanced Weapons Course. Was it a case of the sub-lime to the ridiculous or the other way round?

Editorial Note

A further story of the Saturday night dances in Ballykelly concerned a young pilot, who had just arrived on his first squadron. He was dragged along to the dance and told to put £1 into the kitty, because he was going to take part in a 'grimmy contest.' The senior person present would judge who managed to dance with the grimmest partner, and the winner would take the kitty. After a few drinks, he enthusiastically sought out a candidate and invited her to dance. While they were jigging away, she said to him, "I know what you're doing, you're having a grimmy contest." He strenuously denied that this was the case, but she just grinned and said, "Don't worry, so are we!"

Much later in the evening, the same lady appeared next to him at the bar, smiled sweetly and said, "No hard feelings. Can I buy you a drink?" Our hero, although slightly flattered, was rather nonplussed by this turn of events, until the lady continued, "I won!"

Credit: RuthAS/Wikipedia

Engagement at Shag Cove: 23 May 1982

Reproduced from his book, Hostile Skies, by kind permission of Orion Books and the author, Lt Cdr David HS Morgan DSC

The morning of 23rd May dawned grey and overcast, with regular heavy showers sweeping across the bleak landscape of the Falkland Islands, and making the flight deck of HMS *Hermes* a cold and even more inhospitable place than normal. I had been airborne before dawn, to fly a combat air patrol at low level over the slate-grey waters of Falkland Sound, in an effort to stop Argentine attacks on the armada of ships supporting the landings in San Carlos Water. Over the previous forty-eight hours, since the landings had taken place, the Navy had suffered a number of spirited attacks by Argentine Skyhawk and Dagger fighters. These attacks had been pressed home with vigour, sinking HMS *Ardent* during the previous evening, and damaging a number of other warships. No troop transports had yet been hit, however, and some 3,500 troops had been successfully landed and were now consolidating the beachhead. May 21st, D Day, had been a very busy day, with the Sea Harriers accounting for ten of the twelve enemy aircraft destroyed. Unfortunately, a No 1(F) Squadron Harrier had been shot down near Port Howard but we believed that Flt Lt Jeff Glover, the pilot, had ejected.

The first sortie had been uneventful, although it was very unnerving, as we had been forced to fly our CAP[1] below the 500-foot cloud base, in poor visibility and at low speed, to economise on fuel because of our range from the carrier. This made us very vulnerable to any enemy aircraft that might come across us in the mist, and it was reassuring to know that my No 2 was as keyed up as I was, with his eyes constantly straining and his senses ready for instant explosive action, should we see a 'bogey'. We were both relieved when the time came to climb above the murk and head home into the early morning sun, to return to *Hermes* and a hearty breakfast.

---

[1] CAP – A Combat Air Patrol typically entails fighters flying a tactical pattern around or screening a defended target, while looking for incoming attackers.
[2] 'Bogey' - an unidentified aircraft, possibly hostile.

By the time the sun was approaching its zenith, the weather had changed dramatically, leaving the islands bathed in bright sunshine, with only small amounts of cumulus cloud scattered here and there in east-west lines. My wingman for this sortie was Flt Lt John Leeming, an old buddy of mine from the RAF Germany Harrier force. He had volunteered for exchange service when the conflict had started and had arrived on the ill-fated *Atlantic Conveyor* five days earlier. John had only managed to get a handful of hours in the Sea Harrier before heading for the South Atlantic, and still had to get to grips with the weapons systems. Two days earlier he had been unable to fire a Sidewinder missile at a Skyhawk, and eventually shot it down with guns at very close range, nearly blowing himself to pieces in the process. We subsequently discovered that the reason for the missile not firing was that no one had shown him how to switch it on properly!

As we flew overhead Port Stanley, on the way to our CAP station, we were greeted by a barrage of anti-aircraft fire, despite the fact that we were above 30,000 feet. The 35-millimetre guns were not very accurate at this height and, although the black mushrooms of their explosions looked rather frightening as they burst all around us, a gentle weave was all that was required to render them ineffective. In the distance, we could see the silver specks of the ships in San Carlos Water, and the toy-like outlines of Pucara attack aircraft on the grass strip at Goose Green. Once past Goose Green, we let down to 8,000 feet and set up our patrol on a north-south axis over the 2,000-foot mountains of West Falkland, in an attempt to intercept any aircraft flying through the valleys to attack the landings. Our Blue Fox radar was of very little use over land, so we had to try to guess where the enemy would come from, and put ourselves in a position to acquire them visually and engage them before they reached their targets.

Flying a medium level patrol is rather more relaxing than being at low level, because it is easier to be sure that you and your wingman are not being threatened by a 'bogey'. It also gives you the opportunity to accelerate rapidly as you dive onto the tail of a low level raider, and get a missile in the air before you are seen. What we did not realise, as we cruised back and forth, searching the rolling scree and peat bog for tell-tale flashes of movement, was that the enemy were not aware of the change in the weather and would not be airborne for another couple of hours. The director who was controlling us asked us to confirm our position from time to time, and it was obvious that he, like us, was feeling that things were rather too quiet to last. He could not use his radar because of the surrounding hills, and was relying on us to pick up and report any raids as they crossed the mountains. This would give them a maximum of three minutes warning of an inbound raid. Sooner him than us! There was a great feeling of empathy between us and we were very conscious of being the only ones standing between him and an enemy air attack.

Unbeknownst to us, although the Argentine fighters were not airborne, there was, indeed, some air activity, and it was heading in our direction. A formation of three Argentine Puma helicopters had set off the previous evening, to transport a vital cargo of Blowpipe anti-aircraft missiles and mortar ammunition from Stanley to Port Howard. They had turned back in Falkland Sound when they stumbled across an unidentified ship in poor weather and had spent the night with the Pucara unit at Goose Green.

The following day, after the weather improved, they set off once more for Port Howard. Because of the importance of their cargo, the lead Puma had the company commander on board, and they were escorted by an Agusta 109A gunship, flown by the deputy commander. The Agusta 109A was a fast and very manoeuvrable helicopter, which carried two pods of 2.75-inch rockets and a couple of forward firing machine guns. This could have made life quite embarrassing for us in the right hands. Any fighter pilot who was shot down by a helicopter would never be able to hold his head up in a bar again! This formation crossed the Sound from Goose Green to Shag Cove and had just turned onto a northerly heading, with only about four minutes to go to their destination, when their luck changed abruptly.

John and I had just completed a turn at the southern end of the CAP, and were cruising slowly towards Port Howard, when suddenly a movement caught my eye; a mechanical movement quite alien to the snipe-rich bogs and barren escarpments - the flash of sun on a helicopter rotor disc. There, a couple of miles south of me, was a helicopter skimming over a small inlet a few feet above the glassy water. I yelled to John and asked the controlling ship to confirm that there were no friendlies in the area. At the same time I dived rapidly down to about fifty feet above the valley and accelerated to about 500 mph, running head-on towards the helicopter in an attempt to identify it. Adrenalin pumped as the distance between us closed rapidly until, at about 500 yards, I realised that it was a Puma and, therefore, had to be Argentine.

I shouted 'Hostile, hostile!' over the radio, and John replied that he had a further three in a line behind the leader, and was engaging the gunship escort. I was too close to bring my weapons to bear on the Puma, so flew straight at it, passing as low as I dared over its rotor head. As I passed about ten feet above the enemy, I pulled the Harrier into a 5-G break to the left, in order to fly a dumb-bell back towards it for a guns attack. I strained my head back and to the left under the crushing pressure of the G forces, and I saw the Puma emerge from behind me. It was flying in an extremely unstable fashion and, after a couple of seconds, crashed heavily into the side of the hill, shedding rotor blades and debris before rolling over and exploding in a huge pall of black smoke. I was absolutely amazed! We had previously discussed using wing-tip vortices as a method of downing helicopters, and it was obviously efficacious, although I had not particularly been aiming to try the method out at the time.

As I reversed my turn to the west, I saw John diving down towards a deep stream bed running up into the mountains. As he recovered from the dive, the bottom of the ravine erupted in a storm of explosions from his 30-millimetre cannon, but I could not see the target. As I began my attack, John told me that it was a helicopter gunship in the stream bed 100 yards east of his fall of shot. As I was squinting through the head-up display[2] to find the target I wondered how he could have missed by such a massive distance. This was soon made clear by his next transmission: 'What the hell is the sight setting for guns Moggie?' We had discovered another hole in his briefing on the differences between the Harrier and Sea Harrier weapons system!

My first attack missed, as the pilot manoeuvred his helicopter towards the relative safety of the mountains. I had also fired at rather excessive range in my excitement, which had degraded the accuracy of the guns. My second pass put explosions all around the Agusta 109A, but didn't hit it. I pressed my third at-tack, until the helicopter was filling the sight and I could clearly see the rocket pods attached to either side of the fuselage. As I pulled into a 5-G recovery, I saw

---

[2] Head Up Display - A transparent, electronically generated display that projects data directly ahead of the pilot, thus reducing the need to look inside the cockpit (head down) at instru-mentation

the target disappear under a hail of sparkling explosions from my cannon, followed shortly afterwards by the massive orange bloom of a secondary explosion from the fuel tanks at the rear of the aircraft. The pilot had failed in his task of defending the formation and had paid the price for running away, rather than trying to engage us with his rockets.

As I turned away from the burning wreckage, John located a further helicopter near the smoke of the first one and dived down towards it. He had emptied his cannon in his previous attacks, but flew very low over the new target to show me its position. I followed him down towards the area of scrubby grass and diddle-dee that he had indicated, but could see nothing. As I was about to recover, I realised that my gunsight was sitting directly over a Puma, which had shut down on the rough ground and was being rapidly evacuated by a number of highly excited Argentine soldiers. I pulled the trigger to fire my cannon but only two rounds remained. By a combination of good luck and good shooting, one of these rounds impacted the tail of the Puma, rendering it un-flyable. We re-joined over Falkland Sound in the climb to 36,000 feet for our return to *Hermes*. As we settled down, checked our fuel and began to think about our recovery, our replacement CAP from HMS *Invincible* called us on the radio. We passed them the location of the helicopters, and they set off to complete the destruction of the second Puma.

We had managed to destroy twenty percent of the enemy helicopter force, at a time when they were desperately in need of such transport, but I was not particularly happy at the destruction of the first Puma, as I believed that the crew had perished in the crash. Ironically, I had not meant to attack them on the initial pass and, as a former helicopter pilot, I had a great deal of empathy. After landing back on *Hermes*, I reported to the bridge to brief the captain on our achievements, and was given some information that made me even more concerned. The ship had intercepted a message saying that Jeff Glover was being transferred from Port Howard to Stanley by Puma at about the time of our engagement. For a couple of days I thought that we might have killed one of our own pilots but, eventually, to my great relief, we received intelligence that he had been transferred to the mainland by Hercules.

A visit to the site of the action, after the conflict was over, showed the importance of the cargo, and the subsequent information that the crew had survived also made me feel considerably better. It was also ironic that the aircraft I was flying on this sortie was the same one that I had been flying on the first raid of the war. Then, the Argentines had put a hole through the tail with a 20-millimetre anti-aircraft gun; this time, the boot had been well and truly on the other foot!

Credit: Author

From Aden to UK – By Hunter

All political problems to one side, today, a journey by air from Aden in Yemen to the UK would be a reasonably simple flight in a Boeing 747-400, equipped with triple Inertial Reference Systems, dual GPS, and a range capability of twice the 7 hours 30mins flying time from Aden to London - not to mention a quiet and comfortable flight deck, with a reasonable supply of refreshment en route. Perhaps, not so easy flying a Hawker Hunter FGA9 in 1962. This was the standard single-seat fighter in the RAF Middle East Command of the 60s, with 8, 43 & 208 Squadrons based at RAF Khormaksar, in the then Aden Colony. Each unit was much larger than is the case today, 8 Squadron having an establishment of 24 aircraft, as did our two sister squadrons. All the aircraft suffered from prolonged operations in the heat and dust of the Arabian Peninsula, which meant an occasional ferry to the UK for major servicing; which is why, at our morning briefing one day, the Boss gave two of us the task of ferrying a pair of well-worn Hunter 9s, XE587 & XF455, all the way to England. Flight planning in those distant days did not benefit from the clever computer world of today, so we obtained miles of maps from store, folded them to cockpit size, drew lines to the airfields we hoped to reach, and then calculated the basic time and fuel for the distance. Navigation aids were limited to Tacan[1] and one ADF[2]; even if they worked, much of our route would be out of range from any ground station. With the optimism of youth, tempered with five years experience on type, we reckoned this was all we needed. Diplomatic clearance for two armed warplanes never crossed our minds, as our progress was rarely queried and we were never intercepted en route; some careful staff officer must have done all this on our behalf, so we remained blissfully unaware of potential problems.

There were two possible routes to the UK from Aden: one went north via Sharjah and Bahrain, through Isfahan - we were able to transit Iran back then - to Turkey, Cyprus and Malta, thence to RAF Lyneham. The second, which we

---

[1] Tacan - Tactical Air Navigation, a system that provides a bearing and range from a selected ground station.
[2] ADF - Automatic Direction Finder, a system that gave a bearing only from a selected ground beacon.

chose, was the southern route via Khartoum, El Adem, Malta and Orange to, yes, Lyneham to clear Customs. In the early 60s, the first three stops were all at RAF bases, while Orange was a French Air Force fighter station with an RAF ground crew detachment, the Service being much larger then than now. Maps prepared with tracks, distances and times, the next task was to air-test the Hunters to determine the fuel burn with all the underwing stores. As internal fuel was a mere 400 IG[3], we needed all available external fuel from 2 x 230 plus 2 x100IG drop tanks, giving us a total of 1060 IG, approximately 8500 lbs, enough for 3.25 hours of careful flying. All of this would be needed, as the longest planned leg was three hours, from Khartoum to El Adem over the Sahara desert. Fuel costs were generally unimportant in the Middle East, so an air-test with full load was flown, which proved that one of the internal tanks had a leak; the tank was replaced and, after a series of tests lasting over 3 hours, XF455 was cleared for the ferry. Aden is never cold - even during the Cool Season temperatures match a summer in the Med; however North Africa and Europe were very different, especially as the winter of 62-63 was to become one of the coldest on record. My gallant companion ignored the proffered advice and packed his Khaki Drill lightweight uniform; being rather more cautious, I squashed a blue uniform into my flight-bag. The only luggage space in the Hunter was in the unpressurised gun bay; this was shared by the battery, so any leak would leave small burn holes in the unsuspecting pilot's bag and contents. Anti-G suits[4] were not worn for such a long ferry, but folded and laid on the seat; they provided a rudimentary, but welcome, en-route massage when the test switch was pressed, as three hours on a hard dinghy pack were not as comfortable as the flight deck seat on a 747.

We left at first light; as I walked round my aircraft for the external inspection, my ground crew chief said, "Please don't kick the tyres sir, she's serviceable." So I didn't, as old XF455 was showing the wear and tear of two years' operations in a harsh climate. The first sector was from Aden, overhead Asmara in Ethiopia, to Khartoum, a 2 hour-25 minutes flight, with a brisk low level portion along the White Nile to bring us within landing weight. The Hunter,

---

[3] IG - Imperial Gallons.
[4] Anti-G suits – Worn around the legs and inflated by pressurized air to help a pilot withstand high 'g' loadings.

with all the external tanks, went from too heavy to low fuel in a surprisingly short time. Turnround, with refuel and sandwiches, went pleasingly to schedule, our intention being to reach El Adem before dark; no pilot enjoyed night flying in the Hunter, with no landing lights and dim cockpit lighting. In the event, this was to prove an aim too far; although we had arrived in Khartoum without difficulty, departing was to prove less easy. RAF Khartoum was there to service Transport Command aircraft on their way to East Africa and Aden. Thus, our 'RAFAIR' callsign was considered a transport flight, so the obvious presence of two warplanes on their tarmac produced an official objection from the Sudanese authorities, which took diplomacy an hour to overcome. Eventually, clearance was given to depart, starter master switches to ON, the Avpin[5] starter motor gave its usual high-pitched scream as the Rolls-Royce Avon lit up, and we were on our way once more, now too late to reach El Adem in daylight. Heavyweight, at over 20000lbs, required a long take-off roll; no V1[6] on a single-engine jet, rotation around 150 knots with a lift off nearer 170, made close formation take-off an interesting exercise, normal climb to 40,000 feet was 430 knots to M·85[7], then maintaining a constant Mach Number of ·87, allowing the aircraft to cruise climb to 45,000 feet as weight reduced. There were no assigned flight levels in those days, as there was nobody else flying at our altitude; the age of the jet airliner was still in its infancy.

The direct track from Khartoum to El Adem was unavailable as it would have meant crossing a slice of Egypt, at that time no friend to the UK, so we routed via a point in the desert known as 'Nasser's Corner', which meant a dog-leg, thus extra time and distance. This last was a major consideration, as a three-hour sector meant reaching our destination rather short of gas. None of today's airliner fuel plan of 'alternate plus holding plus contingency' - just 15 minutes to dry tanks on arrival, assuming all went well. Cheered, before leaving Aden, by the news that a Canberra from El Adem would be available to provide guidance over the desert turning point, we were less cheered, on leaving Khartoum, by the

---

[5] Avpin - Aviation Iso-Propyl Nitrate, a particularly nasty monopropellant used in the starting systems of some aircraft of that vintage.
[6] V1 – Applies to multi-engined aircraft and is the speed beyond which a pilot must continue a takeoff, even if an engine fails.
[7] M·85 – Shorthand for Mach, where Mach 1 is the speed of sound.

news that the said Canberra was still on the ground and likely to remain there all day. In typical single-seat fighter pilot mode, we thought the likely reason was that the two navigators in the crew were unable to agree their position. Cruising at M.87, much the same speed as the B747-400 I was to fly some 30 years later, but then sitting on a Martin Baker ejection seat, with a cockpit altitude of 22,000 feet, breathing 100% oxygen, no autopilot, no navigation aids, and no radio contact other than the wingman flying some 800 yards abreast, was very different from the jets of the 21st century. None of this was of the least concern to us at the time until, passing Nasser's Corner near Jebel Uweinat, my colleague reported that one of his 230IG tanks refused to feed fuel to the Avon. Fuel remaining, against distance to destination, meant a walk of approximately 200 miles across the Sahara, so it was unlikely that he would reach El Adem before bar closing time. In those days I carried a camera in the cockpit, so I offered to take a photo when, as looked inevitable, he decided to eject. He seemed unimpressed by my offer; however, before reaching this point, and using what today is known as Crew Resource Management - a rapid look at Pilots' Notes, and a brief discussion of the problem - a decision was reached. He would jettison his now-empty outboard 100IG tanks, in the hope that the pressure surge would encourage the bigger inboard tank to feed. So, off into the desert went the two phenol plastic tanks, in time for me to take a photo of the Hunter now flying on the inboards plus internal fuel. To our mutual, vast relief the plan worked, the fuel started flowing correctly, and we were both now sure of reaching our destination by air.

Fate has a way of catching one out when all seems comfortable. Contacting El Adem, with clear skies, we were cleared for a high-speed descent, from our 45,000 feet cruise in the remaining daylight, direct into the deepening dusk of the airfield. As a considerate leader, I sent my wingman in to land first, then followed some 15 seconds behind. Landing checks in the Hunter were simple: airbrake IN, indicator BLACK, undercarriage DOWN with 3 GREENS... then there was suddenly no point in continuing with the checklist or the circuit, as the green lights remained obdurately out. A quick prod at the indicator showed that, while the lights were working, the undercarriage was not. Hawkers had kindly installed an emergency air bottle for such contingency, with a less kindly side effect. When used, although the wheels would extend, all hydraulic fluid was lost, the result being a landing without power controls, and only one flap selection - full down for landing. For those familiar with the Boeing 737, the manual flying control loads were very similar - hard work, especially after a long day ending with a night landing. This situation was probably all my fault for having offered to photograph my chum in distress; one never learns to 'beware the fickle finger of fate' until too late. So, Air Traffic Control (ATC) was informed, and the emergency services trundled out to meet a Hunter which, though not in distress, was certainly fatigued - as was the pilot.

It took three days for repairs. The weather grew increasingly colder as did my chum, wandering around in the only KD on the station, wishing he had packed his blue uniform and regretting the fruit he had loaded in his bag at Aden – which, by now, was well past any sell-by date. Our transit route could be traced by abandoned mangoes and Hunter drop tanks; however, eventually, our refuelled and repaired aircraft were ready to continue the adventure. A third ferry Hunter from our squadron joined us for our onward leg to Malta; he had come from the Gulf via Cyprus, and would continue as our number 3 to the UK. El Adem to Luqa was a fairly short flight, low level to Benina, then on to Malta before dark in a little over 2 hours. Third to land on the southwest runway, and touching down at 130 knots, I saw the other two Hunters taxi off at the top of a marked slope, so it seemed to this rather unobservant pilot that they had reached the end, and were waiting for their leader. This was not a sound assessment as, on touchdown, my brake chute promptly fell off its attachment; the antiskid brakes were already worn to limits, and my aircraft surged relentlessly towards what I thought was a cliff, the sea and the end. I cut the fuel, mentioned the stopping problem and sat tight. My chums heard my call of brake failure, saw the chute was missing, and kindly pointed out that there was still plenty of tarmac ahead, as, indeed, there was, once I had breasted the hill. So, a quick engine restart was in order, to avoid the humiliation of being towed and, breathing a sigh of relief, I led the formation into dispersal. The local Canberra crews were watching the arrival of three Hunters in their usual critical fashion, so it would have been very bad form to have run off the end in a crumpled heap. We had one night in the transit Officers' Mess at RAF Luqa, which could have been compared to the Black Hole of Calcutta, though not as comfortable. Our Local Overseas Allowance was a handful of British coins, Malta being considered cheaper than Aden, so a quiet and sober night was spent in the bar, planning our next leg to Orange in France. As I was to leave the Service the following year, to join the Viscount flight of BEA, my next Malta night-stop would be based in the splendid Phoenicia Hotel, and funded by a wedge of pound notes - a small wedge perhaps, but a vast increase on the previous visit. However this was the RAF of the time, so we needed our coins, since Aden currency, the East African Shilling, was not recognised in Malta, credit cards were still decades away, and the Mess bar prices were pleasantly affordable to transient crews.

The Hunter could have reached Lyneham, just, from Malta, given a fair wind, or so the planning tables seemed to indicate; however, a refuelling stop in France seemed preferable to arrival over England in winter weather and low on fuel. The old adage that a pilot may worry about the weather or the fuel state, but never the two together, seemed good to us. So did lunch in Orange, as we arrived there in a little over two hours from Luqa. The Armee de l'Air squadrons flew Mystere IV fighters, similar in performance to our Hunters, and made us welcome with an excellent lunch. Fresh bread was a rarity in Aden, as was the French habit of a modest glass of red wine with lunch. We followed their example, not unreasonably, only to be accosted by an RAF Wing Commander, immaculate in No.1 Dress, curious about the presence of three junior officers in shabby tropical flying kit (with equally shabby Hunters) now parked alongside his shining, scarlet Heron of the Queen's Flight. Our account of why and where was accepted, with obvious reservations about an excellent lunch with our French friends; clearly, in his opinion, fighter pilots were an unreliable lot. He may have been right, five days down route, with two days of clean laundry, meant we were far from being as smart as the CO of the Queen's Flight. We never learned why he was in Orange, and he didn't enlighten us. With all three Hunters serviceable for once, I asked Orange ATC if we might do a low level pass to say farewell. This being approved, after takeoff in close Vic, we came past the Heron at 100 feet and 500 knots, an 8 Sqn salute to a senior officer. Cruise climb in wide battle formation over France, well above the civil airways of the time, made for an easy leg to RAF Lyneham to refuel, clear customs and then fly to our respective destinations. The other two were bound for RAF St Athan in South Wales; mine was going to RAF Kemble, not far from Little Rissington. However, we first had to meet Customs, who regarded arrivals from the

Middle East with suspicion. Inspecting my Hunter, the Customs Officer wanted to know what lay behind a panel in the middle of the RAF roundel on the fuselage. I told him I had no idea, other than a Rolls-Royce Avon 203 engine; this aroused official suspicion, so my ground crew, who did know, obediently opened the panel. The triumphant look on the Customs Officer's face vanished as he touched the hot engine turbine outer case, still at a healthy temperature after flight. Unhealthy for human hands however, and the inspection ceased forthwith as he disappeared to seek first aid. No, neither the ground crew nor pilot laughed – out loud, anyway.

So for the last leg to RAF Kemble - not far, however in the gathering gloom of a grey December evening, it took a pilot more accustomed to the clear Arabian skies some 40 minutes to find his destination. No navaids, too proud to ask for radar assistance, I found the airfield eventually, and XF455 landed smoothly on Kemble's runway. It was the end of an adventure, but great fun at the time. If I had been told then about the 747-400, a mere gleam in Joe Sutter's eye at Boeing, I probably would have considered it pure science fiction. It was all very different 52 years ago.

Credit: Author

Whether Decisions

It's 1969 and the RAF is overflowing with pilots. The elderly gentlemen who were recruited for the Korean War had yet to move on, and the youngsters recruited to fill their places found that there was a delay between every stage of their training. 'Holding' it was called, and a lost period it was for most of us. I was more fortunate.

The military is controlled by three forces; the god of surprise posting, the god of nasty surprises, and the fairy godmother. In my case, the fairy godmother was at work, because not for me the dull office jobs of most 'holders'. My holding period after Advanced Flying Training (the last stage before operational flying) was with the Air Experience Flight at Bristol. AEFs used the De Havilland Chipmunk to give schoolboys pleasure flights. Now, the Chipmunk may look like a car engine with wings but, being a tail-wheel aircraft (and not endowed with much power) it could deliver some nasty surprises. Not for nothing did the Flight Safety posters label it a wolf in sheep's clothing. So, any AEF collecting holding pilots was under strict orders as to what we could and could not do; in short, we were to be under the strictest of supervision. It was just like being in flying training, again, and rather stultifying for a forward young man, who had been inculcated with the 'can-do' spirit that was required of a military pilot. Years on, I have to wonder if the strict instructions had filtered down to the boss of the Bristol outfit, or whether he was just one of those people who understood and could empathise with young people.

There were two holding pilots on the unit – myself, bound for Coastal Command, and another bound for Fighter Command (and eventually deputy Commander in Chief of the Command). Once we had settled in, Jim, the boss, gave us our instructions, and then left us to our own devices. One device, with which he entrusted me, was that I should take an aircraft from Bristol to West Malling in Kent, where our major servicing was done. The instructions were very explicit –"Off you go, see you when you get back." The route weather looked fine, so off I went, rather full of myself in this big venture (remember, I was just out of training, and now flying on my own across the breadth of England).

Twenty miles east of Bristol, the ground rises some 400 feet at the start of Salisbury Plain. On this occasion, not only that, but the cloud came down.

'This I can manage', I thought. Up went the ground, down came the cloud. 'I can manage this', I thought. Then a small voice started to repeat: 'This is not a good idea Paul, this is not a good idea Paul' and, eventually, I turned back for Bristol. Fresh from flying training, I was not looking forward to the interrogation which would accompany an early return. 'What was the cloudbase? What was the visibility? Why did you do this? Why did you do that?' And so on, in great depth. As I return to the AEF hut, with leaden feet, Jim looked up from the letter he was writing.

"You're back early!"

"I couldn't get through."

Pause, while I marshal my tale, but Jim just raises his hand and says, "Then you will have to go tomorrow."

Jim, did you ever realise what that gesture did? The first beer that evening tasted especially good. I started the morning as a student pilot, waiting for further training. I ended the day as a pilot in the Royal Air Force.

Credit: Garitzko/Wikipedia

Hidden Hazard

I was at RAF Wildenrath with the RAF Germany Harrier Force, when it consisted of just two squadrons. To practise our war role, the Squadrons, with full support, would regularly deploy to the Sennelager Range area, in the North of Germany. This occurred three times a year; in late spring, in summer, for a TacEval[1], and in the autumn. I seem to recall that a third squadron arrived in the autumn of 1972, thus bringing us up to planned strength. The following January, in order to become operational in time for the spring deployment, they relocated to the far side of the airfield and flew from a prepared strip, rather than the main runway. They even took their own support staff with them and, apart from Air Traffic Control, operated as an independent unit.

However, the weather in Germany being what it was at that time of year, they had not been deployed for very much more than a day when we had a moderate snowfall, and the squadron found itself snowbound. This halted flying operations, so their ground-crew, left with little to do, proceeded to alleviate their boredom by building some large snowmen. They stood, like rather impressive, white sentinels, along a section of the airfield perimeter which was inspected, twice a day, by the RAF Police. The task of the duty police patrol was to drive around very slowly, looking for any signs of illegal entry. Unsurprisingly, the sight of these magnificent snowmen proved too much of a temptation, and they proceeded to demolish each one in turn by driving at it, at high speed, with their Land Rover.

As might be expected, the squadron ground-crew were singularly unimpressed by what they viewed as childish behaviour. So, early the next day, they set to with renewed vigour, and built a further set of (even more impressive) snowmen. Later that morning, the Police sidled around the perimeter track in their Land Rover, lined up with the first snowman and gleefully accelerated towards it. At the moment of impact there was a very loud bang, and the Land Rover came to an abrupt halt in a flurry of snow and a cloud of steam. The ground-crew had constructed the snowman around a substantial concrete post!

---

[1] TacEval - Tactical evaluation of NATO declared units by NATO staff.

How To Get Arrested

Reproduced from his book, 'A Passion For Flying', by kind permission of the author, Tom Eeles, and Pen & Sword Publishing Ltd.

Many years ago, I was an instructor on the Operational Conversion Unit that trained pilots and navigators for the newly-formed RAF Buccaneer squadrons. One of our tasks was to teach night close formation, something few of the students had ever done before, and an activity they viewed with some trepidation. One night, a first tour[1] student navigator and I were programmed to fly in a three-aircraft formation as the lead aircraft. Unusually, it was a very busy night on the airfield, with a number of visiting aircraft, including a twin-engine Andover passenger aircraft which was bringing in a party of VIPs. It was also a very dark night, without moonlight or stars.

All went well with the sortie up to the point when I lined up on the runway as a 3-aircraft formation in Vic, for a 30-second stream take off. I should point out that the mighty Buccaneer, because of its naval origins, was not equipped at that stage of its life with a landing lamp, as it would have been superfluous on an aircraft carrier, so it was not possible to see anything in the darkness ahead apart from the runway edge lighting. Brakes off, up to full power and off I went, expecting my fellow formatees to follow me at 30-second intervals. All seemed OK to begin with, the airspeed indicator began to read at 70 knots but, at about 100 knots, the aircraft rapidly and smoothly decelerated and came to a halt with full power still applied. I thought, at first, that I had inadvertently put the arrestor hook down but, no, the selector was in the up position and there was no green light showing it to be down. Conscious of the imminent arrival of my No 2 up my posterior, I called Air Traffic Control with a message that "I seem to have become stuck on the runway", or words to that effect; luckily none of the aircraft behind had started their take-off roll. Those in Air Traffic, including the Duty Pilot, naturally assumed that I had inadvertently put the hook down – quite easily done – and had engaged the approach end arrestor cable, as had

---

[1] First-tourist – Someone on their first operational posting after completing flying training.

happened previously. Doubtless thinking what an idiot I was – you could tell from the tone of their voices – they sent a vehicle out to have a look at us.

By this time I had throttled back to await developments. The vehicle approached and stopped a short distance away; a man got out and shone a torch towards the aircraft, then quickly rushed back to the vehicle, which rapidly reversed away. Air Traffic, now in a completely different tone of voice, told us to shut down, but not to unstrap or attempt to vacate the aircraft until outside help arrived. My navigator and I were still completely puzzled as to what had happened, but we duly complied. Eventually a team appeared from the darkness with a long set of extending steps, known as a Giraffe, and numerous other vehicles. They gingerly manoeuvred the Giraffe alongside the cockpit, then signalled us from a safe distance to get out. When we climbed down we saw, to our amazement, that the arrestor cable was wrapped around the nosewheel leg. The whole thing was stretched tight to its limit, like some giant catapult; it appeared to be about to launch our Buccaneer backwards, down the runway towards the rest of the formation, who were still patiently sitting there.

By now the Station Commander, a man not noted for his tolerance of professional foul-ups, had arrived on the scene. Breathing fire from his nostrils, he demanded to know precisely who was to blame for this shambles that had closed his airfield in such a thoughtless fashion, and in the middle of a high profile VIP visit! Of course, in the darkness of the night, no one had a clue as to how this had happened, or how to extract the aircraft from its seemingly imminent backwards launch. The debate and argument continued amongst all parties out there on the runway, and, because of a lack of any other ideas, the finger of suspicion inevitably seemed to be pointing more and more at my student and me. In the hubbub we both agreed it would be safer to make ourselves scarce, and to slip away and seek sanctuary in the safety of the Officers' Mess bar.

The answer to this saga only became clear the next morning. Lying on the grass beside the runway was found the shattered remains of a metal stand that the fire crews, who rigged and de-rigged the arrestor cable, had used to hold up the cable about 3 feet above the runway, which allowed them to move the rubber grommets that supported the cable more easily and quickly into position. Whilst re-rigging the cable, after the arrival of the VIP Andover the night before, they were hassled by Air Traffic to hurry up as my formation was already taxiing.

In their haste to get the job done they forgot to remove the stand. I then, inevitably, collected the cable around the nosewheel leg. Amazingly there was little damage to the Buccaneer; it needed a new nosewheel leg and two new underwing tanks where the cable had flailed, but that was all. Not long afterwards, all RAF Buccaneers were equipped with a landing lamp – on the nosewheel leg! Whether this would have influenced the outcome is impossible to say. My navigator also went on to have an illustrious career in the RAF, and is now a Justice of the Peace dealing with more conventional arrests.

Credit: Geoff Lee

RAF Valley and The Gnat - 1968

Having completed my Basic Flying Training in the Spring of 1968, I enjoyed a couple of relaxing months doing not very much before proceeding to RAF Cranwell, in early June, for a 3-day Aviation Medicine Course. This was in preparation for my Advanced Flying Training at RAF Valley. Up to that point it had been a poor summer from the weather perspective, with low temperatures and rainfall levels well above the seasonal norm. This theme continued as I, and my fifteen course-mates, drove west towards Anglesey. However a surprise awaited us as we crossed the Menai Bridge – it was just as if someone had drawn back a curtain - all we could see was blue sky, and that was how it stayed for the bulk of the rest of the summer. Many evenings and weekends were spent on the beach at Trearddur Bay, where the temperature of the sea almost reached an acceptable level.

We soon found out that the pubs were closed on Sundays all over the island; fortunately, however, there were two clubs in the local village of Rhosneigr which were open. One Sunday evening, in early July, a bunch of the course set off in Bob Ruskell's VW Beetle and my Triumph Spitfire to recce these hostelries. A good time was had by all until we set off home at around 10pm, just as it was getting dark. Rounding a corner on the back road to the airfield, and enjoying the ride with the roof down, the occupants of my car suddenly heard singing coming from the middle of the adjacent cornfield. Closer investigation revealed that Bob's Beetle had failed to negotiate the corner and gone through a fairly basic barbed-wire fence. We searched in vain for a gate to the field, so Bob was forced to reverse out the way he had gone in, while the rest of us tried to stretch the barbed-wire. Although the car appeared to have suffered little damage as it entered the field, it certainly acquired major scratches on the roof while being extricated. Suffice to say that we went back to the field the next day to survey the damage to the fence, only to find a gate 20 yards down the hedge!!

Unfortunately we had to endure several weeks of ground-school before we got the chance to climb into the mighty Folland Gnat. It was my birthday, on a Saturday in early September, before I eventually had my first solo flight in that nippy little aircraft, which had the ability to roll at up to 520 degrees per second. We always worked on the first Saturday of the month at Valley, but gained a long weekend downstream in compensation. My birthday culminated in a party at the Trearddur Bay Hotel, after which I was abandoned there as a jape. It was shortly after this that I recall a conversation in the Officers Mess Bar one evening between Bob Iveson, a fellow student, and Bob Jerman, his USAF exchange officer instructor, who were both tall and stocky in build. The subject was the ejection sequence from the Gnat, and Bob Jerman ended the conversation by saying, "Don't worry Bob, if we get into trouble we won't bother to eject, we'll just jettison the aircraft." This created the image of a great cartoon picture in my mind!!

In those days we flew frequently, and the night-flying phase soon arrived. My first dual sortie was quite interesting; as usual, I was sent out ahead of my instructor to do the external checks. To my surprise, on poking my torch down the engine intake, I found a No1 SD Hat and a pair of striped pyjamas nestled against the compressor. On further investigation, it transpired that the aircraft had just returned from a land-away sortie, with the crew's overnight things carried in the cockpit; some items had been sucked into the engine as it ran down post-flight. For most of us, a land-away kit totalled nothing more than a towel and toothbrush; pyjamas were certainly OTT!!

The navigation phase followed thereafter, and included a few solo sorties, during which I have to admit there was the odd occasion when I may have been a little uncertain of my position. I thus approached the Final Navigation Test with some trepidation. When the fateful day dawned, the weather was awful, with an in-flight low-level visibility of no more than 2 miles. I was convinced that the sortie would be cancelled, but no, off we set soon after mid-day. Coasting out from the north coast of Anglesey at 500 feet, towards Morecambe Bay, all I could do was to fly the planned heading at 360 knots, on instruments, and, sure enough, when we hit the coast of Cumbria 7 minutes or so later, I could see little and recognised nothing. However, on a call of 'Press on!' from the rear-seat, I descended to 250 feet and continued to fly the required heading and speed. Now Lady Luck intervened, for I flew the next 40 minutes in the same atrocious weather and found every turning point. There was no navigation involved, and I saw little of the countryside, but I did see each of the turning points about 5 seconds before reaching it. Needless to say, I passed the test with flying colours – there is no doubt that a bit of luck is essential on the odd occasion!!

Indeed, I think the luck stayed with me for my instrument rating, flown later that week, which, again, was conducted in atrocious conditions with 95% of it in cloud. Perhaps, by then, I was getting too confident as, although I passed it, my final handling test was not particularly impressive!! However, it was another hurdle and I had passed the course, my reward being a posting to the Central Flying School. Interestingly, and by way of conclusion, of the 16 students who arrived at Valley for the course that June, a significant number were subsequently killed in flying accidents – either aircraft or ejection seat (Koch[1] fastener) malfunctions. There is no doubt that the aircraft of today are a lot more reliable and forgiving than those that we flew only 50 years ago.

Credit: Arpingstone/Wikipedia

---

[1] Koch - The Koch Fastener was a quick-release device which connected the parachute in the Martin-Baker ejection seat to a torso harness worn by the aircrew. It was originally fitted to the Harrier, Phantom and Jaguar but, after a couple of inadvertent releases, was replaced by the traditional seat harness.

The Cyprus Ranger

This story is very much in the 'I learned about flying from that' category!

On a cold Thursday morning in January 1981, a mixed 4-ship of Jaguars from Nos 41(F) and 54(F) Squadrons launched from RAF Coltishall to seek sunnier parts of the world – namely RAF Akrotiri in Cyprus. As part of the Allied Command Europe's Mobile Force, the Coltishall squadrons could be deployed at short notice to any part of that Command area; for this reason, the squadrons were allocated a number of 'ranger' flights a year. Their purpose was to retain corporate knowledge of routes and areas, as well as providing the opportunity for cross-servicing training for groundcrew not familiar with the Jaguar. Very plausible reasons, which also provided a 'jolly' to somewhere nice every now and again!

So the intrepid team set off, planning to refuel at the international airport at Nice in the south of France, and at the US Navy base at Sigonella on the island of Sicily. I was on 54(F) Squadron, but paired with Flinty from No 41(F) Squadron in the two-seat (T2) trainer, as Number 4 in the formation. The other main player in this story, JDG, was in the lead pair. The plan was for me to fly the T2 to Akrotiri, and then to sit in the back while Flinty flew the return route. All went well until reaching Nice where, during the turn-round, a hydraulic leak was discovered on the T2 - which meant that Flinty and I were going nowhere that day. Meanwhile, JDG was seen taxying out with his link bay[1] door open, being pursued by a Renault van from ground control which was attempting to collect, yes you've guessed it, the various pages of the aircraft F700 (engineering log), which were blowing over the pan towards the sea. JDG was also going nowhere that day, since Akrotiri would be closed by the time his paperwork had been re-assembled, so the other two aircraft carried on without us.

A call to Coltishall resulted in an engineer plus spares being booked to fly (civilian airline) to Nice on the following day. We put the aircraft to bed for the

---

[1] Link Bay – A cavity in which 30mm cannon ammunition links were collected when the gun was being fired, but which could also be used to stow the aircraft technical log, the F700, on deployments.

night, but forgot one action which would have some significance later on. Our kit was left with the British Airways handling agent, who also booked us a rather decent hotel and sorted out transport. A lazy meal and lie-in followed! The next day, Sergeant X turned up as planned and sorted out the hydraulic leak. We had planned to stay the weekend at Nice, since Akrotiri would be closed by the time we could get there the next day (Saturday). However, we then found that the airfield would stay open later, to accommodate the Americans flying their U2 spy plane, so we booked ourselves in. That sorted, we took Sergeant X out for a local speciality seafood meal as a 'thank you' gesture.

The next morning, JDG and Flinty were a bit late on parade. Flinty looked green when he opened his door; JDG had a bit more colour when he opened his. Obviously they had eaten a bad prawn, or perhaps the raw sea urchin (which I had not touched) had got to them. However, JDG thought he was fit enough to fly the single-seater, and Flinty could sit in the back of the 2-seater and let me do the work. All was going well until we checked the aircraft, and found that we had no oxygen; that forgotten, but significant, action was that we had not detached the lox (liquid oxygen) pot from the oxygen system, and its contents had leaked away. The bad news was that there were no facilities at Nice to replenish liquid oxygen pots. Flexibility being the key to airpower, we established that we had enough fuel to re-plan to fly at 10,000 feet (where we did not need oxygen), to Sigonella where we could replenish the lox; so we pressed on.

We reached Sigonella without problem, and were met by an all-female US Navy handling team. JDG and Flinty declined my offer of a burger, and sipped flat coke while they continued their recovery; I enjoyed the burger! Lox pots replenished, we launched off to Akrotiri. The only further problem encountered on the way to the brandy sours was that, short of Akrotiri, we had another hydraulic failure in the 2-seater. A call from Akrotiri to Squadron Leader R (54 Squadron Flight Commander) at Coltishall, informing him of the new hydraulic leak, elicited the response, "Sgt X can sort that out". When we explained that Sgt X was in Nice, the reply was, "Where the hell are you then?" We explained about Akrotiri opening times, U2 flying etc, and he seemed to calm down a bit. Engineers would be despatched on Sunday so, with JDG and Flinty now fully recovered after a good dose of 100 percent oxygen, we settled down to a few brandy sours followed by a meze. A rather pleasant few days followed, with the engineers arriving as planned and fixing the 2-seater.

On the Tuesday, following a successful air test, we planned to leave Akrotiri for Coltishall via Sigonella and, due to the time of day, to night stop in Nice. The airfield at Akrotiri would close shortly after our departure for Sigonella. Off we launched, with Flinty leading JDG, and me in the back of the T2, clutching a large Jasmine plant – a surprise present for Flinty's wife. We had no problem with the hydraulics, but the inertial navigation system in the 2-seater was playing up. JDG asked what our computed wind was since, according to his aircraft's navigation equipment, he thought that, at the level at which we were flying, we had insufficient fuel to reach Sigonella. Since we had duff kit, we went with JDG's plan; we changed flight level, to gain a more favourable wind, and made it comfortably to Sigonella. We were looked after by the same all-female crew, who were very efficient, one of them spotting what they thought was a hydraulic leak from the T2. The fluid appeared to be coming from the gun ammunition trays, in which were stowed our overnight bags. Doubting a hydraulic leak from this area, a quick 'taste test' confirmed my suspicion that one of the bottles of Filfar (Cypriot orange liqueur) had leaked! That problem sorted, we set off for our over-night stop in Nice.

Part-way into the transit, we noticed that the light was beginning to fade. By the time we were with Nice air traffic control, it was definitely dark. Night currency? Not sure about that, but there was no other option at this stage. However, when air traffic insisted on us carrying out a self-positioned, pairs ILS[2] , none of us were very sure about night formation currency! Flinty hung on gamely to JDG's wing as we descended into the darkness (no moon) over the sea – the Nice runway being built on reclaimed land. I could see nothing through the Jasmine plant, until the sea and the end of the runway appeared simultaneously and we landed with a bump. We put the aircraft to bed in swift order (lox pots disconnected this time), left our kit with the British Airways handling agents and checked in to the hotel. Dinner (no raw fish this time) and a few glasses of wine later, we arrived back at the hotel for a final cleansing beer

---

[2] ILS - Instrument Landing System. A system of electronic beams from a transmitter on the ground to receivers in the aircraft which navigate the aircraft to the touchdown point at the end of the runway.

before a relatively early night. However, there appeared to be some other aviators in the bar, who turned out to be the crew of Adnan Khashoggi's private aircraft. A slightly later-to-bed night than planned followed, with a few beers and many interesting stories from his crew.

The phone rang. "Have I over slept?" I thought. No, it was 0600 hours. It was JDG on the line with, "Coltishall have phoned, Station exercise, they want us back as soon as possible". Taxi organised, quick ad-hoc breakfast and we were soon at the British Airways office - to find that it was closed for another hour. Eventually, we got hold of our kit and set off for Coltishall.

Part-way through the climb over the Alps, several things happened in the 2-seater in short order. The pressurisation failed, the cockpit became quite cold, the canopy started to ice up, and the Jasmine plant started to wilt before my eyes – it did not survive the flight. We had plenty of oxygen so, aside from being quite cold, the flight went according to plan. On arrival at Coltishall we were surrounded by armourers and the turn-round team, all keen to get the aircraft replenished and loaded with weapons, so that they could be declared 'on state' as part of the exercise. What the armourers were not prepared for were the fresh Cyprus oranges, which cascaded out of the ammunition bays when they were opened – a rather surreal end to an 'interesting' and, at times, very amusing Cyprus ranger.

Credit: TSgt. Lou Hernandez/Wikipedia

184

Almost Into The Blue
(The Wet Variety)

The flight was being filmed for a TV programme. How often has that sentence appeared in evidence to a Board of Inquiry?

I was flying as No 2 of a pair of Harrier GR3s conducting weapons attacks against a splash target towed by a RN frigate (HMS Eskimo, I think) off the coast of Belize. It was an unusually hazy day, but we were able to do what was required. We dropped practice bombs from the CBLS[1] fitted on the centreline pylon, fired HE[2] 30mm from the 2 Aden cannons, and ended with ripples of HE SNEB[3] from the pods on the outboard pylons.

With the job done, I moved into close formation on my leader for recovery to base, but, after a pause, a request came from the ship for a final flypast for the cameras. Turning back towards them, my leader sought to acquire the grey ship under the grey sky on the grey/blue sea. When he saw it, it was over his right shoulder, necessitating a sharp turn to achieve line-up for a flypast to the right of the ship, with me on my leader's right. He called me out into arrow formation first, to allow more aggressive manoeuvring, and then turned in with about 100° of bank while descending to an appropriate altitude. When on line, he rapidly rolled out and aimed to fly close to the ship at about deck level. What was not apparent to me at first was that the roll out had been from 100° to about 20° of bank. Still maintaining my leader's plane, but out in arrow on the right, I was somewhat lower than he was - and he wasn't high! We had passed the ship, when my peripheral vision caught sight of the Caribbean very close to my right ear. I rolled and pulled (snatched?) back, heard a solid bang, but climbed safely away. Everything appeared to be still working, but I was worried that I might have wiped off the CBLS. In fact, my pull had been sufficiently rapid to overcome the hydraulic up lock of the nose wheel, allowing it to bang against the closed door.

The BBC TV programme appeared as "Inside Story: From Blighty To Belize", which can still be found on-line. The splash firing featured very briefly.

---

[1] CBLS – Carrier Bomb Light Stores.
[2] HE – High Explosive.
[3] SNEB (French: Societe Nouvelle des Etablissements Edgar Brandt) - A forward-firing ground attack rocket system fired from pods carried on wing pylons.

1312 Flight

At the end of the Falklands war in 1982, Port Stanley airfield became a hive of activity as the British Forces moved in large numbers to deter any further aggression from Argentina. The 4000-foot paved runway was covered in Pierced Aluminium Planking (PAP), which extended its length to accommodate F4 Phantoms and to allow the Hercules to operate with a maximum fuel load, a requirement for many of the flights carried out. Personnel were accommodated in portacabins, floating accommodation ships and make-do shelters. It was an interesting time for all, and satisfying, as there was a serious job to be done; thankfully there was little paperwork, with almost everything being organised by word of mouth.

The Hercules detachment, 1312 Flight, consisted of 3 aircraft, 2 in tanker configuration and one in the standard cargo configuration, supported by 3 flight crews and about 45 ground personnel. The Hercules tanker had been thrown together rather rapidly, and was quite a 'Heath Robinson' design, but it worked, providing a single-point refuelling capability. The primary role of the Hercules tankers was to supply fuel to the F4s; therefore, whenever the F4s were flying, a Hercules was also in the air, to refuel the fighters if the sortie required it, and to be available in case the runway became unusable for any reason. The Hercules could also refuel any other equipped aircraft, such as an inbound or outbound Hercules, another Hercules of 1312 Flight or, on one occasion, a visiting Nimrod. The tankers were also often used as practice targets for the fighters, and normally this exercise ended with some fighter affiliation, during which many a new F4 crew was surprised by the agility of the Hercules.

Occasionally the tanker aircraft were used as a replacement for the 'flatbed' C-130 in the maritime reconnaissance role. The 'flatbed' was used every day of the week to carry out a survey of the Falkland Islands Protection Zone, or FIPZ, and to spot and record all activity within the zone. The FIPZ extended out to 150 miles from the centre of the Falklands, covering a vast area of sea. The area was popular with fishing fleets from Japan, East Germany, Russia, Spain, Poland and other nations. Each boat had to be photographed and its position, registration and intentions recorded. On some days, the number of recordings exceeded 100 so the flights were full of activity. It was on one of these lengthy sorties that my crew located the upturned catamaran, Beefeater II, in which Chay Blyth had capsized off Cape Horn, while attempting the record for sailing from New York to San Francisco. Many pictures were taken, which subsequently gained my crew a rather pleasant visit to the Beefeater factory in London. The 'flatbed' was also used for regular supply drops to the detachment on South Georgia, for reconnaissance of the South Sandwich Islands and, at times, it carried communications equipment for monitoring radio transmissions from Argentina.

One tanker was on 24/7 standby, with the crew living within yards of the aircraft. The Hercules was prepared for a quick start and the crews were always ready for the scramble call, be it practice or for real. At the sound of the hooter, engineers and crew reacted like a well-oiled machine, rushing to the aircraft and wasting no time in getting the 4 engines started and the aircraft ready to taxy. 1312 Flight was positioned at the mid-point of the runway, and the C-130 had to wait for the F4s to scramble before making a suitable backtrack of the runway. Most often the Hercules crew were ready and waiting with all engines running before the F4s had even entered the runway. Whilst on Standby or Quick Reaction Alert (QRA), the crew cooked their own meals, watched videos, wrote letters home and also managed to construct improvements to the flight building. The 1312 accommodation consisted of a number of portacabins, which were linked under an umbrella of galvanised sheeting. Some impressive modifications and improvements were undertaken, using great ingenuity and efficacious scavenging of materials. One enviable enhancement was 1312's flushing toilet, commonly known as 'The Turdis'. The crews worked almost every day, only managing 2 days off every 3 weeks, which provided an opportunity for a foray, normally to the West Falklands, to spend an evening or two with one of the families who regularly offered their hospitality; their generosity was always beyond reproach.

During my time as Officer Commanding 1312 Flight, it became the first unit to have a shower and a drying room, all accomplished using ingenuity and scavenging techniques not regularly taught in training. Next door to the Hercules flight was a cabin for the Station Commander who, every other night, would sleep in the cabin whilst on call. It wasn't long before he found out about our shower and came to ask if he could use it; of course, how could I refuse?! The very next day it happened that my crew were on standby, and were woken by a strange voice telling us that breakfast was ready. Our Station Commander had already showered, and had proceeded to cook a breakfast of eggs and bacon, before he called us to the table. How many crew members can claim that? We were all most appreciative of the gesture, and also extremely thankful that he had not noticed the box sitting in the corner of the cabin, leaking oil onto the floor. On one of our visits to a remote island, where we were so generously entertained, we found out that the host's Land Rover needed a new gearbox and it was unlikely that he could ever get it fixed. In the course of another scavenging foray, the Flight acquired a scrapped but serviceable gearbox, which we air-dropped to the island some days later.

A few weeks later, the Station Commander was returning to the UK at the end of his tour, hitching a lift back in a Nimrod which had been in the Falklands for some reconnaissance missions. My crew were flying the tanker that day, tasked to refuel the Nimrod on its journey northbound. The crew hatched a plan, the details of which they released to me just before we departed. As the Nimrod approached our Hercules to take on fuel for its flight to Ascension Island, they could scarcely have missed the message, written in white tape on the underneath of the ramp of the Hercules. Our departing Station Commander came on the radio, to give us some wonderful words of thanks. The message in large print read *'Bye Bye Bobby.'*

Credit: RAF/Crown Copyright

Fear Is Not Confined To Military Flying

The Canadian corporate aircraft scene in 1974 included a wide spectrum of aircraft, all the way from big iron Gulfstreams to lowly Beech 18s (Bug Smashers), and other assorted rubbish. Whatever the type, one might reasonably have expected that the aircraft equipment would generally be well-adapted for the snow and ice conditions found in a Canadian winter. One would be wrong!

Early 1974 was exceptionally cold, and a Commander 500 was far from ideal for navigating in the depth of winter. The one we were flying, that is my RAF friend, Pete, and me, had a history of being used as an asymmetric trainer. The Commander 500 only had a hydraulic pump on one engine (the right), so it is not too hard to guess which engine had been flogged to death during these training flights. General Motors charters were the life blood of small charter outfits like ours, but the redneck running their charter side always asked for a "Beech". So our Boss would always try to be competitive in his quotes, even when we were not!

A flight in the early evening across Lake Ontario was not beyond the Commander 500, but the weather and the awful standard of its instrumentation made it very marginal for IFR (Instrument Flight Rules). We departed for Rochester, intending to stay out of cloud and the attendant possibility of icing. In February, the water temperatures in Lake Ontario are not conducive to swimming, as witnessed by floating patches of ice; thus, ditching was not ideally part of our plan. Pete was in the left seat, with me doing the Radio/Nav knob twiddling. The bang, when it came, was loud and unmistakeable, and the oil all over the right side of the screen did kinda confirm what we both knew. A look out of my side window showed that the right engine had destructed and had distorted the cowling. The next revelation was that the gear was down, and I started the process of using the hand-pump to try and raise it, to reduce drag. Pete struggled to maintain the required single-engine speed, which resulted in a slow descent towards the lake from our initial 3000 feet.

Carburettor icing will stop an engine and, in a Commander, there is a large gauge showing inlet temperature, such that the flap controlling the inlet air can be readily moved to allow more or less hot air into the carb. As we were in misty conditions, that job had priority. Too warm equals less power, too cold risks engine stoppage. I managed a MAYDAY call with our very weak radios, and a British Airways aircraft relayed the call to Rochester. With Pete juggling speed and height, it became all too obvious that a descent into the water was a distinct possibility. Even if we survived that, being rescued was extremely unlikely. Accordingly, we agreed calmly that if he could not hold it, he would half-roll into the lake! The gear situation had resolved itself - after a fashion; I could not get it to lock up, and any cessation of pumping resulted in it flopping back down again. So, we were in a very high drag situation with moderate icing, descending slowly. We had no real communication, so low that both navigation and radio were compromised. There is a good road along the north shore of New York State, and the possibility of landing on it had to be considered, because we did not know if we would have enough height to cross the coast, and stay out of the vegetation until we reached Rochester Airport. The glow of Rochester was enough for us to aim in that direction and we knew where the airport was, luckily this side of the city.

I cannot remember if we got the flaps down (by pumping), but the runway was aligned with our flight path, and by now we were talking to Rochester control. Pete did a masterful job of landing the beast, but then quickly found out that the nose-wheel steering was locked, a by-product of our hydraulic issues. Sadly, it was not locked in the fore-and-aft mode. We shot off down a secondary runway, which just happened to be where the nose-wheel was pointed. Emergency brakes brought us to a stop, and the adrenalin rush was over, that is until we saw that the engine was broken in half, lying in the cowling, and basically held there by the spark plug leads!!

We retired to a late night bar; I really am a non-drinker, but not that night!

Credit: Cdanielsiv/Wikipedia

A Close Shave!

Once upon a time I used to fly single-seat, multi-role jet fighters that hovered. It was a tremendously exciting, highly competitive and demanding business. Life on a squadron was busy; we practised a wide variety of roles (just about everything you could do with a fast jet) and had regular deployments. Constantly changing personnel, along with a strict 'qualification' regime, meant there was always someone to be trained, a skill to be honed or a qualification to be renewed.

I was a senior squadron pilot, one of a few who had just about all the 'boxes ticked' after 12 years of almost non-stop, 'front-line' flying. Consequently, I found myself supervising a couple of newly-arrived pilots, who were progressing through their training towards achieving 'Combat Ready' status.

The Squadron had deployed for a period of intensive training to a remote airfield, in an area known for its constant mist and low cloud (as featured in a song by Paul McCartney); however, the low flying around there was great and we had no distractions. I was programmed to fly as Number 4 of a 4-aircraft formation, with one of the junior pilots leading. We operated in pairs, the Squadron Commander was Number 2 and my leader, Number 3, was another new guy. This was normal practice; the less qualified guys flew as the leader in a pair to gain experience. Our sortie on that day was a complicated mix of low-level simulated ground attacks and a high priority, timed, low-level run at an offshore weapons range, where we would drop a small practice bomb. This would be scored for accuracy and timing. We had also organised some air defence fighters from another base to intercept us en-route. Navigation was done on a map and stopwatch (GPS was still in its infancy) so, as you can imagine, the planning and briefing for such a mission took many hours.

We eventually walked out to our aircraft and strapped in, with the canopies closed to keep out the rain. The weather was awful, but we were told it cleared up a few miles inland, so we had briefed a pairs instrument departure. Eventually we lined up, me and my mate at the threshold, the other 2 about 1000 feet further along the runway. Each aircraft was equipped with 2 radios (Boxes). Box 1 was normally used for external communications, while Box 2 was used for internal formation messages. The Air Traffic Control folk at this airfield were not used to the way we operated and tended to let us get on with things. Although, on this occasion, they could not actually see us through the mist (it subsequently transpired), they cleared us for take-off and waited for our 'going en-route' call on the tower frequency.

Just as we were about to go, the 'Boss' (up front) called on Box 2 that his aircraft had an anti-skid failure, and he was going to taxi along the runway and return to the dispersal. However, our young leader had briefed a 'loser' plan which meant we were to get airborne as a 3-ship in 'V' formation. This required us to renumber and 'shuffle up' to him further along the runway. About one minute later (remember we were on a deadline) the new formation, with lead in the middle, me on the right and my mate on the left was ready to roll. A few hand signals between us and off we went. A 3-ship, close formation take-off in instrument conditions is a demanding exercise; the lead has to keep absolutely straight during the ground roll, fly smoothly and use a series of hand-signals and head-nods to keep everyone informed. A wingman's job is to stick like glue to the leader, whatever happens... with mist, spray, different aircraft engine acceleration rates and crosswind all making life interesting. You really don't want to lose sight of the leader!

Within a couple of seconds we were accelerating through 60 knots. Standard procedure was that the leader would nod his head a moment before he rotated[1]. Just before the nod, and to this day I don't know why, I glanced forward, through the green writing in the Head Up Display[2], into the white mist. For just a split second I could not believe what I saw...there was a tiny speck of red light in the middle of the green symbols against the white background. *The Boss was still on the runway and right in front of me!!* He was crawling along the right hand edge of the runway, looking for the exit. My mind went into hyperdrive. If I transmitted "formation abort" I would definitely hit him. However, if I said nothing, slowed a bit, steered left into lead's wake and then kept going, I might just miss him. So that's what I did...and missed him by a couple of feet. It was

---

[1] Rotated – Uniquely in the Harrier this is the moment when the nozzle lever is moved to a pre-selected setting to vector the thrust for take off.
[2] Head Up Display - A transparent, electronically generated display that projects data directly ahead of the pilot, thus reducing the need to look inside the cockpit (head down) at instrumentation.

a rough ride in the jet-wake of the other two and I briefly considered aborting the take-off. Then I thought 'those guys are not allowed to fly as a pair, I have to supervise them' (strange how your priorities can go haywire sometimes), so I opened the tap again and followed them. As I got airborne I called 'That was close!' on the internal radio and off we went.

We carried on with the mission although it took me almost half an hour to get my heart rate back to normal. I was all over the place. I found it hard to concentrate and flew along just shaking, not caring if the bad guys found me or if I even came close to the targets we had briefed.

The debrief after we had landed was interesting. Unsurprisingly, the Boss was furious that we had nearly taken him out. The poor young guy leading the formation take-off was almost ill in his mask as he got airborne; for a few seconds he thought he had just killed me and the Boss. He had noticed me dropping back on the right, then saw another jet flash past his wing where I had just been. To say that he was mightily relieved to hear my 'That was close!' call was an understatement. The guy on the left was blissfully unaware of the drama until the debrief.

I recall that the world's worst aviation disaster happened when two jumbo jets collided on a runway in poor visibility. We were lucky not to have had a mini version that day.

Credit: Mick Bevan

Black Buck 1
(A Tanker's Tale)

On 18 April 1982, the first wave of five Victor Tankers of Nos 55 and 57 Squadrons deployed to Ascension Island in the South Atlantic. The following day, four more aircraft and crews arrived, forming the nucleus of the only available Forward Operating Base in support of Operation Corporate[1]. Airfield facilities at the ironically named 'Wideawake' Auxiliary Airfield were minimal, to say the least. Aircrews and ground crews worked together in the searing heat to erect the 160-pounder tents on the lava-strewn landscape, next to the single dispersal. Within 48 hours of the first aircraft's arrival, this tented complex was serving as our operations centre, complete with engineering and supporting units. Adjacent to it was sited a Tactical Communications Wing, which linked the newly established airhead to the Air Commander to CTF 317, at Northwood in the UK.

The aircraft and crews were combined to form one tanker unit, colloquially known as '112 Multi-Role Victors', derived from the addition of the two squadron numbers, and a reference to the recently acquired roles of Maritime Radar Reconnaissance (MRR) and Photo Reconnaissance (PR). With the Rolls-Royce Conway engines of the second wave of aircraft barely spooled-down, the first MRR mission was mounted on the night of 20/21 April. Its aim was to provide intelligence of the disposition of Argentinian naval forces, for the Task Group led by HMS Antrim engaged in the re-capture of South Georgia. Lessons were learned quickly, in terms of generating and manoeuvring large formations of aircraft within the confined ramp area, and their sequencing to the single, albeit long, runway. From an air-to-air refuelling (AAR) point of view, however, the launch, rendezvous (RV) and subsequent airborne fuel transfers necessitated by that first mission were relatively straightforward. The expertise of No1 Group's Tanker Planning Cell, coupled with the finely-honed skills of its tanker squadrons in world-wide refuelling operations, were well-recognised. Standard Operating Procedures (SOPs), developed from numerous fighter trails and deployments, were an ideal base upon which to launch the operation from Ascension

---

[1] Operation Corporate - The codename given to the British military operations in the Falklands War.

Island - that is so long as only the Victor K2 was involved! The problems started with the arrival of its unfamiliar and somewhat incompatible stablemate, the Vulcan.

As the only aircraft capable of flying a round-trip mission of almost 8000 nautical miles, and being able to deliver an effective bomb load, the venerable Vulcan was hurriedly prepared for the first offensive air action; bombing of the runway at Port Stanley in the Falkland Islands. The AAR capability within No1 Group's Bomber Force had, however, long since disappeared. Not only did re-fuelling probes need to be found and retro-fitted to the airframes, but also the Vulcan pilots required formation training and, even more importantly, receiver training for in-flight refuelling. All in all, a virtually impossible task within the short time frame available. It was therefore decided that each tasked Vulcan crew would have a Victor AAR instructor onboard to assist during the fuel trans-fers. Our in-theatre experience was that only four tankers were needed on the outbound wave, to get an MRR sweep aircraft (known as the 'Primary') to its operating area in the vicinity of South Georgia. A similar number were then launched on the inbound wave, to enable two tankers, and therefore the choice of two serviceable hoses, to meet the returning Primary aircraft at a pre-deter-mined rendezvous (RV). Eight tanker sorties (plus one reserve) were thus needed to satisfy the MRR task. The predicament, however, was that a heavily-laden Vulcan bomber would need considerably more refuelling support to achieve the mission profile for a variety of reasons: more frequent refuellings (to enable all aircraft to return to Ascension at any stage of the flight); incompatibility between Victor and Vulcan optimum cruising altitudes and speeds; the need to descend to lower altitude and speed during refuelling, and considerably more complicated departure and RV join-up procedures than were catered for in the Standard Operating Procedures (SOPs). All these factors combined to make the refuelling support of such an operation several degrees more difficult than that of the earlier MRR tasking. In reality, it was calculated that eleven tankers would be required on the outbound wave alone, with a further five supporting the inbound recovery wave. At least, that was the plan!

The night of 30 April/01 May provided the opportunity to put to the test the most ambitious bombing mission since the Second World War, which would signal the commencement of offensive air operations in support of the South

Atlantic Fleet. Upon it would rest the RAF's capability (or otherwise) of striking
the enemy at extreme range, and helping establish an air superiority situation
for the South Atlantic Fleet's own offensive aircraft. The buzz of excitement in
the briefing tent was intense, as the scene was set for 'Operation Black Buck'.
Victor and Vulcan crews listened shoulder-to-shoulder as the scenario unfolded.
Three sections, named Red, White and Blue, would form the outbound wave.
Four tankers would make up each of Red and White sections, whilst a further
three would support the Primary Vulcan and its airborne reserve in Blue section.
Five tankers, including an airborne reserve, would comprise the recovery wave,
intended to enable two Victors to meet the post-attack Vulcan at an RV, situated
some distance off the Brazilian coast, abeam Rio de Janeiro. The offer of two
refuelling hoses at the bracket for the Vulcan's final refuelling, to facilitate its
return to Ascension, would reduce the potential for refuelling equipment failure
within a single tanker. In keeping with normal fuel planning criteria, all tankers
in the formation should have been able to return to Wideawake Airfield, albeit
with minimum operationally acceptable fuel reserves. It also had to be borne in
mind that there was no alternate landing airfield available to the Tanker Force
operating from this remote island base. Just as formidable were the demands
placed upon the detachment Engineering Wing. They would be called upon
that night to produce all available airframes, several of which would be required
to fly a second sortie on the recovery wave following immediate turn-rounds.

After the short walk across the cinder track to our aircraft, the operation
began to pick up momentum. One by one, and in the pre-briefed sequence,
callsigns checked in with the minimum of chatter. As the night air was charged
with the sound of 52 Rolls-Royce Conway and Olympus engines, the aircraft
rumbled their way to Runway 14, jostling for position on the crowded pan.
Red One, commanded by Sqn Ldr Martin Todd, then led the thirteen-ship
'snake' climb between the volcanoes into the black South Atlantic skies. (Two
days later, I was to witness a similar spectacle, as Black Buck 2 was launched.
The deafening sound of a dozen 4-jets littered with anti-collision lights, dodging and weaving between the jagged volcanoes either side of the runway, was a
background to the spectacular sight never envisioned in this previously peace-
ful outcrop close to the Equator). Without delay, the next priority for each
airborne tanker was to prove the integrity of its Hose Drum Unit (HDU) by

trailing the hose. Although no guarantee that a subsequent trailing would be assured, at least the early detection of a fault might avoid complications later. To White 4's dismay, this turned out to be the case, as his Navigator Radar (the crew member who controlled the HDU) frantically tried everything possible to achieve a fully trailed hose, but without success. So soon into the mission, the first of a catalogue of surprises surfaced to test the flexibility of the crews and the feasibility of this ambitious plan. With text-book ease however, Flt Lt Steve Biglands, having launched as Blue 3, slid across to White section and assumed White 4's position, which coincidentally elevated his role from that of airborne reserve to Primary outbound tanker. The task would fall upon him, therefore, to anticipate being the last tanker to refuel the Vulcan prior to casting him off some seven hours later!

A more sinister situation was beginning to develop, however, as the formation continued its planned trombone pattern, designed to let all sections join as one formation. Blue 2, the primary Vulcan was unable to pressurise[2] properly and, shortly afterwards, he had to declare his unserviceability also. Flt Lt Martin Withers, as No 4 in Blue section, the designated Vulcan airborne reserve, was now faced with assuming the Primary Vulcan's task. In the new role of Blue 2, he therefore took his place in Blue section as the eleven remaining aircraft climbed to their allocated flight levels. At least the weather factor at Ascension's latitude presented no problems at this stage of the mission. The skies were clear, and visibility in the star-lit night sky was unlimited. Indeed, the only problem was trying to identify which set of lights represented your own section leader. As White 2, and only sixth in the stream, I was able to settle in echelon starboard on my leader without too much difficulty. Nevertheless, it seemed as though the whole sky was awash with flashing red beacons, amidst a clutter of red, white and green navigation lights. On more than one occasion during subsequent missions, section leaders would have to resort to the faithful Very Pistol[3] to assist join-up. Before long however, Red, White and Blue sections were heading just

---

[2] Pressurise – Pressurise the air in the cockpit, without which the crew could not continue the sortie.
[3] Very Pistol - The Very Pistol was named after Edward Wilson Very (1847–1910), an American naval officer who developed and popularized a single-shot, breech-loading, snub-nosed pistol that fired flares.

to the west of south, staggered at their respective flight levels of 360, 340 and 320. The engines settled into their familiar drone, as a comfortable formation position was achieved. There was now time to relax a little, after the anxieties of the less-than-ideal start to what was shaping up to be a night to remember.

Transfer 1 was to take place after approximately 1hr 45mins, some 700 nautical miles (nm) down track. On reaching the refuelling bracket, the four pairs of tankers in Red and White sections prepared to offload to their respective receivers sufficient fuel so that, at the end of the bracket, the latter would be full to the gunwales. This huge transfer of around 50000lbs left each of the fully-laden Victors with 123000lbs of Avtur[4]. The depleted tankers, Red 1 & 3, and White 1 & 3 then turned back for Ascension Island with a 'chicken' fuel sufficient for their recovery plus a small reserve. In the event, the four returning aircraft were all stretched to the limit, and had very little fuel remaining on arrival at Wideawake, to the extent that there was not even time for the first landing aircraft to backtrack the length of the runway and vacate it for the following Victor. The first three aircraft were thus faced with no option but to land in sequence, and position as close to the far end of the landing strip as possible. By the time that Martin Todd was on finals, he was faced with the prospect of completing his landing rollout with his three colleagues blocking the end of the runway. The potential for a major pile-up did not need to be spelled out! In the event, all was well, and the four aircraft were able to taxi back to dispersal, where time was of the essence to prepare the airframes for the recovery wave. However, the initial signs were beginning to appear that the refuelling plan was not going quite according to expectation. The Air Commander on Ascension, Group Captain Jeremy Price, himself a very experienced tanker pilot, was quick to realise that, not only must the aircraft be regenerated as quickly as possible, but any aircraft, additional to the original plan, which might become available, must be offered up for use as Terminal Airborne Tankers (TAT). This reserve refuelling capability, in the form of back-up tankers, would have been built into the original plot, if numbers of available aircraft had not been so limited.

Meanwhile, the remaining tanker with the Vulcan in Blue section had refuelled the bomber, and was staying with the formation prior to offering it a final

---

[4] Avtur – Aviation Turbine fuel.

top-up before departing northbound. This done, the remaining five-ship formation continued to the next refueling bracket, 1900nm south of Ascension. In the early hours of the morning, the physical exertion of upwards of twenty minutes in contact during the first refuelling, and over three hours of concentrated formation flying, was beginning to show. At one stage Steve Biglands, on my right, alerted me as an undetected slow and potentially dangerous roll to port was beginning to develop. Shaking off the momentary drowsiness, I regained my position, and vowed not to let my attention wander again.

More changes of position were to take place during Transfer 2. I took on board around 30000lbs from the recently filled Red 4, who in turn gave a similar amount to Steve Biglands, before turning for home. Red 4, flown by Flt Lt Alan Skelton, was to face a few anxious hours during his recovery as a fuel leak started to eat away at his Island fuel reserve. White 4 (Steve Biglands) and White 2 (myself) were once again full to the gunwales, and proceeding in company with Blue 2 (Martin Withers' Vulcan) towards my final refuelling area, Transfer 3. The chances of further problems were statistically reducing, with only three aircraft remaining. My own aircraft had behaved impeccably so far, and we had plenty of time to prepare for my last planned bracket, expected around 5hrs 30mins after take-off and some 2800nm from Ascension Island. Leading the formation now, my Nav Plotter, Flt Lt John Keable, and Nav Radar, Flt Lt Ernie Wallis, assumed the navigational responsibility for the first time. Our recently acquired Carousel Inertial Navigation System was a great boost to the Victor's otherwise antiquated nav kit. Ernie Wallis's radar system was of no use, however, because we were not only out of range of the nearest landfall, but also intent on limiting all of our electronic transmissions for fear of alerting any possible enemy surface vessels below. Indeed, virtually all of the refuelling procedures up to this point had been accomplished in radio silence throughout. From a communications point of view, Flt Lt Mike Beer, my Air Electronics Officer, had had little to do apart from maintaining a listening watch on his HF equipment. This would be of vital significance to us later, when awaiting the post-attack message with which to gauge the ultimate success of the mission. My co-pilot, Glyn Rees, was meanwhile occupied moving fuel around in the Victor's numerous tanks, in preparation for the final refuellings.

Transfer 3 began without incident, as we passed fuel for the first time. Blue 2 took on around 22000lbs, prior to holding off on my port side. Steve Biglands, in the other remaining tanker (White 4) moved astern, in anticipation of his last onload. Straining to recall the met man's weather brief, concerning frontal activity in the area around 45 degrees south, I started to lose sight of the stars for the first time that night. Unfortunately for us, and for Steve Biglands in particular as the formating receiver pilot, the ride rapidly became very uncomfortable. In next to no time, we encountered the severe turbulence associated with convective cloud in the worsening weather. Considerable St Elmo's Fire[5] was present, as my aircraft started to buck quite violently. Tripping the overworked autopilot, I elected to fly the aircraft manually, in an effort to smooth out the larger flight path disturbances. Ernie Wallis continued to pass fuel to the tanker behind. Brilliantly illuminated by the momentary flashes of lightning, he could see that the hose was becoming increasingly unstable. With less than half the transfer completed, Steve Biglands broke radio silence when his probe fractured under the intense gyrations of my hose and basket. The whole mission was now in serious jeopardy, unless a solution could be found to a rapidly deteriorating situation. Firstly, White 4 had not taken enough fuel to complete the planned profile with the Vulcan. Secondly, even if we were to change places, with me taking back the fuel already transferred to Steve Biglands' aircraft, there was no assurance that my own refuelling basket had not been damaged in the broken probe incident. In that case, my capability to subsequently refuel the Vulcan might be adversely affected, or even made impossible if, for example, the probe tip from the other aircraft was still lodged in my basket. Further delay along track, however, was only going to exacerbate a worsening fuel situation. Any extension outbound by the tankers meant an equal addition to the track miles inbound, incurring a duplicated fuel penalty.

Either way, the initial logical course of action was to change roles with White 4 and attempt to take back the fuel already offloaded, which, together with remainder of the planned transfer that I still held, would put the fuel plan back on track. Racing through the post-tanking checks, and leaving my Nav Radar to sort out the HDU, Glyn Rees set up the refuelling tray for the unscheduled onload.

---

[5] St Elmo's Fire - A weather phenomenon created by a coronal discharge in a strong electric field in the atmosphere, producing a faint glow easily visible in low-light conditions.

Normally, this would be a carefully planned sequence of events that must take account of the critical fuel distribution, otherwise the handling qualities of the Victor, particularly longitudinally, could quickly deteriorate. Hoping that the Vulcan would be able to maintain visual contact with the two of us, I grappled with the controls to place the aircraft astern Steve Biglands' rapidly-trailed hose. With the red signal light out, and thus ready for contact, I fought for some time to achieve a latched contact between probe and basket. Whilst tossing about like ships on a stormy sea, the fuel began to flow. My skills were being tested to the limit, as were the powered flying control units of my airframe, XH189, during what was turning out to be the most demanding refuelling I had encountered during my time in the Tanker Force. A few minutes into the transfer, the hose became unstable with the characteristic whipping up and down its length, causing me to break contact. With insufficient fuel received, it took me three to four more valuable minutes in the turbulent conditions to make a further contact, and re-establish fuel transfer. My workload was so intense that I was barely able to monitor Glyn Rees on the fuel tray as those valuable gallons of fuel were being skilfully directed into the appropriate cells. Equally hectic was the activity amongst my rear crew, who were frantically trying to keep tabs on the much-extended refuelling bracket - which should have been completed some distance back! My first break came just at that moment as the glorious sight of twinkling stars filled the background around the Victor's silhouette above me, and mercifully, the turbulence subsided. As all three aircraft stabilised once more, the transfer was able to proceed amidst a comparative calm. Paramount in my thoughts was the fact that Steve Biglands' aircraft would not be able to receive any more fuel because of his damaged probe. I therefore warned him not to go beyond that chicken fuel which would permit an un-refuelled recovery to Ascension Island. This would mean that I could expect to take on less than the planned transfer originally intended. Furthermore, as both tankers had now proceeded down-route well past the end of the geographical bracket, more fuel would be needed by both aircraft to ensure a safe return. As the implications of the multi-faceted problem began to compound, Steve's refuelling signal lights informed me that I had taken as much fuel as he was able to offer. Accordingly, I eased back and out to the starboard side without delay, to permit his immediate turn to commence his recovery. Hasty farewells were made as I re-engaged the autopilot for a brief respite.

We had been left with two very significant legacies. Firstly, we still had the integrity of the refueling basket to prove, if we were to pass more fuel. Secondly, as anticipated, the reduced uplift left us woefully short of that needed on the master fuel plan to achieve the mission from that geographical position. There was no point in concerning ourselves unduly with the latter situation, as the problem might not arise if the former could not be addressed. Ernie Wallis promptly re-trailed the hose, as Blue 2 was called astern with a view to visually inspecting my refueling equipment. The Vulcan's two pilots indicated no apparent damage. However, to be absolutely certain, there was only one way of proving that the HDU was still capable of functioning normally, and so the Vulcan was cleared for a 'wet' contact. In the restored tranquility, the bomber had no difficulty in quickly making contact, and a nominal transfer of 5000lbs was successfully achieved. The two-ship could at least continue towards the target for the time being.

With the frequent formation changes and the additional refuelling at Transfer 3, we were well over six hours into the mission, around 3200nm from our departure point, and the overriding consideration facing my crew was the worsening fuel situation. The result of hours of formation flying interspersed with high intensity workload refuellings was now glaringly reflected in the much-depleted 'fuel remaining' versus 'planned'. The choices available, as I perceived the situation, were two-fold: as formation leader, I could call it a day right there, and abort the raid whilst my aircraft had more than adequate chicken fuel to return to base; alternatively, the mission could continue, with my own reserves rapidly dwindling to the point where a safe recovery to Ascension could not be achieved without the aid of a rescue tanker. My crew worked feverishly on the options available, calculating points of no return, and flight times against fuel remaining. The reality of our predicament was that, in order to refuel the Vulcan with the expected final transfer necessary for it to reach the target, my own aircraft would be left with insufficient fuel to make the Island. At this stage of Operation Corporate, it must be said that a diversion for a tanker to the South American mainland had not really been considered and, as far as I was concerned, was out of the question. The only viable alternative was to put one's trust in years of experience in the 'system', and in particular our Air

Commander at Ascension Island. We felt certain that he would be only too well aware of the developing fuel crisis. I could not let the AEO get on the HF radio to inform our Headquarters of the predicament, for fear of jeopardizing the as-yet-unfulfilled mission. With so much effort expended by so many professional airmen to keep this show on the road, I was strongly predisposed to press on. Aware, however, that my ultimate consideration must be for the safety of my crew, I felt obliged to hear their individual opinions for the continuance (or otherwise) of the mission. Before giving my own views, I therefore asked my colleagues what their decision would be if they were in command. One by one, they unanimously stated that, having got that far, the mission should continue. The single most difficult operational decision as aircraft Captain that I have ever had to make was thus made much easier with the encouragement and support of my crew.

The final transfer to Blue 2 went without hitch, up to the point of casting him off around 500nm from the Falkland Islands. We calculated that we could offer him a sufficient quantity to enable him to press on with the attack, bearing in mind that the inbound wave of tankers would already have been launched to meet him at the recovery RV. At 58000lbs fuel remaining, I was well below the 78000lbs 'chicken' fuel state that would have enabled me to reach Ascension without refueling. However, I had calculated that it was enough to get me sufficiently close to stand a reasonable chance of linking with a TAT. Then the Vulcan Captain called briefly on the R/T requesting the remainder of his expected transfer. Having stretched ourselves to what we considered to be the reasonable limit, we duly turned north, albeit leaving the hose trailing on offer. Despite turning with us initially, we felt sure that the Vulcan crew, with the experienced tanker AAR instructor on board, would be aware of our ever-worsening fuel predicament. Then, at the next instant, the Vulcan turned back southwards, leaving my aircraft on its own for the first time in seven hours.

A strange silence filled the cabin, as I put the aircraft into a cruise climb to the altitude that would give us best range capability. As nothing was going to happen for at least an hour, there was time for us all to reflect and regain our composure. Although the gross weight of the aircraft was quite light, at a little less than 160000lbs, and the engines close to their peak economy at that altitude, whichever way we looked at it, we could only get to within four or five hundred miles of our safe haven. There would still be a lot of South Atlantic left between that area and Mars Bay, the southerly-most point on Ascension. My hopes were elevated by the expectation of Engineering Wing generating that last airframe, and another tanker crew bringing it south to offer me that precious fuel line.

Suddenly, Mike Beer's excited voice cut through the subdued atmosphere with the announcement of "Superfuse"; the Vulcan's HF transmission signalling a successful bombing run. The elation within my crew that we had really helped achieve the attack on Port Stanley's runway must also have been sensed as far away as Northwood. I recall, however, soon afterwards, the strange sensation of learning of the accomplishment of the bombing mission on none other than the BBC's World Service, to which Mike had been tuned. At the time, we were still some five hours flight time from base, with a little under four hours of fuel remaining! From our viewpoint, the announcement to the World, whilst so much was still at stake, seemed rather premature, and much discussion ensued about the prospect of our not being able to meet up with another tanker. Because of the design of the underside of the nose bay of the Victor, the aircraft had always been considered unsuitable for ditching. The likelihood was that, because of a bulkhead to the rear of the H2S radar scanner, the whole aircraft would dive under on impact. The approved plan for abandoning a Victor in flight was therefore that the rear crew would parachute out of the hatch, followed by a controlled ejection by both pilots. Having talked through the appropriate drills, we placed the plan on the back-burner in favour of concentrating on the more positive prospect of a successful RV.

Mike Beer worked incessantly with the HF radio, attempting to relay our precarious predicament to Ascension, because our situation dictated the need for a tanker to meet us at least one thousand miles south of the Island. We also informed them of the reduced fuel state in the Vulcan so that revised RV arrangements might be made if considered necessary. My hopes and expectations were all realized, with the final confirmation that a TAT was indeed on the way. Some two hours later, after eleven hours of savouring the comforts of the Mk 3 Martin Baker ejection seat, we were all consumed with excitement as five pairs of anxious eyes searched the clear blue Atlantic sky for that unmistakable crescent wing. My Boss, Wg Cdr Colin Seymour, on his second sortie that day, manoeuvred his aircraft directly in front of mine, after a flawless rendezvous, and offered me his trailed centre-line hose. Tiredness was no longer a factor, as the next few minutes would provide the ultimate test of nerve. With hundreds of AAR contacts in the bag, this was to be the most important of my life, literally. There was silence as I took longer than normal to stabilise in the pre-contact position, astern Colin Seymour's hose. There was no point in trying to be too rushed or aggressive. Nor did I feel the usual macho need to make contact in one - a necessity with one's squadron colleagues looking on! The fuel remaining in the tanks, as I moved up towards the basket, would have kept the engines going for perhaps a little over one more hour. Flying the aircraft as smoothly as possible, I narrowly missed the basket, after what I like to think of as the smoothest missed contact that I have ever made. The second approach resulted in my probe clunking home centrally inside the reception coupling. After a brief, uneasy moment, the tanker's Nav Radar transmitted the sweet words "fuel flows": that all-important corollary to the latched contact signifying a positive transfer of fuel. As our tanks filled to that point where recovery to Wideawake Airfield would be possible, the sighs of relief amongst my crew were clearly audible. The final hurdle had been cautiously cleared, and the remainder of the flight was to be entirely uneventful.

Not for us the two hundred or so officers and airmen who met Martin Withers' aircraft to inspect its empty bomb bay, some 1hr 20mins or so after our own arrival. Our experience that night was one to be savoured amongst us and the other tanker crews, some of whom had experienced hair-raising episodes of their own. A total of eighteen tanker sorties were launched during the night of 30 April/1st May 1982 in support of the two Vulcan bombers, and a number of crews were called upon to fly second sorties, either in support of the inbound recovery wave, or as TATs to assist aircraft returning short of fuel. The participating 18 Victor crews flew in excess of 105 hours, with five individual crews amassing flight durations of over 10 hours. Some 23 individual air-to-air refuellings took place, with a total of around 635000lbs of fuel transferred. Beyond any doubt, the refuelling of the Vulcan, in support of Operation Black Buck One, had needed every bit of expertise that No 1 Group's Tanker Force could muster. Ultimately though, we had ensured the success of the longest bombing mission in the history of aerial warfare.

So That's What Friends Are For!

Back in the mists of time, the RAF training pattern had produced too many pilots (does that sound familiar?) and there were a range of 'Holding Postings' on offer. One of these was to be sent to RAF Germany for a Forward Air Controller (FAC) course, after which we happy few were allocated to various Army units. I was doubly lucky – I was not only posted to a very famous and senior Scottish Infantry battalion, but was also given to a very competent Platoon Sergeant (most definitely with capital letters) who guided a very young Pilot Officer through the intricacies of running a platoon of hardened Glaswegians. A real education for a young officer, whose two and a half years at Cranwell had hardly prepared him for such a role.

Those familiar with infantry regiments will know that the fresh-faced 2nd Lieutenants, or their equivalents, were a long way down the pecking order in status. Everything depended on having a sympathetic platoon sergeant (see above) and, very largely, the support of one's fellow 2nd Lieutenants. In my case I certainly got both, but one comrade in particular was alongside (and usually leading) during many, somewhat unfortunate, adventures with me. Plonky, as he may have been colloquially known, shared with me a rampant curiosity about what we might get away with, from (nearly) sinking an armoured personnel carrier, when trying to cross a fast flowing major river during a lunch break (when no-one was watching), to wandering around the then East Berlin, 'borrowing' unattended, East German Army helmets. By such means are strong bonds made.

Fast forward a few years, and the famous Scottish Infantry battalion is now based in Cyprus, at the Joint Services base at Episkopi. I was, by then, just starting my tour as the youngest captain on the Victor fleet. Having survived probation, we, the squadron junior crew, were let loose on a weekend Ranger Exercise to Cyprus, so I contacted Plonky in advance to find out what goodies the troops might be short of in the Mediterranean sun. Strangely, the garrison was apparently short of corn flakes and washing powder (don't ask me why), so, with easy access to the capacious storage in the Back Hatch at the rear of the Victor, we loaded up our Red Cross parcel of these supplies.

On our arrival on the Friday afternoon, we were met by our enthusiastic and grateful Royal Scots friends, and were immediately invited to the Officers' Mess at Epi for the traditional Happy Hour. Well, strangely enough, one thing led to another, and we were delighted to accept the invitation to dinner there and join in the ongoing festivities. As these things will, the volume was turned up to full, and various silly games got going. Determined not to be outdone, the crew set to with a will to show the RAF to best advantage. At a fairly late stage, the challenge was to get on the large table and down a succession of flaming drinks – and we did really well! So well, in fact, that a very irate RAF Wing Commander, who was the PMC (President of the Mess Committee, in charge of the Officers' Mess), roared into the room and declared that this was the last straw in the misbehaviour of the young Army officers – they would be immediately banned from the Mess. Whereupon, with a seraphic smile, Plonky gestured winningly to the PMC and revealed that the rapidly sobering team standing on the table, were, in fact, proud members of Her Majesty's Royal Air Force. So that's what friends are for!

I am delighted to say that the PMC realised that it was not just we who had been set up, but that the net had been cast wide enough to wrap him in its embrace as well. Whilst not exactly pleased with us, he did, at least, have the grace not to do much more than accept our rapid withdrawal from a distinctly untenable position.

As an afternote, we were due to leave RAF Akrotiri on the Monday morning. However, in the Operations block prior to the flight, we were briefed that there was a spot of bother at the gates of the base. Local passions had been inflamed, for some reason or another, and protesters had arrived in an ugly mood. The day was being saved by the presence of Plonky and his men, who had reinforced the defences. Given the calm surface wind, we were offered a choice of runways, but nobody had immediate knowledge of the state of play at the gate, where, were we take off on the westerly runway, we could possibly be within shooting distance of the protesters. During a quick call to Plonky, on a frequency that only he and I knew (and anyone else who was listening!), he vouchsafed that a couple of shots had been fired, but that nothing too serious had broken out. Nonetheless, he advised that, if we had a choice, a departure out to the east might well be the better option, so as not to stir things up further. For the second time that weekend I followed Plonky's advice, but this time with happier consequences.

The Hunter In The Far East

The Hunter Squadrons in the Far East in the 1960s (Nos 20 and 28 Squadrons) were equipped with the latest Day Fighter Ground Attack (DF/GA) Mk 9 variant of the Hawker Hunter. I was posted to No 20 Squadron, at RAF Tengah in Singapore, in mid-1966, as a third-tourist, initially as the Squadron Pilot Attack Instructor (PAI), responsible for all weapons training and delivery, and later 'promoted' (in hierarchy not rank!) to command A Flight, in early 1968. At this distance in time, some 40 years after leaving the Squadron, one's recollections become clouded with nostalgia, and probably also a number of inaccuracies - for which, dear reader, I can only apologise. The advancing years play tricks on one's addled brain-cells! However, I am not addled about the Hunter's role as part of Tengah's Strike Wing, during the latter days of 'Confrontation' with Indonesia.

Our role on 20 Squadron was, principally, to deter and, by default, to attack any intruders by air, sea or land against Malaysia or Singapore. To this end, we trained in Practice Interceptions (PIs) at high and low level, Close Air Support (CAS), in support of ground forces, and 'Strike' (but not as in NATO's nuclear strike!) missions, against ground targets anywhere in Malaysia. These would, had actual hostilities developed, have typically included convoys, troop concentrations, lines of communication, command and control centres, supply depots etc. In the more benign environment that prevailed in the late 60s, such targets had, of course, to be simulated, with suitable examples being few and far between in the sparsely-populated areas of mainly jungle over which we operated. Over time, we built-up quite a library of strike targets - such as bridges, kampongs, small clearings used as football pitches(!), isolated buildings etc. Many of these we established using our own F95[1]-equipped Hunters, but we were grateful for the support of the PR[2] Canberras of No 81 Squadron, co-located with us at Tengah. A typical training strike sortie, involving a 4-ship armed with simulated 3 inch rockets and 4 x 30mm Aden cannons, against a target up-country would,

---

[1] F95 - A downward, and sideways-facing, reconnaissance camera, made by Vinten, and mounted in the starboard side of the FGA9 nose section.

[2] PR – Photo Reconnaissance.

because of the distance involved, require a Hi-Lo-Hi profile. The profile would include a climb-out and transit at high-level for about 30 minutes, a let-down for a 20-minute low-level approach and attack, and a 30-minute return at high level.

Sounds simple enough, and not materially different in concept from standard Hi-Lo-Hi profiles practised in other theatres. Except! Except that navigation in FEAF[3] was something of an occult art! Firstly, the Hunter had none of the sophisticated navigation aids that make life so easy for today's generation of fighter/attack pilots. SatNav had yet to be invented, as had any sort of Inertial Navigation equipment or moving-map display, as later seen in the Jaguars and Harriers which superseded the Hunter. We had to rely on the time-honoured principle of heading/speed/distance to give time en-route, hoping that the forecast wind was accurate! Add to this, of course, a map, the details on which were hazy at best (areas uncharted!) and the jungle beneath, which, to the untutored eye, seemed completely featureless. Many an experienced Hunter pilot, new in theatre, was humbled to become 'temporarily uncertain of his position' (and I certainly counted myself amongst their number), when a first-tourist, with a year or so in theatre, was able to find the target. One quickly got to learn that skill and experience were no substitute for local knowledge!

We devoted at least 25% of our training time to weapons delivery, and this was always a highlight of the programme. In addition to using local ranges at Ulu Tiram, Asahan and China Rock, once a year the Squadron moved up to the RAAF[4] Base at Butterworth in the north-west corner of Malaysia, opposite Penang, for its Armament Practice Camp (APC), using primarily the coastal Range at Song-Song, about which more in a moment. One of the more contentious weapons that we trained to deliver in theatre (but not up at Butterworth!) was napalm – a fire-bomb, described in media-hype as 'indiscriminate burning of women and children', as a result of some unfortunate footage from Vietnam. Consequently, our training was never described as 'napalm' delivery (although we had stocks of 100-gallon tanks of the stuff); but, it would be right to place napalm in context, as it was hardly a new weapon. Napalm was, in essence, a

---

[3] FEAF – Far East Air Force.
[4] RAAF – Royal Australian Air Force.

fire-bomb/fuel gel mixture, designed to stick to – and burn - its target, rather than to spread widely. It was composed of polystyrene plus benzene, to solidify the gasoline, and was, despite fears to the contrary, remarkably stable, requiring an igniter to set it off. Napalm had been in use since WW2, most notably in reducing much of Dresden to ashes in early 1945, and has been widely used – although not much reported – in every war since. Had we been called upon to use it, it would have been controversially effective in clearing jungle hide-outs etc, whilst demoralizing the enemy. The preferred method of delivery was a level drop from 50 feet and 420 knots, as the target disappeared under the nose. Hence our training in this method of delivery was with 25-lb practice bombs, whose aerodynamics were designed to be similar to that of the napalm tank - but sometimes things do not go as planned!

These 25 lb practice bombs were crutched in pairs into an open bomb carrier, usually mounted on the Hunter's inboard pylons[5], if the range was close enough not to need the external fuel tanks. The Hunter's armament circuits were pretty basic; if the pilot selected the appropriate pylon, armed that circuit, and 'pickled' the release button, the store on that pylon would release. Easy! Except that, if the practice carrier were on that pylon, it would be necessary to check that an additional switch within the pylon was set to ensure that the release pulse went to the bombs and not to the carrier. Obvious really! And certainly, this requirement was repeatedly reinforced to all armourers and pilots. Does anyone see Murphy's Law coming into play here? Sure enough, both armourer and pilot screwed-up one day with the result that, when the pilot pickled, the carrier released with both bombs still aboard, and plummeted to earth well short of the target. This was colloquially known as a 'switch-pigs' and, despite protestations from the pilot about an 'inadvertent (and thus not recordable) release', I insisted that the scores for both bombs stand, and that both armourer and pilot retrieve the carrier from the Range. They did so with considerable loss of dignity!

Song-Song was an unpretentious, over-water weapons range, a short flight to the south-west of Butterworth, but with limited facilities. It did, however, have some excellent, clearly-defined, 15 foot square hessian targets, which were ideal for air-ground gunnery, and for which we carried 60 rounds of 30mm ball

---

[5] Pylons - A pylon connects the frame of an aircraft to an item or object that is being carried.

ammunition, using one of the 4 selectable Aden cannons. Each pair of aircraft normally had a 15-minute range slot, which allowed for one practice 'dry' run, plus up to five live 'hot' runs, to fire off the 60 rounds. The Range Safety Officer (RSO), whose word was law, strictly controlled time on target, and he (rightly) never allowed any of us to extend the range slot to accommodate anyone who had been unable to 'bring their guns to bear' in the allotted time. One of the features at Song-Song was the cross-wind, which was usually benign at dawn, increasing steadily throughout the day. Every pilot therefore wanted the first slot of the day and, as the PAI in charge, I was responsible for ensuring that each had his fair share, me included. To add spice to the event, the APC featured an inter-Flight competition, with the ground-crew running a 'book' on the outcome, plus a sweepstake on each individual pilot. I was sufficiently young, arrogant and confident to fancy my chances as an individual winner, and thus lead the Flight to victory! Pride before a fall, indeed! On the morning to which this story relates, I led our pair to the Range for the first slot at 0900 hours. The weather was perfect with not a breath of wind. I had selected a well-harmonised aircraft, firing an inner gun, and was fully expecting to 'fill my boots'. However, we arrived to find the Range closed; a Malay fishing boat was illegally casting its nets just within the Danger Area, and the RSO would allow no firing until it cleared off. Steam rising from every orifice, I cajoled and pleaded, even abusing such authority as I had as the Sqn PAI (which cut no ice at all!) to shift the whole morning's programme by 30 minutes. I then lost control, and threatened to 'fire a warning shot across the boat's bow' to encourage him to move on, whereupon, I was told to 'leave the Range immediately'. Oh what shame and humiliation! Later, I grovelled an apology to the RSO and to my Boss, and was lucky that this potential 'international incident' did not turn out to be entirely career-limiting!

Following the withdrawal of No 28 Squadron's Hunters from RAF Kai Tak, Hong Kong, in 1967, 20 Squadron was authorised to detach a Flight up there twice a year to 'maintain an RAF presence'. On each detachment, because there wasn't much else to do in such a restricted area, we used Port Shelter Range - a flat rocky promontory on the east side of the New Territories coastline. The range included a 'dive circle', shaped like a dart board, in the centre of which was a prominent Bull's Eye, the striking of which was awarded a DH (Direct Hit), and much kudos. This was an ideal target on which to practise our 25 degree rocketry. That day, when I was assessing the morning's results, I noticed that the scores were all over the place, with a few pilots being unable to fire even remotely accurately. The cine film, from the cameras recording the image through the gun-sights, displayed a lack of concentration, leading to sloppy tracking and poor accuracy. And then the story emerged! Apparently, on the night before, a posse of pilots had made a foray into downtown Kowloon to sample the delights therein. After probably more libations than was wise, they had been lured into the back streets to see a 'movie'- colour not specified! The star of this movie was a young lady of ample charms and dubious virtue, who was performing 'an unnatural act' right there on top of the Port Shelter Bull's Eye. The following morning on the Range, the young pilots, when turning in to attack, were diverted from their purpose of tracking the target by haunting images of this young lady performing on the Bull's Eye. Clearly, this was a novel diversionary tactic, which offered great potential for an enemy to develop. The mind boggles!

And finally, although nothing to do with weaponry but everything to do with flying in Hong Kong, we turn to night flying – a nemesis for most day-fighter boys. For reasons that escaped me at the time (and even now leave me bemused), we were tasked to go night flying whilst based at RAF Kai Tak, where, let it be remembered, we shared the only runway with all Hong Kong's civil airline traffic, the latter invariably expecting priority for landing. The night in question was overcast, with light rain and a strong-ish wind from the South, making for a tricky approach and landing on the duty Runway 13. The approach on the base leg to this runway, heading North-East, was over the middle of Kowloon – a mass of flashing and disorientating neon lights. You headed for what was known locally as The Checker Board, fortunately illuminated and easy enough to see, but itself mounted on a hill-side. You aimed directly for this feature until you could pick up the runway lights, out to your right, whereupon you turned on to finals, passing high-rise buildings on your wing-tip, and manoeuvred to make a successful landing. On a clear day, it certainly concentrated the mind but, on a dark and rainy night with a cross-wind, it was sufficient to make one contemplate a change of underwear. I have been lucky enough to survive many dicey landings before and since, but none was more scary than that first night landing on Kai Tak's Runway 13.

And so, how should one sum up flying Hunters in the Far East in the 1960s, as opposed to flying them in any other theatre? Flying a Hunter anywhere was always a joy, because it was truly a gentleman's aircraft. But it was especially a joy in the Far East, because of the frisson of the role within the large Strike Wing, which included four other Squadrons at Tengah. In those days, one could fly almost anywhere, at any height (within reason), as very little of the airspace was controlled and most of the terrain was uninhabited. There was always a sense of purpose, with a grumbling Indonesia to the South, and a full-blown war to the North in Vietnam. Add in a colonial life-style in the splendid Officers' Mess, together with the many social and sporting delights in Singapore itself, and those of us privileged and lucky enough to have been a part of them were blessed indeed. Those were the Golden Years!

Credit: Geoff Lee

The Unkindest (Defence) Cut of All

I'm the last man left in the Air Force, I've an office in MoD.
And a copy of Queen's Regulations, which only apply to me.
I can post myself to Leuchars, and detach me from there to Kinloss
Or send me on courses to Innsworth, then cancel the lot - I'm the Boss.

I'm the last man left in the Air Force, but the great parliamentary brains
Omitted, when cancelling people, to sell off the stations and planes,
The result is, my inventory bulges with KD and camp stools and Quarters,
Plus a signed book of speeches by Trenchard that I keep to impress the reporters.

I'm the last man left in the Air Force, I suppose you imagine it's great
To be master of all you survey, but I tell you, it's difficult, mate.
I inspected three units last Thursday, as AOC. (Acting) of Strike,
Then I swept half the runway at Laarbruch and repaired Saxa Vord's station bike.

I'm the last man left in the Air Force, my wife says I'm never at home,
When I'm not flying Hercs, I'm at Manston, laying gallons and gallons of foam,
Or I'm in my Marine Craft at Plymouth, shooting flares at the crowds on the Ho,
Or I'm Orderly Corporal at Uxbridge, it's an interesting life, but all go.

I'm the last man left in the Air Force, I'm ADC to the Queen,
I'm Duty Clerk at St. Mawgan, I'm the RAF rugby team,
Tomorrow I'm painting a guardroom, and air-testing several planes,
The day after that I'm in London, to preach at St. Clement Danes.

I'm the last man left in the Air Force, and I'm due to retire before long,
There's no talk of any replacement, and I won't even let me sign on.
I hope to enjoy my retirement, I've put up a pretty good show,
But I won't cut myself off entirely. There are always reunions, y'know.

© Peter Wyton

Night Fright

The place was RAF Bruggen, the date 27th August 1953, the time about 1030pm. I was serving with No 112(Shark) Squadron, having arrived at RAF Jever, in the north of Germany, in late 1952. The Squadron had recently moved to Bruggen and would be joined later by No 130 Squadron, which was in the process of reforming. Both squadrons were flying Vampires but were about to be re-equipped with the new, Canadian-built F86 Sabre, to form No 135 Wing. Two years later, the Sabres would be replaced by Hawker Hunters (with superior performance) which were being built by Hawker Siddeley.

Bruggen was a new NATO airfield, built close to the Dutch border near Roermond, about 40 miles to the west of Dusseldorf. It was the most northerly of the three 'Clutch' airfields, all built to the same pattern and spaced about 10 miles apart; the others were RAF Wildenrath and RAF Geilenkirchen. All three were strategically placed, with reference to the East German border, and designed to accept the higher-performance fighters. The airfield consisted of one east/west concrete runway (8000 feet long, cut out of a forest of fir trees), with dispersals at either end. RAF Laarbruch, to the north, would be built some years later, but the clearing in the forest was already easily seen from above. The three airfields all looked the same from the air, so, in the early days, one or two squadron pilots, following a 'run in and break' at the end of their sorties, landed at the wrong airfield. 'Not visual' calls from Air Traffic Control (ATC) did not seem to deter them. In fact, one pilot, after landing and realizing the awful truth, taxied past the three hangars, still on his own local radio frequency, and took off again in the forlorn hope that his Boss wouldn't get to find out. There, but for the grace of God etc!

The Station Commander was Group Captain Crawford Compton, CBE, DSO, DFC and Bar, (and Croix de Guerre), who had distinguished himself during the Battle of Britain although, oddly, none of us were aware of his past. He was a very fit New Zealander, who had joined the RAFVR and trained as a Sergeant Pilot, after working his passage to Liverpool as a ship's carpenter. He was a tough but well-liked commander, who subsequently captained the RAF Ski team in his mid-fifties, and was eventually promoted to Air Marshal. He also became the stepfather of Duncan Goodhew, the Olympic swimmer, and I met him again, quite by chance, at Suez in 1956, after we had both volunteered to take part in the invasion. He sadly died of cancer, aged 71, a few years after his retirement.

The building programme at Bruggen was behind schedule when the squadron flew in; and, although the airfield and hangars had been completed, many other buildings were still under construction. I have memories of large piles of sand and earth-moving vehicles working round the clock in the months that followed. We were part of the 2nd ATAF (Allied Tactical Air Force), whose task was to oppose the Russian threat from Eastern Germany. At that time, there were many RAF squadrons operating out of at least seven airfields, all in support of BAOR (The British Army of the Rhine). The American Zone (1st ATAF) covered the southern, more scenic, part of the country, including Bavaria. At that time, the USAF was operating Sabres fitted with the more powerful 'Orenda' engine. Flying into their zone without warning was one of the standard exercises; waiting for their GCI[1] stations to locate us and hoping that their aircraft would be scrambled to intercept. The ensuing free-for-alls were very hairy, and there was always a risk of collision when up to six of our aircraft would be doing their best to get behind one of theirs. If fortunate, you might get close enough to record a Sabre on your gun-sight camera and could claim some success. They, in turn, would occasionally penetrate into our airspace, but they knew we couldn't catch them in our Vampires unless we had the advantage of being up there first; even then, they could easily outrun us. Operating in both the air-to-air and air-to-ground roles was a lot of fun and very testing, but the Vampire would have been no match for the Russian MiG 17. As things turned out, we never got to see one.

Prior to our conversion on to the F86, a night flying programme was planned, which would make us night-current again after a number of previous cancellations. The Met Forecaster was a German who had previously briefed Luftwaffe pilots; his English was quite good but, naturally, with a distinct Teutonic accent. Fog (in reality more like smog) often drifted in from the highly industrialised Ruhr valley, about 40 miles to the east and, if he mentioned "clout" or "tic fok", night flying would be instantly postponed to a future, unspecified

---

[1] GCI – Ground-Control Interception.

date. However, on this particular night, the area forecast was good throughout the flying period, and the night flying programme was confirmed. At the brief, we were all given the choice of taking off at dusk (and landing after dark) or delaying for a night take off. As far as I remember, nearly all of us opted to delay, and were briefed for a 45 minute sortie which would include general handling, aerobatics, circuits and roller landings[2]. After landing, and before repairing to the bar, we always planned to head straight to the Airmen's Mess for a night flying supper; they were not to be missed and would have done justice to any hotel breakfast!

I took off on Runway 27, towards the Dutch border, and then climbed east towards Cologne. I recall the crystal clear conditions, and seeing Dusseldorf and Cologne all lit up. Large towns were easy to identify, the winding, unlit course of the Rhine well defined and, above the horizon, the starlit sky was spectacular. I was between 8000 and 9000 feet and still climbing when, without warning, there was a very loud 'pop' followed by a rapid decrease in engine RPM. At the same time, the engine 'whine' faded quickly until everything went very quiet (the Vampire was sometimes referred to as the "Tin Whistle" because of the constant high pitched whine, which was associated with the Rolls-Royce Goblin engine's centrifugal compressor). Within seconds the cockpit flood-lighting had failed, but I could still see some of the flight instruments, so I suspected that the ultra-violet lights were working. For a moment I was concerned that I must have forgotten something and would be in trouble. After strapping in, connecting the oxygen hose, R/T lead etc., checking for full fuel and pressing the starter button, there was little else to remember. The important thing was not to be the last to start and to be the first in the air if you possibly could. You had to know the contents of the Flight Reference Cards (FRCs), which were stowed in a flying suit pocket; but the Emergency Drills, at the back of the FRCs, were just for ground school exams or preparing for a pilots' quiz. I mean, emergencies didn't actually happen in the air!

I instinctively set a glide attitude, headed back west and looked round the cockpit for whatever it was that I must have forgotten. All the levers and

---

[2] Roller landings – where an aircraft comes in to land but, instead of stopping, the pilot applies power and takes off again.

switches appeared to be in the correct positions and, although I can't remember now, I expect that many of the electrical instruments would have failed. The prescribed drill, in event of engine failure at night, was to abandon the aircraft - we had no ejection seats then but we did have a standard seat parachute. Abandoning meant unplugging your helmet R/T lead, jettisoning the canopy, inverting the aircraft, undoing the seat harness and dropping out (leaving the aircraft in a normal, upright attitude would result in striking the twin tail-boom). After releasing the seat harness you were supposed to push the stick forward to assist in making a clean exit. Then you would need to locate your parachute release handle and wait for it to open. However, the thought of falling, head-first into the inky black, put the fear of God into me and I gave up the idea immediately. I didn't think anyone had ever done it at night and I wasn't keen to be a trend-setter.

In the cockpit, apart from the eerie silence, things didn't seem too bad; I could see the airfield lights very clearly below me and, with ample height, decided to force-land on the runway. I remember making a rather feeble, non-standard, emergency radio call, saying that I had had an 'engine failure' but was 'too low to bale out' (not true, but I felt slightly guilty and needed to cover myself). Fortunately for me, Air Traffic Control only heard the first part, and landed or diverted those aircraft that were still airborne. In the event, I did not get any reply because the aircraft battery had failed at the same time as the generator. According to what we had been told in ground-school, the 28 volt DC supply was good for 15 minutes after a total engine failure; but my battery must have been well past its sell-by date, because it lasted less than a minute. The same instructor had also explained that, in the event of a hydraulic pump failure, there was an accumulator that would allow a (down) selection of the undercarriage and one application of the wheel brakes. Operating the airbrakes would result in dumping this precious reserve of pressure so, in the event of a hydraulic pump failure, it was important not to use them. Having got the answer right in the exam, I was about to demonstrate that I had forgotten all about it when it mattered most.

I had learnt to glide as a CCF cadet and had stayed on as a staff cadet, which meant you got some extra launches and became more confident. Fortunately for me, the Vampire controls were manual (not hydraulically or electrically assisted), and the gliding qualities were almost too good. I was able to make a couple of descending orbits over the airfield prior to planning the approach, but ended up rather high and fast – at which point I selected the airbrakes! They came out halfway and stuck. I then selected the flaps, which immediately retracted when the slipstream forced them up again. I might have been able to hand-pump the undercarriage down, had I thought about it, which would have slowed me; however, wheels didn't seem important at the time and, in any case, they may not have locked fully down. I flew over the runway caravan at about 50 feet going much too fast for comfort and scaring the runway caravan controller[3]. He later confessed that it gave him quite a fright when a black shape passed over his head, unannounced, showing no lights and accompanied only by the sound of rushing air - in the excitement, ATC had forgotten to warn him!

I was still airborne with over half the runway length now behind me and I didn't look like stopping, so I remember deciding to put the aircraft on the runway, regardless of the speed. Fortunately it was a very smooth touchdown on the belly, and the aircraft came to rest about 150 yards from the end of the runway. The metal band around the wooden fuselage had caused an impressive shower of sparks and exciting sound effects, before the aircraft came to rest; this alerted some of the squadron pilots who, unaware of my adventure, gathered around the open hangar doors. I knew that the friction had started a small fire beneath the cockpit and, in my haste to get clear, I ran about fifty yards, still wearing my parachute! The entire flight had taken less than ten minutes, and the fire crew quickly extinguished the hot bit.

I think 'Big G' must have been with me that night, as I survived, despite having forgotten the correct drills, and think I must have had a large bucket of good luck to counter my inexperience. The Master Engineer groundschool instructor would not have been impressed! The aircraft sustained relatively minor damage, and I believe that she was made airworthy again by a team from the Maintenance Unit about eight weeks later, but I'm not certain. I was most relieved to learn the following day that the Quill drive (thinner than a pencil), which connected the fuel pump to the gearbox, had sheared due to metal fatigue. When that happened, the engine, generator, hydraulic pump and nearly

---

[3] The runway controller sat in a small caravan adjacent to the runway threshold and monitored aircraft about to take-off or land. The controller used an Aldis lamp to communicate with aircraft, and by flashing a green or red he indicated whether it was clear to proceed.

everything that a pilot would depend on, failed at the same time.

With the runway obstructed, the night flying programme was cancelled, much to the delight of everyone, including the hierarchy. Unfortunately the night flying suppers were cancelled too, so everyone went straight to the Mess bar. The drinking went on to the early hours, but we all flew the next day - after a late start.

Credit: Arnaud Gaillard/Wikipedia

Bored by a Life of Routine?
(Then Come And Fly With A Blue Steel)

What is the last thing that a pilot would want in or near his aeroplane? Perhaps something that can spontaneously set light to any combustible material it touches, something that will do serious injury if it gets onto skin, something that will emit a cloud of vapour, which is a mixture of fire-producing droplets and oxygen that will keep the fire going nicely. Not only would such a substance be dangerous near aeroplanes, but you could add to the excitement by making it so temperamental that it sits around quietly until such time as it decides to go unstable, whereupon it starts to get hotter and hotter, eventually creating a self-sustaining and spectacular fire. What might they call such a substance? How about High Test Peroxide or HTP?

Now, what did they do with this HTP? They put it into Blue Steel missiles, which were slung underneath our Vulcan Mk 2s of the RAF Scampton Wing. True, we did not have to sit on top of HTP the whole time, for we mostly flew with training rounds (with no innards other than the INS[1]), or inert rounds which had engines etc, but no fuel. When we did fly with a fuelled missile, we had to carry a large box in the rear cockpit containing two sets of protective clothing, to be put on by the Plotter[2] and Nav Rad[2] who, following an emergency in the air, had to off-load the HTP from the missile, once we got the temperamental beast back on the ground.

I had one such experience in 1964. We were flying late at night, heading for Northern Scotland, when my nocturnal dreaming was rudely shattered by a very loud and repeated banging. I was instantly fully alert and did a rapid scan of the cockpit instruments, all of which were indicating that the aircraft was behaving normally; but the banging continued. I called up the crew, "Does anyone know what that banging noise is?" "It's only Tony trying to open his soup can with the fire axe", came the calm reply. The Nav Rad had forgotten his tin opener, which he needed for piercing his can, before putting it into one of the can heaters which allowed all of us in Eating Command to dine with a soup course, before

---

[1] INS – Inertial Navigation System.
[2] The two navigators in a Vulcan crew.

moving onto a steak sandwich or cold roast chicken. Tony eventually managed to pierce his can of Heinz tomato, and we all relaxed again.

About an hour after the incident with Tony's soup, the AEO[3], who was monitoring the HTP-filled missile beneath us, said, "The HTP temp has risen a bit". After another twenty minutes, this was followed by, "Temp's still rising but now more quickly". I decided it was time to get the Vulcan on the ground as soon as possible and turned towards RAF Leuchars, initiating a PAN[4] call. I told Leuchars we were diverting to them with a hot missile on board and, when we landed, it seemed that the whole station was waiting for us. There were fire engines, ambulances, RAF Police, the Station Commander and lots of engineers milling around. By this time, though, the protective suits had been donned by the Navs, and the resident firemen were spraying water all over the place. Under the aircraft, however, the HTP seemed to have stabilised itself and we had no need for an emergency off-load. It was all a bit of an anti-climax, and the highly trained HTP handling specialists seemed quite disappointed.

Our next experience with HTP was one of pure amusement for my crew, but not for the star of the show. Before HTP came into service with Blue Steel, open pits were dug around the Scampton perimeter, and also at all the V- Force dispersal locations and RAF master diversion airfields. These pits were about 20 yards by 15 yards, and about 6 feet deep at the centre, and were placed beside designated HTP off-load dispersals. Now, what HTP really enjoys is a good piece of rubbish, to act as a catalyst to start it going. Half-eaten NAAFI sausage rolls and discarded tabloid newspapers are ideal, and where were such things to be found in quantity? At the bottom of all the open HTP off-load pits. After an HTP off-load into one of these rubbish filled pits, it wasn't long before a cloud of HTP vapour would start drifting across the airfield and, if it passed any lit cigarette dangling from the lips of an unwary airman, his fag would burst into flame thus ruining his smoke, and also his moustache if he had one. After several HTP incidents, these open pits were abandoned, and replaced by vertical shafts about 8 feet in diameter, dug into the ground and capped with a concrete pad and a large man-hole cover.

---

[3] AEO - Air Electronics Officer.
[4] PAN - A state of urgency exists, although there is no imminent danger to life or the continued viability of the aircraft.

It was a lovely sunny summer's day, and my crew had come onto QRA[5] duty about two hours earlier. We had checked our QRA aircraft, with its loaded weapon, and set the systems and switches to allow us to taxi with the minimum of delay, should we get a practice scramble. We had time to spare before we needed to be elsewhere, so we just lay in the sun on the grass, watching the airfield activity, chewing grass stalks and listening to the skylarks singing away overhead. Nearby was one of the new-model HTP off-load pits and, as the odd wisp of vapour squeezed itself from the edge of the man-hole cover, it was obvious that an HTP off-load had recently taken place. The vapour wisps grew denser and more frequent, and eventually the edge of the cover lifted and released a small vapour cloud before the pressure dropped and the lid fell back in place. Our attention was now firmly fixed on the drama that was rapidly unfolding before us. Eventually the lid was lifted clear of the manhole and a volcano-like eruption developed, with a huge cloud of HTP vapour emerging, apparently from the centre of the earth.

We were about to call someone to tell them what was happening when an RAF Police Land-Rover appeared so, as everything was now presumably under control, we didn't bother. The policeman got out of his vehicle, wandered over to the edge of the eruption and stared at it, whilst reporting the situation to his control office by radio. This was obviously the Corporal's first encounter with HTP, otherwise he would not have parked his canvas-covered vehicle downwind of the off-load pit in the midst of the HTP cloud. Having reported the situation to his superiors, he climbed back into the Land-Rover and drove away. We watched him go with a certain degree of apprehension and, sure enough, when he had gone about 200 yards, the Land-Rover cover burst into flames and a very startled Corporal fell out of the driver's door.

The introduction of Blue Steel with its HTP fuel certainly added a new dimension to life at Scampton!

---

[5] QRA – Quick Reaction Alert.

A First Night Landing

A pilot's confidence and ability go through various stages during his career. There are times when over-confidence makes him think he knows everything and is invincible. This usually occurred, with the fighter pilots of my generation, when they had achieved about five or six hundred hours, and it was a very dangerous stage. However, before that there was another period which flying instructors warned against. This happened to student pilots who had qualified for their initial licence in the civil world, and had altogether flown about fifty hours. In military flying, this would occur as the successful end of basic training came in sight. In their own minds, these pilots had no more to learn. The sky was theirs and they could do anything with their aircraft.

It was early February 1949, and I thought that I was the bee's knees! The previous autumn I had come ashore, after serving at sea as an apprentice in the Merchant Navy, and immediately joined the West London Flying Club at White Waltham. I had a very happy time there, and obtained my 'A' Licence flying Tiger Moths - the 'A' Licence being the equivalent of today's Private Pilot's Licence. The West London Flying Club grew out of the wartime Air Transport Auxiliary, the ATA. Most of the staff, and many of the members too, had been ferry pilots during the war, and I became steeped in ATA lore, absorbing their stories and experiences as only a brand-new trainee pilot, such as I was, could. I listened avidly to all of the bar talk and, looking back, I think that some of the cautionary tales were designed to kick some flying sense into me, while they thought there was still a chance!

I had about forty hours in my log book, and was quite sure that I knew all about it. Also, I had, by then, walked into a recruiting office and joined the Royal Air Force. That led to aircrew selection at Hornchurch, where I had been passed fit for pilot training, and I was now awaiting orders to report to RAF Cardington. There, I would actually become immersed in the RAF. I just knew it; a flying future would all be mine.

Unfortunately, I had just about used up all my money, and was working for my keep on my brother's farm near Salisbury. It was no longer possible for me to fly at White Waltham, but Thruxton was nearby. I therefore joined the Wiltshire School of Flying and, occasionally, as wages for farm work, my brother stood the cost of an hour or two in the air. This was no longer on Tiger Moths, because the school used Austers. However, I was already a type-hunter, so that was fine by me, and I found the Auster's enclosed cabin very luxurious compared to the Tiger's open cockpit. At Thruxton, I was also introduced to my first low-wing monoplane, the Miles Magister, which was used to teach spinning and aerobatics. That brought my total of different types up to five, and definitely added to my swelled head. I was surely heading for trouble.

At Hornchurch, I had made friends with another successful candidate named Bill. He flew out of Fairoaks, and suggested that I should come over in an Auster one day and meet up with him. Thruxton to Fairoaks was easy; virtually all I had to do was to pick up the main Southern Railway line at Andover, follow it past Basingstoke and Farnborough, then turn left at Woking. Fairoaks should be there in front of me! It was a bright clear day, with good visibility, and Fairoaks was there, right on my nose, just where it should have been. Feeling very pleased with myself, I joined the circuit in the prescribed manner, and landed. There were no special entry lanes or routes as such in those days, one just obeyed the regular rules of the air and got on with it.

I was, in fact, slightly worried, as I rather felt that I had got too close to Farnborough. It had been drummed into me that I must keep line features on my left when following them; that went with the bit about making sure that you were following the correct railway. However, Farnborough was also on the right of the line, and I was sure it was less than two miles away. Even the few regulations that there were in those days could catch a new pilot out, however good he thought he might be. I therefore hoped that I had not been noticed, and I was all right, I never heard a thing about it.

Bill and I sat and talked excitedly about our futures in the RAF as the afternoon slipped by. Afternoons do not last long in February anyway, and Bill still wanted a flight in the Auster, so off we went. It was just for twenty minutes around the local area, but suddenly it was dusk. Oh-oh!

"Bill, I must go. I'll be flying in the dark." I had never done any night flying at all and was a bit worried. He replied that I'd be alright, but I was not so confident. I got airborne and, by then, dusk was rapidly approaching. The flight would take about forty minutes and, by the time I reached Thruxton, I had visions of it being quite dark. I had done a stupid thing, it was all my fault and I had got properly caught out. Firstly there was night navigation; how did one find one's way around in the dark? I had no torch and knew nothing of the set-up for the aircraft's night flying equipment, where the light switches were or even if it had any. I could no longer see the instruments properly, was being thoroughly stupid, but I still decided that I must press on. Obviously the railway line that I had followed to Fairoaks, earlier in the day, would take me back down into Wiltshire. Then I remembered all the stories that I had heard in the bar at White Waltham from the ATA pilots. Following the wrong railway, road or river was common and good for a laugh in the bar, but not now, especially now, late on a February afternoon.

There were many more railway lines running across the country then than there are now, with large steam locomotives on all of them. These were easy to see in the dark. They had great big fires that poured light out of the cab whenever the fire door was opened and, because there was no more black-out, light also streamed out of the coach windows. The line of a railway was easy to see, but now there seemed to be railway lines running all over the place. In the event I was lucky, and picked up the same, main Southern Railway line to the west that I had followed earlier in the day.

With all the light from the carriages and the engines, I had no difficulty following it, and saw Basingstoke slide underneath, just as it should have done. By that time, lights were on all across the country, and I was amazed how I could pick out the bigger towns. Winchester was obvious, away to the south of me, and Andover was coming up ahead. Luckily it was a fine evening, in spite of being February when all sorts of poor visibility might be expected, especially in those days of coal fires. This was the first time that I had seen the countryside from the air in anything like the dark, and it fascinated me. However, my fascination was somewhat damped by the thought of how I was going to locate Thruxton and get back onto the ground when I did.

There seemed a long way to go and I was quite sure the coming darkness would beat me to it. I was also unsure about the route after Andover. The railway turned away to the southwest, in the direction of Salisbury, and there was nothing but countryside, with the possible help of the A303. Undaunted, I set off in what I thought was the right direction and was lucky. The road was not difficult to pick out and Thruxton was not very far along it. With great relief I saw the black bulk of the hangar, which then stood near the road at the edge of the airfield. The clubhouse and offices were in the old RAF control tower and, with its greyish colour and the lights from the windows, it was reasonably visible. I was orientated, knew where I was and could join the circuit. I felt pretty pleased with myself.

There was no flare path, which was probably a good thing as I certainly would not have known how to use it. I just went round the circuit, and set up an approach at what I thought was the right place. The wide expanse of the airfield was a dark hole in front of me, so I glided on towards where I thought the ground was and the touch down point should be. The lights from the clubhouse gave me a good mark to keep straight on, and it must still have been less than fully dark, because I saw the ground in time to round out and did not bounce too badly after touch down. I taxied up to the club house, parked and shut down the engine.

The instructor hierarchy at Thruxton was very different from the friendly atmosphere that I had known at White Waltham. Here, the Club was run by a retired squadron leader who always had to be addressed as 'Sir'. The instructor, whose job it was to look after me, was an ex-NCO pilot, so way down the pecking order. He had completed a tour on Lancasters, was, I thought, a very good instructor, and I certainly enjoyed flying with him. By contrast, the second-in-line was a friend of the squadron leader. He was very unpopular and had very little flying experience, not having been a wartime pilot it was said, but held a lot of sway in the organisation. He lived in a caravan, parked not far from the clubhouse, from where he would watch everything that was going on and dish out adverse comments to people about the way that they flew.

The sound of my taxying aircraft brought him rushing out to greet me. As I parked, I knew that I would be in trouble and fully expected my instructor to descend on me like a ton of bricks. I knew that I had done a stupid thing. I had hung around Fairoaks for much too long before starting back, but I felt that it was nothing to do with someone who nobody liked, nor had any respect for. I stood by the cabin door as he blasted away at me. However, during the course of his rant I realised, much to my amusement, that he did not even know my name. Then the clubhouse door swung open and a shaft of bright light shone out across the grass. There stood my instructor. He smiled and said, "Well done

Mike! That was really good, particularly considering that you've had no night flying training. To have found the airfield, and then make a decent landing when it's as dark as this, is great."

That started it. The unpopular instructor tore into mine with all the power that being a friend of the management could generate. My instructor responded by telling him that it was none of his business. As for me, I crept off and left them to it, slogging away at one another. After booking in, I taxied the Auster down to the hangar, put it away and went home.

It turned out to be a good lesson, but I was lucky to get away with it!

Credit: Arpingstone/Wikipedia

Who Wants To Be a QFI? I Didn't!

My first tour was eventful. Joining No 1(F) Squadron to fly the Harrier GR3, within days I was off to Decimomannu (on Sardinia) for an Armament Practice Camp (APC), followed rapidly by the first rush to Belize (which settled into a 10 weeks out, 10 weeks back routine), with regular deployments to Norway, Denmark, Germany and so on. I attended courses, to become a CSRO[1], EWO[2] and FRI[3], while my wife had two babies. And, after 2 ½ years of this, I was still a flying officer, struggling to make ends meet on the poor RAF pay of the day.

My second tour was enjoyable. As an FRI on IV(AC) Squadron, the Harrier reconnaissance[4] squadron, based at RAF Gütersloh, it was professionally rewarding. With promotion to flight lieutenant, the new military salary, Local Overseas Allowance and access to duty-free goods, fun became affordable. Nordrhein-Westfahlen was a great place for my two, blond-haired, blue-eyed boys to grow up. For 2 years, in addition to the normal fun and games of an RAFG squadron, I got to enjoy travelling around Europe, displaying the Harrier.

My third tour? Looking for something to surpass the first two, I volunteered[5] to go and fly the new Sea Harrier, which was just being introduced. However, a friend, who had taken that route a few months before me, reported back with tales of life on the ocean wave that somewhat dulled my enthusiasm. I called my desk officer[6] at Barnwood, and requested a change of posting plot. To my chagrin, I was told that becoming a QFI[7] at Valley was the only option. Apparently, too few fast-jet pilots, particularly Harrier pilots, had been allowed to go to the QFI empire in recent times, so 3 of us, from the same squadron,

---

[1] CSRO - Combat Survival and Rescue Officer
[2] EWO - Electronic Warfare Officer
[3] FRI - Fighter Reconnaissance Instructor.
[4] The FRI course taught me both how to spell reconnaissance and the advanced origami needed for multi-target missions.
[5] I should have known by this stage never to volunteer, but it seems to be a lesson that evades me to this day.
[6] Desk officer – The person who is responsible for your next posting. He reportedly told my flight commander that I had abused the open-door system, whereby 'negotiations' take place over the telephone or by letter.
[7] QFI – Qualified Flying Instructor.

were posted in quick succession. My brief look at the system suggested that there were some 250 RAF QFIs at that time, 100 of whom were engaged in teaching, standardising and examining the other 150, so I argued that I ought really not to be needed, or certainly not for so long. Nobody wanted to hear, so off I went.

The route from RAF Germany to RAF Valley in Anglesey was not so direct at that time, and required a detour to Yorkshire, for the CFS[8] ground-school and introductory flying at RAF Leeming. With the children growing, the ground-school period seemed like a good opportunity to get a vasectomy. I paid for the walk-in, crawl-out service in Leeds, ready to sit quietly in a classroom for recuperation. Inevitably, this was immediately followed by a surprise 'good deal', and off we went to Valley, for an early familiarisation trip in the Hawk. The demonstration of how much 'g' could be pulled, and for how long, particularly lingers in my memory, somewhere deep down. From the classroom, we progressed to the Jet Provost, for lessons in basic airborne teaching. I managed to shake off the habit of adding power just before touchdown, got used to moving my thumb along a map at such a slow rate, and duly set off to Valley to fly the Hawk. When I went to Valley as a student, there had been two aircraft types, the Gnat and the Hunter. I was tall, so I was too big for the Gnat and flew the Hunter. Returning to become an instructor, the two aircraft I faced were the Hawk and the Hunter. I was, apparently, too tall for the Hunter, so went to the Hawk.

On completion of the course, I joined 1 Squadron of No 4 Flying Training School. A new student course started as I arrived and, as the new B2 QFI, I got the 2 students at the end of the alphabetical list, both with surnames beginning with W. Exposure to real students began to show me some of the real benefits to be gained from being an instructor, firstly in terms of self-preservation. Once, on a glide approach, I allowed the student to press on until he too could see that we wouldn't reach the runway. Taking control, I applied full power, and was immediately reminded that the engine was an Adour, not a Pegasus (as fitted to the Harrier). The power 'bit' just in time to make it an acceptable roller landing but, considering that my aim had been to overshoot, that was too close for comfort. Then again, flying with a previously unknown student who was nearing the end of the course, we flew a low-level navex around Wales. His flying and navigation

---

[8] CFS – Central Flying School.

were very good. At the end, the syllabus called for me to fly a demonstration re-covery through the A5 pass. The student said that he had already seen the demo and, as he had flown so well, I agreed to let him fly this bit too. As he came to the corner where the valley bottom descends, he rolled the Hawk to a semi-inverted attitude, so as to use positive 'g' to turn the aircraft and to descend. That, I had expected; but not what came next. He snatched to 8g, already at low level, and with our heads pointing towards the ground. I took control, recovered to wings level, and climbed gently to check the aircraft...and prepare my explanation for the overstressed airframe.

Night teaching sorties had a limited repertoire of events, one being a simu-lated rapid descent from high level, as would be necessary in case of pressurisa-tion failure. During one such sortie, we talked through the procedure as the student climbed to height, then I closed the throttle to indicate to him that he should initiate the procedure. Sure enough, the aircraft rolled, albeit rather slowly, into a steeply banked attitude, and the 'g' increased as we spiralled down. I allowed this to continue until the control of bank and pitch became so erratic that I had to comment. The student's response was that he was not flying the aircraft; he had assumed that I was taking control when I closed the throttle!

The Valley high life was not to last for long. I settled in, and prepared for the QPNI[9] course, but the Mafia escape committee had been working on my be-half, and a request came in for me to go to the Harrier Operational Conversion Unit (OCU) as a QFI. It was agreed that I would become a B1 on the Hawk, and then move to Wittering. So my final Hawk flying was a landaway, with the Chief Instructor in the back seat, leading a pair, teaching low-level navigation on the way out and high-level formation on the way back. The champagne greeting on the pan at Valley conflicted somewhat with the CI's desire to complete the B1 ground test, but I was soon heading back across the Pennines in the car. I had spent just 6 months seeing through the course with the 2 Ws, who both became air defenders, so I don't know what I did wrong there. However, both are still flying in 2013, albeit commercially.

Working as a QFI on the Harrier brought a whole new range of challenges. Things happened very quickly in that jet and, in particular, the 2 levers by the left

---

[9] QPNI – Qualified Pilot Navigation Instructor.

hand have to be carefully monitored. Either the throttle or the nozzle lever can, and indeed should, be moved rapidly by the student, with significant effect. The QFI needs a strong left hand to be able to prevent the wrong one being used. By the time I started flying the Harrier, the old days of learning in the single-seater alone had long gone. We still had the 'horror film', from the days when student efforts were filmed from a safe distance; this was shown to students once they had completed the conversion phase of the OCU course. But we still needed to do a lot of supervision from outside the cockpit. For instance, the dual sortie on vertical take-off and landing typically lasted for less than 10 minutes, due to the low fuel load needed to achieve adequate performance. So, the student had flown perhaps 3 or 4 such manoeuvres before practising in the GR3. The QFI would then sit in a Land Rover, with a radio to enable instructions to be passed to the student. I watched one such exercise, with a student whose first language was not English, positioning the vehicle so that I could observe the aircraft from the side. I could see and hear as the student tested the engine and reaction controls, lowered the nozzles to the hover stop, and opened the throttle, all correctly. At this point, it is important to keep the control column central, so as not to invoke any of the reaction controls unnecessarily. In particular, if the control column is pulled back, this opens the pitch reaction control duct under the nose, from where hot air shoots down, stirring up potential FOD[10] which can then bounce back off the ground and into the engine air intakes, possibly leading to a surge. Well, this time I saw the rear of the tailplane move up, indicating that the experienced pilot had reverted to the conventional habit of pulling back to get airborne. I therefore called on the radio, "Close the throttle, close the throttle," but, almost immediately, saw the aircraft leave the ground. My instruction therefore changed to, "Keep the power on", as I attempted to keep in phase with events in the aircraft. Needless to say, the pilot heard little of this, student hearing being the first sense to disappear under pressure, even when the instructions are in their own language.

Another of my non-Anglophone students might have been expected to speak the language better, having come to us via advanced flying training in the USA. However, the United States Air Force appeared to have provided Spanish

---

[10] FOD – Foreign Object Damage. Refers to debris that may cause damage to an aircraft.

speaking instructors, so the English words didn't always flow well. I was supervising from the air traffic tower when the student called, "Downwind to slow land on the Alpha South." The controller turned to me for clarification, as a slow landing is at about 120 knots, while the Alpha South is an 80 foot square of concrete. I said to leave him alone, as there were no other aircraft in the circuit, so the student could either slow land on the main runway, or land vertically on the A South, doing no harm in either case. But he did neither; he performed a vertical landing on the blacktop of the main runway, burning yet another two scars in the surface.

Even from a greater distance, students could catch you out. One night, we sent two non-RAF students on a practice diversion to Valley, about 20 minutes apart. They were recalled, due to impending fog, and their tracks crossed as one turned back, with the other already heading for Wittering. Somehow, the one that had been 2000 feet higher departed from controlled flight, recovering at about 5000 feet after cruising at 35,000! He returned very sheepishly, without a convincing explanation that did not involve a turn-in to his mate's 6 o'clock.

While on 233 OCU I was also able to enjoy another 2 years of display flying, but, eventually, I had to comply with the system, and qualified as an A2 QFI on the Harrier before being promoted and posted back to Germany. That might have been the end of my instructional career, except that I took up gliding, and glider instructing, as a pastime. This introduced me to a whole new type of pilot, one that pays per lesson and carries on as long as he wants to. I could ensure safety by not letting them fly solo, and advise them if they were unlikely to do so but, if they wanted to carry on, they could. One very difficult solo decision was whether my son should do his first solo on his 16th birthday. This was a nice aim, but the wind was a bit gamey for such an exercise. He did do it but, while he was in the circuit, I did worry about how I would explain any mishap to Mum.

After Staff College and promotion, I returned to the front line as a Jaguar pilot but, subsequently, the QFI ticket again came in useful. I did a couple of staff tours (with flying) in the light aircraft business, before retiring with a CFS refresher course as resettlement training prior to becoming an FTRS[11] QFI. This took me into yet another corner of the instructional world, teaching

---

[11] FTRS - Full Time Reserve Service.

undergraduates with no proven aptitude, but with demonstrable academic potential and motivation. I soon discovered that the academic bit bore little relevance to practical airborne intelligence. I saw the complete spectrum of pilot aptitude, with a solid core of future professionals in the student body surrounded by an assortment of amusing aspirants. There was great satisfaction in seeing many students reaching first solo standard, though quite a few of them then needed to be advised that this, or maybe a Private Pilot's Licence, was as far as they were likely to progress. While the RN and Army run separate grading establishments, this function of the University Air Squadron system served the RAF well, adjusting ambitions at an early stage.

Becoming a reservist instructor provided me with several more years of paid flying, and a couple of thousand hours on another aircraft type, at the end of my RAF career. Once again, this proved how worthwhile it is to be a QFI, just like I had always said...

Credit: Geoff Lee

Trucky Stuff

On long, tedious, oceanic flights, trucky[1] crews needed something to help pass the time. A cargo of soldiers often provided a source of amusement and, of particular entertainment, was the use of the 'voice-responsive autopilot'. The loadmaster was tasked with selecting a suitable officer, hereinafter referred to as 'the grunt', who would be invited to have a change of scenery by visiting the flight deck. After a few minutes of general chat, the captain would throw into the conversation the fact that this particular C130 Hercules was fitted with an experimental autopilot. The grunt would inevitably ask for a demonstration, which would only be given reluctantly, because the equipment was still 'under development'. The captain would then point out the grille in the centre pedestal (actually for equipment ventilation), explaining that beneath it sat the microphone into which the voice instructions were delivered. He would then simply say, 'turn right', whereupon the navigator, pre-briefed and sitting behind the grunt, would input a right displacement of the Doppler (navigation) track which the autopilot was following. The unsuspecting grunt would be duly impressed, particularly when the command 'return to track' was equally smartly complied with by the voice-responsive system. Naturally, the grunt would then ask to control the autopilot himself, and the captain would respond that only he and other 'qualified' crew were voice-trained with the correct degree of authority in their commands to the autopilot. Grunt would reply that, being an infantry officer, he was quite used to using authoritative tones, and the captain would reluctantly permit him to try. For several minutes, with the grunt's face becoming ever redder, the veins standing out in his neck as he screeched into the 'microphone', the aircraft would steadfastly maintain an undeviating course. Suitably chagrined, the grunt would descend to the hellish freight bay of the C130 - to be greeted by the barely-concealed merriment of his men.

I once worked alongside Fleet Air Arm colleagues on a basic naval flying training unit in Yorkshire. Much banter between light- and dark-blue uniformed QFIs[2] was the norm, and we (RAF) were referred to as crabs. At

---

[1] trucky – A (complimentary?) term used to describe those who fly transport aircraft.

[2] QFI – Qualified Flying Instructor.

course graduation time, it was customary for the naval students to carry out some prank at the expense of their host RAF station - lifting one of the QFIs' cars into the mess foyer, hauling assorted ladies' undergarments up the flagpole instead of the ensign etc. One course appeared to have done nothing by which to be remembered, and were quickly forgotten. That is until about three weeks later, when - upon over-flying the RAF airfield - the words 'FLY NAVY, EAT CRABS' were clearly visible in huge letters, produced by weedkiller applied to the grass by the departed course.

Truckies didn't just amuse themselves at the expense of hapless passengers, however; new co-pilots were especially singled out, and spent many frustrating hours, bellowing on HF[3] frequencies and trying to decipher the static-ridden replies. One such lad thought he had saved the day when, out of the ether, he heard the words, 'Ascot aircraft (Ascot was a favoured trucky callsign, reputed to be an acronym for Air Support Command Operational Task) this is Space Shuttle Endeavour requesting a relay to Houston'. A detailed message, concerning a serious malfunction of the Shuttle, would be laboriously copied down and then, eventually, the perspiring co-pilot would present his jottings to his captain, only to find him drying tears of mirth from his eyes. He had played the part of the Shuttle pilot over the intercom, also being monitored by the co-pilot, accompanied by suitable crackling and hissing.

Credit: RAF/Crown Copyright

---

[3] HF – High Frequency radio.

Turnback Trouble

Following Duncan Sandys' cut-back of Fighter Command, for my sins – which must have been considerable - I was given a posting to the Maintenance Command Communications Squadron at RAF Andover, a triangular grass airfield just outside the town. Besides the ubiquitous Ansons and Devons, the squadron also had Chipmunks.

Extant philosophy regarding engine failure after take-off in the single-engined Chipmunk demanded a subsequent straight-ahead landing. However, this airfield was surrounded by rail embankments, roads and dense housing, making safe recovery from such an unhappy event an alarming, not to say impossible, proposition.

Accordingly, I did some investigative work on 'Turnbacks', as later taught on Jet Provosts and Hawks. I even wrote a paper on how the technique should be employed on the Chipmunk, which included the caveat that the climb needed to be flown at 70 knots. The report went to Command Headquarters, where it was investigated and cautiously accepted, and I subsequently flew the manoeuvre many times with my Boss and Flight Commander. By judicious use of the triangle, it was always possible to have some runway alongside you!!

On said day, I was authorised to practice EFATOs[1], and did so several times. Take-off, climb at 70 knots, close throttle, initiate turn back, make it back to the runway I had just left, then throttle up for overshoot. Easy – only this time, at about 100 feet, the engine crankshaft broke, leaving me going the wrong way with a tailwind AND way down the runway.

I entered a highly yawed turn, using what little speed I had, and knowing that this was going to be painful. Since I now found myself heading straight for the windsock, I was forced to just pull. The aircraft was fully stalled as I hit the wet grass, covered in oil, and the main wheels travelled a little more than one aircraft length before stopping in the very soft ground.

Unsurprisingly, the Boss appeared at high speed in his chariot, and I was torn off a major strip, before it became apparent what had happened. What can go wrong, will go wrong, and at the most inconvenient moment! Whose law was that...?

---

[1] EFATO – Engine Failure After Take Off.

The Towing Arm at Tangier

It was the late summer of 1980 in Gibraltar, and I had been on the Fleet Requirement and Air Direction Unit (FRADU) for about 18 months. We had all the benefits of military aviation, with none of the bullshit; all right, the money was rubbish, but we were living in Somerset, and that had to be good. I was flying the Canberra, Marks TT18 and T22. On this particular day, we were just finishing an exercise with HMS Battleaxe, one of the shiny new Type 22 frigates in Her Majesty's Grey Funnel Line. The exercise area was east of 'the Rock' and the weather was good, so a quick recovery to Gibraltar was in order followed by a few green bottles at the North Front Mess.

I had flown a lot with Brian, my navigator on that day, and, once in sight of the Rock, he started packing up the navigator's station. Over to tower frequency, and we were cleared for run and break on Runway 27. I eased down to 300 feet and 300 knots, and lined up (not too soon, lest the Spaniards get upset) with the runway. What a beautiful sight, 'the Rock' on the left and the marina ahead. Ease up, break left as fast as the old girl would go at that speed, and down the bay at 1000 feet. Speed reducing, round Europa Point, undercarriage selected down. I waited for the rumbling but there was none. Dead silence. No lights - not even red unlocked to show that the undercarriage had started to travel. Round I went again, advising the tower that we had a gear problem, and Brian got the checklist out of his bag again. "No, there is no hydraulic pressure," I replied to the first question, having looked at the gauge over the entrance door. A quick check of fuel indicated that we had enough for Tangier, but not enough for Faro – one was not allowed to land at Gib with any sort of control or gear problem, so recovery there was out of the question. We advised Gibraltar that we needed to start heading for Tangier, while trying to sort the problem out, so I climbed to 3000 feet and headed southwest. The checklist basically said that we would be flapless[1] when we eventually landed, and that the landing gear had to be pumped down if possible, on the hand pump by my right hand. Also, braking was courtesy of accumulator pressure only, and therefore very limited.

---

[1] flapless – Aircraft normally land with wing flaps extended that reduce landing speed and improve controllability.

My mind was trying to evaluate all the possibilities and combinations of circumstance, and one of the least attractive was a wheels-up landing on the only runway at Tangier International. I voiced this concern to Brian; I said the Moroccans would, in all probability, bulldoze the Canberra off the runway to allow their 727s to land ASAP. I said that, if it came to it, perhaps we would be better taking the aircraft out to just off Europa Point, heading it east, and ejecting. "Not with my back, you're not!" said Brian's voice from the hole. I heard the sound of seat straps being unbuckled and, like the good trooper he was, he appeared by my side, saying, "I'll pump the bloody gear down don't worry. Just head for the Tangier VOR[2]". Needless to say, the gear duly came down, and Brian stood by my side, admiring the view of the Straits of Gibraltar, whilst I made a real flapless approach to the easterly runway at Tangier off a left hand downwind position. All went well, and we touched down at about 160 knots and I applied the brakes. Sure enough, we slowed down and, when under control, slipped off the runway on the first high speed exit to the right. We stopped. Instructions came over the radio: "Take first right, second left, up the hill and parking on the left with the marshaller", or something equally impossible given our situation. "Would the crew please report to the tower?" "Roger to that, but we are unable to comply. We have no brakes!" At this point, Brian said that he was looking at the ground plate[3] for Tangier and confided, rather comfortingly, "I don't think they are going to be very pleased with us stuck here. It's the main exit off the runway to the terminal and Royal Air Maroc are very busy". "Standby" said the tower. Wheels chocked with Brian's navigation bag, we waited. A few minutes later, a fire truck appeared at the aircraft. I got out and went to meet the Chief. He introduced himself, and said, "We will tow you to dispersal." Wonderful, I thought, and replied, "I am surprised that you have a tow bar to fit a Canberra." "We don't...we have a rope". OK, I thought, I have no choice, having parked the thing here; I am in their hands. A cursory inspection of the outside of the Canberra revealed a very new coat of something red all over the fuselage, roughly the colour of hydraulic fluid. "Where are we going?" I asked. He pointed to a parking spot, some distance away over some very undulating

---

[2] VOR – VHF Omni-directional Radio Range. A type of short-range radio navigation system for aircraft.
[3] ground plate – A chart detailing information about the airfield.

ground. I reminded him of our problem, namely that we had no brakes, and asked what was going to happen when we went downhill. "No problem," he said, "we have Ahmed." "Ahmed!" he cried. There appeared a Moroccan fireman, about 5 feet tall and about 3 feet wide, carrying what can only be described as a 2/3-size railway sleeper. "No problem," the Chief said, "When we go downhill, Ahmed will put the wood ahead of the nosewheel and take up the slack. Then, when the aircraft has passed, he will pick it up, catch us up and do it again as required". Not having much say in all of this, I agreed and the rope was tied to the nose wheel.

We set off. I was in the cockpit, Brian in the fire truck with Ahmed running alongside the Canberra. All went well. We came to the downhill stretch. Sure enough, the aircraft started to catch up the fire truck. Ahmed heaved the railway sleeper in front of the nose wheel and the Canberra reared up and over it like a good'un. Not wishing to dwell on what this might be doing to the nose wheel, I concentrated on the procession. We came to a long uphill stretch. Half way up, there was an almighty "twang" and the rope broke! Far from worrying about the nose wheel, it was the rope that was quite literally the weak link in the chain. This was new to me; I was now going backwards downhill with no brakes. Even if I had any, I was reluctant to use them for fear of sitting the Canberra on its tail. We came to the bottom and slowly settled in the hollow. Fire Chief and truck re-appeared, tied the rope together, and off we went again, this time without incident, to our parking.

The rest of the story is for another time, and involves our lack of passports/IDs/rank insignia/military aircraft combination, and an explanation of this which, I felt, was not wholly believed! I had heard that Moroccan jails had improved a lot in the 70s, but we were, fortunately, allowed a phone call across the Straits. This soon had our engineers on their way in the hydrofoil, with every part of a Canberra hydraulic system they could muster. Suffice to say, the next day, after a very pleasant night in Tangier, the aircraft was fixed and we flew back to Gibraltar to those green bottles.

Good Call!

It was in the days of the Jet Provost (JP) TMk5A, a little single-jet basic training aircraft. As with all pilots, we had to pass regular checks in various disciplines and, in our role, instructors had to be checked, not only for how they flew the aircraft but also for how effective their instruction was.

I was airborne with another instructor on the squadron, who was doing his low-flying check ride. The JP used to trundle around at 250 feet and 300 knots for an hour or so before it ran out of fuel but, in that time, the test profile had to run through a simulated emergency or two. One scenario was that, when getting close to the end of the sortie, a serious problem had to be introduced, so that simulated emergency engine shutdown drills could be run through; almost invariably, this would lead to some form of practice forced-landing (PFL), with the engine completely throttled back.

To make the situation as realistic as possible, on this occasion I elected to simulate a birdstrike (a not uncommon event in real life), which would lead to the desired, simulated engine failure. The procedure required that I would announce something along the lines of, "For simulated emergency only - you now have a multiple birdstrike", immediately after which the pilot under test was expected to raise the nose, climb to height, and then work his way through the emergency procedures.

I waited until I was pretty sure that, if the drills were carried out correctly, we would be able to complete the exercise with a PFL back at base. So, once comfortable that we could indeed make it back to the airfield, I turned to Bob and trotted out my little speech. I was expecting a smooth transition into the practice drills but, as I finished my oration, we smacked into a whole flock of wood-pigeons. Not in the least bit fazed by this, Bob immediately turned to me and added the classic line "How the **** did you do that?"

I was still smiling when he put the wheels of the battered jet back on the runway at RAF Leeming.

What Could Possibly Go Wrong?

It all started out so innocently, as these things often do, over a pint of beer in the bar. Pete, who was an Air Traffic Control Officer, told me that he had a share in a Cessna 172, based at Aberdeen airport.

"Have you ever flown a little Cessna?"

"No, I haven't, Pete".

"Would you like to?"

"Yeah, why not".

So it was that, early one autumnal Sunday, we set off for Aberdeen. Our plan was to fly over to Inverness, have a coffee and fly back. We dutifully consulted the weather, which told us it was going to be a reasonable day with light winds, no cloud forecast below 2000 feet, and quite warm for the time of year, but there was a chance of an isolated shower. What could possibly go wrong?

Our departure from Aberdeen was uneventful. In fact, the entire leg across to Inverness passed without incident. Initially, we followed the A96 (why make life more difficult than necessary!) to overhead RAF Lossiemouth, where we turned left and flew just inland from the coast, at around 2000 feet. I had checked the day before that Lossie would be closed, and a quick courtesy call on the radio confirmed that all was quiet at RAF Kinloss. However, Air Traffic did advise us that there were isolated, heavy rain showers to the south. No sweat! We weren't going anywhere near them.

We had shared the flying on the first leg, and I found the Cessna to be very stable - so stable, in fact, that it required some persuasion to deviate from the straight and level – very different from what I had been used to. Nevertheless, it was enjoyable enough, and I sat back and admired the scenery as Pete did the approach and landing at Inverness, with the promise that it would be my turn back at Aberdeen.

After shutting down the Cessna, we climbed up the steps into the Air Traffic tower to blag a free coffee. There were a few commercial flights coming and going, but it was a quiet Sunday afternoon, and Pete was busy chatting to the guys on duty when the first spots of rain appeared on the windows. I was leafing through the Sunday paper, and only noticed them because of the noise they made as they hit the glass. Strange really, because the cloud base still looked OK, and the wind was...where was the windspeed readout? In the space of a couple of minutes, it went from 3 to 5 knots up to 15, and the rain started coming down hard. Fortunately we had parked the little Cessna facing into the wind, so the only thing we could do was sit tight until it cleared. Thirty minutes later it was still raining, the visibility was rubbish, the gulls were walking, and Pete was becoming concerned about getting back in daylight. He only had a basic licence, so he wasn't qualified to fly at night and, in the north of Scotland, it got dark quite early at that time of year.

Eventually the rain stopped, the visibility improved, and we hurriedly did our checks before starting up and setting off eastwards. The plan (yes, we did have one of sorts) was to land at Lossiemouth if necessary, and only press on to Aberdeen if we were confident of making it before darkness fell. As we passed abeam Lossie, our calculations showed that we would be on the ground at Aberdeen with ten to fifteen minutes to spare. So, press on! However, just as a precaution, we turned on all the cockpit lighting we could find, and the external navigation lights.

Our plan started to fall apart when I called up Aberdeen Approach to let them know we were inbound. I was told to hold overhead Kintore, and it was evident from the radio chatter that the airport was busy. We had plenty of fuel, so that wasn't a problem but, fifteen minutes later, it was certainly getting gloomier, both outside and inside the cockpit. We discussed requesting a priority landing because Pete wasn't night qualified, and probably, with hindsight, should have done some time before, but then we received inbound clearance, and were told to call tower frequency.

I checked in with the tower, confirmed that the airfield was in sight...and was told to join dead-side at 1000 feet! This meant that we would have to carry out at least one full circuit of the airfield before landing, by which time it would be dark. As the Cessna is not the fastest form of aviation known to man, there was plenty of time to discuss our predicament as we trundled around the circuit. We agreed that I would do the landing, purely on the basis that I was the only one with night experience, and I duly managed to get us back on the ground without mishap; however, it did involve giving the Boeing 757 in front a fairly wide berth, to avoid any possibility of wake turbulence. In so doing, I incurred the displeasure of air traffic as there was a rapidly closing 737 behind us in the queue. Fortunately, we managed to turn off the runway in time for the 737 to land, and tentatively picked our way back to the light aircraft park.

Nobody queried our late return, and no-one questioned the night landing, so we just said nothing. However, what this little adventure clearly demonstrated is that unconnected events can, and often will, conspire against you, if you have an aeroplane of any sort strapped to your backside. What could possibly go wrong? The answer is, invariably, more than you can imagine.

Credit: Adrian Pingstone/Wikipedia

The One That Got Away

The part that 'Bravo November', the one Chinook to survive the sinking of Atlantic Conveyor, played in the Falklands Campaign, and the events that transpired on shore, have been well documented. However, how this came about has not, and so I decided to put pen to paper...

"You take my crew and do the task while I stay here in case any important information comes in". These were the words of the Flight Commander to me in the late afternoon of 25 May 1982, on board the SS Atlantic Conveyor, some 70 or 80 miles to the east of the Falklands.

Some weeks before, 18 Squadron, just newly equipped with the Chinook, had flown four aircraft to Southampton, where they were loaded on board Conveyor, along with Royal Air Force Harriers and Navy Wessex, to set sail south with the task force; a small party of ground crew accompanied them on board. As the task force arrived at Ascension Island, the remaining aircrew and groundcrew flew from UK to embark. The majority embarked on Norland, a North Sea ferry; two crews, mine – consisting of Flt Lt Andy Strachan, FS Brian Jopling and Sgt Don Maxwell – and the Flight Commander's, plus a dozen groundcrew, boarded Conveyor to sail south with the aircraft. To protect the aircraft from the elements during the sail south, they had been smothered with a corrosion inhibitor, not unlike a thick WD40, and then placed in large, all-enveloping plastic bags or cocoons. Containers, which held various support equipment, were stacked either side of the deck to provide additional protection from the elements.

Life on board Conveyor was relative luxury compared to that on other ships. Due to the small number of personnel on board there was plenty of space, and the Merchant Navy certainly knew how to eat well; there was a large refrigerated container on a lower deck, full of some choice items. We had eaten our way through the container to the crayfish tails; these were next on the menu, but events overtook the meal that evening. As the task force progressed south, those Harriers which had not flown off while at anchor at Ascension Island were prepared for flight and, one by one, positioned across deck to depart for the carriers. That day, the ship was rolling by some degrees, and the Harrier pilots had to judge the exact moment to apply full power, so that the aircraft lifted when the deck was level. If this was not done, the aircraft would rise at an angle, with the possibility of not clearing the deck safely. This spectacle provided a couple of hours of great entertainment for those on board, if not for the Harrier pilots, some of whom were not relishing the task in hand; there were one or two close calls but, in the end, they all made it safely.

Once the Harriers had departed, the helicopters on the forward deck could be repositioned. One of the aircraft, ZA 718 (Bravo November), was taken out of its cocoon, bladed up and prepared for flight, with the intention of operating from the forward deck area to carry out inter-ship tasking. This was breaking new ground for the Chinook, which was still under introductory trials, so no limits for operating from ships had been formulated. The seas in the South Atlantic were not the calmest but, even with the ship pitching and rolling at least 10 to 15°, there were no great problems with operating, although this was well in excess of the limits imposed post-Operation Corporate[1]. Tasking was successfully carried out during the journey south, consisting mainly of the movement of Harrier ordnance from Conveyor to the two carriers. Conveyor, with other ships of the task force, was planned to sail into San Carlos Water during the night of 25/26 May, disembark the aircraft and start offloading the immense amount of equipment on board. In anticipation of this, another Chinook (Bravo Tango), which was on the small rear deck behind the ship's superstructure, was bladed up and ground run. In order to allow the blades to turn, the large rear ramp of the ship had to be partially lowered; this entailed some sweet-talking of the ship's captain, as it was normally only allowed in dock. When completed, it allowed the aircraft to be positioned so that the rear blades overhung the stern, giving the forward blades clearance from a Sea King, which was folded and tucked away by the superstructure. Once the successful ground runs had been carried out, Bravo Tango was moved forward, to allow the rear ramp to be raised once again. For this reason, when Conveyor was hit (some time later), it was impossible for the remaining crew to start the aircraft and fly her off; the rear blades would have hit the ramp and the forward ones the Sea King.

During the afternoon of 25th May, we received a task to collect a spare

---

[1] Operation Corporate – The codename given to British military operations in the Falklands War.

engine and gearbox from HMS Glasgow for her Lynx helicopter, to undergo repairs by the specialist Mobile Aircraft Repair, Transport and Salvage Unit (MARTSU), based on Conveyor. HMS Glasgow had taken a hit from an Argentinian bomb, and was sailing north out of the immediate area to undergo repairs. On board Conveyor we had been taking it in turns to do the tasking, and it was the Flight Commander's turn next. However, due to the plan to sail into San Carlos later that evening, he elected to stay on board and be available for the important communications that were bound to be received, so I took his crew (Flt Lt Andy Tailby, MALM Jim Savage and Sgt Paul 'Gibbo' Gibson) to carry out the task. Mail from the task force, which was on board Conveyor for forwarding back to UK, was loaded and we departed in the late afternoon. HMS Glasgow was some 40nm to the east of the main task force, and was located without any undue problems. The intention was to lower the mail by winch, and then pick up the Lynx engine and gearbox as a netted, underslung load. We had just been given clearance to approach the rear deck when we were instructed to hold off a short distance to the east. There was an air raid developing to the west of the task force and Glasgow was preparing to fire her missiles. Shortly after this we witnessed the spectacular sight of Sea Darts[2], which are about the size of telegraph poles, being launched in the half-light, something which, when seen from such relatively close quarters, stays in the memory! After about 15 minutes we were, once again, cleared to approach the rear deck and pick up the load. We were informed that there had been an air raid, in which one ship had been slightly damaged, but that was all. We winched down the mail, picked up the load and, with it hanging beneath the aircraft, set off back towards the task force as night finally fell.

HMS Invincible was controlling air operations in and around the task force and initially we headed towards her; there seemed to be some confusion in the air, but nothing to make us think anything was amiss. As we approached, we could see what appeared to be Invincible with deck lights on and the anti-collision lights of Harriers recovering. We then requested 'pigeons for mother' (a bearing and distance to fly from Invincible to Conveyor) and were told 340° at 12 miles. Off we set into the darkness. As 12 miles approached, the first inklings

---

[2] Sea Dart – A type of ship-mounted anti-aircraft missile.

that all was not well were starting to stir in my mind. Normally, even at night, ships could be made out below, but this time there was nothing to be seen. On reaching 15 miles, with nothing at all spotted, the aircraft was turned and a reciprocal course flown. Still nothing was seen, so we continued back towards Invincible. On reaching what we assumed to be overhead, the situation slowly started to clarify. What initially we had assumed was Invincible recovering her aircraft had in fact been Conveyor; the 'deck lights' were the fires starting to break out on the deck; and the 'Harriers recovering' were, in fact, helicopters starting to evacuate survivors from the ship. In the aftermath of the air raid there was confusion, even for the air controller. By now the fires had really got hold, and the sight below was one that made all on board fall silent.

For how long we orbited in silence, each crewmember with his individual thoughts, it is hard to say; it may have been 30 seconds, it may have been 3 minutes. It was a sight you never expect to see and, therefore, personal reaction is unpredictable. I will always remember the way the inaction was broken. "Captain", came Gibbo's voice, "You couldn't get on the radio and order two late meals from the Sergeants' Mess could you?" The realisation that here we were, orbiting somewhere in the South Atlantic, with a netted load of Lynx spares and the fuel gauge starting to indicate it was time to do something, suddenly hit home. Firstly, the worsening fuel situation prompted us to release the netted load into the sea. There was also a suggestion that we should go down to help evacuate survivors but, tempting as that was, I thought we would just get in the way. We did not know who was controlling the rescue operation or the relevant radio frequencies, and a Chinook, pitching up in the darkness unannounced, would have caused more problems than could be imagined. With the fuel still decreasing, finding somewhere to either refuel or land was the priority. We were still in radio contact with Invincible and, after some confusing discussion with the controller, it was decided that we would land the aircraft on HMS Hermes.

Our arrival at Hermes caused surprise and some consternation, but we were eventually cleared to approach and land on the starboard rear of the flight deck. After we had shut down, a member of the Sea King ASW[3] squadron met us, and I was taken to the control room to discuss the situation with the ship's

---

[3] ASW – Anti-Submarine Warfare.

commanders. The Chinook was taking up valuable deck space that was required for critical Harrier operations, so it obviously could not stay there. Various options were considered but, although they alleviated the problem, I did not find any of them acceptable. They included sawing off the blades, so that the airframe could be tucked away somewhere on the deck, or even pushing the aircraft over the side. Thanks to the support of our friendly Sea King pilot, common sense eventually prevailed and the decision was made that, after refuelling early the next morning, we would fly the aircraft ashore. It still wasn't clear exactly how this would be achieved but, nevertheless, I found the crew and told them of the intention. Meanwhile, some of the rescued groundcrew had arrived on board, so we made a visit to the sick bay to see them. Smoke inhalation had been the biggest problem but, by donning their respirators, they had been able to breathe and see sufficiently long enough to make it onto deck. My original crew were not on board Hermes, but I later found out they were all safe. They had all had to abandon ship, and had spent varying times in the water and in dinghies. Brian Jopling was awarded the Queen's Gallantry Medal for his part in rescuing survivors from the water and ensuring they were put into, or safely fastened onto, a dinghy. The Flight Commander, Squadron Leader Kim Smith, and all the groundcrew had also abandoned ship, but were safe. For our part, we were fed, found camp beds and shown to the Admiral's Cabin for the night. All we had was what we stood up in, immersion suits with flying kit underneath and trainers on our feet. On Conveyor, spilt fluid from aircraft had made the decks treacherous for anyone in flying boots; trainers, on the other hand, still gave a good amount of grip and were therefore the preferred footwear.

Early the next morning, more detailed plans were formulated to get the aircraft ashore, but the Navy's solution did not appeal at all. It was to fly towards the islands under control of Hermes, climb as the edge of radar cover was reached and call HMS Ambuscade, the Local Anti-Air Warfare Co-ordinator (LAAWC) for the day. Ambuscade was sitting in Falkland Sound, and getting identified on her radar would have meant flying over Stanley at 7000 feet or above; not an attractive option, particularly when a Harrier had been hit by a SAM[4] at 13,000 feet over Stanley on the previous day. It was obvious that

---

[4] SAM – Surface to Air Missile.

a different plan was needed, and this is where those many hours of 'budgie-baiting'[5] at Happy Hour in the bar at RAF Gutersloh paid off. Many of the pilots on board Hermes were from, or had been on, the Harrier at Gutersloh, where I was stationed on 18 Squadron's Wessex helicopters in the latter half of the 70s. Armed with directions from a friendly Lieutenant Commander, we successfully negotiated the maze of corridors, ladders and bulkhead doors, in a bizarre sort of game of snakes and ladders, until we found the Harrier pilots. Face-to-face discussion soon produced a feasible plan. Armed with the radio frequencies for the Harrier Combat Air Patrol (CAP), and the call signs of the pairs of aircraft carrying out the CAP over the next few hours, we would fly at 50 feet above sea level to ensure we remained below the radar horizon of any land-based Argentinian radar. We would approach Falkland Sound from the north, thence into San Carlos Water and would establish communication with the CAP, which would relay our progress to the LAAWC. As each CAP went off station, we would re-establish comms with the oncoming pair of aircraft. An accurate position of the ship would be fed into our Tactical Air Navigation System (TANS) before set off, because the only map the second pilot could get his hands on was a naval 1:2,000,000 chart. This meant that our planned ground track, via four waypoints from the ship to Eddystone Rock (just to the north of Falkland Sound), although 120nm[6] in length, was only about two inches long on the chart. Thank heavens for aircrew eyesight!

The plan was firmed up and put to the Royal Navy, who agreed the concept. However, the crew had only just been briefed when we were asked if it was possible to take some of the Atlantic Conveyor survivors and winch them onto British Tay, a merchant tanker supporting the fleet, that was about to set off north to replenish before re-joining the task force. Our aircraft had a winch fitted; no-one had used it before, but a winch is a winch and so we agreed. We would fly the survivors and some mail to British Tay, return to Hermes to top up with fuel, then set off for the trip ashore. The Navy found us some extra clothing by way of trousers, shirts, jumpers and socks; all dark blue but still gratefully received. In fact, I still have the flight deck foul-weather clothing they also gave us! Then,

---

[5] budgie-baiting – The practice of taking the mickey out of helicopter aircrew.
[6] nm – nautical miles.

just before setting off, I received some fairly worrying news in an intelligence update. The helicopters, that were already off-loading the ships in San Carlos Water, were inhibiting the firing of Rapier anti-aircraft missiles on those units fitted with Blindfire. Blindfire uses radar to track a target, but a safety interlock inhibits missile launch if the system detects a friendly squawk[7] transmission. As air raids were a regular occurrence in San Carlos Water this was definitely not ideal, therefore 'Guns Tight' had been declared on all helicopters[8], and they were not to squawk. This was fine for the Wessex and Sea Kings in San Carlos Water, but we were shortly to arrive in a Chinook and, at that stage, it was believed that there were still Argentinian Chinooks on West Island. On top of this, two Rapier fire units had been positioned on the north and south headlands to guard the entrance to San Carlos Water. They were not in radio contact with the LAAWC and so could not be notified of our intended arrival. What to do about this situation was still occupying our thoughts as we prepared to get airborne.

On returning from delivering the survivors to British Tay we took on fuel, got an updated position and set off for San Carlos. The plan worked exactly as hoped. We called the first pair of Harriers on CAP, got an immediate reply and the flight leader then informed LAAWC that Bravo November (our callsign) was on its way. As each pair handed over to the next, we would establish comms and continue to give updates as to our progress. When we set off from Hermes the weather had been ideal, with 8/8 cover of stratus at around 800 feet, reasonable visibility and a fairly strong westerly that made the sea quite rough. The TANS was being operated by the second pilot in Sea Rough mode, with only limited data input available and, at the same time, he was carrying out a manual air plot of our heading and time. However, as each notional waypoint was reached, the air plot and TANS position were agreeing fairly well. About halfway through the flight the weather changed; the stratus cover started to thin and breaks began to appear. The day before, an Army Air Corps helicopter had been bounced by an Argentinian Pucara aircraft over the sea to the north of Falkland Sound; the

---

[7] squawk – Aircraft carry transponders that emit a selectable coded signal to aid in their identification. Transmitting this 'electronic number plate' is known as "squawking".

[8] Guns tight – In this context it means that all helicopters were deemed friendly and would not be fired upon.

pilot had successfully evaded but it was still a worrying possibility. With the cloud cover, which had been giving us protection from this eventuality, beginning to break, the possibility of the same thing happening to us began to enter my mind. We still had two waypoints to go before the turn south to Eddystone Rock and, as we approached the next one, patches of blue sky were evident. Under the circumstances, I made the decision to miss out the final waypoint, and route directly towards Eddystone Rock. As we neared the rock, a quick comparison of the Tactical Air Navigation System (TANS) and the manual air plot revealed that the TANS was in error by only about three quarters of a mile and the air plot by about half a mile. Considering there had been no way of updating our position since leaving Hermes, some 150nm or so previously, the results were quite impressive; who says heading and time does not work? Full marks to the second pilot! By the time we reached Eddystone Rock, the clouds had all but disappeared and our next problem was fast approaching. We would shortly be in sight and range of the two Rapier sites on the headlands protecting San Carlos. Contrary to the briefing that friendly helicopters were not to squawk, we checked we had the correct codes for Modes 1 and 3 for the hour set, and started squawking to the world. In an additional attempt to ensure that we appeared as friendly as possible, we also increased our height to about 500 feet and put on both landing lamps. In this configuration, we progressed down Falkland Sound towards San Carlos, but not without some apprehension. If we'd had some Union Jacks on board, they would have been flying out of every window we could open. However, something must have worked because we entered San Carlos without incident and made contact with HMS Fearless, which was controlling operations in the area. Where to land was the next problem; we had no maps and the directions being given from the controller were confusing. We were assisted by a Sea King that, on hearing the exchanges on the radio, popped up to a high hover in the area where they wanted us to land. At last the wheels touched the ground and the aircraft was shut down. When we landed, Bravo November had about 18 hours total flying on the airframe. As we climbed out, we were met by two people standing right by the aircraft, the commander of an SAS unit and his Warrant Officer, who enquired if the aircraft was serviceable as they wanted to use it that night. How they knew where we were going to land is still a mystery. Then, to cap that, our Squadron Commander and other squadron members appeared from behind nearby rocks! It transpired that they had been somewhat surprised to find themselves in San Carlos, along with the rest of the task force, when it sailed in for the landings. Norland had 2 Para on board and, of course, had to be there to off-load them. After off-loading she had set sail towards South Georgia to trans-ship more troops from the QE2, and so the squadron personnel were transferred to HMS Fearless. During the ensuing air raids, sitting below decks listening to the shrapnel pinging off the sides, was not ideal and so, early each morning, the squadron would go ashore on a landing craft and spend the day on a hillside, safely hidden among the rocks and with a grandstand view of the action in San Carlos Water, before returning in the evening to eat and sleep. After deciding to leave two crews and supporting groundcrew ashore with Bravo November, the rest of the squadron embarked on Europic Ferry to sail out of San Carlos and await the arrival of replacement aircraft from UK.

The next time I flew in Bravo November was the day after the surrender. The previous day I had accompanied the Boss ashore on the first replacement aircraft, Bravo Uniform. Having done it before, I was asked to go along as the intention was to follow a nearly identical plan; depart Europic Ferry, refuel on Hermes and follow a very similar route. We landed at San Carlos mid-afternoon. Squadron Leader Dick Langworthy and his crew, who had done so much well-documented work during the battle, landed from tasking in Bravo November about an hour later and announced the surrender of Stanley. The following morning, I was back in Bravo November. By then she had amassed about 120 hours on the airframe, and that day we did another 7 or so, ferrying fuel bladders from San Carlos to Fitzroy and Stanley Racecourse, to keep the naval Wessex and Sea Kings in the air. Since I had last flown her she had lost the port cabin door, the compasses no longer worked, various automatic systems now needed to be operated manually and there were a host of other problems. However, she was still deemed to be airworthy!

As I conclude my story I reflect on the fact that a lot has been written about the Falklands Conflict, much of it true, but there is some I read, even to this day, which is not. Hopefully, with the passage of time, a full and accurate picture will appear.

Buccaneer Ejection

Out Of The Blue Volume 1 included a tale [Near Mid-Air No 1] of a near collision in South Wales between a Buccaneer and a Hunter, told from the Hunter pilot's perspective. Here is the same event, as recalled by the Buccaneer navigator.

It was in the mid 70s, those heady days for the Buccaneer overland force, when most of England, Wales and Scotland were our stomping ground. We spent most of our time at 250 feet agl[1] in 4-ship formations, attacking simulated targets (SAPs), dropping bombs on a variety of coastal ranges, avoiding marauding fighters and occasionally topping up our fuel from Victor or Buccaneer 'buddy-buddy' tankers. On this occasion, however, I was flying a conversion exercise sortie with Terry, a pilot who had recently joined the squadron and was on his Combat-Ready work-up.

On that typical early April morning, with strong westerlies and lumps of scudding cumulus at around 2000 feet, we got airborne, alone, from RAF Honington, and set off at 250 feet towards Holbeach Range in the Wash for an FRA (First Run Attack). We then flew west through the tactical link routes to mid-Wales, to make simulated attacks on a couple of targets, remaining at low level and winding northwards through the A5 pass for further FRAs on the ranges at Jurby, Cowden and Wainfleet, before returning to base. We had completed the Holbeach FRA, and were approaching our IP (initial point) before pulling up for our first SAP: a bunt-retard shallow dive attack on the dam at the end of the Claerwen reservoir. The aircraft would top out at around 1300 feet, before tipping in and diving at 500 knots to a simulated bomb-release point at around 500 feet. During the dive, my main responsibility was to call out the heights and bomb release point.

All went according to plan until we saw two Hunters, at some 2000 yards in our 1 o'clock, just before we began to dive. Their close formation positioning indicated that they were probably part of a four-ship. I called the spot to Terry, who was now concentrating on lining up his gun-sight with the target, and had

---

[1] agl – above ground level.

a quick look in the area where I expected the other pair of Hunters to be, before getting my head in to call out the heights. Seconds later, in the dive, I experienced a violent onset of positive 'g' coupled with a shout from the front seat. I blacked out, but was still acutely aware of the loud and rather disconcertingly deepening tones of the ADD[2], only previously heard in the simulator. A wing rock to the right, some heavy buffet, and a couple of loud thuds immediately followed.

I lost no time in surmising that it was no longer safe to remain where I was, reached for the nearest ejection seat handle and was probably gone within a couple of seconds of it all turning to worms. As the other two Hunters (of the four-ship formation) flew across our nose, some 50 yards ahead, and blocked Terry's view of the target, he pulled hard back on the control column and, with no computer to adjust his input, boldly reached just over 9g. As I now know, although possibly not according to Brough[3], that was a bit too much for the tail! He then, almost immediately pushed the stick back forward, and the aircraft bunted. Initially Terry assumed this was as a result of his input, but it more likely resulted from the airframe now being tailless. Quickly realising he was no longer in charge of this rolling and pitching machine, and possibly hearing a loud bang from my seat, he decided to join me outside.

My own arrival in the fresh air, at some 480 knots, broke both my helmet visors and my arms flailed wildly, as our seats were not then fitted with arm restraint. As a consequence, my left arm broke (along with some ribs) as it struck the distress radio in my life-jacket. I recovered consciousness hanging in my parachute, after what seemed like a long sleep but was only a few seconds, and, feeling euphoric, offered up a thankful prayer to my maker that I was still in this world! Unfortunately, I could not breathe, a sensation overshadowed by the realisation that I was fast approaching terra firma, although unable to see it. I therefore adopted a position vaguely remembered from mogul skiing, rather than parachute instruction, and awaited the worst. I had no idea whether I was

---

[2] ADD - Airstream Direction Detector; an angle of attack indicator including an audio warning.

[3] Brough – Where the Blackburn Aircraft Company, manufacturer of the Buccaneer, was located, near Kingston-upon-Hull.

attempting a front, right or rear left approach[4]. As I pulled my knees up, almost blind, I just made out our stricken jet, tailess and upside down (well, that's how it looked to me) plunging towards its penultimate resting place in the reservoir.

Terry wisely elected for a wet landing beside the plane, where he sensibly inflated his dinghy and laid claim to an extra badge, mine was just the caterpillar[5]. I was less fortunate, hitting the ground in some 25 knots of wind, which kept my parachute inflated and dragged me along on my back as I struggled with the Koch fasteners[6]. The recent addition of a safety pin to prevent premature release in high speed ejections (for which I was thankful) was now making them even harder to undo. Unfastening the right one with a broken left arm wasn't easy, and I kept sliding on my back until it dawned on me that, by undoing the easy one first, it would collapse the chute and stop my ever-faster sleigh ride. With vision in one eye now improving, I gave a friendly wave to one of the Hunter pilots, who had kindly stayed to cover the action. It occurred to me that I might fire a flare to indicate my wellbeing but, as the RAF had recently introduced blunt dinghy knives[7], I found it impossible to open the plastic wrapping (plus ça change, plus c'est la même chose!). So, instead, I sat on my dinghy and monitored the approach of a man in a brown raincoat. This Welsh shepherd stopped some 10 yards away, and looked at me cautiously as if I were an invading German soldier. Eventually he inquired whether I would be needing anything 'boyo', to which I responded by asking him for a cigarette. Though I smoked a pipe, a fag seemed more appropriate under the circumstances.

---

[4] Approach - Ejection seat parachutes are not as steerable as their sports counterparts, and the direction and attitude of landing very much depended on the direction and strength of the wind. Different attitudes demanded different techniques.

[5] Caterpillar - A small gold brooch of a silkworm, presented by the parachute manufacturers, Irvin, to those who have survived by virtue of using their product. The Goldfish Club is a worldwide association of people who have jumped by parachute from an aircraft into the water, or whose aircraft crashed in the water, and whose lives were saved by a life jacket, inflatable dinghy, or similar device.

[6] Koch Fastener – A quick-release device which connected the parachute in the Martin-Baker ejection seat to a torso harness worn by the aircrew. It was originally fitted to a number of different types of fast-jet but, after a couple of inadvertent releases, was replaced by the traditional seat harness.

[7] Dinghy knife- A curved implement with a blade on the inside of the curve, but no point. This was deemed to reduce the risk of personal injury or punctured dinghies.

He felt in his pockets, produced a yellow packet of some rare make, and held it out. I couldn't get up, but he wasn't going to risk getting closer. The moment of frustration passed when he announced that he hadn't got a light 'boyo'. Searching for matches in my dinghy pack was not an option, so I sat back to await the arrival of a helicopter from the Search and Rescue Flight at RAF Valley. I was not disappointed to see them. They saved me from the ministrations of some local firemen, who had fitted me with a leaking rubber splint, and nearly dropped me out of the stretcher as they stumbled down the hillside. We were delivered to the nearby hospital at Aberystwyth, where Terry and I were both rewarded with a plethora of medical staff, who had been briefed about an air disaster with many injured passengers. They seemed rather let down with just the two of us! The highlight of my stay was waking from an operation to find a Catholic Padre beside my bed. Expecting the worst, I began to tentatively examine myself but he opened his cassock to reveal four cans of Guinness, and I converted to Catholicism on the spot! I managed to call my mother to pacify her, as we had been mentioned on the news, whereupon she immediately called my sister and said, "It's Peter, but don't worry, he's alright, he's just ejaculated over Wales."

Some months later, I received a very detailed report which was supported by photographs from the British Aerospace Group at Brough. It attempted to pin the blame for the failure of the Buccaneer's tail-fin on to my ejection seat. Allegedly, due to my premature ejection, my seat struck the tailplane at some 500 mph, causing severe damage which broke the front spar, before moving inboard along the under surface of the tailplane, causing further damage to the rear spar before falling away. Reading this, I recalled the Test Pilot sketch from Hancock's Half Hour (you can see it on YouTube), and idly wondered why the one pain my body hadn't suffered was a headache. Martin-Baker were none too pleased either, as a major failure of the seat would have had to occur to achieve such a trajectory. The tail-strike theory was happily discredited by a famous RAF aeromedical doctor, Group Captain Tony Barwood, who, together with the Air Accident Investigation Board (AAIB) at Farnborough, proved that the marks on the tail were not from the sear pin on the top of my seat, but from the tail hook on the underside of the aircraft, which had hit the tail plane as it folded and broke away. My seat had worked perfectly; I duly thanked Martin-Baker, spent three months in Headley Court, got my tie and tried to avoid 9g thereafter.

Interestingly, the view of the Board of Inquiry was that the problem of seeing high-speed, camouflaged aircraft at low-level requires excellent look-out, but also calls for an element of luck!

Credit: Geoff Lee

A Reet Grobbly Day

After receiving my pilot's wings, I was posted to hold at RAF Wyton as an Operations Officer, as there weren't any slots available on my advanced flying course for some months. Due to the nature of some of the operations at Wyton during the '60s, I was only told what I needed to know, which was pretty much how to switch on the kettle and turn off the lights. Being a sensitive 19-year-old, and still very new to the way of things in the RAF, I did what I was told and tried not to question much in this new posting.

Crews came in and out of the Operations Centre, picked up folders, returned folders, checked weather conditions and, I hoped, would not ask me any questions for which I usually had no answer. I didn't really feel that I was contributing much to the smooth and efficient running of the UK's defence system, but smiled and wished them a safe flight. This sometimes raised a few eyebrows, as I suspect they thought I knew a lot more than I should have. I might add that I was rarely by myself, and that I was relieved to have an extremely capable Corporal, who seemed to know everything; well, he was able to satisfy any questions directed at our side of the counter, and I expect it was a huge loss to Ops when he was eventually posted.

Feeling a little under-valued in my new post, I quickly became bored and wandered around to see if anything of interest could be found. Every hour, a mechanical chattering could be heard from an adjacent room; it lasted for about five minutes and then stopped. The Corporal would pop in, return with a roll of paper, and then nip up a ladder in front of a huge vertical map of the UK and Europe which was positioned on one of the walls. Clutching a handful of ½-inch circular magnets of various colours, he then went round selected military airfields on the map, updating their weather state as dictated by reference to a table. We had a lot more airfields then! For those not familiar, a table was devised to give a quick guide to the weather at a station by using colour coding, so Blue meant it was a lovely day, working down through White, Green, Yellow, Amber and finally Red, which represented very low cloud or fog. Actually, there was another colour – Black - only used when the airfield was closed for any reason not necessarily related to weather, like an aircraft suffering a tyre burst on landing, thus blocking the runway. I believe that these colour codes are still in use today. The idea was to give a broad picture of the UK weather at various selected airfields at a glance, and it was quite effective.

In aforementioned, adjacent room, I found what appeared to be an electric typewriter with lots of wires coming from it; it sat, for the most part, quietly whirring, in what must have been standby mode. At that time, this was cutting edge stuff and the machine seemed to have a life all of its own. Just before each hour, it would start up and begin printing. It had a circular ring of mechanical key rods, located within what looked like a small wheel above the keyboard, set centrally in front of the platen; the wheel would rotate at a furious pace, while the electronics would cause selected rods to produce characters through the ribbon onto the paper, which was on a roll. All the weather information for each station came through in coded form, and I was fascinated by this "high-tech" machine. When it wasn't downloading information, I found that I could use the keyboard like a typewriter. I remember seeing something like this on TV when the football results came in.

Imagination flourishes in an idle mind, so one day I went through to the printer room and typed up my own weather for the UK, tore it off the roll and handed it to the Corporal. He went up the ladder and proceeded to put red and black magnets over the whole of the UK, whilst making comments of surprise. It gave the impression that the RAF had closed for the day and it all looked pretty ominous. Of course, this was as far as I had intended the joke to go but, before I had a chance to say anything, a few 'wheels' came in, including the Station Commander who was hosting an important visit. I can still remember the look on his face, as he took in what appeared to be a dire situation developing, and checked with the Corporal that this was the latest weather report. I was beginning to feel very uncomfortable as the Corporal handed him the print-out but, of course, dared not say anything as the situation escalated. The Station Commander had to agree that the map correctly showed the met situation, and quickly realised the implications of diverting aircraft – but, of course, where could they divert to? I was hoping for a small miracle at this point, when the printer started up with the real weather. After it had stopped, the Corporal came back and handed the print-out to the Station Commander, who was relieved to see a more normal picture. He went back to the other print-out and, when he reached the bottom, he softly read aloud "...and I wish our readers a Reet Grobbly Day. Hmm!" He looked slowly at me, then the Corporal, before turning on his heels and departing with his guests, leaving me, perhaps, the most relieved of all.

No Place To Go

It was January 1981, and this tale started with a plan to take two Phantom FGR2s from RAF Wildenrath to Portugal for the weekend. With two days to go, everything was planned for two leisurely outbound legs on Friday and two equally leisurely return legs on Monday. The engineers would remove the gun pods, and we would go in two-tank fit[1]. Then, on the Wednesday morning, a message came from HQRAF Germany that our Diplomatic Clearance for Portugal had been cancelled; they did, however, offer an alternative weekend in Cyprus. After some hurried planning, we aimed to leave Wildenrath on Thursday afternoon and fly to Decimomannu in Sardinia. After a night stop, we would stage via Souda Bay, in Crete, to arrive at Akrotiri for Happy Hour (1230) on the Friday. Although we asked for centreline tanks to be fitted to the two aircraft, the engineers said there was not enough time; later on, how we would wish that we had insisted! The plan for the Monday return was Akrotiri, Souda, Deci and home.

The trip out went without too many problems and, DCO (Duty Carried Out), we were at Happy Hour on time. On the Sunday, the lead navigator got a meteorological brief for the following day. The tailwinds that we had enjoyed for the trip out were still there! They would now be eighty-knot headwinds to Deci, and then one hundred knots plus up over France. We would be very tight on fuel with just our two wing tanks; if only we had insisted on the extra 5000 pounds provided by the centreline! The two legs to Deci went without a hitch, apart from having to do a pairs TACAN[2] approach at Deci, followed by a landing with the crosswind on limits. Whilst turning the aircraft round, the Operations Officer appeared and advised us that we had been ordered by our Flight Commander to stay in Deci for the night, and stage back through Baden Söllingen on the Tuesday. Oh dear, another night of Deci Red[3].

Tuesday morning arrived and time to head for home. The weather for our

---

[1] Two-tank fit – two underwing drop tanks, one under each wing, to extend the unrefuelled range.
[2] TACAN –Tactical Air Navigation equipment.
[3] The local brew. Rough, but by no means lacking in alcohol, not for nothing was it known as 'The Purple Infuriator'.

diversion airfields, Söllingen and Lahr was forecast to be no worse than GREEN[4]. The 100-knot-plus headwind was still there, so fuel would again be tight. On our way up France, the winds were even stronger than forecast. Both navigators tried to get weather updates on the HF[5] from base, but to no avail. Moreover, there was no ATIS[6] at Söllingen or Lahr in those days. As long as the forecasts we had received prior to takeoff were accurate, we were still alright! At Dijon, we turned onto an easterly heading and put the wind on the beam; the fuel was still OK - just. As we approached the German border, we requested a cruise descent; this was denied by French Air Traffic Control (ATC). Ahead, there was a lot of cloud build-up, possibly CBs (thunder clouds), over the Black Forest.

Eventually we got a handover to Söllingen Approach. As we came on frequency, we heard a Canadian F104 diverting to Ramstein due to the weather. We quickly asked for the latest weather and were given 'Cloudbase 100 feet, visibility 600 meters in snow, with snow on the runway'. We then requested the weather at Lahr and were told that it was the same. ATC requested our intentions. We did not have the fuel to divert to Ramstein so that was out of the question; we were going nowhere. It was decided that we had enough fuel to attempt two approaches to land at Söllingen, prior to engine flameout. I was then the first to descend, as my fuel was a couple of hundred pounds lower.

The GCA[7] controller sounded very confident, which is always a bonus in such a situation. As we approached 5 miles from touchdown, we entered blizzard conditions. Approaching 200 feet on finals, I looked up - nothing. I had unconsciously reduced the rate of descent and gone high on the glide slope. Immediately and simultaneously, my navigator and ATC said, "Keep going down". Soon afterwards, there was a glimmer of lights through the driving snow. At 100 feet there were two distinct rows of runway lights, but it was solid white between them. The good thing about the Phantom was that you didn't have to flare or kick off drift so, as soon as we were down, I deployed the brake parachute

---

[4] GREEN - NATO airbases used a colour coding system to indicate the prevailing meteorological conditions in relation to cloud base and visibility. Starting with the best they were BLUE, WHITE, GREEN, YELLOW, AMBER and RED.
[5] HF – High Frequency radio. A type used for long range communication.
[6] ATIS – Air Traffic Information Service.
[7] GCA – Ground Controlled Approach radar.

and heaved a sigh of relief. The next second, the aircraft was swinging quickly towards the runway edge. Opposite rudder and brake took effect and we were quickly heading for the other side of the runway. As I reversed the controls, I dumped the chute and lowered the hook (a trick that I heard from an Old Pro). At this point my navigator asked, "Have you got it?" I answered something like "I think so", completely lacking in any conviction. We managed to stop before the end and vacate the runway prior to the other aircraft landing.

After shutdown, we were met by some Canadian F104 pilots who were somewhat bemused that we had landed in such adverse conditions. It is as well we got in on the first attempt, because the snow continued for an hour. If only we had had that centreline tank, we could have diverted to Ramstein and not frightened ourselves to death. Some time after the incident, my navigator told me that he had very nearly ejected us both as we inspected the edge of the runway for the second time.

Credit: Geoff Lee

I Wish We Had Left That Man At Home

In a career of many years as an air force fighter pilot, there is almost no avoiding it – suddenly, unexpectedly and without preparation, the Grim Reaper stares you in the eyes. Deep in the eyes!

It happened to me on 26th August 1985, in peacetime, and flying over 'friendly' Scotland. Was I on his list that day? Had my final hour struck? Not only was I shot at that day, by a Dutch F-16, but what's more, I was hit too! The bullets struck holes in my aircraft, and literally buzzed around my ears. Had The Reaper maybe wanted those bullets to hit at a slightly different position? Ten centimetres to the left, and critical control components would have been hit; fifty centimetres forward, and fuel tanks would have exploded. However, that was not to be; this time only the engine nozzle and horizontal stabiliser had been hit. The aircraft remained controllable, I medically fit to complete the flight, and the other bullets ended up somewhere in the Scottish Highlands. So what had led up to this?

As part of a squadron rotation[1] (a mutual exchange between my own squadron, No 322 from Leeuwarden Air Base in the Netherlands, and the British 237 Operational Conversion Unit at RAF Lossiemouth in Scotland) we, somewhat unusually, took along a pilot from the other Leeuwarden squadron, No 323. During the rotation, we were flying our F-16s and they, the Brits, their Buccaneers. One sunny Monday, a cunning and special training scenario was planned. Two F-16s and four Buccaneers would depart, together, for a training mission to a firing range situated in the north. They were going to practice dropping laser-guided weapons, a new air-to-ground technique in those days.

Fifteen minutes later, two additional F-16s would get airborne, with an entirely separate role. Their mission was to intercept the other six aircraft, on their way back from the bombing range. This was an air-to-air scenario, and I was the leader of the second pair of F-16s. After the planned interception, the four Buccaneers would continue back to base, while we, the four F-16s, would become a new formation. We would then set course for a more southerly firing

---

[1] Known in the RAF as a Squadron Exchange, this was an annual programme of mutual visits between NATO squadrons for the dual purposes of professional and social interaction.

range, where we would use our guns to fire at ground targets.

At first, everything went according to plan, and the first six aircraft departed for their mission. Fifteen minutes later, while starting our engines, my wingman developed a technical problem and had to ground-abort. Now what? After some consultation on the radio, we decided that I would go on my own. Just me against six aircraft? Stupid maybe, but a challenging exercise!

So there I was, flying low-level over the Scottish Highlands towards 'the enemy', where I set up a Combat Air Patrol (CAP), in a race-track pattern at about 500 feet above ground level. After completing about 3 circuits, I struck gold. Six blips on my radar - they were coming! I banked 30° left, descended to 250 feet, and accelerated. After two minutes, I saw them on the horizon; first one, then two, then all six. I made a sharp turn back, and selected full military power[2]. In the run, I kept my eyes on all of them, and selected a simulated air-to-air weapons mode, using the buttons on my stick and throttle. The Buccaneers ran away immediately! That was nice because it left me with just two F-16s as opponents, a 2 v 1 aerial battle. Cool, that meant I had a slightly better than zero chance. They turned towards me; I passed the leader head-on, and pointed my aircraft at his wingman. Immediately after we passed each other, I turned back in afterburner[3]. A low-level dogfight! They came back towards me again. After about 1½ turns, I was slightly offensive on one of them, while the other was no threat – yet. I evaluated my chances; if I could quickly succeed in eliminating the first one (that is, to bring my weapons to bear and simulate 'shooting him down'), I might be able to stay out of the other one's gunsight; and I was always ready to engage in a 1 v 1 aerial battle which would ensue thereafter. I could win that one too, I thought.

It all seemed to be working out. I looked at my direct opponent ahead of me, and over my shoulder at his wingman. He was quite far away, and was definitely not supporting his leader at that range. Of course, I was happy to see that, but knew that he would be back in no time, like a 'deus ex machina', I had to be quick. My direct opponent was manoeuvring frantically to shake me off,

---

[2] Full dry power, ie without afterburner.
[3] afterburner - AKA reheat, produces considerable, additional thrust by injecting fuel near the rear of the engine.

but things were OK – I only needed half a turn before I could 'fire'. All of a sudden, though, my 'victim' called over the radio, "Knock it Off, Knock it Off, Knock it Off[4]." 'The coward', I thought. 'Just when he's about to lose, he stops the fight! But, admittedly, we had already turned and battled far longer than the rules allowed at low altitude. I acknowledged the termination of the fight over the radio.

We then flew to the air-to ground range in a tactical 3-ship formation, and there, one by one, we dived to strafe the ground target with our guns. After that, we left the range, returned to RAF Lossiemouth and landed. As I climbed down the ladder at the side of the aircraft, my crew chief approached, and looked at me enquiringly, with wide eyes. I wanted to say 'Hi' to him but, before I could do so, he stuttered, "Matta (my tactical callsign), what the hell have you been through?" Not comprehending, I followed him to the back of my F-16. There, to my utter amazement, I saw several real bullet holes in my aircraft.

It transpired that, in the dogfight, the opposing wingman (who just happened to be the pilot from 323 Squadron!) had selected air-to-air mode, and also left the main armament switch on 'Hot'; the position it had been in for the first part of his mission, dropping laser-guided bombs. This was an unforgiveable error. In the subsequent dogfight he had, inadvertently, fired some haphazard shots from long range, and just happened to hit my F-16!

Fortunately, it all ended well, and The Grim Reaper did not come for me that day. But, by Jove, I really wished that we had left that man at home...

Credit: Senior Airman Thomas Trower/U.S. Air Force

---

[4] Terminate the engagement.

Manna From Heaven

One useful lesson to be learned from this cautionary tale is that initiative doesn't pay. I certainly believe so, although I should explain that the story I shall tell concerned a close, a very close, friend of mine who wishes to remain anonymous. There may be occasions when I slip into the first person, but it's really my friend who is speaking, and I hope you will remember that. It was, after all, about the biggest cock-up since Narvik (in purely personal terms, as far as my friend was concerned) and who would want to be associated with anything like that? I hope I make myself clear – or that he does, if you get my meaning.

It was a nice day in early May: spring was springing, and the birds outside the crewroom window were looking at each other in a contemplative sort of way. "I was reminded," my friend later explained, "of a middle-aged chap getting back on a bike for the first time in a year or two. The idea seemed a good one, but the execution was probably going to be absurdly inept, until memory and instinct came to the rescue." If only instinct had played a better part in the tale that follows.

As I have said, it was early May and also a Friday. It promised well since there was a plan, a plan devised by those in authority, who ran the operations desk and handed out goodies for the weekend. One Canberra was to man up and pop down from West Raynham to Chivenor (for the younger readers both these establishments were once owned and operated by the RAF, full of aeroplanes of a British make and overall good quality). There the jet was to be refuelled and, after a suitable period of briefing, take off again and escort a Hunter to Gibraltar. Once again, younger readers, for some years we maintained a detachment of Hunters at Gibraltar, intended to dissuade the Spanish ne'er-do-wells from threatening the Crown Colony. They were usually drawn from the Chivenor Hunter fleet, and one of the Gibraltar echelon was due for routine rotation. The powers that be deemed it appropriate to provide an escort on such occasions. The theory being that the Hunter was a bit poorly placed for navigation aids, and the Canberra could allegedly do something to assist (little did they know how little that could be). In any case, Hunter pilots tended to get lonely if left on their own. Have you noticed that single-seat jocks are always thinking of ways to 'enhance their tactical flexibility.' This just means that they like the company of their buddies, and prefer at least two, if not four, in the same piece of sky. But I digress – enough psychology for now.

Before I go further, I should mention that a single-seat chap would seldom (Never – Ed) admit to a liking for a navigator for company in his aircraft. That's going too far. Anyway, my friend explained that, on this occasion, his navigator was Jim, and Jim was starting to feel his age. You know the symptoms; hairs on your legs are going grey, you can't/don't feel the urge to run for the bus, and your girth is increasing. It was the latter that caused the first problem of the day. Once on the ground at Chivenor, my friend and Jim made arrangements for refuelling, and then set off across the airfield to meet their intended airborne companion. They gratefully accepted a lift in a passing Bird-Control Land Rover, because the duty Flying Prevention Officer (otherwise known as the Air Traffic Controller) had invited the gallant pair to park their aircraft at a point on the airfield furthest from the Operations block. En route, Jim gave vent to a few thoughts about that ATC fellow, as the Land Rover bounced along the perimeter-track. They were loud, concise and far from complimentary, which was unfortunate. His ample girth had switched on part of the vehicle radio system, thus allowing him to share his thoughts with everyone on the local airfield frequency. Unaware of this faux-pas, they were somewhat surprised by the hostile reception that awaited them from a tight-lipped OC Operations, who put them into a tastefully furnished shed to await the Hunter pilot – that sun-bronzed, golden-haired, demi-god of the air.

He turned out to have a hangover and no cigarettes, and his realisation that they were free of the former and devoid of the latter did nothing to improve his opinion of them as lesser mortals. But he announced himself prepared to follow them, as soon as they were ready to get airborne, and showed them his one and only navigation aid. It was a crumpled map, of such a scale as to enable the entire Chivenor to Gibraltar route to be shown on an eight-inch long chart that measured no more than twenty scale miles across. There seemed little point in entering into discussion on the finer points of navigation; so radio frequencies for use en-route were agreed, as were emergency procedures should things go seriously Tango Uniform at any stage. The two Canberra chaps returned to their aircraft and, fifteen minutes later, the pair were up and away, heading for Flight Level 400 and Gibraltar.

Three hours later, the welcoming party gathered round the aircraft, and the crack and hiss of the opening beer cans made sweet music on the afternoon air. Less sweet was the sight of the demi-god reverently removing his cellophane-sheathed Dinner Jacket from some hatch or other in the side of the Hunter. "I presume you've brought yours," he said. "There's a big party in the Mess tonight." Our Canberra lads shook their heads thoughtfully – obviously a lack of communication somewhere. "We needn't have bothered anyway," said my friend. On arrival at the Mess, they were greeted by a friendly member of the permanent staff, and told that 'transients' were not invited. The implication was clear, so our gallant lads made other, fairly predictable arrangements for their couple of days in Gibraltar.

The weekend passed in a blur of cultural and mind-improving activities. Monday dawned, and with it came two discoveries. The first was perhaps predictable; the demi-god had supped unwisely. Great-uncle Bacchus had slipped him a quart or two of duty-free Fundador, and the golden hair hung limply over a pale, troubled face. But help was at hand, in the shape of the second discovery. The Hunter due to return to UK on this rotation had developed a sympathetic mechanical problem, which could only be solved by fitting a new nosewheel and undercarriage leg. No spares in Gib. No chance of having one flown out from UK until Thursday at the earliest. Demi-god took the news cheerfully. There were definite signs of a return to health, before he slipped back beneath his bedclothes and began, once more, to sleep.

At this point a degree of initiative was shown which brought the operation to an ignominious end. "Surely", said my friend "we could go and collect the spare parts. We could have them back here by nightfall and the Hunter could be ready to fly back to Chivenor tomorrow." Nobody found fault with the proposal – it seemed totally sensible. As they used to say at Staff College, it was the 'pink', the DS solution[1]. If only someone had found fault. But the fourth Earl of Chesterfield said it all, when he said that idleness was only the refuge of weak minds. Uplifted by this moral precept, the gallant Canberra crew made arrangements for an early departure, which translated to Jim sharpening his pencils and

---

[1] DS solution – The Directing Staff's solution to a task at Staff College was known as a 'pink.'

getting on with some compulsive drawing of lines on charts and twirling of his Dalton Computer[2].

Shortly after ten, the Rolls-Royce Avons burst into life and all went so well that, just after one that afternoon, our heroes were back on the ground again at Chivenor. And there was a spot on the airfield further away from the Ops block – thank you OC Ops! Naturally there was no transport, so there was much muttering as the two good Samaritans trudged across the English landscape. Refuelling was arranged, the spares were taken to the Canberra and lashed into the bomb-bay crate, and a request was made for some in-flight rations. Items one and two were completed without a problem, but the catering flight said "no entitlement". Free and collective bargaining was undertaken by Jim, and the Corporal got enough of the message to realise that a packet of corned beef sandwiches – although not much – would be enough to keep Jim from committing some ritual disembowelling. They turned out to be door stops – doorstops for the sort of door a Devonian castle might have sported. Never mind; take a bite and get on with it. Pausing only to spit out a bit of broken filling, Jim clambered into the back seat while I – or rather, my friend – checked the security of the bomb-bay load, parked the unexpired portion of the day's rations just by Jim's feet, climbed into his own seat, strapped in and got ready for start-up.

There was a spot of bother with the aircraft door, it seemed to be very difficult to shut tight. In the event, some hefty wellying from outside did the trick, once again the Rolls-Royce masterpieces fired up, brakes were released and the Wright brothers' calculations were confirmed yet again, as 48,000 lbs of British engineering climbed up into the azure whatnot. "Should be back in Gib just after four-thirty, in time for tea; no problem."

"Oh, I have slipped the surly bonds of earth" murmured my friend as the layers of low cloud fell away beneath.

"Bang," said the aircraft, unappreciatively, and all Hell broke loose.

Jim said many things in succession which we shall not repeat here.

My friend surveyed the situation calmly. The door – yes, that wretched, resistant door – was open. It seemed likely that it had disappeared completely. In

---

[2] Dalton Computer – an ancient form of rotary slide rule (for those who remember such things) used to compute navigation data.

the awful cacophony of the 400 knots of airflow rushing past the opening, and rushing in and out again, the one lasting impression was nevertheless a visual one. Out of the doorway were disappearing, in apparent slow motion, the entire contents of Jim's navigation bag: maps, charts, old cigarette packets, a note from someone at Station Headquarters asking him to pop in and sign Confidential Orders for last year and the pencil box with a spare ten-bob note in (younger readers, ask for guidance here). Finally the vacuum cleaner effect overcame the inertia of one last object, and out went the corned beef sandwich doorstops.

There's not much more to tell. Our heroes elected to land forthwith at the nearest suitable airfield – St Mawgan got the vote. During the descent, reduced speed brought a lowering of the noise level. It also brought the door back into view, hanging by one distorted hinge. After landing, the Hunter spares were un-loaded, taken back to Chivenor by road and flown out to Gib on the Thursday. The demi-god duly flew his Hunter home, with another Canberra sent out to give him company. Our heroes' Canberra was semi-repaired, covered in duct tape, and flown gently back to RAF West Raynham at a thousand feet, landing gear down, and at 180 knots. Minor admin items, like the return of our heroes' kit from the Gib Mess, were all completed by mid-June.

There were no reports of unexplained fatalities in Cornwall that might have been ascribed to a blow on the head from a corned beef sandwich at terminal velocity. So really everything turned out all right in the end. But if only the ini-tiative had remained untaken. How much simpler it would have been.

I tried to comfort my friend with the Earl of Lytton's words, drawn from his "Last Words of a Sensitive, Second-Rate Poet":

"Genius does what it must, and Talent does what it can." He was not consoled.

Credit: MoD/Crown copyright

I Learnt About Test Flying From That

July 1968, and I was on A Squadron at RAF Boscombe Down. That morning I had drawn the short straw and was 'on the desk', which meant that I was the authorising officer, and running the flying programme. So I was generally minding my own business, drinking a cup of coffee, when the phone rang. I picked it up, and it was ETPS[1] on the other end, asking if we could help them out with a little problem they had. It seemed that they had a serviceable Lightning T4 two-seater, and a student ready to do some particular exercise but they had no-one qualified to fly the Lightning as captain. The Lightning had appeared on ETPS in 1966 and, whilst students did an exercise in it, they were not allowed to go solo. So, normally, a tutor would sit in the right hand seat whilst the student did silly things to the aircraft at ridiculous speeds. In fact, I had done my preview exercise on this aircraft whilst on the course in 1966, when it first arrived; but two years had passed and I had not flown it since.

I asked around, and there was no-one Lightning-qualified and available on A Squadron except me – and I was already employed on the desk. I also did a quick check of my log book and, since it was some time since I had flown a Lightning (at that time we had about 6 of them on A Squadron) and I was also not a WIWOL[2] merchant, I ruled myself out on grounds of lack of currency. We did have a couple of other ex-Lightning pilots, but they were not around at the time. So, I answered the ETPS query, saying that there was no one available. I was the only one vaguely qualified to do it, but did not feel that I was sufficiently current to go supervising an ETPS student. Half an hour later the phone rang again and it was ETPS on the line, begging me to go and act as captain of the aircraft. They really needed to complete the exercise, and there was absolutely no one else who could do it. Once again I refused. Ten minutes later the phone went again, and I then made a big mistake by succumbing to their pleas. They assured me that the student in question was very capable, and that all I would have do was sit there.

The exercise was something to do with stability, exactly what I cannot

---

[1] ETPS - The Empire Test Pilot School, also based at Boscombe Down.
[2] WIWOL - 'When I Was On Lightnings'. If you haven't stood at the bar and been bored to death by WIWOL stories, you haven't lived.

remember - except that it involved doing all sorts of unspeakable things to the aircraft, including stick jerks at up to Mach 1.6 at 36,000 feet; not something that I would have chosen to do myself, but then the choice was not up to me. The weather was not that good, with mandatory GCAs[3] for recovery. However, off we went, but the cloud cover meant that we were unable to do the low-level part of the exercise, so we climbed to 36,000 feet, just out of the cloud tops, for supersonic runs down the Channel. Whilst the student was busy doing whatever it was he was trying to do, I amused myself looking around the cockpit, to re-familiarise myself with where everything was, particularly as I had never flown in the right-hand seat. The activities being conducted from the left-hand seat did not make for a particularly comfortable ride; but one thing that I did notice, with some surprise, was that, as well as engine relight switches on the left-hand side of the cockpit, there was a duplicate set on the right. Quite why, I never discovered; but, presumably, it had something to do with the fact that this aircraft was the original two-seat prototype, and they had been put there for trials purposes. It turned out to be an extremely significant observation.

Now the Lightning is not exactly over-endowed with fuel and, by the time we had done two runs down the Channel, we were down to 800 lbs a side, at which fuel state you would normally expect to be in the circuit to land. Even I realised that we were going to be a little tight on fuel, and I got the student to point the aircraft in the direction of Boscombe Down, so that we could be fed directly into the GCA. As we went into the cloud tops at 36,000 feet, I instructed the student to throttle back to idle/idle to conserve fuel. A quick word of explanation here: the Lightning has two engine idle positions, idle/idle and idle/fast idle, the latter so that one engine always remains at sufficiently high RPM to keep the electrics on line. This is only really required somewhere below 20,000 feet, as the idle RPM reduces in the descent. Normally you only used the idle/fast idle setting, but if you were really tight on fuel, as we were, you could conserve a little bit by going to idle/idle at high level and then, as the RPM decreased in the descent, setting the engines to idle/fast idle. However, the throttle stops could be a little confusing if you were not used to them, as exhibited by my student, who pulled both throttles back through the HP cocks[4],

---

[4] HP cocks – High Pressure fuel valves that were actuated by pulling the throttles fully closed through an inhibiting "gate". This action shut off the fuel supply to the engines.

thus causing the engines to flame out.

There was a pregnant silence, followed by a number of expletives (from me) and I immediately took control. The instrument panels did their best to impersonate a couple of Christmas trees, and I do not think that I have ever seen so many warning lights in a cockpit in my whole life. We were now in cloud, on emergency instruments and above the relight envelope[5] – but descending rapidly, as the Lightning is not one of the best gliders in the world; and it was at this stage that I remembered seeing the extra relight switches on my side of the cockpit.

I do not know what Air Traffic Control is like today, but it was extremely good then, and the handover from Southern Radar to Boscombe was always very slick. In fact, Boscombe Tower would always keep an eye on you whenever they could; and they were pretty switched on that day, as they responded immediately to my MAYDAY call, and proceeded to give us headings to feed directly into the GCA. My knowledge of the systems on the T4 was not, perhaps, as encyclopaedic as it should have been, so I was not certain of the relight envelope, or of how many relight attempts the batteries would give you (no doubt someone is going to tell me). So I left it until we got below 20,000 feet and then tried it. One engine immediately wound up and, once we had the electrics on line, we got the other engine going as well. Air Traffic fed us straight into the GCA, and we landed, low on fuel but not as low as I had expected, and all in one piece. Shutting down the engines saves even more fuel than just going to idle/idle, but it is not to be recommended!

So what did I learn from all of that? Firstly, beware the siren voices of temptation (ETPS tutors in particular!), and do not believe everything you are told; it can get you into situations that would be better avoided. It also turned out that the student in question was a maritime pilot, who had never been near a fast-jet before arriving at ETPS. So do not get suckered into something without checking the facts beforehand, and ensuring that you are prepared for the worst.

Finally, I find it somewhat ironic that the aircraft in question is now the gate-guardian at Boscombe. It reminds me forcibly of that incident every time I pass by!

---

[5] Relight envelope – Constraints of height and speed, outside of which it was not appropriate to attempt an engine relight.

Memories Of 8 Squadron In Aden

In the early 1950s, I was a Flight Commander on 8 Squadron, equipped with Vampire 9s. As a squadron, we had been having a busy time. First a detachment in Kenya on anti-Mau Mau operations and, later, fairly continuous bombing, rocket and cannon strikes, in the Aden Protectorate, against dissident tribesmen who were killing and robbing neighbours and travellers. Our Air Officer Commanding decided that it was time to demonstrate our offensive ability to a number of so-far-friendly sheikhs at an up-country gathering, near the town of Nisab. The squadron was to demonstrate dive-bombing, low-level bombing, rocketing and strafe attacks. I chose the low level bombing, as I loved low flying.

A number of targets were prepared and reconnoitred by those of us taking part and, on the appointed day, several bigwigs, including our CO, were flown up to the area by the Aden Support Flight. My No2 and I were the last to perform. Our target was a 10 foot square cloth, mounted on a wooden frame. Full of dash, and determined to put on a good show, I pulled in as low as I could, and released my two 500-pound bombs from where I just could not miss. Great! A piece of cake, I thought, right through the centre of the target. No need to pull up, so continue up the wadi[1] climbing slowly and back to Aden for a nice refreshing drink. Two hours later, my CO burst into my office. "Geoff", he yelled, "I've never seen anything so hairy in my life. Those bombs hit the rock, missed your trailing edge[2] by inches, bounced to above your height, and followed you up the wadi, slowly dropping behind. How you weren't killed I have no idea." Luckily for me, the Sergeant Armourer had asked me what delay I wanted in the bomb fuses, and I had chosen 45 seconds. Oh well, old pilots and bold pilots etc... I should add that the dissident attacks continued unabated...

One of the perils of flying over the highly mountainous Aden Protectorate in a single-engined aircraft was the possibility of an engine failure, and the subsequent bale-out over very unfriendly tribesmen. The locals were known to torture and kill their unfortunate infidel captives by cutting off their crown

---

[1] wadi – The local name for a dried up river bed.
[2] trailing edge – The rear edge of the wing.

jewels and stuffing them into their mouths - a rather unpleasant fate! As a result, besides our lightweight flying suits and Mae Wests[3], we always flew with our .38 Smith and Wesson revolvers, an ammunition belt and pouch. In the extreme heat and humidity of Aden, this rendered us wet through by the time we had taxied to the runway, and it was a great relief to get airborne.

However, the aces in our protective measures were our two blood chits, known locally as 'goolie chits.' These were written in Arabic and in English, and were a brilliant example of the Civil Service (probably Treasury) obsession with saving money at any cost – the potential cost, in this case, being our private parts. The procedure, if one was in the unfortunate position of having been captured, was to present the first card to the captors. This promised a reward of 40 Maria Theresa Dollars for the safe and complete return of the captive to the nearest British outpost - in our view a derisory offer. If, however, they started to sharpen their knives, we were authorised to produce our second card, which upped it to 400 Maria Theresa Dollars. Thus comforted, we flew over the Protectorate without worries. But were we right? In later years I have reflected on the fact that 99.9 per cent of the local populace were unable to read or write! Somehow or other, I feel that the desire for revenge would have overtaken their wish to walk miles in that heat looking for someone who could read. We owe our personal contribution to the nation`s gene pool to the Goblin engine that, certainly in Kenya and Aden, never failed us. Thank you Messrs Rolls-Royce!

DE HAV. LAND MADE GHOST

Our usual working day in Aden was from 7am to 1pm because, by midday, it was always too hot and humid to work, even in the winter. We usually managed 3 sorties in the time available but, as the political position worsened, it soon became the norm to work from dawn to dusk. The Aden Protectorate Levies (APL) were local tribesmen, trained and officered by the RAF Regiment. They were a very smart, and seemingly efficient, body of men, and we often provided air support for them. Up-country, at the end of a very long and deep wadi, the APL maintained an outpost known as Rabat Fort. It was a very isolated spot, surrounded by threatening mountains and ridges, and was used as a means of

---

[3] Mae Wests - During World War II, Allied aircrew called their yellow inflatable, vest-like life preserver jackets "Mae Wests" partly from rhyming slang for "breasts" and "life vest" and partly because of the resemblance to her torso.

maintaining a British presence in the area. The small detachment that manned the fort was commanded by one RAF Regiment officer, and personnel were rotated every month. Unfortunately, as the situation worsened, Rabat Fort became a target for local tribesmen, who would fire at the fort and retire when the return fire became annoying. This had to be stopped, so it was decided to keep 2 aircraft on standby during daylight hours, so that such attacks could be repulsed forcefully and thereby deterred. A radio in the fort allowed the detachment to call for help and, 15 minutes later, the squadron would arrive and spray the appropriate ridge with cannon fire. To our surprise, this did not seem to deter the locals and the number of attacks actually increased for a while. This mystery was finally solved when our used cannon shells started to appear in local markets in the form of potato peelers or cigarette lighters. Enterprising tribesmen were climbing the blind sides of the ridges and popping off a few shots before retiring to the safety of the lee slopes and awaiting our attack. When the aircraft had gone, they whipped back over the ridge to retrieve the spent shell cases. Never let it be said that air attacks are always detrimental to a local economy!

Credit: Adrian Pingstone/Wikipedia

La Plume De Ma Tante

Whilst flying Vulcans in the early sixties, I was once loaned a French Canadian co-pilot for an overseas trip. He initially made a good impression by performing all the pre-flight co-pilot duties with skill and determination. This included carrying the crew's ration box from the kitchens to the aircraft, and loading it into the rear cabin with great care. We eventually got airborne and, while we remained in UK airspace, all continued to go well. However, when we entered French airspace there was a dramatic change, as our temporary co-pilot made the fatal mistake of talking to the radar controller in French, or, to be more precise, French-Canadian French. Once the controller heard familiar vowel sounds, he refused to change back into English; he gabbled away so fast that I could not clearly understand what he was on about. It soon became apparent that our Francophone co-pilot was also having difficulty in understanding what he had previously thought was his mother tongue. We continued south across France, replying 'Oui' or 'Non', as we guessed to be appropriate, and were very relieved when we left the French behind us, and were once again able to talk English - to the Italians.

Since those early days in the V-Force, I have had to speak some French on a couple of my tours. I was even given formal French language training, but they don't teach you French body-language on these courses. One of the bits of Gallic body-language that I learned to dread, particularly whilst involved with French air shows in the mid-sixties, yet also learned to accept as indicating the end of the discussion, was the raised shoulders accompanied by spread forearms, the palms of the hands raised to heaven and the raised, quizzical eyebrows. The most dramatic demonstration of this silent, but expressive, Gallic method of visual communication was an incident I witnessed in the control tower of the French Naval airfield, at Landivisiau in Brittany.

It was in the late 1970s and, at the time, I was OC Ops at RAF Wyton. One of the resident Wyton Squadrons was No 360, equipped with T17 ECM Canberras, and some of their aircraft were detached to Landivisiau for a NATO exercise. I went with them as their liaison man on the ground and, when needed, as duty pilot in the air traffic tower. Staying with the French Navy was an interesting experience. The resident squadrons were flying Chance-Vought

Crusaders; the French aircrew were friendly, welcoming and had the attitudes and spirit which set all aircrew apart from ground-based mortals. I did, however, notice a marked difference amongst our French hosts when it came to eating. In the Mess dining room, sitting at long tables set with bottles of wine, as soon as the food was served, they frequently began a heated discussion on the quality of the cooking, and whether or not the chef's choice of sauce was the best for the species of fish that was on the menu. Every lunch-time, the Station Commander, accompanied by all his senior executives, would march through the main dining room and disappear into his private dining room next door. I never did see them emerge again, and they were possibly there for a couple of hours or so. One spell of duty I had in the Landivisiau tower turned into a memorable demonstration of French body-language. I had watched all the 360 Squadron aircraft take off, and then spent two hours or so watching the weather deteriorate much more seriously than we had been told was likely. Shortly before our aircraft were due to start their recovery back into Landivisiau, I unobtrusively crept into the radar room of the control tower. I stayed well out of the way, while keeping an eye on the radar screens and an ear open to monitor the conversations between our pilots and the French radar controllers; controllers that our pilots were relying on to get them safely back on the ground through the lowering cloud base and decreasing visibility.

As the weather deteriorated, first of all the Senior Air Traffic Control Officer came into the radar room to keep an eye on things, and he was soon followed by the French OC Flying. Eventually the Station Commander himself arrived in the darkened radar room and all this high powered help started to ask questions, look at the radar screens over the shoulders of the controllers and frequently gave what they thought was helpful advice. All they succeeded in doing was to create an atmosphere, and distract the controllers from their difficult and vitally important task of getting the aeroplanes safely back on the ground.

In spite of the increasing tension in the radar room, one by one, 360's aircraft landed safely, until there was just one of them left in the air, waiting to be guided back down. I knew that I would not be able to relax until that had happened, but, by then, the weather was very bad and on the minimum limits for landing. However, the last aircraft had already been handed over from the approach controller to the final radar controller, who would talk the pilot down the glide path onto the runway. I knew that this particular pilot was very experienced, and had doubtless met similar situations before, though it did cross my mind that he would probably have been given his instructions by someone whose native tongue was English. In addition, they would not have had those excitable genes which, under circumstances such as these, seem to come to the fore in those with Latin blood in their veins.

With this last aircraft just about half way down the glide path, I noted with some satisfaction that the French NCO[1] controller was talking him down in a calm and very professional way. I was thankful that the last of the 360 crews would soon be safely on the ground, in spite of the weather which was now technically below limits. My interpretation of the situation was not at all how the French senior officers saw it, and they started advising the poor NCO on what they thought he should be doing. The closer the remaining aircraft got to the ground, the more the advice, interruptions and taps on the shoulder increased in frequency, until the poor NCO could stand it no longer. He slid his chair back from the radar screen, stood up and raised his forearms to the heavens. The message was clear. "I will serve no more. You do it." Fortunately our pilot, though abandoned at a critical stage, managed to see the approach lights and then the runway threshold, and much to my relief landed safely. As I descended the control tower staircase, on my way to the Mess and a well needed drink, I could hear the raised voices in the radar room, and could imagine the waving arms and possibly the forehead-smacking which would be the visual accompaniment to the verbal conflict that was taking place. They never do teach you that, in certain parts of the world, language often includes vision to accompany the sound.

Credit: SSgt. David S. Nolan, USAF/Wikipedia

---

[1] NCO – Non Commissioned Officer.

Gulf War One

It was January 19th 1991, not the date of the first ever Jaguar operational mission, but my first time nonetheless. The day before yesterday, we had all gone out in buoyant mood to greet the first 8-ship as they returned, but the smiles were soon wiped from our faces when we realised that two of the aircraft had fired their air-to-air missiles and two were without their centreline fuel tanks. Had they got involved in some incredible dogfight just off the coast of Kuwait?

Beads of sweat were now emerging on our foreheads, as we realised that tomorrow we were up for the same thing. Our mission was led by the then Flt Lt Stevie Thomas – QWI[1], hard man, and just the sort you wanted up the front, to instil confidence in us more junior types. We were to attack an SA-2 missile site in the Kuwait Theatre of Operations (KTO) – mad mission if you applied logic to it, as we were going in at medium level and there was no chance of us climbing above the missile engagement envelope. Anticipation and nervous trepidation hung over the brief like a cloud but, now that we were ready, it was just a case of wanting to get the job done.

We outbriefed with some last-minute intelligence and a pat on the back from the GLO[2], Pat King, and then wandered out to the aircraft, dispersed behind concrete revetments at what had once been RAF Muharraq but was now Bahrain International Airport, our new home. My walk-round checks were a little more thorough than usual and the four 1000lb bombs, hanging from the tandem beams on my inboard pylons[3], got a very close inspection. As I strapped in though, and started my left-to-right cockpit checks, it became readily apparent that this jet was very unserviceable, and was going nowhere. To cries of 'I just don't believe it' and 'Not today, of all days', I ran to the spare aircraft, cursing the fact that I'd just lost all my spare 'walk time', and was now in a complete rush to make the check-in. I briefed my liney[4] to do the external checks, and to make sure all the weapons safety pins were out, as I strapped in and fired up as quickly

---

[1] QWI – Qualified Weapons Instructor.
[2] GLO - Ground Liaison Officer.
[3] pylons - A pylon connects the frame of an aircraft to an item or object that is being carried.
[4] liney – An affectionate name for a line mechanic (Airman) who prepares the aircraft for flight.

as I could. Just the way you want it on your first operational mission – I don't think! Still, there was no time for worry now and, as we taxied out, I was fully focused on what lay ahead.

Stevie called 'Keeper 01, ready for take-off' and Air Traffic enquired as to how long we would be away. 'No answer' was the reply, for obvious reasons, and we got airborne and departed to the north. There was rather too much cloud around for my liking and, as I led the back 4 up the transit corridor, we went IMC[5] at about 10,000 feet. With only the Air-to-Air Tacan[6] as our friend, in 10-second pairs trail as an 8-ship, this definitely wasn't what we had practised day-to-day during the work-up; but hey, this was war, and things would surely get better as we approached the KTO. The word from the front was that we would press to the target area and, if we didn't get sight of the ground, RTB[7]. We checked in with AWACS[8], were declared 'sweet'[9], and continued in eerie silence towards Kuwait.

As we crossed the border into enemy territory, I made sure all my weapons switches were live, and glued my eyes to the Radar Warning Receiver. "Time to descend," called Stevie, and down we went, breaking cloud at exactly 15,000 feet. What were we to do now? How could we do a dive attack, if were not supposed to go below 15,000 feet? Well, no time for thoughts like that and, as I scanned the ground, looking for the familiar circular shape of the SA-2 site, I incredibly saw one, right 2 o'clock at about 8 miles! Letting Mike Rondot, my wingman, know where the target was, I tipped into the attack, releasing my stick of weapons at about 9000 feet, a perilously low height considering that the target could shoot back.

It was now every man for himself, as I became aware of bombs going off north and south of my position, and tracer fire was everywhere, highlighted by the poor light conditions prevalent below the overcast skies. For some reason, I

---

[5] IMC – Instrument Meteorological Conditions; in other words, in cloud.
[6] TACAN - Tactical Air Navigation equipment, normally used to give a bearing and range to a designated ground beacon but, when used in air-to-air mode, gave a range only between equipped aircraft.
[7] RTB – Return To Base.
[8] AWACS - Airborne Warning And Control System aircraft.
[9] sweet – Being recognised by the AWACS' on-board identification equipment.

desperately wanted to get back into cloud, in the vain hope that it would offer me some protection from the forces below. We now had 8 separate Jaguars, in cloud, heading as fast as possible towards the safety of the Saudi border – thank God for the 'big sky' theory. As our heart rates slowed, we joined back up for the recovery into Bahrain, laden with the mixed emotions of euphoria at surviving and concern at what we'd just done. As the Authorisation Sheets recorded, one aircraft, 'X', suffered minor flak damage, but otherwise no harm done. We, however, were somehow much wiser as to what an operational mission was all about, and the kinds of danger we faced – which weren't always attributable to the enemy. Six weeks, and 617 Jaguar missions later, I'm pleased to say that we had all survived to tell the tales.

Credit: Tech. Sgt. Rose S. Reynolds/Wikipedia

A Miraculous Escape

In 1970, I was serving on No 4 (FR) squadron at RAF Gutersloh, in the low level Fighter Reconnaissance role; this was a squadron that had won the prestigious Royal Flush[1] in 1969, and was rightly recognised as the best Fighter Reconnaissance squadron in either of NATO's Allied Tactical Air Forces, 2 and 4 ATAF.

My involvement in the 1970 Royal Flush began in the early part of the year. I was selected, along with six other FR pilots, to work up to a high standard from which four of us would be selected to represent the squadron in the last ever NATO Royal Flush competition, to be held at the Royal Netherlands Air Force (RNlAF) Base Deelen. The aim of the competition was not only to identify the best reconnaissance squadron and pilot, but also to recognise the top Photo Recce Unit (Photographic Interpreters). After four months of flying two missions a day in some pretty atrocious winter weather across North and South Germany, Holland, France and Belgium, I was selected as one of our four Squadron representatives - an achievement which made me feel proud to be considered as one of the elite.

On 9 May 1970, five Hawker Hunter FR10s detached (with the Squadron Commander flying the spare aircraft) to Deelen, a helicopter airfield with only a short North-South runway, and no barriers[2]. The next day was given over to each of us flying a practice sortie, to familiarise ourselves with the local area and procedures associated with the airfield. On the first morning of the competition, 11 May 1970, I was selected to fly the first mission which involved 2 static targets (a complex structured bridge and a military vehicle depot, with some 8 different vehicle types) and a very demanding 40 km line-search, covering mainly 'B' and 'C' class roads, in the notorious Ardennes region of Belgium. The mission was to be timed from take-off to crossing an imaginary line on return, between the airfield Air Traffic Control tower and the umpires' control tent on the opposite side of the main runway. Points would be deducted for any deviation of more than 5 seconds from the target time.

---

[1] Royal Flush – A reconnaissance competition for NATO squadrons.
[2] Barrier(s) – A mechanical arresting system, designed to stop an aircraft from going off the end of a runway.

I took off in Hunter FR10 XF428 and overflew the two static targets dead
on schedule, achieving good photo cover and transmitting a comprehensive
and accurate in-flight report to the airfield. I then navigated my way, on the
1:500,000 scale map, to an Initial Point (IP) which would lead me straight to
the start point of the line search. While navigating the twisting and difficult line,
and about 20 kms into the search, I identified camouflaged bridging equipment,
which was well hidden some 200 metres in from the side of the road. I managed
to plot its position accurately on my 1: 50,000 map, and recorded the number
of bridging equipments, types and defensive weapons. So far all had gone exactly
to plan, and I had turned my aircraft for Deelen when I suddenly noticed that
my fuel was much lower than the planned figure. I continued for a short time,
monitoring the fuel gauge, at which point, to my real concern, it became quite
obvious that either my Hunter was losing fuel fast, or the fuel gauges were faulty.

With the pressure of having to make my airfield overhead time, I aborted
the remaining low level part of the mission and commenced a gentle climb to
gain height (in order to reduce the fuel consumption), but was restricted by
the plethora of airways crossing overhead in Belgian and Dutch airspace. The
aircraft's 2 'Bingo lights' then suddenly illuminated, signifying that there was
only 600 lbs of fuel remaining in each wing. With growing apprehension, I
quickly calculated that I was going to be hard-pushed to make the airfield, let
alone the competition 'overhead time'. However, if I aborted the mission the
Squadron would be severely penalised, resulting in minimal chance of us being
top Squadron. Therefore, and against my basic survival instinct, I elected to
continue. Eventually Deelen came into view, just as the fuel gauges were starting
to indicate empty. The Deelen runway was 01/19; at this time, 01 was in use
with a 10-15 knot wind from the North (the same direction from which I was
approaching), so I called the tower and requested priority landing on runway
19. Clearance was confirmed and, at the point from which I judged I could glide
the aircraft, I moved the throttle to idle and commenced a straight-in, descending approach.

When certain that I was going to make the touchdown point, I selected the
undercarriage down, but, unfortunately, with the throttle at idle, the time for it
to travel fully was some 30 seconds. So, as I crossed the threshold, I had green
under-carriage locked-down lights on the nose wheel and starboard side, with

a red on the port wheel indicating that it was still unlocked. I then selected full flap, which also took time to extend. With no fuel remaining, I touched down deliberately on the starboard wheel, and held the port wing up for a further 3-4 seconds until the port wheel locked down. Meanwhile, the flaps were still extending and, because of the lack of flap (less drag) and a tailwind, I had landed some 20 knots above normal touch-down speed. I streamed the brake parachute at about 150 knots (the normal limit for the chute), but it immediately burst, thus offering minimal retardation. It later transpired that this was the parachute's 50th opening, at which point it would have normally been replaced - just my bad luck!

The flaps had now fully lowered but, with a short runway of only 4,500 feet, I realised that, even with full braking, I was unlikely to stop. As, by then, I had passed the competition timing line (with no penalty points!), there were three options open: with no arrester gear or barrier net, I could go off the end of the runway and hit all the poles supporting the approach lighting; I could raise the undercarriage, and slide along the runway; or I could put on full power, hoping there was sufficient residual fuel to become airborne and 'dumbbell' back to runway 01. I selected the last and, to my delight, the Avon engine wound up, and I lifted-off at the far end of the runway with fuel gauges indicating empty. I then commenced a low level turn to port but, as I climbed through 3-400 feet, the engine flamed-out.

With undercarriage still down and full flap, I managed to glide and turn the aircraft round through 150° back towards Runway 01. At about 100 feet, and descending rapidly, I passed over and just cleared two PR Canberra aircraft, which were at the marshalling point ready for take-off. I glided over the threshold at about 40° to the runway heading and, while I was banking to port to line the aircraft on the centre line, the aircraft literally fell out of the sky since I was well below stalling speed. The magical Hunter wing just seemed to pick itself up, and landed me perfectly on 3 wheels on the runway centre-line, down which I rolled to my turn-off point. I then turned left, to freewheel down the taxiway gradient to my Squadron dispersal site, coming to a halt only 10 yards short of the chocks! I extracted myself from the cockpit and, with my film, completed the mission report with photos of the targets. I received no penalties as I had also made the return time at base.

After completing the reports I suddenly felt a little traumatised, but so grateful to that beautiful and iconic fighter aircraft. That evening, in the mess, I was supplied with beers all night, not least by the Canberra crews, who reported that they thought they had 'bought it.'

Oh, and the engineering investigation of the aircraft revealed a major fuel pipe fracture of one of the coupling joints!

Credit: Author

Piano-Smashing Competitions

Reproduced from his book 'Cold War, Hot Wings', by kind permission of the author, Chris Bain, and Pen & Sword Publishing Ltd.

When I was on 54 Squadron at RAF West Raynham, I joined not just the only UK-based Hunter Wing alongside No 1(F) Squadron, but also the home of the Piano-Smashing Competition. Indeed, the UK Hunter Wing had refined the operation to a fine art form! The Wing already had permanent advertisements in the Eastern Daily Press, looking for old pianos, and stating, "going to a good home"! It was amazing how many pianos were donated in this way!

Every formal dining-in-night terminated with a competition between 1 and 54 Squadrons for the highest throw and fastest piano-smashing. The event occurred outside the front of the Mess, sometime around midnight, and conformed to only two rules: to win, every piece of the piano had to be smashed small enough to be passed through a toilet seat, and the two pianos had to be burnt after the competition, in order that the local volunteer fire brigade could earn its crust. The local Massingham civilian Fire Brigade loved turning out after midnight, because they were then on double-time (some collusion here?), the fire was easy to extinguish and their drinks were on us. All we had to do to ensure their enjoyment, and to maximize the double-time, was to pinch the keys of their fire engine.

Laying into pianos with axes and sledge hammers is hard work, even when sober, and a more modern, refined method was always being sought. We invented the simple 'Insertion of a box of twelve Thunderflashes' method! It required a team of seven pilots, irresponsible for the items below:

- One match box
- One match
- One thunderflash
- One tin with the other 11 thunderflashes
- One tin lid
- One piece of tape - to hold the lid in place
- One holding the top of the piano open

The instructions were: *Light the single thunderflash, pop in tin with other eleven, tape the lid down, throw into top of piano, slam piano lid down and run like hell!* Believe me, twelve Thunderflashes exploding inside a piano makes an indescribable, multi-toned but harmonious, cascading reverberation!

Subsequently, the piano pieces were picked up, fed through the toilet-seat, petrol poured over them, and then the 999 call! The added bonus of this explosive method is that it takes a much shorter time thus not only winning the competition but also leading to more drinking time!

Finals, Two Greens

I was not the only one of my family who flew with the RAF; my uncle Steve flew for many years in Shackletons and had a host of tales of misfortune. The one that I found the most amusing involved an incident with an MR3 at RAF Ballykelly, in Northern Ireland, in the 1960s.

Once again it helps to know a bit about the aircraft's working parts. The MR3 version of the Shackleton had, amongst many other modifications, a tricycle undercarriage arrangement as opposed to the original tail-wheel option. Unfortunately, in some of the earlier models, the nose wheel had a tendency to stay retracted when the undercarriage was selected 'down'. Conversely, the sequencing of retracting the aircraft's undercarriage would not start unless the nose wheel was correctly 'locked down' to begin with. This generated a further problem because, in the event of an undercarriage malfunction, it was often better to land 'all up' rather than some up and some down.

On this particular day, Uncle Steve was returning with his crew but, when they got into the circuit and selected the undercarriage, they only got two green lights, indicating they had a wheel that was not properly down. Initial checks showed that it was not an electrical fault, and that the nose-wheel was still firmly up. They were not short of fuel, so a number of tricks were tried in an attempt to get the wheel to unlock and come down, but all to no avail. They were now committed to landing with the nose wheel retracted, so there was a bit of preparatory work to do. The first thing was to get some foam laid on the runway, to reduce the danger of fire caused by the inevitable sparks once the nose touched the ground. This would take some time, as it was not a regularly-practised exercise; moreover, once the foam was down, the runway would be blocked for quite a while, so all other aircraft had to be recovered beforehand or diverted. Still, while they waited they could continue experimenting with ways of trying to get the nose-wheel to lower, and also consider the crew egress procedures and other such minor post-arrival problems (and that is another tale).

Eventually they were informed that the foam had been laid and they returned to the circuit. My uncle said he was horrified at what he saw. He had expected the whole runway to be covered in foam but, instead, there was just a 'pencil thin' strip down the centreline, from about the half-way point to the far end of the runway. It was certainly not the sea of foam they had all expected! After a quick inspection they started their approach, touched down where they intended and held the nose off the runway (no braking!) as the speed decreased. Eventually, just before they ran out of aerodynamics to keep the nose up, they reached the halfway point; the nose was lowered onto the foam, the engines were shut down and the 'Shack' ground to a halt. Job done! However, everyone knows that counting chickens is bad form, and so it proved in this instance.

It is probably useful to mention at this point that, with the aircraft 'standing on its nose', the nose wheel bay resembled an inclined telephone box, with its base sitting slightly above ground level. Also, in these situations, the engineers were always very keen to find out what had gone wrong. So it was that a senior engineering officer quickly arrived on the scene to investigate the situation, and was soon joined by another, even more senior officer from the station. In order to get a close look at what had transpired, they both climbed up into the nose wheel bay. Unfortunately, none of the aircrew or the onlookers, who were all gathered around discussing the event and generally congratulating themselves on a job well done, noticed this.

After a little while, the officer in charge of the Crash Rescue team (apparently a very keen young fellow) came up to the crew and asked for the captain. My uncle went with him to see what he wanted and was shown a slowly growing pool of liquid, just in front of the open nose wheel bay doors. Steve bent down and dipped a finger in the liquid, felt it, smelt it and thought for a moment what it might be and where it had come from. He then declared that it was possibly hydraulic fluid, maybe from a pipe connected to the nose landing gear that had ruptured during the 'landing'. On hearing this the young lad immediately decided that, despite the foam already laid, there was still a risk of fire from the residual heat generated by the friction of skidding along the runway. He duly sprang into action and ordered one of his men to fill the nose-wheel bay with foam.

Shortly thereafter, two 'snowmen', each displaying a considerable amount of rank braid, were observed making a very rapid exit from the wheel bay. Subsequent discussions were not recorded; suffice to say that that was something they were not expecting - 'Out of the Blue', might one suggest?

No Need To Be Too Brave In Peacetime

During the summer of 1978, BBC TV ran a live series called Summer Sunday, about people who worked on Sunday afternoons, not a common activity in those days. On August Bank Holiday, Sunday 30th August, the programme featured the Quick Reaction Alert (QRA) role at RAF Leuchars. To meet the needs of the programme, the two Phantom FGR2 aircraft in the Q-shed were allocated to the programme, while two further aircraft, operating from the 111 (F) Squadron Line, covered the QRA task; my navigator, Tony Stephens, and I were the crew of one of these aircraft, XT 424.

Half way through the live TV programme, we were called to the cockpit and launched to intercept a Bear Foxtrot (Russian bomber), which was transiting up the west coast of Scotland, en-route to its home base in the Kola Peninsula, from an exercise with Soviet vessels in the Bay of Biscay. As we turned to head west after take-off, the weather was superb and the whole of Scotland was mapped out before us. Tony got an early radar pick-up on the Bear, which was travelling over the sea at low level, I called an early 'Judy'[1] and we set about completing the intercept, so that we could photograph the aircraft and get its Door (Registration) Number.

As we descended to low level, with some 20 miles to go, we lost radio contact with the GCI[2] Station and, I suspect, disappeared from their radar screens. We also found ourselves confronted with a layer of sea fog about 2,000 feet thick. Undeterred, and knowing that our target was flying in the sea fog at around 500 feet, we set about flying a Low Level Visual Identification Procedure. This involved approaching the target from the rear and then moving, in the final stages of the approach, to a position above, but stepped to one side of, the target, at a range of 300 yards; roughly in the target's 4 or 8 o'clock position. The procedure complete, the cloud was so thick that I could see nothing of the Bear. We could, however, hear the sweep of its radar-laid tail gun radar on our Radar Warning Receiver (RWR).

---

[1] Judy - Indicates that the fighter crew has contact with the target and is happy to take over responsibility for the intercept.
[2] GCI – Ground Controlled Interception.

Suddenly the noise went to a radar-locked indication, and Tony said, from the back seat, "You do realise that, as we are out of GCI radar and radio cover, they can shoot us out of the sky and no-one will ever be any the wiser – it would probably be assumed that we have just flown into the sea." This comment was all the more relevant, as the Squadron had lost two crews during the previous year due to aircraft accidents over the sea. A shiver ran down my spine; that was it, there was no rush to complete the identification. I applied power, pulled-up to 2,500 feet and we dropped back to shadow the Bear from a mile astern. Some 20 minutes later, it appeared out of the fog bank and we closed visually to complete our task. This time the RWR remained silent.

The rest of the sortie was uneventful, and we returned to Leuchars in time for our evening meal. Even better, we were released from QRA duties, as the TV programme was over and the aircraft in the Q-shed had taken back the formal task.

Credit: Geoff Lee

What's In A Name?

I was a very young Junior Pilot – newly arrived on No 20 Squadron at RAF Tengah in Singapore. One of the second tourists - Flying Officer Heinz Frick by name – was programmed to lead me on a 1 v 1 combat sortie, and had been quietly told to 'wax my arse', thus performing a public service by lowering my self-esteem. So it was that we ended up 'dogfighting' over the South China Sea at around 20,000 feet. As so often happened on such occasions, by design, desire or accident, we ended up in a very slow-speed 'scissors' with both aircraft weaving in close proximity, both to each other and the stalling speed of the Hunter FGA 9. Of course, because the use of flap in combat was not permitted by the Release to Service, we weren't using it – much!

I like to think that I was getting the better of Heinz in the scissors, because he suddenly rolled away and started spiralling earthwards, in a manoeuvre that I found impossible to follow. Imagine my surprise when his ejection seat suddenly emerged from the cockpit! Needless to say, the aircraft stopped spinning immediately, and continued its dive into the Malaysian coastline, closely followed by Heinz, on his parachute, who fortunately landed on a beach. So much for his waxing my arse!

The outcome of the subsequent Board of Inquiry was entirely predictable; not so the 'clip' that appeared in The Straits Times the next day, which reported that, 'Flying Officer Prick, a pilot on 20 Squadron from RAF Tengah, was forced to ejaculate over the Malacca Straits yesterday.' I kid you not; it was either some cub journalist having a laugh, and not expecting the story to get past the gimlet eye of his editor, or an unfortunate and unwitting malapropism by a gentleman whose first language was not English. I still have the press cutting somewhere; needless to say, my self-esteem remained undented.

A Trip Down Memory Lane

In the course of a career in aviation, one occasionally meets a character who, for whatever reason – be it personality, leadership, flying ability or a mixture of all of them – stands out. One of my memories is of my short time on No 1066 Flight, which flew the Handley Page Hastings whilst part of No 230 Operational Conversion Unit, and particularly of my own aviation hero – Sqn Ldr Ken "Jacko" Jackson, now sadly with us no longer. If you want his whole story take a look at his autobiography "Fifty Four Years in the Cockpit" but, in short, his career goes from wartime Halton "brat", to Spitfire pilot and subsequently to, amongst other aircraft, Hastings, Belfast and Lancaster. Whilst the Hastings is a story in its own right, I just want to tell a couple of stories of a great man from a time before diversity, equality, health and safety, human factors, the breathalizer et al. It's the early summer of 1974 and I'm passing the time before starting my Vulcan conversion by flying air cadets in the Chipmunk at RAF Colerne...

I enter my flight commander's office on Day 1 for the arrival chat, where I'm joined by a (to me) elderly squadron leader. We receive a lengthy brief culminating in the tricky art of landing a tail dragger in a crosswind. This is illustrated by our mentor with the aid of a 12 inch ruler clipped into his Parker biro, which he lands rather skilfully on his desktop. I'm amazed as Jacko rolls his eyes skywards in my general direction. A squadron leader just shared his derision with me - an Acting Pilot Officer! Later, he briefs me that we are to go to his old local pub in Castle Combe, and I am to drive him in his huge Ford Zephyr. The quid pro quo, he assures me, is that the landlady has three lovely daughters. To my surprise, when we get there, it is staffed by middle-aged women. He smiles and points out that his last visit was in nineteen fifty-something! Over a few beers he invites me to come to Scampton and wait for my Vulcan conversion by flying with 1066 Hastings Flight (which he commands as a day job). Naturally I accept, and somehow I get the Zephyr back to Colerne in one piece.

It's week 1 at RAF Scampton, and the RAF is halfway through changing from the wearing of WW2 battledress (with brevet) to woolly, army style jumpers (without brevet). A new (Vulcan) captain sits awaiting his arrival brief, in "woolly pully"; Jacko sails past without a word. Next day, same scenario but Stuart (the

Vulcan captain) is dressed in his battledress with brevet. "Sorry mate...", says Jacko, "Thought you were a navigator...". I should perhaps point out that Jacko despised the Vulcan possibly even more passionately than navigators!

It's a deep February fog at Scampton. Nothing stirs, unless...could that have been the sound of a Hastings taxiing in the distant stillness? We are drinking coffee in the crewroom of No 35 Squadron, when my harassed flight commander (who is the Duty Commander Flying at Scampton that day) comes in muttering darkly, "That bloody Jacko, demands a take-off clearance, I refuse and say there are no UK diversions, and he just takes off whilst transmitting *Heathrow's open!*"

Just in case you thought Jacko was totally unique, let me give you a moment from our sister Vulcan flight. Young Irish co-pilot, invited into new (slightly unpopular) flight commander's office for chat.

Flight commander:- "So young WC what do you think of the new office arrangements?"

WC(deadpan and with Irish brogue):- "I notice you're sitting where the waste paper bin used to be sorr!"

As it's almost the festive season as I write this, I am reminded of one further Jacko tale. It involved a Hastings going to RAF Machrihanish in early December, to collect Christmas trees and fresh fish for the good folk of RAF Scampton. As he often did, Jacko selected a crew to get to Machrihanish (including me), and took a spare crew to fly us back. After arrival Jacko, the Air Engineer and I set off for refreshment in our respective Messes – actually two ends of the same building at a very bleak airfield, if memory serves. There was no-one but a lonely receptionist in the Officers' Mess, who sent us next door to the Sergeants' Mess to get the key to our honesty bar. Having been invited into this tiny Mess (as tradition demands), an unbelievable din breaks out as it becomes apparent that we have stumbled into a major Christmas party. Undeterred, I down several pints, whilst Jacko despatches a number of his favourite G&Ts. Back at the aircraft we climb carefully through the cargo door to find the whole interior decked out like a Santa's grotto, full of fresh Christmas trees and, rather bizarrely, evil-eyed dead salmon and the like staring blindly at us. We settle into 2 seats at the H2S (navigation) station, and off we go. As we get airborne, and over the bellowing of the four mighty Bristol Hercules, Jacko turns to me and shouts, "Bloomin' lovely!" You could tell he meant it. Yes, things like this could and did happen in those days.

Years later I am a Qualified Flying Instructor on the Central Flying School Jet Provost Squadron at RAF Leeming. An even older Jacko arrives for a, would you believe it, Chipmunk refresher course! I fly him on a Jet Provost Mark 5 low-level navigation exercise, landing away at RAF Wittering. Guess what – he flys the ar*e off it and lands it beautifully.

What an absolute gentleman and star.

Credit: RuthAS/Wikipedia

Pressing On Regardless

Looking back through my logbook the other day, I came across 4 entries for 1987 which brought back some vivid memories. They were:

DateAircraft No.DutyDayNightIFApp
22 NovPhantom XV404Nellis - Goose (AAR)4.301.101.00PAR 1
23 NovPhantom XV404Goose - Goose Eng Fail (AAR)2.000.20PAR 1
27 NovPhantom XV404Eng Air Test0.40
28 NovPhantom XV404Goose Wild Turb Fail (AAR)3.002.400.30PAR 1

These four lines encompass an interesting series of events, but I should probably start off by sketching in some of the background. In 1987, I was based at RAF Wildenrath in Germany, and held the post of Staneval[1] (Flying). I had flown the Phantom for about 2400 hours, and was thus quite experienced on type. In October and November, RAF Wildenrath sent a combined detachment of 19 and 92 Squadron aircraft to Nellis Air Force Base (Las Vegas), to participate in two, back-to-back, 2-week Red Flag[2] Exercises. For the recovery back to RAF Wildenrath at the end of the detachment, I was detailed, with a 19 Squadron navigator, to fly XV 404 back home. Now this was a pretty sick machine. The air-to-air radar, which also had a ground mapping mode, was completely dead. In addition, the Inertial Navigation Attack System (INAS) was unserviceable. This left the TACAN[3] system as the only navigation equipment which, unfortunately, relied on ground-based beacons (in short supply across the Atlantic). On the bright side, the aircraft was part of a 4-ship formation allocated to a dedicated tanker, so all we had to do was follow the others. The aircraft was configured with 3 external fuel tanks and 2 baggage pods containing personal belongings, service equipment and some spares – the Phantom freighter!

---

[1] Staneval – Standardisation and Evaluation.
[2] Red Flag - An advanced aerial combat training exercise, hosted at Nellis Air Force Base, Nevada and Eielson Air Force Base Alaska. Its purpose is to train aircrew from the United States and other NATO countries. In a typical Red Flag exercise, Blue Forces (friendly) engage Red Forces (hostile) in realistic combat situations.
[3] TACAN - Tactical Air Navigation equipment.

On 22nd November, we departed Nellis in good order, and headed across the USA for Goose Bay in Canada, using Air-to-Air Refuelling (AAR) to make the long distance. If you note the time of year, you can imagine the contrast between the deserts of Nevada and the Canadian snows at the beginning of winter. As we approached Goose Bay, the weather deteriorated and the end of the sortie culminated in some formation flying in cloud, and at night, before we split up into individual aircraft and were talked down by Precision Approach Radar, for an uneventful arrival at the snow covered airfield.

The following day, after briefing, we took off for home. The route would take us out of Canada, over the Atlantic to the southern tip of Greenland, south of Iceland, down past the Hebrides and over the North Sea to Germany. Our formation of 4 aircraft had a Tristar tanker to refuel us 4 times on our transatlantic crossing. The plan was to keep each aircraft topped up with fuel so that, in the event of any emergency or unserviceability, sufficient fuel was available to divert to an airfield en-route. After take-off, we joined up with the tanker and set off down route. XV 404 still had no navigation aids, and had now also developed a noticeable vibration through the airframe. Although a little worrying, after discussion with the navigator, I made the decision to press on. Mistake Number 1!

Now, AAR with the Phantom in the freighter configuration required a bit of finesse. As the fuel flowed, and the aircraft got heavier, more and more power was needed until eventually afterburner[4] on one engine was required to stay in contact. In the aircrew manual for the Phantom, this was described as an 'emergency procedure'; however, it was used routinely. The problem was that it took 4 seconds to light the afterburner and then it would cut in with a surge of thrust – a little disconcerting when plugged into the refuelling basket and only a few yards from ramming the tanker. The trick was to select half reheat on one engine, put your hand on the other throttle, count to 4 and smartly throttle back this engine as the reheat lit. This throttle was then used to maintain the correct distance for refuelling.

Whilst plugged into the tanker, and taking on fuel during the first refuel

---

[4] afterburner – AKA reheat, produces considerable, additional thrust by injecting fuel near the rear of the engine.

between Canada and Greenland, it became progressively more difficult to push the refuelling hose in, and a glance down at the engine instruments showed that the nozzle of the engine not in reheat was stuck fully open. The nozzle, at the back end of the Rolls-Royce Spey engine fitted in the Phantom, automatically adjusts itself to maintain optimum airflow through the engine at all rpm and during the operation of the afterburner. With it failed fully open there was no major problem, just a reduction of maximum thrust from that engine. Now it was decision time! Disconnecting from the tanker and turning round we set heading back towards Goose Bay with the suspect engine at a low power setting. After discussion with other members in the formation, I had made the decision that, as it was just a nozzle failure, we did not need an escort back to Goose. Mistake Number 2! The rest of the formation continued with the tanker, and quickly went out of radio range.

So, in summary, we were now halfway between Canada and Greenland in November, with no navigation aids and one damaged engine. On the bright side, we were at height and should be able to talk on the radio and get assistance. However, things then started to go seriously wrong. The engine with the failed nozzle gradually started to vibrate more heavily, and eventually I had no choice but to shut it down.

The following points now needed to be considered. The generator on the failed engine was not working, but the electrical system had operated correctly and all electrical systems were operating normally on the remaining generator. Two of the Phantom's four hydraulic pumps were now of limited use, but the aircraft was flyable at reduced speed and sufficient power was available to operate services like the undercarriage. Of more immediate concern, half the aircraft's thrust was gone, and we had additional drag from the shut-down engine. In the aircraft's operating manual I could remember that, with our external load, the stabilised height on one engine without reheat was quoted as 500 feet. We also had a reduced range compared to two-engined flight. However, having just filled up to 21,000lbs of fuel, range was not a problem. Nevertheless, we could not maintain height. The option of jettisoning the external tanks to reduce weight was available, but I was wary about throwing away all that potentially useful fuel. We could also jettison the baggage pods with all our personal stuff in them, but were naturally reluctant to take this course of action. Therefore, with the airspeed adjusted to give the optimum angle of attack for range, and the good engine set to maximum continuous rpm, we headed for Canada in a gradual descent. In fact, eventually, having descended through patchy cloud we stabilised at about 5,000ft above a very grey cold looking sea, still well out of sight of the coast. The very low air temperatures must have given us more thrust than calculated. Thanks for small mercies!

Crossing the North Atlantic in winter meant wearing full survival equipment, in case we ended up in the sea. This normally included waterproof gloves with thick rubber wrist seals. I hated the feel of them and had positioned mine on the aircraft's coaming above the instrument panel, and was wearing ordinary flying gloves. As we started our descent I rapidly changed gloves, which shows how concerned I was with our situation. The next problem was to find our way back to Goose Bay. Of course we had no navigational equipment; in addition, as we had no Inertial Navigation System (INAS), we were left with just a magnetic compass. The variation between true north and magnetic north at that latitude was 28^0 which made life more difficult than usual. However, on the plus side, I had a large scale topographical map of northern Canada. Usually, on long transits, we only carried a chart with airspace details on it but, fortunately, at some time in the past, an old pilot had told me it was a good idea to carry a map with ground features on it. The trick to finding Goose Bay would be to locate the very large inlet that led from the coast to the airfield, which was where 'The Chichester Principle' (named after Sir Francis Chichester) came into play. Basically, if you are aiming at a point on a line feature, like an inlet on the coastline, you deliberately aim off to one side. Then, when you reach the line feature and cannot see your point, you know which way to turn in order to find it. It worked!

The next problem was to let someone know we were in trouble. The rest of the formation were out of radio range and we were so low that, for half an hour or so, we could not talk to anyone. Eventually, having hopped around various frequencies, we spoke to a Delta Airlines aircraft on a civilian frequency, and we asked him to forward a message to Goose Bay to let them know we were on our way back. Having found the coast and the inlet, we made our way visually to Goose Bay for a straight-in radar approach. All this time, the vibration level from the damaged, rotating engine was gradually increasing. It was so bad on final approach that the whole instrument panel was shaking and the instruments were difficult to read. Having landed uneventfully and taxied back to dispersal, we shut down, climbed out and had a look at the rear of the aircraft. The tail of the jet pipe normally contained rings of guttering for the reheat - there was nothing left but a big black hole. In the ensuing 1½ hours since the engine had failed, it had eaten itself to death. After examination, the groundcrew told us that the vibration had been so bad that the main steel fuel delivery pipe, of some considerable diameter, had sheared. In addition, the large oil breather pipe on the upper fuselage side had also sheared.

So we were now stuck at Goose Bay. Fortunately for us, the groundcrew, who were following behind on a Hercules aircraft with all the detachment spares, were still there. They had a spare engine and, four days later, it was fitted and the aircraft was ready for engine ground runs. These were duly completed, after which we got airborne for a successful engine air test in the local area. I remember thinking that the terrain around Goose Bay, in late November, certainly did not look very inviting.

The RAF kindly deployed a Tristar tanker to refuel us on the way home. The plan was for the Phantom to get airborne before the Tristar and, if we were serviceable, we would orbit the airfield where, from long finals, I would tell the Tristar pilot when to release brakes. Remember - we had no radar or INAS, so we needed to get into close formation for the climb; if we lost the Tristar in cloud, we had no way of finding him again. The Hercules aircraft would get airborne last and follow wherever we ended up! I *now* know that a Tristar takes a long time to get airborne and climbs out at an incredibly slow speed compared to the Phantom. We very quickly overtook, and ended up desperately doing a lag pursuit roll round him and wingovers in order to stay behind before he went into cloud. Eventually we slotted into formation, climbed up and headed for Germany.

The flight proceeded as planned, but I was surprised at how quickly it got dark. After four mid-air refuels, and a lot of close formation, we were on the last leg of our crossing and approaching the Outer Hebrides. It was a beautiful clear night, and the lights of Scotland were in view, when there was a thunderous explosion from the front of the aircraft. It was so violent that the throttles were wrenched from my hand. I knew immediately what it was. The equipment cooling turbine, which was located somewhere forward of my left knee, had disintegrated. High pressure air from the engine was compressed, passed through a cooling heat exchanger and exhausted through a turbine, to drive the whole thing round at a rumoured 40,000rpm. Apocryphal stories of the early days of the Phantom told of pilots losing their lower left leg when the turbine blew up. However, we had been informed that RAF aircraft were modified with a steel shroud that would contain any explosion.

So we now had no equipment cooling, but the irony was that, apart from a radio and some lights, we actually had no operating equipment to cool! I therefore decided to continue to Wildenrath, and not divert to any open RAF airfields in Scotland. Eventually we passed over Holland and the Tristar took spacing behind us, as we commenced our descent into Germany and led the way home. After an uneventful approach we landed at Wildenrath, but The Fates had not finished with us yet. The Phantom has very poor brakes[5], and the use of a brake parachute is normal on landing. I dutifully deployed the brake chute, but it left the aircraft still in its bag - a large frozen lump. Quickly selecting full power, I took off again and entered the visual circuit. The runway controller left his caravan and retrieved the offending brake chute from the runway, as I set up for an arrested landing into the approach cable. This was the standard operating procedure for the loss of a brake chute. In the meantime the Tristar, full of equipment and groundcrew, circled overhead.

Finally, after a normal arrested landing, I taxied back to 19 Squadron's dispersal for an engine-running winch-back into our allocated Hardened Aircraft Shelter (HAS). It was now late in the evening, and a reception committee of senior officers had left a social function in the Officers' Mess to welcome home the last aircraft from our detachment. As we slowly moved backwards into the HAS, I observed that they were looking at the front left hand side of the aircraft with some interest. After I had completed all the shut-down checks, and was climbing down the aircraft ladder, I could see why. There was a jagged hole in the side of the aircraft where the Equipment Cooling Turbine had exploded and punched its way out just in front of the left engine intake ramp. Obviously the

---

[5] Poor brakes – The Phantom was originally designed to be a carrier-borne, naval fighter, and was fitted with an arrestor hook as the main means of stopping. In such circumstances, brakes would only be required for taxying around the flight deck.

steel shroud was not designed to completely contain an explosion, just to protect the pilot's leg. Nobody had told us this important bit of information! Subsequent examination showed no damage to the left engine, and the only mark on the airframe was a small nick on the left hand external fuel tank.

So that is the story of me pressing on for home. You can probably identify all the bad decisions I made, and imagine how much worse it could have been. Coincidentally, the next time I flew the same aircraft, on 7th January 1988, the equipment cooling turbine failed again. However, this time, it was a gradually increasing whine and rumble that warned us of the impending event. The cooling turbine was quickly shut down before it could explode and, as it turned out, I never flew that aircraft again. What a relief!

Credit: Geoff Lee

Getting Away With It

In 1954, on my second squadron tour, flying the armed version of the Harvard with 1340 Flight in Kenya, I found myself deep in a hole, which very nearly caused dire problems for me in more ways than one. But, as had happened before, I was lucky and got away with it.

One morning, on the way back to Eastleigh after that morning's second strike in the mountains, the CO and I landed on a bush airstrip at the company headquarters of a battalion of the Buffs, that famous regiment which, like much of the old backbone of the British Army, has now disappeared. I remember that it was a very short strip, and I only just managed to stop my aircraft from rolling gently off the end into the bush. Right in full view, in front of the Army and my CO, that would really have let the side down; the CO would never have forgiven me, and rightly so.

Various aspects of co-operation and air support were discussed, after which we took off to fly back to our base near Nairobi. I followed the Boss, as he climbed to ten thousand feet. This was very unusual as we normally flew around Kenya at a maximum of no more than about ten feet above the bush, often lower. So, as I tucked in on his wing tip, high up over Kikuyuland, I wondered just what he had in mind this time. I soon found out! He rolled over, calling out over the R/T, "Follow me Mike". He need not have done so; I was a well-trained fighter pilot and always followed my leader. It was 'fighter law', and an unmentionable crime to lose one's leader at any time.

Far below were two neat, straight rows of khaki tents; between them was an open space, possibly the parade ground. The RAF considered that the Army always had parade grounds in their camps, wherever they were in the world, and however far out in the bush, jungle or desert they might be. "You take the right row, I'll take the left", called the Boss.

Our Harvards were red-lined at 257 knots Vne but, in a vertical dive from ten thousand feet, the airspeed needle could easily pass that figure. Vne is the never exceed speed for an aircraft, and it is very stupid and a heinous crime to do so; I would never even consider it now. In those days, however, we were young and, some would say, stupid, but fighters were very strongly built, and we always flew our aircraft to the uttermost limits. It was part of our training and the way of life on a fighter squadron, very necessary if you were to win in battle. 1340 was not a fighter squadron, and the Harvard was far from being a fighter, but our morale was high and that was the way that we operated.

We came over the Buffs' camp, in battle formation at about 300 knots, and we must have made a wonderful Harvard noise. As I reached a point about half way down the line of tents there was a sudden and ghastly great crash. My aircraft yawed mightily to the left, totally out of control; it was no longer flying, just hurtling through the air sideways. Luckily, for some reason, it hurtled up not down and, after a bit, I found that it did fly in a rather unwilling manner, but needed a great bootful of right rudder, with a lot of right aileron, to maintain straight and level. The left wing, which seemed somewhat bent, had parts missing, with small splinters of flagpole stuck in the mangled leading edge. The Boss flew in close to inspect the damage. I could see him looking at it rather grimly and shaking his head.

We arrived back at Eastleigh, where I landed, again in a somewhat unconventional manner, and then taxied in. I shut the engine down and, as it cooled and ticked away, just sat there in total misery. 'This is the end', I thought. 'This will mean Courts Martial. I will be drummed out of the Service and will never fly again'.

The Boss walked over and looked at the mess, shaking his head. His face wore the grim expression of fury that I had expected; then he looked up at me. "You must learn to avoid all these great big birds that we have in Kenya", he growled.

The world suddenly turned golden. I would get away with it. I would fly again. I did not realise it at the time but, had the true story come out, he would have been far deeper in the dwang, with far more to lose than ever I could have been. A new wing was soon fitted to my aircraft, and the battered old one was dumped in a corner of what served as our maintenance hangar. She then flew as well as she ever had.

A few days later, on a Sunday morning of low grey cloud and drizzle, we carried out our two normal early strikes with four aircraft, after which the other three pilots went over to the civil side of the airport for breakfast. It was my turn to sit by the phone, in case of a call to scramble for some reason, but I hoped that it would remain silent. Two goes at hunting for targets, hidden somewhere in the drizzle-shrouded, misty peaks and valleys of the mountains, was quite enough for one morning. The tourist brochures don't mention it, but that sort of weather is quite common in Kikuyuland at some times of the year.

Sitting in our cold damp tent, feeling hungry, I noticed the Air Commodore doing one of his morning wander-rounds. It being Sunday, he wore a blue battledress top, had his hat on the back of his head, his hands in the pockets of his khaki shorts, and his pipe in his mouth. He drifted into our hangar. Chiefy, our superb and long-suffering Flight Sergeant, walked over to him and saluted smartly. I watched them go round the hangar together, and stop at the remains of my wing. Together they stood there, looking down at it with much nodding and shaking of heads. Their expressions were very serious.

Chiefy pointed at the Ops tent where I sat. The Air Commodore headed my way; his grim expression was very obvious. I was scared stiff and stood rigidly to attention; this was definitely the end now. All my previous visions of Courts Martial returned, more vividly than ever before, and I shivered with cold, fright and misery.

"That was not a bird strike, was it Holmes?"

"No Sir", I gasped.

"What actually happened then?"

'Oh Lord', I thought, 'What can I say? I can't tell the truth, but what can possibly have a chance of holding water?' I was near to panic. "I flew too low on a strafing run, and hit the top of a big tree", I managed to get out. "Oh, where was that, and when?" 'Oh Lord, what can I say that may sound anything like the truth?' One hope came to mind. On the Southwest corner of the Mount Kenya Massif were two small round hills, which we naturally called 'Twin Tits'. They were a Mau Mau gathering point and, to try to break up these gatherings, we bombed and strafed them regularly, two or three times each week.

"The morning strike on Twin Tits the other day", I stuttered, and showed him the point on the damp wall map.

"Thank you Mike, for telling the truth", he said. "It will remain a bird strike, and you will hear no more about it".

He smiled and laughed, and we chatted about flying in general for a little, while I just burbled and continued to stutter, but now with utter relief. When the Boss came back from breakfast I told him what had happened and, once again, there was head-shaking with a serious expression, but I never did hear anything more about it.

We have 1340 Flight reunions, but there is only one other pilot who is left and able to get to them now. All the others who attend are the one time National Service airmen, who worked so hard on our aircraft out in the bush, and kept us continually flying when there were no spares, and the servicing schedule was born of Chiefy's ingenuity. It's a very happy get-together, and the ghastly old rank barriers have long since disappeared.

At the October 2003 meeting, I was presented with a beautiful Airfix model of a Harvard, with a flagpole embedded in the left wing.

On the stand is inscribed, 'IT WAS A BIRD WOT DONE IT.'

Credit: Dim Jones

It's Not Just the Enemy...

My third mission was far deeper inside Iraq than I'd been previously, to a target only about 40 miles west of Baghdad, and just beside the large airbase of Al Taqqadam. This was going very much into the heart of Iraq, and we could expect it to be defended accordingly. It was also a long way for CSAR[1] forces to come if we were shot down, and we nervously bantered during our pre-flight planning about how short a car ride it would be into the centre of Baghdad if we ended up on the ground. I was aware also of the rich RAF history in this part of Iraq. This was the area of RAF Habbaniyah, which had existed from well before WW2, in the days of air policing of the Empire, and right through to the 1950s. There was something ironic in the RAF bombing Habbaniyah in 1991 and, on at least one mission, we attacked hangars that we had constructed a number of decades previously. As someone once said, history may not exactly repeat itself, but it certainly has some interesting rhymes, perhaps especially if you have recently lost an empire.

All went fine on this mission until we were off the tanker, lights out and approaching the Iraqi border in almost complete darkness. There was plenty of cloud about, including high cirrus, so there wasn't even starlight to break the uniform blackness, and we could see no other aircraft although there were hundreds of them out there. We were in our standard formation of wide 'card' - two flying line abreast by about 2-3 miles on separate but parallel tracks, followed by another two flying about one minute in trail on the lead element. That allowed us to provide good cross-cover for each other, particularly with what might be happening in the blind area underneath us. The separation also gave us a decent margin of error for deconfliction purposes, although it was still important to keep any weaves to the 'outside' of track and back, and to be 'on time'. We were especially fixated by timing – it was always at the heart of minimising the risk of running into each other. All of our operational planning was conducted on the basis that we might have to fly the plan by night and in cloud – that was what the aircraft had been designed to do – so timing for us was life. You were either

---

[1] CSAR - Combat Search & Rescue.

in the right place at the right time, or you weren't – there was no grey area.

As we headed up to and across the border, I spotted a dull red glow a little off to the right of the nose of my Tornado. The glow seemed to be staying in the same place in the canopy as we turned slightly at each waypoint, which indicated that it wasn't a glow on the ground; it was also sitting about level with the horizon, so it would have had to be a long way off if it was on the ground, and it didn't have that look to it. My next thought was that it might be a reflection from my cockpit lights in the canopy, but turning them down even further (they were already very dim, to give my eyes the maximum chance of picking up things happening outside the aircraft) didn't make any difference. I then asked my navigator if his lights were a bit bright, but that didn't change anything either; he couldn't see the glow that had my attention, as angles and reflections tended anyway to obscure the area either side of the nose from the back seat. I was still puzzling over this red glow – in reality probably only for about 30 seconds in total – and getting increasingly uncomfortable, as we reached the next waypoint. The red glow stayed in the same place as we gently turned, and it was just starting to dawn on me what this light could be, when there was a sudden explosion of light and noise at what seemed touching distance to the right of me. Instant recognition … a Tornado going into reheat[2], very, very close to us. Instinctively, and all at the same time, I swore, rolled to the left and pushed down, away from the reheat plume, followed by a roll back right underneath the other aircraft as it accelerated away, now out to our left. There was no problem diagnosing what was wrong – someone was on the wrong side of the formation. It would take a few moments to work out who, but in the meantime we couldn't afford to drop too far back, otherwise we would start to conflict with the trailing elements.

The likely problem was almost certainly an obvious one, and very quickly came to mind. The Tornado navigation kit could have two routes loaded into it. If a parallel track route was planned - as on this mission - then odd-numbered aircraft in the formation used the first route and even-numbered aircraft the second. Crucially though, both routes were loaded and available in the kit, you just

---

[2] reheat – AKA afterburner, produces considerable, additional thrust by injecting fuel near the rear of the engine.

needed to select the right one pre-flight. On this sortie, we'd had to go late for one of the 'hot-spare' aircraft, after an unserviceability with our primary aircraft during start-up. In the rush, we had not cross-checked the routes and Murphy's Law applied - if something can go wrong, it will - so we'd been using the wrong route. We'd been flying precisely on time, but on precisely the wrong side of the formation, and precisely right next to our element leader. How close is close? Well, once we had got the right route loaded, and had got ourselves across to our track and back on time, I had the opportunity to reflect on what that red glow had been. I realised that there could only be one source of lighting coming from our leader's aircraft, his own cockpit lights. The red glow which I had been watching was the red lights above the radar display immediately in front of the navigator. That is very close indeed! It was really only luck that had kept us from bumping into each other, and relying on luck to keep you safe has never been part of my personal philosophy – and certainly not when you're in the middle of enemy territory.

At least the next lot of excitement was not self-generated in our cockpit. As we headed further north, with the Tigris river running west to east in front of us, and Al Taqqadam airfield still off in about the right two o'clock position and about 20 miles away, our constant checking of the RHWR[3] drew our attention to a 'spot' in the direction of the airfield. This 'spot' suggested that the surveillance radar from a SAM[4] system was emitting out there. It was not unusual to see these spots come up, normally only briefly, and often they were false indications, so it was something to note rather than to action. But this particular spot was unusual, in that it not only stayed on the screen but, as we turned, the position of the spot gradually moved too, maintaining the same relative position in the display. There was no doubt about it, we were being watched by a SAM radar, and we were shortly going to turn right and fly into the heart of its envelope – this felt a bit personal. Further confirmation came over the radio. We were being escorted by a flight of four F4G 'Wild Weasel' aircraft, providing us with SEAD[5] cover through the target. Their mission was to find and destroy

---

[3] RHWR – Radar Homing and Warning Receiver that gives visual and audio alerts in the cockpit.
[4] SAM – Surface to Air Missile.
[5] SEAD – Suppression of Enemy Air Defences.

enemy radars, so their RWR[6] kit was the best around – and, using codewords, they also called a SAM active at Al Taqqadam. Shortly afterwards, there was a radio call of 'Magnum, Magnum'. I'd never heard that one before, and I was just about to look down at my kneepad to see if I'd missed one of the codewords (there were lots of them and they changed weekly) when a rocket streaked over the top of the canopy from directly behind me, at very close range, lighting up my cockpit and my little part of the sky. I ducked instinctively, swore (again), and started, just as instinctively, to turn the aircraft to counter this threat, but quickly checked myself as the rocket flew rapidly ahead in front of me and then down to my right side - rapid realisation, enemy missiles went upwards not downwards! Further rapid realisation – I'd just witnessed a HARM[7] being fired from one of the F4Gs. More calmly now, I watched with fascination as the missile corrected its course, snaking back and forth as it tracked downwards, clearly off in the direction of that 'spot' on my RHWR. I lost sight of it as its rocket motor burned out, the rear-end cooled and it became enveloped in the darkness. At the point where I was about to forget about it and focus on the target run, there was a distant small bright flash and a glow from a detonation on the ground, just in the right place. I glanced again at the RHWR, just in time to see the 'spot' disappear. I liked that a lot. I might not have appreciated the rocket-over-the-head trick, and I rather suspect that the F4Gs had not even appreciated that I was between them and their target, but it was worth it to see the threat knocked out. I had also learnt what 'Magnum, Magnum' meant – Anti-Radar Missile being fired – a previously unfamiliar part of the US lexicon, but one which I was reassured to hear again on a number of occasions during the conflict.

With some of my attention elsewhere, we were a bit late turning onto our easterly heading for the target run. It was not far to go so there was not much time to catch up and we needed more speed, quickly. I was already at maximum dry power to turn at this height and weight and, with only 3 minutes or so to the target, and plenty of AAA[8] already visible below, plus the possibility of other SAMs from around Al Taqqadam to the right, this didn't seem like a good time

[6] RWR – A variant of RHWR.
[7] HARM - High-speed Anti-Radiation Missile.
[8] AAA – Anti Aircraft Artillery.

to highlight our position to everyone in Iraq by lighting up the night sky with reheat. There was, however, an alternative. A switch on the Engine Control Panel, by my right thigh, tagged 'for operational/emergency use', increased the top end temperature limit of the engines. This would give me a bit more power, but the down side was that it put a fair strain on the engines, such that afterwards they had to be inspected for damage by the engineers. This seemed as good a time as any though, so I broke the wire lock, moved the switch forwards and got an increase in power, but then could only watch the engine temperature gauges with some consternation, as they swung a good way past the normal maximum limit. Did I really want to be operating my engines to their very limits, only 40 miles away from Baghdad? I had enough experience of Tornado engines to know that they could be fickle (it was a good job that there were two of them) and, at that moment, maximum reliability seemed rather more important! So I quickly put the switch back to the normal position and selected minimum reheat instead. This produced some extra power, but with only a dull red glow at the back of the aircraft's tailpipes, rather than the large, white, tell-tale plume associated with a maximum selection. A small personal faff in the big scheme of things, but I was at least as concerned about the considerable dependency I was placing on my Tornado's serviceability as I was about the efforts of the Iraqis. I remember nothing else of the target run, or indeed the rest of this mission, save for looking left towards Baghdad as we turned south and exited the target area. After all these months here I was a few minutes' flying time (and still a relatively short road journey) away from the source of all this trouble; but on that night there was nothing to see other than the all-enveloping darkness.

On the long transit back to the border and subsequently to base, I had time to reflect, once again, that even on operational missions, the enemy is not necessarily the biggest risk that you might have to confront. You may, in fact, find yourself becoming your own worst enemy.

Don't Increase Speed – The Queen is Late!

At the beginning of 1965 I was told that, as the boss of No II(AC) Squadron, I would lead a Royal Flypast at RAF Gütersloh for Her Majesty Queen Elizabeth's visit to Germany in May. All the operational squadrons in Germany would participate, and I was to be at the helm with six single-seat Hunter FR10s, followed by ten other 'six-ships' of Hunters, Javelins and Canberras, with each section in close formation, but well separated and stepped down in a twelve-mile long, line-astern trail. This would be 'Hacker Formation' (not my choice of title). With three tours of fast-jet, low-level flying behind me, one in the Swift FR5 at Gütersloh, I was quite happy with the task, in principle – but I was not to know then what lay ahead.

I should have become a little uneasy when I heard that the 'experts' at HQ RAF Germany were to prescribe the route, be responsible for all the planning, seek the necessary clearances and make all the weather decisions. We could all comment, but otherwise I simply had to do what I was told. On the crucial matter of weather limits, I was assured that a 'senior worthy' in the Air Traffic Tower at Gütersloh would ensure that, if the cloud base was below 1500 feet and/or the visibility was less than 3 nautical miles, anywhere along the route, we would not fly. Really?

I had no argument with the route they chose, although it passed through the perennial murk in the north of the Ruhr, beyond which I would be joined first by the Javelins and then the Canberras. Nor was I worried about the featureless, final run-in, despite its alignment with Gütersloh's airfield servicing platform (ASP), rather than the more familiar, extended centreline to Runway 09. What did concern me was the confidence within 'higher management' that they could get Her Majesty from the Royal Train, at Gütersloh Bahnhof, onto the saluting base, a mere couple of minutes before I was due to be overhead at 1100 hrs. The assignment of this responsibility to a 'highly reliable officer' gave me little comfort. Accordingly, I begged that the Queen be invited to inspect the line of static aircraft first, to ensure that she could be guided from there to the saluting base to coincide with a revised overhead time for me, but this logic did not prevail; my commitment to the original overhead time must remain sacrosanct. Moreover, I was advised that if I were more than three seconds early or late, it would be best for me to continue heading east for the German Democratic Republic (GDR). Ours was not to reason why!

With this inviolate plan, it was reasonable to assume that the 'highly reliable officer' could ensure that the Queen did not mount the saluting base too early, but what if the apparently impossible happened, and Her Majesty was late? I had no flexibility on the final run-in, other than to adjust our speed, within the very narrow bracket I was given, between the lowest manoeuvring speed demanded by the Javelins and the highest declared by the Canberras. A 'dog-leg' or orbit might be considered, but only if I was told exactly how late the Queen was to be, we were far enough out from Gütersloh and the weather allowed it. Even then, these latter options always carried the grave risk of throwing my 12 miles of aircraft into disarray.

A number of rehearsals, first involving the leaders only and then all the players, were largely uneventful, but one or two lessons were re-learned, and there were some amusing incidents. On the one occasion when the visibility fell below limits en route, I had to make a small adjustment to our heading at a late stage, and this brought angry cries from the rear of the formation, and promises from the front to do better next time. After that, the experts at Rheindahlen decided that I needed some help on the final run-in, and ordered that the RAF Regiment be deployed to light fires for some 20 miles (4 minutes) back along the route. Perhaps taking umbrage at this intrusion, the local German farmers decided to join the party with a few bonfires of their own, thereby helping to fill the whole area with distracting smoke. Undaunted, we held our heading and made our time on target.

On the first full-scale rehearsal, one Canberra squadron could not raise the required minimum number of serviceable aircraft, and was allowed to fly its leader only. This was made clear to the next section leader in line, who found a lone aircraft at approximately the right position, and followed it, albeit with a somewhat alarming number of twists and turns in poor visibility, until it broke into the circuit to land at RAF Laarbruch – after an air test! Laarbruch Air Traffic Control (ATC) was no doubt bemused by the successive groups of Canberras which had followed their aircraft in, and this tail end of the formation, now being too late to join the big parade, then skulked home to their respective bases.

Came the big day, 26 May 1965, a glance out of my bedroom window and a quick call to the Met office, suggested that the flypast would be cancelled: heavy rain, a low cloudbase and poor visibility being likely to persist until mid-morning. However, there was a chance that, by then, the weather could be improving slowly from the west, wherein lay our route, and the senior worthy quite rightly deferred the ultimate decision until nearer our take-off time. I was to be present for his crucial decision. Final preparations for the arrival of the Queen at Gütersloh were well in hand as I cycled to the ATC Tower (no cars allowed) in the rain. There had been little improvement in either cloudbase or visibility, but the senior worthy greeted me with an invitation to 'give it a try'. In short, it was all left up to me.

The FR10 pilots of Nos II(AC) and IV(AC) Squadrons were all in their cockpits when I arrived on my bike at the usually deserted southern dispersal, and we were soon taxying out to Runway 27. With the conditions so poor, I changed the take-off instructions for my squadron from three pairs to two 'threes', the second formation launching 10 sec after me, for an instrument departure and radar-monitored low level 'snake', with me calling all height, speed and heading changes, hoping that we would break out for a visual rejoin as we headed south-west. We entered cloud before the wheels were 'in the well', which was not the best time for ATC to ask me what the weather was like. Indeed, the senior worthy in the Tower was heard to observe that my reply was less than helpful, but after this period of high concentration by all involved, I was able to report that all the Hunter sections had the necessary visual contact, and had formed up as planned. Together we passed through the Ruhr gloom, and began picking up the remaining elements of the formation until all 66 aircraft were in place - but there was more drama to come.

Several wind shifts around our route had lost us a few seconds and, six minutes out, I called for an increase in speed to 310 knots. This seemed to awaken a hitherto dormant Gütersloh ATC which intruded with: "Don't increase speed, Hacker leader, the Queen is late". My question: "How late?" elicited the anguished reply: "Sorry Leader, we don't know". As far as I can remember, nothing more was heard from ATC until we joined the circuit to land. From somewhere deep in the formation, a voice was heard to murmur 'God save the Queen' – but I had a more immediate problem on my mind.

With no new timing to go on, and now only five minutes out, with twelve miles of aircraft behind me, I saw no alternative but to hold my heading, pull the speed back to the minimum acceptable to the Javelins, and hope for the best. In the event, I saw Her Majesty's car rounding the last bend on to the ASP, at very high speed, as I approached the saluting base. It was far from what was wanted and planned for, but I suppose it could have been worse; I might have been encouraged to continue eastbound to the GDR!

The Hunter elements then broke away from the formation to rejoin the Gütersloh circuit (quietly), to land downwind on Runway 09 and disappear (quietly) into the southern dispersal, for the pilots to leave the station (quietly), by the back gate, while the more worthy enjoyed the well-rehearsed luncheon with the Queen. No II(AC) Squadron did as it was told, and made for a local hostelry to drink large quantities of beer, where talk of the flypast was prohibited; in the days and weeks to follow, it seems that this was also the rule within the hierarchy and among the 'experts' on the HQ staff. I certainly heard nothing of it during the rest of my tour in Germany; it was as if it had never happened.

Many years later, while lunching with a friend at the Royal College of Defence Studies, an Air Vice-Marshal joined us uninvited and, quite incidentally, began telling his tale of a Royal flypast over Gütersloh in 1965, in which he had taken part as a Canberra navigator. Seeing which way his version of the story was heading, and being a non-violent man, I stopped him in his tracks, but I'm under no illusion that there were - and probably still are - many of our kind who would have known what to do in the air – had they been at the helm when the call came: "...The Queen is late". Such is life!

Credit: Geoff Lee

Operation Energise

Operation Energise was an attempt, in the early 1960s, to calibrate all the early warning radar stations that had recently been built in many of the NATO countries. The Royal Air Force 'won' the contract to carry out this flying, and to organise the calibration of the ground stations. I was on a five-year commission and, after training, had been posted to Canberra B2s on 35 Squadron at RAF Upwood. With a year of my commission left, I was sent, along with another five or six crews, to RAF Tangmere to join 245 Squadron, a Canberra radar calibration squadron. We were to await the start of Energise in early 1962, and I managed to extend my service to 7 years so as not to miss out. A bachelor friend and I had volunteered to do all the detachments, to give the married folk some time at home and to enjoy the fun of travelling. We started in Norway, flying out of Gardermoen for a month from snow-covered runways. We also enjoyed lots of skiing, once we had twigged that, to ski downhill, one needed edges on the skis; the skis we had originally borrowed turned out to be for cross country use! In that first year we went on to Denmark, Germany, back up to Bodo in Northern Norway and then down to Stavanger. At Bodo we did a lot of fishing up in the fjords. After one particularly successful day, we decided to have a barbecue on the beach by the airfield, and built a large fire to cook our catch. As we were enjoying the repast we were illuminated by the station fire service, who demanded we put the fire out immediately – we had managed to build it on top of the station fuel dump(underground tanks). We had no difficulty in co-operating fully with their request.

The second year started at Aviano in Italy, where we were accommodated at a USAF base. Some kind Americans lent us a car, a Renault 5 (or was it a 2½?) that took a few of us to see the sights of northern Italy, including the glorious ski slopes of Cortina d'Ampezzo. We were by no means expert skiers but, after our experience in Norway, we could manage a reasonable downhill run without letting the side down too badly. I also recall, on one occasion, giving an American a lift back to UK when rotating aircraft[1]. He was most amused when the navigator talked about our 'Most Probable Position'; he obviously thought that a navigator

[1] rotating aircraft – Bringing one aircraft back for servicing in exchange for another.

ought to know where he was, and could not understand the 'navspeak'.

From Italy we went to Turkey where we were based at an airfield called Murted, about 20 miles north-west of Ankara. We lived in hotels in Ankara, and ate and passed the evening at the American Officers' Club on Cankaya Hill, among the embassies. Flying out of Murted was reasonably straightforward as, in the event of any weather below 5000 feet base, we were required to call for a GCA[2] on the emergency frequency. However, our navigation fit was not designed to operate in Turkey. We only had ADF[3], on which we could not rely, as it always pointed north, regardless of the beacon it was tuned to, understandable as most of our flying was over northern Turkey. We thus flew in good VMC[4], with the navigator lying in the nose map reading and, from 45,000 feet, the view was delightful. Occasionally, the nav got so comfortable that he tended to nod off, and the pilot had to keep him awake with a carefully-aimed nudge from his boot.

One of the radar units was on the north Turkish coast, near Trabzon. One of our senior crews took some equipment up to Trabzon by Canberra and, unfortunately, when selecting the flap up after landing, the pilot pressed the wrong knob and the undercarriage collapsed, or mostly collapsed. It was certainly enough to give the detachment engineer a moment of consternation. He called up the Trabzon docks and got a large crane, big enough to lift a Canberra, to come up to the airfield. He slung the aircraft on some strong webbing, and then tried to describe what he wanted of the non-English-speaking crane driver. What he wanted was for the crane to ease the aircraft up, very slowly and gently, so that the undercarriage locks could be put in place. Unfortunately, either the crane driver did not understand or he did not press his buttons in the right order. He jerked the aircraft up quickly and then let it fall back to earth with a distressing thump. Happily, little further damage was done on top of the first incident and, on the second attempt, the locks were inserted satisfactorily. The tip tanks had also been damaged and so could contain no fuel, which limited the aircraft range. It was positioned back to Murted, but it was then decided to fly

---

[2] GCA – Ground Controlled Approach radar.
[3] ADF – Automatic Direction Finding.
[4] VMC – Visual Meteorological Conditions.

it to the MU[5] at RAF Akrotiri in Cyprus, possibly for scrap. I was given the job of flying this trip. It had been arranged with the Turkish MOD, and we planned to refuel at Konya - where the whirling dervishes live. We set off at fairly low level as there was no cabin pressurisation and, with the undercarriage extended, we were limited to 170 knots maximum. We landed at Konya with no trouble but, when we parked and opened the door, I was met by a fierce looking, non-English-speaking Turkish soldier/airman, with his gun levelled at my head and little sign of a welcoming smile. After some discussion, where I used my less than fluent Turkish to ask for an officer (Binbasha is Turkish for Major, the nickname we gave to our Boss), I seemed finally to get a result. We were whisked off to the station commander's office, where we were made most welcome and given several cups of chay to drink while he chatted about his wartime experiences in UK, including asking us if we had met a girl he knew in Birmingham! Our visit to Konya ended later than we had intended, but we set off for Cyprus, where we had to explain to Nicosia Centre that we were RAF and had come from Konya. There followed a lot of questions but, in the end, the clearly English accent convinced them we were legitimate and could continue to Akrotiri.

We had two radars to calibrate in Turkey, the second one being in the deepest, darkest remote east of the country. In order to ease the administrative jungle, we were moved down to Nicosia, in Cyprus, as the detachment base. To get to the remote east and do the job, we had to refuel at Diyarbakir, close to the town of that name. There being no refuelling personnel who understood either English or the Canberra, this entailed us clambering over the aircraft to fuel it ourselves. Normally, we ate packed lunches, although the American Services variety is not the most succulent of feasts, especially on a very hot, dry day in Dyarbakir. After a few visits, we managed to find a small American unit, based nearby, where we were given food; it was not a huge improvement, but it was better! After the calibration trip, and another refuel, we transited back to Cyprus via Adana, overhead the US Base at Incirlik. Returning by this route, after one sortie, I was letting down through 15,000 feet, north east of Cyprus, when I saw a Javelin on my wing, having some formation practice - or so I thought. I continued back to Nicosia, where I was met by the OC Ops, Wing Commander Peter

---

[5] MU – Maintenance Unit.

Bairsto, and put under close arrest. Apparently the Javelin had been scrambled by Cape Gata radar, to intercept a contact that had been chasing along the south coast of Turkey heading east, then turning, climbing rapidly to 15,000 feet and heading for Cyprus. The Javelin had its radar locked on to the contact for most of this time, including the rapid climb and turn towards Cyprus. When I was finally allowed to defend my action, I asked the Nicosia staff to check what time I had passed over Incirlik on their radar, and what time I had made contact with Nicosia Centre. By a simple bit of maths, I was able to prove that, to do all that I had been accused of and still manage to meet the timings, the Canberra would have been flying at Mach[6] 1.3, a little beyond its capability! I never did find the answer to what had happened, but clearly there were some red faces around who shunned any more publicity.

While we were there, the RC Padre became a friend of ours, and enjoyed celebrating his birthdays and unbirthdays – any excuse – with Benedictine. He had been seconded into the Royal Air Force from Ampleforth Abbey. Apparently, when Dom Hume was told to nominate one of his staff to be sent to the RAF, he selected Father Duffy with little hesitation. Duffy had been famous for driving his motor bike round the cloisters of the Abbey – or so the stories go. He was posted to Nicosia, where he had responsibility for Ayia Napa and other out stations, for which, of course, he needed transport. Accordingly, he managed to persuade the Abbot to buy him a rather excellent 1000cc superbike, which he collected with glee and insisted on demonstrating for us. This entailed a quick once round the hut, or so we thought. Two of us were put on the bike, one on the handlebars and one on the rear seat, and Father Duffy proceeded to show off his new bike all around the station, to the embarrassment of the two of us, who were dressed only in our undies. One evening he asked us to dress as vicars for a special dinner, and lent us dog-collars to complete the transformation. While he was entertaining us, as was his wont, to a pre-prandial drink in the mess bar he was called away, but said we should continue with the vicars' dinner. During the meal there was a phone call for the Padre, and the receptionist, seeing so many vicars dining, asked if one of us would take the call. One brave fellow did, and found himself on the phone to an Irish woman who appeared to be at the end

---

[6] Mach - A measurement of velocity, where Mach 1 is the speed of sound.

of her tether. Her husband had walked out, her children were in a bad state and she desperately wanted the Padre's help. With some spluttering sympathy for her predicament, our 'vicar' attempted to assure her that Father Duffy would come to her aid as soon as he could. Unfortunately, this backfired spectacularly, and the woman became almost hysterical at the news that she was not going to get any immediate assistance. Things then continued to deteriorate until, as she paused for breath, there was just a hint of a snigger in the midst of the protestations. Yes, it was Duffy, thoroughly enjoying the joke at our expense. In spite of this, we still took him flying with us on several occasions, where he expressed delight at being nearer to his God! All in all a wonderful man, who thoroughly enjoyed his detachment to the RAF.

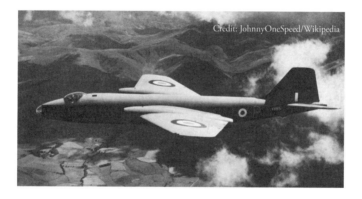

Credit: JohnnyOneSpeed/Wikipedia

Know Your Geography

Shortly after joining the RAF, I was given the opportunity of studying French and taking some exams. It was a 'no-brainer' for me; there was no downside as I liked French, and it made a pleasant break from the more technical subjects on my curriculum. Success would not only mean some sort of Civil Service Certificate, but also (and far more useful to an impoverished young cadet like myself) a cheque for £100. I did the course, passed the exam and received my £100. Happy days!

Annual reports in those days used to ask for details of any language qualification, and each year I would dutifully mention my French qualification. However, I was increasingly mindful that my French was not quite what it had been, as I had had no cause to either speak the language or visit France since my earlier studies. So, it was with a frisson of excitement and trepidation that I received a call from my desk (postings) officer, almost 8 years later, asking me if my French was still current, because he was thinking of sending me to a post where my language skills would be needed. It took me only seconds to recall the word 'Oui' and I confirmed, with as much confidence as I could muster, that I was indeed still fluent and very willing to accept such a post. The desk officer was slightly reluctant to tell me where, exactly, I might be sent, but eventually informed me that the location was a place called Tongeren. Desk officers didn't divulge very much in those days, and I have to say I was slightly puzzled as to why there was an RAF French-speaking post in the Tonga Islands, in the South Pacific, but it was not for me to reason why and I was delighted when the posting was subsequently confirmed. You can well imagine that my joy was somewhat tempered when a colleague subsequently informed me, with great mirth, that Tongeren was in fact in Belgium, and that I would be using my French, not in the South Pacific, but from a support unit in Liege, which was described as an industrial city the size of Sheffield!

In the end, I went to my Belgian Sheffield, had a great tour and returned to the UK fluent in French and with a marked Walloon accent!

The Case Of The Runaway Kettle

My story goes back to 1977, when I was flying the venerable AEW Shackleton on 8 Squadron, based at RAF Lossiemouth in the wilds of Scotland. For those who are not as mature in years as myself, 1977 was the year in which the Nation celebrated the Queen's Silver Jubilee. As with all these major anniversaries, 'Their Airships' down in London decreed that the Royal Air Force would commemorate the occasion by mounting a flypast over Buckingham Palace that July, an event which was to involve every single aircraft type which the RAF had in service at the time. I'm afraid that my memory-bank is not what it used to be (even then, it was quite small), and I can no longer recall the total number of aircraft involved; suffice it to say that it must have approached the Grand Century. Naturally, the flypast comprised everything from basic trainers and rotorheads to fast-jets, with every other type in between; and certain bases in RAF East Anglia were nominated to play host to visiting types, particularly the slower varieties, of which we were one. Our host Station was RAF Coningsby, where we camped out for virtually the entire month, with other elements of 11 Group.

As with all these major events, in addition to the primary aircraft, participating units were required to provide both an airborne spare and a ground spare; moreover, all the crews were expected to take part in at least one practice flypast. As you can imagine, with upwards of 100 aircraft, all required to be in perfect formation over the Palace at a nominated time but with widely-varying airspeeds, several holding areas were nominated over East Anglia and the North Sea. The majority of the join-ups were done on a visual basis, but the holding patterns were adjacent to the UK's busiest Terminal Control Areas - with civil airliners departing from, and arriving at, all the civil airports in the south-east. In addition, there were the summertime private flyers in their 'puddle-jumpers', so it called for all crews to have their eyes out and their wits about them.

To digress slightly, this was in an era before atomic clocks and accurate quartz watches, and all time-hacks were taken from BT's speaking clock. It transpired that, on one occasion, when the MR[1] Nimrod from RAF Kinloss was over 30 seconds adrift in joining the formation, that none of BT's regional

---

[1] MR – Maritime Reconnaissance.

clocks were synchronised! After that incident, we all had to phone a central number for a time hack.

However, back to the story. For one particular rehearsal, my crew was pro-grammed as the ground spare. This meant that we would start up with the primary flypast aircraft and the airborne spare but, as soon as both aircraft were safely airborne, we would taxy back to dispersal and shut down. The time came for all three aircraft to start, which we duly did, and we all taxied out to the holding point. Being a mighty piston-engined machine, part of our pre-take-off checks was to carry out engine runs; with these runs complete, we were then forced to wait for about 15 minutes for the Shackleton slot time. With the two other Shacks both serviceable, it was highly unlikely that we would be getting airborne, so time to relax a little – and what better way to do that than to have a cup of tea and a cake; we all know that, like the Army, Shackleton crews worked best on a full stomach!

To digress slightly again, the Shackleton's galley was originally designed and equipped with a water tank, situated immediately adjacent to the wall-mounted kettle and the sink; however, over the years, some of these water tanks had seen better times and been withdrawn from use. The tanks had been replaced by a couple of large jerry-cans, with a length of hose routed through a hand-pump and thence to the kettle.

Back to the holding point. As the navigator, it fell to me to make the first round of drinks. So, leaping swiftly over both spars[2] – at the time, I was in the halcyon days of my youth and a squash-player of some repute – and settling into the galley, I pumped away on the hand-pump to provide enough water for six teas, and turned the kettle timer on. The little red power light came on as advertised and, after several minutes, the water boiled and I brewed the drinks. I should say, at this stage, that the kettle took 200 amps directly out of the main busbar[3], and its only protection was a circuit-breaker on the front of the galley unit. Drinks made, and time to hand them round, but what's this? The timer had timed out but the red light was still on!

---

[2] spars – The main structural members of the wing, running at right angles (or thereabouts) to the fuselage.
[3] main busbar – The primary electrical circuit in the aircraft.

If I recall correctly, no emergency checklist had been written for the galley, other than to isolate it from the busbar by tripping the circuit-breaker; remember, the Shackleton was designed and built in the days before the Nanny State, and common sense ruled, OK. So, 'recycle the timer and pump some more water into the kettle' seemed to be the order of the day. Again, the timer timed out but, again, the red light stayed on. After a quick call on the intercom to the Flight Engineer (God bless 'em – a finer bunch of aircrew you could never have wished to meet), confirming that it was in order to trip the galley circuit-breaker, gloves on and execute the drill! What's this? The circuit-breaker won't budge. By now, I'm like Robert the Bruce – keep on trying to trip the circuit-breaker whilst, at the same time, maintaining a constant flow of water into the kettle, to prevent the element from burning out.

At this point, the remainder of the 11 Group formations of Phantoms, Lightnings and Hunters were taxying past our Shackleton which, by now, was beginning to resemble a roadside café, with steam pouring out of the overflow vents. Of course, no comments were made by the fast-jet mateys, were they? Well, as we couldn't isolate the power to the kettle, the only alternative was to de-energise the main busbar, by shutting down all four engines. So, with steam pouring out behind, we limped back to dispersal and shut down. I suspect that this was the first time a Shackleton had DNCO'd[4] for a runaway kettle!

On a more serious note, had this happened while the aircraft was flying over the Atlantic, several hours out from land, and had the crew been unable to isolate the kettle, the consequences when the water ran out don't bear thinking about.

---

[4] DNCO'd – Duty Not Carried Out.

No, The Rocket Thingy Shouldn't Look Like That

The entry in the log book is cursory, as usual – none of the splendid stories you find in the records of the Old and Bold of WWII. The date was August 1st 1972, which would mean that I was about halfway through my first tour, with just over 400 hours on type – smack-dab in that window where the chasm between perceived and actual ability is at its widest. The aircraft was a Lightning Mk3 – sports car extraordinaire, but not over-endowed with either weaponry or endurance. The sortie profile is recorded as a Contex 3B which, as I recall, was low-level random set-up intercepts, real one-armed paperhanger stuff. There was also a tanker involved, always a useful thing in a Mk3.

Met briefing had said something about CuNim[1] activity later, but it was clear-and-a-million as we got airborne and headed off towards the North Sea. I can't remember anything much about the sortie itself, which does not necessarily mean that it went well, but it would certainly have been busy. The GCI[2] station at Bawdsey would be have been able to set the intercepts up with both target and fighter at medium level but, as soon as the target descended to low level inbound, the fighter would have been on his own. I can't recall at what point I stopped peering down the rubber radar boot and trying to beat the radar hand controller into submission, but it eventually registered that Bawdsey were talking about weather at base, and increased diversion fuel. Needless to say, it was the last intercept, we were already down to original recovery fuel, and none of the diversion bases were any closer than Wattisham. We had taken off on the south-westerly runway, so the approach would be effectively straight-in. When we finally got to talk to Air Traffic, we were informed that a large and malevolent CuNim was currently parked over the field, discharging its contents without fear or favour, and that a PAR[3] would be our best course of action. It will come as no surprise that a PAR had not figured in our fuel calculations, radar-to-visual being the worst that had been contemplated. Neither was a pairs approach the ideal solution, but the consequences for the No 2 of a delay for separation were

---

[1] CuNim – Cumulo Nimbus. A cloud type associated with thunderstorms.
[2] GCI – Ground Controlled Interception.
[3] PAR – Precision Approach Radar.

worse. Furthermore, we were reassured that our pitiful cries of Fuel Priority had been heeded, and we were 'Number One' – a guarantee which must rank alongside 'Cheque's in the mail', 'I'll respect you in the morning' and something else which escapes me, as one of the world's greatest lies.

Onwards and downwards we pressed until, when level at 1500 feet and, therefore, using the greatest amount of fuel for the least forward movement, we were informed that a runway change was in progress, and that we would be making our way south-westwards on a great circle route to intercept the centreline inbound to Runway 06. Nibbled to death by ducks crossed our minds, but it did not appear that we had much choice. We were, of course, extended even further south-west than normal, while they turned the PAR round or something, but eventually we were inbound in weather which was getting increasingly 'smeggy.' It was at this point that we discovered that 'Number One' did not necessarily mean that we took priority over departing traffic, and that the official runway change had been delayed to allow the last aircraft to get airborne on Runway 24. Through a helpful break in the weather, we observed him as he zipped past us in the opposite direction, at which point Air Traffic declared that the runway was officially flooded, with the crosswind gusting out of limits.

Those of you familiar with the undercarriage of the Lightning will recall that, in order to get the mainwheels inside the skinny wings, the tyres were about the width of a razor blade and, because they had many tons of aircraft to support, the tyre pressure was stratospheric (or, more accurately, the exact opposite); 240psi rings a bell which, by my $9\sqrt{P}$ calculation, gave an aquaplaning speed of about 140knots, and we were going to be trying to stop these two rocket-powered roller-skates on the same piece of runway (or lake) at the same time. We hadn't said much to each other during this developing drama, but we now arrived at an inescapable and simultaneous conclusion that enough was enough.

'You go to Bentwaters, I'll go to Honington' seemed like the best idea we'd had all day. How to find them in this weather was another thing. Naturally the Bentwaters/ Woodbridge TACAN[4] was out; we had a natty little device called an offset computer, which applied a bearing and distance from another TACAN to find a new destination, but it was helpfully situated between the knees, and I

---

[4]TACAN –Tactical Air Navigation equipment.

had other places to be looking. So, I set sail in a generally south-easterly direction in order to pick up a landmark even I might recognise - Ipswich. In the event, about the only things I could recognise were Portman Road (the Ipswich Town football ground) and the River Orwell. From here, my plan was to find the coast and chunter up it until I found Bentwaters. The only trouble was that between me and Bentwaters was Woodbridge - another USAF F-4 Phantom base - and I would have to cross their centreline. However, I reckoned that, if they were recovering aircraft, one place they wouldn't be was 3 miles on the centreline at 200 feet, so that's where I planned to be. And it all worked out fine, except that the weather continued to alternate between clear patches and real dark and incredibly noisy bits. I had long ago shut down an engine, a last-resort fuel-saving measure. I hadn't a hope of wrestling the Red Book[5] out of my flying suit pocket to find the Bentwaters Approach frequency, so I resorted to Guard[6], repeated the PAN[7] call, hoped that Wattisham had talked to them, and broadcast what I intended to do instead of asking permission to do it.

As I cleared the Bentwater's runway at the far end, I made a mental 'Note to Self' not to shut down an engine as per the After-Landers checks, otherwise it would all go quiet. I also elected not to consult the fuel gauges to find out how long it might be before it all went quiet anyway. Suffice to say that I made it to the ramp but, after completing the paperwork and applying the fudge factors for US gallons to pounds, and JP-4 SG (fuel) as opposed to AVTUR, I had the greatest difficulty in making the total fuel capacity, minus the fuel put in, add up to a positive figure. In a closing scene to this drama, the USAF weapons technician assigned to the turn-round asked me to explain how exactly the seeker heads on the two Red Top missiles worked. At that point I realised that what should have been the seeker heads were instead mangled messes of twisted metal sans glass, and the noisy interludes over the back streets of Ipswich had been my aircraft being attacked by hail, as witnessed by some nice little dents in the leading edges of the wings and elsewhere.

---

[5] Red Book – Slang for the En Route Supplement, a book that contained details of all operational airfields in the UK.

[6] Guard – Emergency radio frequency.

[7] PAN - A state of urgency exists although there is no imminent danger to life or the continued viability of the aircraft.

After waiting for some back-up from the Squadron at Wattisham - an armourer to download the remnants of the Red Tops, a rigger to OK the wings, and a 'sooty' to clamber down the intake and look at the engine compressors, I carried out a slightly more sedate return to homebase. The logbook records, however, that early evening saw me airborne again for a flypast at the Colchester Tattoo, so clearly this was a case of 'no sense, no sensibility'.

'Aug 01 1972 - Lightning F3 XP700 - Self- Solo - Contex 3B + AAR Div B'Waters - 1 hr 30m' doesn't really tell the whole story, does it?

Credit: Author

P-P-Parachute

When I was undergoing air signaller training at RAF Topcliffe, we had an air-crew cadet who stuttered badly. He was prescribed some appropriate medicine by the Medical Officer, and was crewed to fly a check trip with instructor Flt Lt Tommy Shean, a wartime signaller and a gruff chap, of whom we cadets were all petrified.

During the flight, the staff pilot came on to the intercom stating "For Practice - For Practice - Crew put on parachutes" (We wore the harness all the time, but the chutes were in bins in strategic locations). Our cadet, light-headed under the influence of the drugs, picked up his parachute by the D-ring and it deployed.

"If we have to bale out for real, that's your bloody parachute," responded Tommy.

A little later, the staff pilot came on the intercom again "For Cadet X only - For Practice - For Practice - Put on parachutes." The cadet picked up a different chute – and, again, deployed it after lifting it by the D-ring. "Whooosss parachute is tthhiss one going to be, Sir?" he enquired of Tommy!

Needless to say, the tablets were not adjudged to have been a success.

A Tale of a Hunter T7

This is a little tale, concerning a ferry trip carried out in August 1965 when I was serving in Aden. As was the custom, every two months or so, we would take a couple of old aircraft back from Aden to the UK for refurbishment, and pick up a couple of new ones. On this particular occasion I had to pick up a new Hunter TMk7 (XF321) and my number 2, a certain Flt Lt R E Johns[1] of 1417 Flt, had a brand new Hunter FR10 as his mount. The T7 had 4 x 100 gallon under-wing fuel tanks, and the FR10 had the usual 2 x 230 plus 2 x 100 gallon tanks. The discrepancy in performance between the two aircraft was quite marked, and the FR10 on my wing could easily outperform my T7, despite the significantly greater weight.

All went well for the first 5 legs; Kemble to Lyneham to clear customs, Lyneham to Istres, Istres to Luqa, Luqa to Akrotiri and, finally, Akrotiri to Diyarbakir. It is a long time since I have been to Diyarbakir but, in those days, to describe it as a dump was being kind. It was somewhere in the middle of Turkey, in the back of beyond, with only very basic facilities; not a place that any sane man would schedule a night stop. Some years before I had been arrested there, while ferrying a Hunter T7 (XF310) out to the Far East, when they claimed that I had landed without diplomatic clearance. On that occasion, a very stressed United States Air Force exchange pilot – they were flying F86 Sabres at the time – had very kindly rescued me from my predicament. He had been, in fact, the only man on the base who spoke English (after a fashion), and he went everywhere with an interpreter. He must have done something very bad to get such a punishment posting. But I was under no illusions; this time I did not want to stop at Diyarbakir. Not under any circumstances.

We refuelled and taxied out for take-off, and that was when I discovered that I could not get the T7 into powered controls. Every time I selected ailerons and elevator into power, the dolls'-eyes[2] remained white. Flying a Hunter in manual

[1] Flt Lt R E Johns - Later Air Chief Marshal Sir Richard Johns, Chief of the Air Staff 1997-2000.
[2] Dolls' eyes - Cockpit indicators, which turned from white to black to indicate system functions.

control is an emergency situation and, while it cannot be said to be that difficult, the controls are extremely heavy and usually require two hands on the stick. We did practise manual landings from time to time, but manual take-offs were not in the Pilots' Notes. So, there I am, taxying out and wondering quite what to do. My instinct was to avoid going unserviceable at Diyarbakir, but I did not like to say anything over the radio to Dick Johns. My thoughts tended to anticipate the subsequent Board of Inquiry; therefore, the less anybody knew about what I was about to do, the better.

So, I committed myself to a manual take-off, not a recommended practice or one that I had ever tried before. In fact, I don't know of anyone who has tried it, although I am prepared to bet there are a few who have done it inadvertently. The only aspect that really worried me was where to put the elevator trim. Too much tail-down and I might not be able to control the pitch-up; too little and I would have trouble getting the nosewheel off the ground. However, Diyarbakir's runway was quite long, and I guessed that I would have time to get airborne even if I had too little tail-down trim; so, I erred in that direction to avoid the nose pitching up, which could definitely be embarrassing. Off we went down the runway and, quite apart from the inferior performance of the T7, it became clear to Dick that nothing much seemed to be happening with regard to getting airborne. After a while, he gave up any attempt to remain on my wing, and accelerated past me into the air. I actually got airborne at the end of the concrete in a flurry of dust, sorted out the trim, raised the undercarriage and flaps, and climbed nonchalantly away.

It was not until we had landed at Tehran that I was able to tell him what the problem was; and, because there was no one to rectify the problem, I had to do the next leg in manual as well. But this time Dick was prepared for the take-off, and I had learnt from my previous experience what to expect. When we got to Muharraq (Bahrain), I managed to find a knowledgeable technician, who took one look at it and diagnosed blown fuses – which, indeed, it was. So, we were able to continue on our way on to Khormaksar, via Masirah, in fairly good order, although the last leg was not without a few 'moments'. Going direct from Masirah to Khormaksar in the T7, with its restricted fuel load, could be marginal with any sort of headwind, and, needless to say, we had a headwind, which meant that the prudent thing to do was to land and refuel at Salalah. However,

I was keen to get home and, as we passed over Salalah, I decided to press on. We did make it, but only just. The Line Chief said that, when he refuelled the aircraft, he put more fuel in than the book said was possible. It was not a trip that I shall forget; indeed, ferry trips hardly ever failed to test one's ingenuity, resourcefulness and initiative. They were always a challenge, but also great fun and you never failed to learn a thing or two!

Credit: Arpingstone/Wikipedia

Thank You, Messrs Martin-Baker

In August 1952, I was A Flight Commander on 263 Squadron, based at RAF Wattisham, with 11 Meteor Mk8s and 14 pilots on my Flight. I had one new pilot, who had completed 11 of the 12 exercises required before he could be counted as operational, and I was keen to get him trained to that state. I had already flown once that morning and, although the weather was a bit bumpy, I thought that he was advanced enough to fly the next exercise, so I briefed him and another 2 pilots for a pairs snake climb with him as my No 2.

By the time we taxied out, the wind had increased considerably and the sky was full of developing cumulus. We took off and entered cloud at about 1100 feet, and there was considerably more turbulence than I had experienced on my first flight that day. I had my head in the cockpit, concentrating on the instruments, when there was a loud bang; the stick was stuck against my knee and the aircraft started gyrating. I could not budge the stick but a look out to the wings showed that they were OK; however the aircraft was, by this time, un-controllable, so I decided it was time to leave. I jettisoned the hood, pulled the face-blind handle and went. The blind blew away from my face, and the aircraft passed below me and disappeared; it was only then that I discovered why the aircraft was out of control - the last 12 feet of the fuselage were missing!

However, at that moment I was more intent on survival than on contem-plating the damage. I should explain, at this point, that the early ejection seats were not automatic, and it was up to the pilot to separate himself from the seat and deploy the parachute. So I undid the seatbelt, threw myself out of the seat and pulled the ripcord. Mercifully the chute opened with a jerk and, 2 or 3 seconds later, I broke cloud, only to see the second pair about half a mile south, following me in the climb and with an F86 Sabre from USAF Bentwaters on their tail! I was, by now, drifting quite alarmingly across the ground. A minute or so later, I realised that I was likely to land in a large tree, so I just went com-pletely limp and hoped for the best. Luckily, the ground effect must have saved me and I thumped into a ploughed field - head down, of course, and covered in ...well you can guess.

Having regained my breath, I staggered to my feet, only to be grabbed by the wind and dragged across the field until the parachute caught on a hedge; that did not improve my appearance either, but at least I could extricate myself from the 'chute and stand up. "Ah," I thought, "Someone must have seen this drama." But no, there was not a person in sight. Eventually, a tractor came and I was able to buy a fag from the driver. Then a couple of aircraft from 257, our sister squadron, found me and did a reassuring beat up, so I knew that rescue was on the way. The tractor driver took me to a small country pub, where they insisted that hot sweet tea was what I needed (??) and, from there, I was collected by our Station Doc in his blood-wagon.

My No 2 had never called to tell me that he had lost contact with me in cloud and, not surprisingly, was in a distressed state as he thought that he had killed me. He did eventually land his aircraft but, like mine, it never flew again. He later became a very reliable fighter pilot and flew with me many times, before converting to heavies and subsequently doing an exchange posting to the USA. Happy days!

The Tale of the Potless Knocker

1971, and Britain is beginning to draw its military back to base. 'Withdrawing from East of Suez', it was called. Until the final move I was a co-pilot on Shackletons, flying out of Sharjah in the Trucial States. Not a lot to do and we only flew once a week.

One of our sorties involved following the coast north, through the straits of Hormuz, and then on past Oman to the island of Masirah. We would then head north, across the desert, for our home base. There was not much to be seen, save sand, for the 500 mile transit, except for the Burami oasis, bang on the mid-point. Burami also sported an outcrop of rock which went up over 1000 feet so, to be on the safe side, our transits were conducted at 5,000 feet – which was close to earth orbit for the Mk2 Shackleton. Now comes the technical bit; the Shackleton was powered by Rolls-Royce Griffons – the biggest piston engine ever manufactured in the UK. So powerful was our version of the engine that one propeller disc was not sufficient to absorb the power, so we had two, each turning in a different direction. More technical bits; the engine drove the front propeller disc, and the remaining power was transferred to the back disc by a device called a Translation Unit (TU). Still with me? Good. The weakness in all this was that, if the TU failed, the back prop went fully fine[1]. In effect, it became a solid disc which you had to drag through the air.

Now for the fun! Thirty minutes into the transit, the TU of the right outer engine failed and the disc went fully fine. We put power on the remaining engines but, in the Arabian summer, the engine temperatures began to climb, and we had to reduce the power otherwise those engines would have failed as well. So, even applying as much power as we could, we began to slowly descend towards the sands. I could occasionally persuade the beast to climb, but the overall direction was most certainly down. As the inevitable crash landing would be delicate, my revered captain left me to fly, so that he would be fresh for the drama.

Now, on the maritime fleet, the search sensors were operated by a fine body

---

[1] fully fine – Variable pitch propellers permit the angle of the blade in relation to the airflow to be altered. This is akin to changing gear in a car. The limits of travel are fully coarse (top gear) and fully fine (first gear).

of malcontents, officially rated as SNCOs[2] but colloquially known as the Knockers. Impressed with my flying skills, this fine body of men retreated to the galley area of the aircraft. There, fortified by the occasional hip flask of tea, they began to run a sweepstake on how far from Sharjah we would crash. Down we went, and up on the horizon came Burami and that blasted bit of rock. As happens in flying when things go wrong, they go wrong in spades. The rock was directly on track - and above us. "Left or right?" says I to the Captain. He replies in Anglo-Saxon dialect, which I was eventually to master when I became a captain.

To this day, I know not why I went left, but left I went. Glider pilots will probably be able to explain it but, as we passed to the left of the rock, we found some lift from somewhere and began to climb. Not a lot, but just enough to hold our own and reach Sharjah. I was even allowed to do the landing which, for me, was a good one - I only bounced twice. I turned and looked down the aircraft, expecting a round of applause, only to be greeted by the angry face of our senior Knocker who had organised the sweep stake. "I suppose you think that was great? Well it truly [more Anglo Saxon] me; I've 'ad to give the pot back. Not only that, sprog, but I would've won!"

Credit: RuthAS/Wikipedia

---

[2] SNCOs – Senior Non-Commissioned Officers.

Mission – Operation DENY FLIGHT

It was August 1993, and the Squadron premises at RAF Coltishall were deserted. I had just arrived, fresh from the OCU[1], and had missed the Squadron by a week or so as they had detached to Gioia Del Colle, in southern Italy, for the Jaguar forces' latest mission – Operation DENY FLIGHT. Five months later, I stepped off the Hercules at Gioia, the newest Combat Ready pilot on the force. After a daunting theatre arrival brief, and having attempted to navigate my way around the SPINS[2], it was with some trepidation that I awaited my first trip.

The first trip came and went and, 6 months later, I switched off my hotel television, having just watched the latest CNN analysis of the likelihood of the Serbs removing their artillery and tanks from the exclusion zone around Sarajevo. The Serbs had been in this situation some months ago and had, on that occasion, capitulated. Replete, after another fine meal in the Hotel Suevo restaurant, I drifted into sleep, wondering whether tomorrow would be the day on which I would actually drop my bombs, after months of flying over the AOR[3].

Another sunny, but hazy, day dawned. On arrival at the JagDet accommodation on Gioia del Colle airbase, the daily intelligence brief unfolded. The Serb armour was still in place and the deadline for its removal was approaching. The flying programme had changed somewhat and I was now on RS30[4], as No 2 to Flight Lieutenant Dave Foote. We drew our weapons, goolie chits[5], Deutschmarks etc, and donned our CSWs[6] and sat around. After a couple of hours, the phones and communications networks started to heat up. The Serbs had missed the deadline and there was talk of launching to attack their armour. Finally the call came, and the other pair on RS30 were launched. At this stage, Footey and I were champing at the bit, not wanting to be left out of the action. However, as

---

[1] OCU – Operational Conversion Unit.
[2] SPINS - Special Instructions.
[3] AOR - Area of Operational Responsibility.
[4] RS30 - Readiness State 30 minutes.
[5] goolie chit – A letter that encouraged locals to assist a downed airman, usually by way of financial reward. 'Goolie' is Hindustani for ball – which is probably all the reader needs to know.
[6] CSWs - Combat Survival Waistcoats.

the second 'alert pair', I felt we would not be required. An hour later, we moved to cockpit readiness; then, unbelievably, it happened – we were scrambled. The first pair had been frustratingly held off and run out of gas so, with no tanker available to them, we were launched. We set off towards the gate[7], my leader barely visible in the thick haze. After the 20-minute transit my aircraft was prepared, but then the controlling AWACS[8] called us - "Crest, Magic 40, return to base, target has already been attacked." An American A-10 had strafed the target, and the Serbs had started to withdraw their tanks.

This was an atypical day on Op DENY FLIGHT. Most days involved a 60/40 split of Close Air Support (CAS) and reconnaissance flights, and we worked a regime of 6 days on and 2 off. Periods of RS 30 were not uncommon and involved much sitting around, waiting for nothing to happen. This is not to say that there weren't moments of excitement. I remember assisting a Forward Air Controller, who was under attack, by flying repeated, high-dive passes overhead the enemies' position. The fact that he lived to fight another day gave meaning to our efforts.

Perhaps the most exciting moment of our time over the Former Yugoslavia was due not to enemy action, but to the vagaries of the Jaguar fuel system. One day, after air refuelling, our brave airman flew up to Tuzla, in the far north-east of the AOR, to conduct a CAS sortie. Due to the nature of the mission, the magnetic indicators, which show whether the underwing tanks are feeding or not, were either not checked or gave an erroneous indication. Therefore, relying only on the detotaliser[9] clicking down throughout the sortie, our intrepid aviator left Tuzla with what he fondly believed to be the minimum fuel required to get back to Italy. It rapidly transpired that he had 2000 kgs less usable fuel than he had thought. The remaining fuel was trapped in his drop-tanks, and was not available at all, leaving him with around 300 kgs! Faced with only one choice, he diverted into Sarajevo.

Although run by the French UN peacekeepers, this was by no means a diversion of choice; in fact, it was never briefed as one. Welcomed by the French, and

---

[7] gate – A designated entry point.
[8] AWACS - Airborne Warning And Control System aircraft.
[9] Detotaliser - A mechanical, numerical indicator, showing total fuel remaining.

donning a flak-jacket, our intrepid aviator assisted them with hiding his aeroplane behind some lorries. This was later followed by a sumptuous dining-in night, courtesy of the French. The following morning, our pilot helped to sweep the snow off his aircraft and carried out a gravity refuelling from a Hercules, which had flown in to assist. After a low departure and zoom climb into cloud, the Jaguar was escorted by two American F-18s out of the AOR and flew back to Italy.

The Jaguar force handed over Op DENY FLIGHT to the Harrier force in August 1995. Approximately one month later, 2 Jaguars from 6 Squadron flew back out to Gioia, and conducted numerous missions designating LGBs[10] for the Harriers. The professionalism displayed by these two pilots was a fitting footnote to the 2 years during which the Squadron helped to patrol the skies over the Former Yugoslavia.

Credit: Geoff Lee

[10] LGBs – Laser Guided Bombs.

Where's 'My' Jacket?

In my position as Senior Engineering Officer of 543 Squadron - which operated the four-jet Victor 2 in the Strategic Reconnaissance role - it fell to me to lead a hand-picked engineering team in support of a detachment of aircraft to Midway Island in the Pacific. The whole island was a United States Navy base and was a pleasant change from our UK home station, offering as it did such off-duty treats as access to the US Navy duty free stores, where we could and did buy wholly unsuitable flared trousers in tropical colours, together with snorkelling, BBQs on the beach and more than the UK ration of sunshine.

One other element that came to my attention was a particularly striking US Navy dark brown leather jacket. Though such a garment was not the sort of thing I would normally have worn, the usual bizarre judgement that surfaces during detachments took over, and such a jacket became hugely desirable in my eyes. Now as anybody who has been in the services knows well - the go-to fixers in any military are the SNCOs[1]. As it happens, in this case this was an aircraft crew chief - one George Fidler. I spoke to George on the subject, and he duly took it on board and wandered off.

Nothing happened for some time, until one day, working away in my island office, George came in wearing one of these jackets. I perked up and asked him where he had got it; he was fairly noncommittal, and I emphasised my continuing interest. Half an hour later another stalwart of the team, one Sergeant Kitchen, briefly sauntered in, resplendent in just such a jacket. This time I was a little more forceful in my request, vaguely mentioning advancing career prospects for any successful provider of my sartorial update. Not long after that a third individual, Senior Aircraftsman (SAC) Peach, arrived; he too was attired in one of the jackets that I coveted. This time I really felt that, the carrot of promotion not having worked, the stick of potential demotion could be wielded for any who failed to acquire a jacket for me. A somewhat idle threat as SAC Peach was on one of the lower rungs of the promotional ladder.

Now you are probably ahead of me here, in that, no sooner had Peach left the office than laughter was heard outside, where a considerable number of people were drawing straws to see who would be the next one to don the *one-and-only* jacket to wear into my office and further wind me up!

I have usually admired the unashamed joy with which the British service-man will find ways to wind up any senior officer, but this time it took a little longer to fully appreciate the richness of the situation. But I never got a jacket.

Note: SAC Peach was a one-off. He was notionally my clerk, (in the Detach-ment Order he was designated as "locally cross trained in supply procedures", which probably cheered up the station Supply Officer enormously, or is it Lo-gistics now?) but he had transformed himself into a kind of 'Radar' (from the M.A.S.H. television programme). He always correctly anticipated the squadron requirements and was extremely efficient and adaptable. One "duty", which he took on himself, was that whenever any squadron member, or even a family member, was in hospital, Peach would visit them and, at his own expense, take them grapes or some small token. A very human personality, and, I am glad to say, ultimately I initiated his receiving an Air Officer Commanding's Com-mendation - which in my experience was the only time an SAC received such an award.

---

[1] SNCOs - Senior Non-Commissioned Officer

Hyeres We Go
(A camping trip to France)

Do you remember the days when we had very few Buccaneers to fly, and many of us became unwilling members of 2-seat Hunter squadrons? A couple of accidents put us in that position for quite a while in the early 80s. The pilot fraternity were kept busy doing day checks, captaincy checks, Instrument Rating Tests, Friday checks, Monday post-weekend refreshers etc, following a training programme gleefully arranged by the QFIs[1]. The navigators, meanwhile, made a lot of coffee and grumbled.

After a few months of this ill treatment, there was a minor mutiny and insistence that some fun was put back into life again; to wit an unofficial squadron exchange to somewhere 'nice and warm'. The Execs – particularly those with QFI sympathies – were dead against the idea of slackening their grip on their toys, but we eventually persuaded the Boss that a long weekend away on a site recce would boost morale - for four of us, at least. The proviso was that it had to be done at no cost to Her Majesty's Government (HMG); in other words, try to find somewhere that has on-base accommodation and the beer is free. Maps were spread, the bit of string that was the Hunter fuel endurance computer pinned to RAF Laarbruch, and a sweeping arc drawn through most of Western Europe. "Anywhere in there, then". Some hours of telephone calls later, and we were running into problems. No room on the ramp, no room at the inn, bar closed for redecoration, pool closed for cleaning....eventually we found that the French Navy Etendards seemed keen, they could also look after the cabs[2] for the weekend, but had no spare rooms until Sunday night. "No problem," says I, "It's July in the South of France. We can take tents and camp on the beach! What could possibly go wrong?" While this suggestion wasn't met with universal approval, we'd run out of other ideas by then.

Hyeres we go, then...

The run down with two cabs was uneventful, but it was clear as soon as we arrived that the state of the runway would make a Buccaneer landing extremely

---

[1] QFI – Qualified Flying Instructor.
[2] cab –Slang term for an aircraft.

exciting. Nevertheless, as we were in place we might as well make the best of it! The French fish-heads were very welcoming, and by that I mean a bloke with a broom pitched up as we were unpacking the gun bays of Boy Scout gear. He squinted under his beret and over his Gauloise, pointed to the hangar and shook his head, and towards the bowser and nodded, from which we interpreted as, "No accommodation for you or the cabs and now you know where the hose is". It was at this point that one of the pilots discovered he hadn't packed a sleeping bag...

We hired a car and headed up the coast to find Fun and Sun. Both appeared to be severely rationed. The anticipated clear blue skies hadn't appeared and, in fact, it seemed that autumn had started two months early – a Baltic draught, raining domestic pets and, on top of that, all the beaches (and their accompanying attractions) were for the exclusive use of the extremely exclusive hotels - as well as being windswept and deserted. We had a splendid evening nonetheless, and that even included pitching the tents, in driving rain, in the corner of a field. We slept well, except for the aforementioned Bagless One (TBO). He shivered the night away, while wrapped in two copies of Le Figaro and wet socks.

Saturday dawned grey, wet and windy. We quickly packed up and legged it, as what had seemed to be a field last night turned out to be a vineyard this morning, complete with grumpy owner and noisy tractor. Ablutions were dealt with in the loos at the nearest petrol station and, over a bucket of coffee and a fag, we sat in a café, watched the rain fall and worried about the cabs. The Hunter canopy seal was for keeping air in not water out, so we'd taped over the gaps, much to the amusement of the French liney[3], but doubts remained as to the effectiveness of this ploy, given the tropical storm we were now enjoying. Contact was eventually made with Operations at Hyeres, once we'd found a serviceable phone box, and they had already found some space in the hangar for our aircraft and tucked them safely out of the weather. With consciences now clear, we only had to wait for the sun to come out, which it eventually did.....on Sunday. By this time, The Bagless One was on the verge of hypothermia, despite us spending a fortune at the newspaper stands. We returned to Hyeres, and the hospitality of the Aeronavale, for a last night, to find that the bar was indeed

---

[3] liney – Slang term for a mechanic who works on aircraft at the dispersal (or line).

closed, the nearest pub was seven miles away and we'd returned the hire car!

Monday morning arrived; Flight Plan filed, bags stowed, cartridges primed and all set to go home. It took some time to get the lid off the cockpit, and our wingman left us to it as we struggled with instructions relayed from home which involved the use of spanners. At last we gained entry, and made haste to beat the 're-filing' deadline for the flight plan. As we taxied out, it was becoming obvious that the gaffer tape hadn't been overly efficient at keeping the water out of the cockpit; we were steaming up. Confident that the cabin conditioning would cope with that once we got the engine properly wound up, we continued, busily mopping the canopy and vaguely following the centreline. It wasn't until Vr[4] that the extent of the problem became surprisingly obvious. As the nose came up, a wall of water came down from somewhere forward of our feet and The Bagless One got wet socks again. Too late to abort, we climbed above the airfield with quite a lot to occupy us – the undercarriage wouldn't come up, the IFIS[5] was having a fit, and the radio was rather quiet. Clearly we weren't going anywhere in a hurry and tried to communicate the fact to Air Traffic. They, equally clearly, weren't responding to a word we said. A minute or two later and we'd settled into a medium-level orbit of the TACAN[6], squawking 7600[7] and burning off fuel. TBO and I spent an amusing half-hour watching the French fire trucks shadowing us by endlessly circling the peri-track[8]. We debriefed the weekend's events, particularly the lack of entertainment available on-base, and our assumptions about how French matelots got their fun. It subsequently turned out that our radio was on permanent transmit...!

The descent to warmer air reaffirmed that the cockpit was wetter than an otter's pocket, but we managed to get on the ground before it got so bad we couldn't see outside. Once clear of the runway, we tried to open the lid a little, but it wouldn't respond to any of the usual methods of achieving this, so taxied

---

[4] Vr – Rotate speed, at which the pilot starts to raise the nose of the aircraft to initiate the take off.

[5] IFIS – Integrated Flight Information System.

[6] TACAN – TACtical Air Navigation system.

[7] squawking 7600 - The term "squawk" is used when assigning an aircraft a transponder code. 7600 indicates radio failure.

[8] peri-track – The perimeter road around an airfield.

back to our start point very warily. The Gauloise-equipped liney was still there, leaning on his broom, watching us sitting there all steamed-up, but with no particular interest in doing much to help. After a minute or two, he flipped his dog-end away and advanced curiously as we tried to attract his attention from our shower cubicle. Eventually he understood. I knew this because I saw him pull a hammer out of his pocket and advance towards the Emergency Canopy Release. I managed, through frantic wiping and waving, to stop him doing anything explosive, at which point he lost interest and wandered away. We sat and considered our options. I remembered that, during one of those interminable Friday afternoon QFI quiz sessions, we'd been told how to unlatch the canopy at the hinge and "then you can push the thing up and climb out". Well, you can - in theory. I didn't believe anyone had actually tried it, and I still believe that we were the first, but hey, when needs must...In case you're wondering, the Hunter canopy weighs about 100 lbs. The only way to lift it is to unstrap, stand on the seat facing backwards, lift it with your back and shoulders, until you can jam your flying helmet under the rim, and slither out from under it, hoping that nothing goes wrong or it'll cut your legs off. Then fall off the back deck onto the ground. Oh, and don't be a tubby git either. That's why TBO had to wait for the matelots to organise a crane to get the lid off, by which time his skin had gone all white and wrinkly.

We then began a 4 day game of 'Find 'n Fix'. Careful reading of the turn-round guide allowed us to pump up the accumulator and get the canopy sorted out. On the phone, the squadron engineers had us listing the symptoms of the other snags, so they could come equipped with the right spares to mend us, and it was then that I was introduced to the deeper recesses of the aircraft's electrical system. Upside down in the cockpit, peering under the seats, we found banks of fuses that would safeguard the National Grid. Far from pristine, they were covered in the slimy fungus that old torch batteries grow after a year or two, so clearly there was a bigger problem than a dud radio and a sticky canopy. Further telephone discussions later, and we'd worked out a list of possible fixes and prepared to host a party of Menders. While we waited, we got busy with mops and buckets to dry out the small pond that had now collected on the cockpit floor. The engineers duly arrived, identified within 30 seconds that they'd brought the wrong bits, and the cycle began again. The improving weather helped combat our disappointment, of course, since, apart from providing the Menders with copious quantities of water and Sandwiches de Jambon, TBO and I had little to do but bronze ourselves and sample the local delights - which we did. Shamelessly, now that HMG was picking up the tab.

As the week passed, the snag list grew as the engineers got deeper into the soggy bowels of the jet. The fire lights came on and wouldn't go out, the canopy hydraulics developed Machiavellian tendencies, and one of the Menders spent an interesting afternoon in his own personal sauna when it jammed shut with him under it. A faulty canopy motor relay was diagnosed, the canopy electrics had to be re-wired through the standby compass light switch, and the complement of engineers grew steadily as more and more trade experts were needed. Repeated engine starts used up all our cartridges, and 3 of the 4 replacements turned out to be duds. Attempts to fix the radio had us once again on permanent transmit and filling the tower frequency with hammering noises and curses for an afternoon. An irate Gallic airtrafficker turned up to remonstrate and suggest that we desist, and on departure drove over our aircraft's radio bay door.

At last, a week after arriving at Hyeres, we managed to get airborne for the return trip. It'd taken all our negotiating skills to persuade Air Traffic to stay open, since they normally packed up at lunchtime on Fridays, and it was a lovely evening across Europe with unlimited visibility. Just as well. The TACAN packed up before the first turn, the radio died again and 400 lbs of fuel wouldn't come out of one of the underwing tanks. Having had enough of France by then and, as most of it was closed for the weekend, we 'proceeded as per flight plan' and landed safely back at Laarbruch, once we'd managed to get the fuel snag cleared. On touchdown we deployed the drag 'chute, which, predictably, fell out of the back of the aircraft and lay uselessly on the runway.

All true – well, you couldn't make it up, could you?

What Goes Around, Comes Around

As a single-seat, fast- jet pilot, I, of course, felt that I could learn nothing from the rotary world. But despite my denial, I did pick up a few lessons over the years. It began with the pre-Harrier-OCU helicopter flying course. This consisted of 6 hours of rotary-wing flying, with no ground school or simulator, but with a Qualified Helicopter Instructor (QHI) to take care of all the checks and limitations. Concentrating just on the flying, it was amazing how much you could achieve in that short time. *Lesson 1: The traditional Central Flying School way of doing things is not always the best.*

As a first tour flying officer, I experienced RAF, Royal Navy and Army helicopter operations in Belize. I was in the front left-hand seat of a Puma, as we flew down to the bottom left corner of the country to re-supply an Army outpost atop a hill overlooking the border. After many miles of jungle, I was surprised to see a sign of comparative civilisation, so I remarked to the Puma captain, "Hey, I didn't know that there was a road down here - and there are trucks on that road... And they look to me like Guatemalan army trucks!" After a quick about turn, we approached our intended destination, but from the wrong direction. Unfortunately, the occupants had radioed back to HQ reporting our first fly-by. By the time we got back to base, it was already past opening time, so I repaired to the bar to recount my adventures. Before my lips touched the glass, I was ordered to report to the Air Commander, with my hat on. From him, I received a stiff telling off for allowing the Puma pilot to stray into the wrong (enemy) country. Later, seeking sympathy from other aircrew, I got a response from the Puma guys along the lines of, "Oh, did nobody tell you about his legendary navigation, and the Irish border incursions?"
Lesson 2: It's the junior officer's fault.

The RN couldn't fly with us in Belize, where we had only single-seat aircraft, so they came to visit Wittering for T-bird (2-seater version) trips. During one such visit, I flew with a Qualified Helicopter Instructor in a Wasp. Noting that I had flown helicopters before, he decided to make things more interesting, and asked if I had tried auto-rotation. I said yes, accustomed to the secure feeling of power being available as a back-up if needed. He then handed control to me and shut down the engine.

Lesson 3: The Navy often do things differently.

I flew a close air support training mission in Belize, with the FAC (Forward Air Controller) in an Army Sioux helicopter. I called, "Running in from the IP (Initial Point)", and the FAC replied, "Your reference point will be orange smoke." He then ignited a smoke grenade and threw it from the helicopter. His next call was, "Disregard smoke. It is in the back of a truck moving west. New reference point is a bushy-topped tree" (this, in the land of a million trees).

Lesson 4: Look before you chuck.

As a flight lieutenant, I served as the wing FRI (Fighter Reconnaissance Instructor) on the Harrier recce squadron, on a station where there were also two helicopter squadrons. We had some pre-planned war missions, with recce targets to the west of the IGB (Inner German Border), but within the buffer zone where we could not fly in peacetime. With video technology becoming available, it seemed like a good idea to go and film the target areas, flying in a helicopter (which could go into the buffer zone). So, I spent a couple of days sitting in the front of a Wessex, looking through the monocular viewfinder of a huge VHS camera at the targets, mostly along various, more or less winding roads. By the end of Day 2, I felt distinctly queasy. The cause may have been the nature of the task, the Wessex cockpit environment, or the huge meal, beers and very dodgy cabaret in Braunschweig that I had shared with the helicopter crew on Night 1.

Lesson 5: Support Helicopter flying etc can be sickening.

As a squadron leader, again in Germany, I spent a day out in the countryside with various senior Army and RAF officers on a TEWT (Tactical Exercise Without Troops). After a long day on the mostly flat North German Plain, considering potential reactions to moves by the 3rd Shock Army, we were ready for the long haul back to RAF Gütersloh. Fortunately, we had in our syndicate the CO of an RAF helicopter squadron, so we relaxed at the top of a small hill waiting for our lift to arrive. Despite this being before the days of mobile phones, we were confident as we heard, and then saw, the unmistakeable helicopter approach in the gathering darkness. However, as it passed at the nearest point some 1 mile from us, we ran to catch the last Army officer in his departing Land Rover. Through him, we were able to summon more wheels for the long drive home.

Lesson 6: Beware of tasks on which the Boss's reputation may depend.

For its Cold War role, the RAFG Harrier Force would disperse to 10 locations, and this plan was exercised three times a year. Before the sites were activated, the various Execs (Force, Squadron and Site Commanders) would be taken on a recce to see the initial locations for the exercise. The most convenient means by which to do this was in a helicopter. On one such occasion, after a walk around one of the sites, I was still strapping in to the back of the helicopter when I saw all the other passengers jumping out and running away with cries of "Fire!" Fortunately, it was not as serious as it might have been, but it did lead to a policy change.

Lesson 7: Don't put all your eggs in one basket, or all your execs in one Puma.

As a wing commander, I flew Jaguars at Coltishall, where there was a Wessex Search and Rescue flight. One day, I flew in the left-hand seat of the Wessex, with a flying officer as captain in the right-hand seat. The flight commander was a rear-crew squadron leader, who flew with us that day. We went out off the east coast, to rendezvous with a marine craft and practise some winching. First, the flight commander went on the end of the cable, and was lowered to the deck of the marine craft. We then flew away and returned to pick him up. The marine craft had come to a halt, and was wallowing around in the sea, with its various antennae waving around high above the deck. We came to a hover over the boat, and the cable was lowered, allowing the squadron leader to attach himself to it. At this point, the Wessex drifted to the right (or the boat went left). The winch operator instructed the pilot to move left, and became concerned about losing sight of the deck. The pilot also shared this concern and asked me (the spare guy in the left seat) if I could see; I could not. Evidently the concern became too great for the winch operator, who promptly operated the cable guillotine, leaving the flight commander shaking his fist on the deck and the Coltishall sector SAR helicopter without any winching capability. The flying officer captain had the half hour transit back to base, plus the time to get the spare aircraft out to the marine craft, in which to get his story straight. Sadly, the flight commander had the same time to think of a suitable punishment.

Lesson 8: Same as Lesson 2, with a touch of Lesson 6.

After a tour of Jaguar flying, including hours over Bosnia pitying the poor souls down below, I was posted to ... Sarajevo, with UNPROFOR[1]. I got there by RAF Hercules to Split, then French Puma (calling in for fuel on a desolate hillside) to just outside the hostile bit around the city, then driving the final few miles. Not a nice journey. When the time came to leave, I was waiting at Sarajevo airport, vainly hoping for a break in the weather, when I saw the new American 3-Star commander arrive. Not quite believing what I heard, I peered out and saw a rather special looking MH53 helicopter emerging from the dense fog, taxying towards the terminal building. As it slowed, the ramp lowered and troops ran out in a fan, adopting prone firing positions to secure this part of the international airport before the admiral disembarked. I managed to scrounge a lift out some 24 hours later, on an RAF aircraft.

Lesson 9: Senior officers get bigger, more capable choppers.

So perhaps the biggest lesson of all is:

Lesson 10: There is always something to be learned in any form of aviation. Whatever your professional specialisation, it pays to watch what is going on around you whenever engaged in any flying activity.

Credit: Geoff Lee

---

[1] UNPROFOR – United Nations Protection Force

Dominie Double Flameout

In September 2005, I was the pilot of a Dominie aircraft conducting a 55(R) Squadron training sortie from RAF Cranwell. At the time, I had been flying for 34 years and had accumulated 6500 hours flying experience of which over 5500 hours was on fast jets and 650 hours on the Dominie. The sortie briefing included a Met Briefing which warned that, in the Borders area, severe icing could be expected up to Flight Level 220 in nimbo-stratus cloud. The sortie went as planned throughout the route up to RAF Kinloss and across to Aberdeen. However, on the return leg, while flying at Flight Level 270, 50 nautical miles north-west of Newcastle, the aircraft approached cloud which may have contained icing conditions. At the time, there was a student navigator in the right hand seat and an instructor on the jump seat. I duly carried out the Precautionary Icing Drill prior to entering cloud, in accordance with the Flight Reference Cards (FRCs) and, as this was being done, the instructor briefed the student on the importance of the drill and the aircraft's vulnerability to icing. After a short time in cloud, a small amount of ice had accumulated on the windscreen, but the ice detection light had not illuminated and the aircraft surfaces and engine intakes were clear of ice. I then requested a climb to Flight Level 290, to achieve VMC[1] on top. Scottish Military (Radar) cleared us to climb but, as I advanced the throttles, both engines flamed out within two seconds of each other. There was no sign of engine surge, overtemp or malfunction from either engine.

I maintained speed in a shallow descent, while we put out a MAYDAY[2] call, and selected both engine relights to ON. Scottish Military advised me that the closest airfield was Edinburgh, in my 5 o'clock at 25 nm. However, I elected to continue to Newcastle, which was ahead at 47 nm; it was within gliding distance, and I knew the prevailing weather there. We had only recently copied the weather for Newcastle and Edinburgh, Newcastle being BLUE[3] whilst Edinburgh was YELLOW and underneath the worst of the weather.

---

[1] VMC – Visual Meteorological Conditions.
[2] MAYDAY - A distress signal that indicates a life-threatening emergency.
[3] NATO airbases used a colour coding system to indicate the prevailing meteorological conditions in relation to cloud base and visibility. Starting with the best they were BLUE, WHITE, GREEN, YELLOW, AMBER and RED.

Both engines re-lit within 20 seconds, without any abnormal indications, and I continued descending to VMC at Flight Level 150. During the descent, the aircraft became heavily contaminated with ice, but both engines performed normally. Once we were VMC, all the ice on the aircraft melted within a couple of minutes. Having levelled out, I assessed the situation and downgraded the emergency to a PAN[4]. As a crew, we then had a detailed discussion about why the engines had flamed out, and whether any damage had been done. We assessed that neither engine had surged or malfunctioned in any way, and it was apparent that we could recover to base VMC, thus avoiding any further icing conditions. We also assessed that the aircraft would always be within a safe distance of a suitable diversion airfield, and duly notified Air Traffic Control of our intention to continue to Cranwell for a straight-in approach. The rest of the sortie was completed without further event, although the crew members were quieter than normal.

Once back in the Squadron, we in-briefed and informed the Duty Aircrew Officer that we would be reporting an incident. As a crew, we debriefed our sortie and agreed on the order in which the events had taken place. I then debriefed the engineers in detail, and filed an Incident Report. The Boss came into the crew room a while later and asked what had happened. Having heard our story, he thanked us for returning the aircraft to base. However, within a couple of hours, and after a few phone calls to and from Group Headquarters, it became clear that all was not well; a number of assumptions were being made, without any evidence.

At 5 o'clock, there was only one place to go - York House Officers' Mess bar. After a quick pint and a few war stories, it was time for home. As I walked across the car park, I was surprised to see a very senior officer heading in my direction. After a cursory greeting, I was debriefed, accused, found guilty and hung, all in the space of about two minutes! Why had I flown into icing conditions? Why had the engines flamed out? Why had I returned to Cranwell? Why many other things too? The screwdriver was out and turning.

Over the following days it was discovered that the ice detector in that

---

[4] PAN - A state of urgency exists although there is no imminent danger to life or the continued viability of the aircraft .

aircraft was unserviceable. It was also determined that the pre-flight check of the ice detector (which had been carried out in the same way for many years) was invalid. Detailed discussions with the Rolls-Royce Viper engine specialist confirmed that the engine was very susceptible to flame-out from ice ingestion. It was also discovered that the RAF version of HS125 (Dominie) Icing Drills were totally different from those recommended by Rolls-Royce and performed by all other HS125 operators. Over the following week a number of procedures were changed, and the Aircrew Manual and Flight Reference Cards amended. The Dominie had never had an approved Flame-Out Procedure, or any advice on how the aircraft performed with no power, only word-of-mouth advice passed on through the generations.

Almost immediately a Unit Inquiry was initiated but, due to the chosen investigating officer not being available, the first interviews did not start for almost a week; not great for getting immediate recall from each crew member. Thereafter, it soon became apparent, from the way the Inquiry was being conducted, that 'those on high' expected someone to shoulder the blame. It was a sobering and saddening experience to witness this. While we on the squadron were liaising with everyone from Rolls-Royce and the Civil Aviation Authority to the aircraft icing experts in the Federal Aviation Authority, the screw kept turning. Eventually, to placate the powers that be, I compiled a Human Factors Report...to make others aware of my transgression.

The immediate aftermath of this incident was a classic, knee-jerk example of the wrong people getting too involved. In the end, all the corrective work was done at local, squadron level. Lessons were learnt and errors corrected, but it was never actually discovered why the aircraft operating procedures had drifted so far away from the manufacturer's advice.

That Sinking Feeling

In the old Whirlwind Mk10, a second pilot was optional. The cyclic stick[1] in the left hand seat was removable, and the seat itself was hinged at the rear, so it could be lifted up. In this way, it was possible for a crewman to get into the front, to assist with navigation and lookout, and get back down to the 'hold' if required to supervise loading or unloading. The stick could also be removed or replaced in flight, as it (initially) had no electrical connections but, instead, had a simple bayonet fit with a safety locking 'pip-pin'. The left-seat collective lever[2] – which did include electric and engine control functions - was not "in-flight-removable".

Now, on one particular trip, a new and inexperienced crewman asked if he could 'sit up front'? "No problem", I said. Pip-pin removed, stick twisted and lifted out of its socket, anti-FOD[3] cover re-zipped, and stick stowed below – job almost done. When I confirmed I was happy, Sgt 'Funk-knuckle' eased himself halfway up the bulkhead underneath the seat and then lifted the seat from below with his head (think of getting through a loft trap-door).

Now keep thinking loft. How do you get up? You reach up through the hole as far as you can, put your elbows on the edge of the hole, and sort of spring and do a parallel-bar straight-arm push at the same time. Are you still with me? Well he nearly wasn't.

The lever in my left hand (with about 60-70% of power selected) suddenly tried to go through the floor. The aircraft waited a millisecond and then tried to follow it, while the rotor went from cruise pitch to minimum pitch, slightly faster than the engine could decelerate in order to keep the revs inside limits. We are now into 'Gerard Hoffnung and the Barrel' territory. The aircraft's sudden plummet caused the crewman to slip back down into the cabin and, in so doing, he let go of the collective lever. At the same time however, I was trying to lift the lever - and, initially, also the crewman's weight - up from somewhere

---

[1] cyclic stick - Movement of the cyclic stick tilts the helicopter's rotor disk, causing it to move in that direction.
[2] collective lever – Controls the lifting capability of the helicopter's rotor.
[3] FOD – Foreign Object Damage.

near my toes, to arrest the downward trajectory of our transport. Now, pure power-operated controls, with no damping or feel, respond very quickly, as did the old Gnome engine. Thankfully, in those days, so did my reactions, so the subsequent over-swing[4] was not that marked. However, it took somewhat longer for my heart to recover to normal!

I certainly learned about flying from that! It was subsequently decided that 'in-flight' movement between cabin and cockpit had to be practised on the ground before being attempted in the air. However, a year or two later, the left-hand stick routinely had the electrics connected, so it was no longer possible to do an unplanned airborne change. I do recall that some of the slimmer navigators could negotiate the route with the stick still in place, but I don't know of anyone who actually did it airborne!

Credit: Crown Copyright

---

[4] over-swing – In this context, temporarily outside operating limits.

Monty 67

On the evening of 27th February 1991, two Hercules of 47 Squadron Special Forces flight deployed from their forward operating base at Al Jouf to King Fahd International Airport. This new airport, never used before Gulf War 1, had become the headquarters of US Special Operation Command. I believe the airport is still the largest, by area, in the world and is now Dhahran International Airport. After extensive briefings and detailed planning, Callsign Monty 66 departed the following morning for Kuwait, taking some signals equipment and personnel. Although the Iraqi forces had destroyed a British Airways 747, and caused severe damage to the terminal buildings, they had surprisingly not damaged the main runway. The intention was for Monty 66 to unload its cargo, and take off immediately to return to Saudi territory.

Shortly after Monty 66 departed, my crew in Monty 67 also took off, carrying further signals vehicles and equipment to set up a forward Air Refuelling Point (FARP), from which to replenish British helicopters prior to the retaking of the British Embassy. US helicopters, carrying their special forces troops, would be retaking the US embassy as part of a co-ordinated assault. We departed King Fahd carrying maximum fuel, as it was our intention to refuel the helicopters twice each, once on arrival in Kuwait and once before departure for base. We planned to fly a route through the area where the oil fields were aflame, as this seemed ideal for giving us cover. We did not expect any active aggression, but there were pockets of Iraqi troops on our route. As we took off, the sun had risen and was shining brightly, and we had clear skies ahead of us. I settled the Hercules at 250kts and around 50-100ft. Our protection wasn't up to the standard of the US aircraft, but we had a form of radar warning receiver called Orange Crop, some chaff and flare dispensers, and a gunner at the rear door. That was it, apart from a great aircraft and crew.

It wasn't too long before we crossed the border into Kuwait and, at once, signs of the struggle that had recently taken place were evident, with burned-out tanks and vehicles, and the infamous anti-tank berms (mounds). In the distance, the smoke and fires from the oil wells came closer and closer, and the skies became blacker and blacker, eventually resembling the conditions one would expect at dusk. It was a sight to behold, a scene of devastation, with fires as far as the eye could see which, I must admit, wasn't that far. Eventually we cleared the oilfields and headed for Kuwait airfield, passing by pockets of Iraqi troops, mostly evident by the white flags they were waving.

We made a quick slowdown, and lined up for the runway at Kuwait to make an uneventful touchdown. The destruction was quickly evident, as was the BA 747 with its tail still standing upright. We parked up, quickly unloaded the signals vehicles, then rolled out the FARP equipment, to await the arrival of the British Chinooks and Sea Kings. The FARP equipment was quite "Heath Robinson", and involved taking a pipe from the refuel coupling of the Hercules to a small pump, and then to two refuelling pipes, which were positioned to each side of the rear of the Hercules, allowing 2 helicopters to refuel at the same time. The system was simple but it worked and was quite quick and easy to deploy. It wasn't long before the first British helicopters arrived, and promptly took on fuel prior to departing for the Embassy retaking operation.

During this time, the US helicopter fleet arrived, and quickly found out that the fuel tanks on the airfield, although they were still intact and containing fuel, had been contaminated. Fortunately for the US aircraft, Monty 67 still had quite a lot of extra fuel available, and this became a rather valuable commodity. American colonels came to us begging for an upload and, of course, we obliged; Monty 67 rapidly became known as the "Fuel Pit".

At some stage around midday, the winds changed direction and the clear skies over Kuwait quickly took on a very dark hue. Within minutes it could well have been late in the evening. It was impossible for us to see the helicopters refuelling, only a mere 100ft from the back of our aircraft; fortunately these conditions did not last too long. More and more US helicopters seemed to appear, and our fuel state reduced to a critical level for a return to Saudi. I made the decision to carry on refuelling the helicopters, as that was the most important issue, and we would be able to call for Monty 66 to return with fuel for us and any other aircraft.

At about this time a Hercules landed on the runway and promptly deployed a Union Jack from the top hatch. We were surprised, but very pleased, as our instant thoughts were that it might have some extra fuel. The captain rushed to speak with us, his first words being: "How long have you been here?", to which I replied: "All day now - have you any spare fuel?". It would appear that this Hercules, from 70 Squadron, had arrived with the British Ambassador on board, and they had been under the impression that theirs would be the first aircraft to land in Kuwait. The captain had checked all tasking for the day, but had not realised that our Special Forces tasking did not appear on the normal operational orders. I have to say that he was not amused, and was even more upset when we got him to back his aircraft onto ours, so that we could take extra fuel on board. That done, the Hercules departed back whence it had come, but this time not displaying the Union Jack. It's interesting to note that rumours circulated that a Special Forces Hercules had diverted into Kuwait to be the first to land there!

The helicopters carried out their missions without any problems or major contact with the Iraqi forces and, thankfully, Monty 66 arrived back full of fuel, ready to take over our "Fuel Pit" duties. We finally departed, having played a small but vital role, refuelling far more helicopters than we ever thought we would have to.

Credit: RAF/Crown Copyright

The Final Engagement

The morning of 8th June 1982 started much the same as any other during the Falklands conflict. The ritual of a shower, putting on clean underwear and 'lucky' flying suit (which was, by now rather high!) and a good breakfast, before checking the briefing room for the day's commitments as dawn was breaking. It transpired that I was unlikely to be needed before midday, as I was due to carry out the final part of my night qualification that evening. I therefore volunteered to fly in the left hand seat of one of the Wessex helicopters, which had been saved after the ATLANTIC CONVEYOR was hit by an Exocet missile. It had been nearly ten years since I had flown the Wessex full time, but I found it soon came back, and I spent a happy couple of hours delivering mail and supplies around the fleet.

After lunch, I flew a mission patrolling to the north of Falkland Sound. The weather had cleared beautifully by then, with very little cloud over the islands and just the odd thunderstorm over the sea. At this stage of the conflict, we were normally using the metal landing strip at Port San Carlos to refuel between sorties. Unfortunately, Wing Commander Peter Squire, the Commanding Officer No 1(F) squadron, had experienced an engine problem whilst landing there that morning and spread his aircraft all over the strip, coming to rest on top of a slit trench. My sortie was completely uneventful but, very soon after we set off back to HERMES, HMS PLYMOUTH was attacked by a formation of Argentinian Air Force Daggers, a frustrating but not unusual occurrence, and we were glad to hear that her damage had not been serious.

That evening, Dave Smith and I strapped ourselves into our aircraft to come to five-minute alert, with our minds fairly full of the night landing to come. Shortly before we were planned to launch, we were jolted back to reality by the broadcast 'Stand clear of intakes and jet pipes, scramble the alert 5 Sea Harriers!' We had a job to do. We were airborne within three minutes, and streaking towards the sun, which was now low on the western horizon. For the next quarter of an hour, we flew in silence, both wondering what we would find when we got to the islands. Finally, approaching the CAP[1] station, I radioed the pair of Sea

---

[1] CAP – Combat Air Patrol.

Harriers that we were relieving, to get an update, and was told that they were 'over the action' to the north of our briefed station. As we got closer, I saw a huge vertical column of oily black smoke rising from a bay to the southwest of Stanley. When we arrived overhead, the grim reality unfolded. Two landing craft were at anchor in the bay, wreathed in a nightmare of smoke and explosions. From our perch, high in the halls of the sky, we could only watch, with increasing concern and frustration, as the living beetles of lifeboats crawled back and forth between ship and shore, with their desperate human cargoes. There was little we could do but search the lengthening shadows for further attackers, as we ploughed our parallel furrows back and forth, a couple of miles above their heads. To fly lower would have denied us radio contact with our controller in San Carlos, and risked spooking the troops on the ground into thinking we were the enemy, returning to cause further chaos.

Some five miles to the south of our racetrack in the sky, I noticed a small landing craft, leaving Choiseul Sound and heading up the coast towards us. On checking, this was identified as friendly, and became a particular point to check each time I turned back onto a westerly heading. I felt great empathy with them, as I imagined the crew, cold and tired in their tiny boat, and I wondered if they had any idea that we were watching over them. The next forty minutes crept by as we circled, using the minimum possible amount of fuel, neither of us talking and both of us very much aware of the tragedy being enacted below us. Finally, I made a routine check of the fuel gauges as I rolled into another turn to reverse track, and realised that I now had only four minutes flying before I had to turn east, into the rapidly darkening evening sky, for HERMES. I flicked my eyes out of the cockpit and searched the gathering dusk below me for the small landing craft and soon picked it out, butting its way through the South Atlantic rollers towards Port Pleasant, with white water breaking over its bows.

It was in that instant that I spotted something which triggered the explosive action which lies, like a tightly coiled spring, beneath the outwardly calm carapace of the fighter pilot. My worst fears and fondest dreams had, in a single instant, been realised. A mere mile to the east of the vessel was the camouflaged outline of an Argentinian A4 Skyhawk fighter, hugging the sea and heading directly for the landing craft, which had become a very personal part of my existence for the last forty minutes. This was the very thing that we had been anticipating and dreading so much. I jammed the throttle fully open, shouted over the radio 'A4s attacking the boat, follow me down!' and peeled off into a sixty degree dive towards the attackers. Dave Smith wrenched his Sea Harrier around after me, but lost sight of my machine as we plunged downwards, with the airspeed rocketing from the economic 240 knots on CAP, to over 600 knots, as we strained to catch the enemy before he could reach his target.

I watched impotently, urging my aircraft onwards and downwards, as the first A4 opened fire with his 20-millimetre cannon, bracketing the tiny matchbox of a craft. My heart soared as his bomb exploded a good 100 feet beyond them, but then sank as I realised that a further A4 was running in behind him. The second pilot did not miss and I bore mute and frustrated witness to the violent fire-bright petals of the explosion which obliterated the stern, killing the crew and mortally wounding the landing craft. All-consuming anger welled in my throat, and I determined, in that instant, that this pilot was going to die! As I closed rapidly on his tail, I noticed, in my peripheral vision, a further A4, paralleling his track to my left. I hauled my aircraft to the left and rolled out less than half a mile behind the third fighter, closing like a runaway train. I had both missiles and guns selected and, within seconds, I heard the growl in my earphones telling me that my missile could see the heat from his engine. My right thumb pressed the lock button on the stick, and instantly the small green missile cross in the head-up display transformed itself into a diamond, sitting squarely over the back end of the Skyhawk. At the same time, the growl of the missile became an urgent, high-pitched chirp, telling me that the infrared homing head of the weapon was locked on and ready to fire.

I raised the safety catch, and mashed the red, recessed firing button with all the strength I could muster. There was a short delay as the missile's thermal battery ignited and its voltage increased to that required to launch the weapon. In less than half a second, the Sidewinder was transformed from an inert, eleven-foot long tube, into a living, fire breathing monster, as it accelerated to nearly three times the speed of sound, and streaked towards the nearest enemy aircraft. As it left the rails, the rocket efflux and supersonic shock wave over the left wing rolled my charging Sea Harrier rapidly to the right, throwing me onto my right wing tip at less than 100 feet above the sea. As I rolled erect, the missile started to guide towards the Skyhawk's jet pipe, leaving a white corkscrew of smoke against the slate-grey sea. Within two seconds, the missile disappeared directly up his jet pipe, and what had been a living, vibrant, flying machine was completely obliterated in an instant as the missile tore into its vitals and ripped it apart. The pilot had no chance of survival and, within a further two seconds, the ocean had swallowed all trace of him and his aeroplane, as if they had never been.

There was no time for elation. As I was righting my machine after the first missile launch, I realised that I was pointing directly at another Argentine aircraft, at a range of about one mile; the one I had seen hit the landing craft. I mashed the lock button again, with strength born of righteous anger, and my second missile immediately locked onto his jet efflux, as he started a panic break towards me. As I was about to fire, the homing head lost lock and the missile cross wandered drunkenly onto the sea, some 50 feet below him. Cursing, I rejected the false lock, mashed the lock button again and fired, the missile whipping across my nose and taking a handful of lead to the left, to head him off. He obviously saw the Sidewinder launch, because he immediately reversed his break and pulled his aircraft into a screaming turn away from it. His best efforts were to no avail, however, and the thin grey missile flashed back across my nose and impacted his machine directly behind the cockpit. The complete rear half of the airframe simply disintegrated, as if a shotgun had been fired at a plastic model from close range. As the aluminium confetti of destruction fluttered seawards, I watched, fascinated, as the disembodied cockpit yawed rapidly through ninety degrees and splashed violently into the freezing water.

I felt a terrific surge of elation at the demise of the second A4, and started to scan ahead, in the murk, for the others. I had just picked out the next one, fleeing west, his belly only feet from the water, when a parachute snapped open right in front of my face. The pilot had somehow managed to eject from the gyrating cockpit, in the second before it hit the water, and flashed over my right wing so close that I saw every detail of the rag-doll figure with its arms and legs thrown out in a grotesque star shape by the deceleration of the canopy. My feelings of anger and elation instantly changed to relief, as I realised that a fellow pilot had survived. An instant later, immense anger returned as I started to run down the next victim, before he could make good his escape in the gloom. Now that I had launched both missiles, I had only guns with which to despatch the remaining Skyhawks and, as I lifted the safety slide on the trigger, I realised that my head-up display had disappeared and I had no gunsight. This was a well-known 'glitch' in the HUD[2] software and could be cured easily by selecting the HUD off and then on again. This I duly did but, in the ten seconds it took for the sight to reappear, it was all over. The A4 broke rapidly towards me, as I screamed up behind him with a good 150 knots overtake. I pulled his blurred outline to the bottom of the windscreen and opened fire. The roar of the 30-millimetre rounds leaving the guns at the rate of forty per second filled the cockpit. I kept my finger on the trigger and relaxed and then re-applied the G, in order to 'walk' the rounds through him as best I could.

Suddenly, over the radio came an urgent shout from Dave Smith, 'Pull up, pull up, you're being fired at!' All he had seen of the fight up until now, because of the failing light, was two missile launches followed by two explosions. He then saw an aircraft only feet above the water, flying through a hail of explosions and assumed it to be me. By now I had run out of ammunition and, at Dave's cry, pulled up into the vertical, through the setting sun and in a big lazy looping manoeuvre, rolled out at 12,000 feet heading northeast for HERMES. In the vertical climb, I looked back down over Choiseul Sound and saw a white trail appear, accelerating towards the fleeing A4. The trail was so low to the water that my first crazy thought was that it was a torpedo! I soon realised, however, that it was a missile and watched mesmerised as it headed for the enemy fighter. About halfway to the target, the rocket motor burnt out and for a few maddening seconds, I thought it had been fired out of range and would drop into the water. Dave had not misjudged it though, and after some seven seconds of flight, there was a brilliant white flash as the zirconium disc in the warhead ignited. The Skyhawk was so low that the flash of the warhead merged with its reflection in the water of the Sound. A fraction of a second later, the aircraft disappeared in a huge yellow-orange fireball, as it spread its burning remains over the sand dunes on the north coast of Lafonia.

Climbing rapidly through 20,000 feet, I checked my engine and fuel gauges, and realised that we were going to be very tight for gas. We used a figure of 2,000

---

[2] HUD - Head Up Display. A transparent, electronically generated display that projects data directly ahead of the pilot, thus reducing the need to look inside the cockpit (head down) at instrumentation.

lbs of fuel overhead Port Stanley as a good rule of thumb for returning to the ship, and my gauges were reading less than 1,400 lbs. As I overflew the battered runway, climbing through 25,000 feet between the odd burst of anti-aircraft fire, my low-level fuel lights came on, indicating 1,300 lbs remaining. At 40,000 feet, I called the carrier and told them that I was returning short of fuel, and they obliged by heading towards us to close the distance. Even so, when I closed the throttle to start a cruise descent from ninety miles out, I was still uncertain that I was going to make it before I flamed out and took an unwanted bath. At 40,000 feet the sun was still a blaze of orange on the western horizon but, as I descended, the light became progressively worse. By the time I had descended to 10,000 feet, my world had become an extremely dark and lonely place. The adrenalin levels, which had been recovering to normal during the twenty minutes after the engagement, now started to increase again in anticipation of my first night deck landing. To compound the problem and to give final proof of 'Sod's law', HERMES had managed to find one of the massive thunderstorms, and was in heavy rain. I realised that I did not have sufficient fuel to carry out a proper radar approach, and asked the controller to just talk me onto the centreline, whilst I adjusted my glide so that I would not have to touch the throttle until the last minute.

With three miles to run, descending through 1500 feet, I was still in thick, turbulent cloud when my fuel warning lights began to flash urgently, telling me that I had 500 lbs of fuel remaining. At two miles, I saw a glimmer of light emerging through the rain and, at 800 feet, the lights fused into the recognisable outline of the carrier. I slammed the nozzle lever into the hover stop, selected full flap and punched the undercarriage button to lower the wheels. I picked up the mirror sight, which confirmed that I was well above the ideal glide path, but dropping rapidly towards the invisible sea. With about half a mile to run, I added a handful of power, and felt the Pegasus engine's instant response, stopping my descent at about 300 feet. The wheels locked down as I applied full braking stop to position myself off the port side of the deck and, seconds later, I was transitioning sideways to hover over the centreline of the deck, level with the aft end of the superstructure. I knew that I had very little fuel remaining, so finesse went out of the window as I closed the throttle and banged the machine down on the rain-streaked deck. Once safely taxied forward into the aptly named 'Graveyard' and lashed in place, I shut down the engine and heard Dave's jet landing on behind me. My fuel gauges were showing 300 lbs, sufficient for a further two minutes flying!

Our debrief took place in the Wardroom bar, which John Locke, the ship's universally-loved and respected Commander, had kept open for us. Here we discovered that a pilot from our sister squadron in INVINCIBLE had reported seeing four aircraft destroyed during our engagement. Neither of us could give a satisfactory explanation of the fourth kill but this version was sent back to UK, describing the mission as a night training sortie. This elicited the following amusing response from CinC Fleet:

CONGRATULATIONS YOUR EVENING SORTIE. IF THIS IS WHAT YOU DO ON A TRAINING MISSION, I CAN'T WAIT TO SEE WHAT YOU DO WHEN YOU ARE OPERATIONAL!

I discovered some years later that the fourth pilot, Hector Sanchez, had, in fact, escaped after jettisoning his fuel tanks. He made it to the C130 tanker with a teaspoonful of fuel, having received some small arms damage to his aircraft. Hector survived the war and recently retired from the Argentine Air Force. In the summer of 1993, through the good auspices of Maxi Gainza, a mutual friend, we met in London and spent the afternoon flying Maxi's Zlin at White Waltham. A few days later Hector and his wife stayed with us in our Somerset cottage and, after several pints of scrumpy, we discovered what had really happened that evening more than eleven years earlier. To my dismay, I found out that I had ended up in front of Hector in the heat of the engagement and, had it not been for the fact that his gun had jammed, he might have been the only Argentine pilot to shoot down a Sea Harrier!

Credit: Geoff Lee

A Thousand Hours On Type – But Only Just

The 30th of March 1977, the last official flying day of the RAF Germany Lightning Force, dawned bright and clear. 19(F) Squadron had already converted to the Phantom and 92(F) Squadron was due to do the same on the following day. To mark the end of the Lightning era, Ed Durham, the Squadron Boss, had been tasked to lead a diamond-16 formation flypast over our Rheindahlen Headquarters. I was to fly in the No2 slot in Lightning FMk2A, number XM 793. The sortie and flypast went without a hitch until the formation broke into the circuit back at Gutersloh when, downwind to land, I found I had 2 not 3 green lights on the undercarriage indicator. A flypast of the Air Traffic Control Tower confirmed that the left main wheel was only half way down, and that it appeared to have snagged on the undercarriage door.

At this stage I had over 20 minutes fuel remaining but, to increase my endurance further, I closed down the No2 Engine, as was standard practice; this, however, left me with only one hydraulic system powering the flying controls. I then climbed to height, where an airborne visual inspection confirmed the original diagnosis of the problem, and tried every trick in the book to entice the left main wheel to lower; all to no avail. As I was fast running out of fuel, time and ideas, Ed Durham, who by now had landed and made his way to the Tower, authorised me to use the Emergency Undercarriage Lowering System. This I did apprehensively as, only 3 weeks prior, Mike Lawrance, when faced with a similar problem in the Squadron's T4[1], had used the emergency system and subsequently suffered a total hydraulics failure. He had then been forced to eject[2], along with his passenger, Hoppy Granville-White, a Harrier pilot. In my case, after a few anxious seconds the aircraft was still flying, but there was no change to the status of the undercarriage.

Now completely out of ideas and time, I turned the aircraft north towards the Dummersee (a nearby lake, which served as the designated Ejection Area), tightening my straps and preparing for an ejection while in transit. However,

---

[1] T4 – 2-seater version of the Lightning.
[2] – A total hydraulics failure in the Lightning included the powered flying controls, for which there was no manual back-up system.

just as I was about to pull the ejection seat handle, the aircraft shook violently for a second. I now had 3 green lights! A quick scan of the cockpit led me to conclude that I had just enough fuel to get back to Gutersloh, with the undercarriage down. Air Traffic came up trumps with an expeditious routeing and I landed a few minutes later. However, half way down the runway, I experienced a total hydraulics failure and was forced to abandon the aircraft where it came to rest. So ended my last ever Lightning sortie, which incidentally gave me my 1,000th hour on the aircraft type. Interestingly, if I had been forced to use a Martin-Baker let down[3] I would have been left a few minutes short of the magic target!!

The subsequent engineering investigation concluded that the left undercarriage leg had not lowered because it had snagged on the undercarriage door, which had come off its hinges and jammed. The extra pressure from the Emergency Lowering System had eventually forced the undercarriage door free, which then detached from the aircraft and fell to the ground; this, in turn, had allowed the undercarriage leg to lower fully. Unfortunately, as it came off its hinges, the door hit and damaged the hydraulic pipes that ran through the undercarriage bay, which led to a leak and the total hydraulics failure that occurred during the landing roll. After a few pints of Warsteiner I slept well that night!!

Credit: Geoff Lee

---

[3] Martin Baker let down – Aircrew slang for using the ejection seat, which was manufactured by Martin Baker.